Matthew Henry's Concise Commentary of the Bible V
(Romans to Revelation)

Romans

The scope or design of the apostle in writing to the Romans appears to have been, to answer the unbelieving, and to teach the believing Jew; to confirm the Christian and to convert the idolatrous Gentile; and to show the Gentile convert as equal with the Jewish, in respect of his religious condition, and his rank in the Divine favour. These several designs are brought into on view, by opposing or arguing with the infidel or unbelieving Jew, in favour of the Christian or believing Gentile. The way of a sinner's acceptance with God, or justification in his sight, merely by grace, through faith in the righteousness of Christ, without distinction of nations, is plainly stated. This doctrine is cleared from the objections raised by Judaizing Christians, who were for making terms of acceptance with God by a mixture of the law and the gospel, and for shutting out the Gentiles from any share in the blessings of salvation brought in by the Messiah. In the conclusion, holiness is further enforced by practical exhortations.

Chapter 1

Chapter Outline

Verses 1-7

The doctrine of which the apostle Paul wrote, set forth the fulfilment of the promises by the prophets. It spoke of the Son of God, even Jesus the Saviour, the promised Messiah, who came from David as to his human nature, but was also declared to be the Son of God, by the Divine power which raised him from the dead. The Christian profession does not consist in a notional knowledge or a bare assent, much less in perverse disputings, but in obedience. And all those, and those only, are brought to obedience of the faith, who are effectually called of Jesus Christ. Here is, 1. The privilege of Christians; they are beloved of God, and are members of that body which is beloved. 2. The duty of Christians; to be holy, hereunto are they called, called to be saints. These the apostle saluted, by wishing them grace to sanctify their souls, and peace to comfort their hearts, as springing from the free mercy of God, the reconciled Father of all believers, and coming to them through the Lord Jesus Christ.

Verses 8-15

We must show love for our friends, not only by praying for them, but by praising God for them. As in our purposes, so in our desires, we must remember to say, If the Lord will, Jas 4:15. Our journeys are made prosperous or otherwise, according to the will of God. We should readily impart to others what God has trusted to us, rejoicing to make others joyful, especially taking pleasure in communing with those who believe the same things with us. If redeemed by the blood, and converted by the grace of the Lord Jesus, we are altogether his; and for his sake we are debtors to all men, to do all the good we can. Such services are our duty.

Verses 16, 17

In these verses the apostle opens the design of the whole epistle, in which he brings forward a charge of sinfulness against all flesh; declares the only method of deliverance from condemnation, by faith in the mercy of God, through Jesus Christ; and then builds upon it purity of heart, grateful obedience, and earnest desires to improve in all those Christian graces and tempers, which nothing but a lively faith in Christ can bring forth. God is a just and holy God, and we are guilty sinners. It is necessary that we have a righteousness to appear in before him: there is such a righteousness brought in by the Messiah, and made known in the gospel; a gracious method of acceptance, notwithstanding the guilt of our sins. It is the righteousness of Christ, who is God, coming from a satisfaction of infinite value. Faith is all in all, both in the beginning and progress of Christian life. It is not from faith to works, as if faith put us into a justified state, and then works kept us in it; but it is all along from faith to faith; it is faith pressing forward, and gaining the victory over unbelief.

Verses 18-25

The apostle begins to show that all mankind need the salvation of the gospel, because none could obtain the favour of God, or escape his wrath by their own works. For no man can plead that he has fulfilled all his obligations to God and to his neighbour; nor can any truly say that he has fully acted up to the light afforded him. The sinfulness of man is described as ungodliness against the laws of the first table, and unrighteousness against those of the second. The cause of that sinfulness is holding the truth in unrighteousness. All, more or less, do what they know to be wrong, and omit what they know to be right, so that the plea of ignorance cannot be allowed from any. Our Creator's invisible power and Godhead are so clearly shown in the works he has made, that even idolaters and wicked Gentiles are left without excuse. They foolishly followed idolatry; and rational creatures changed the worship of the glorious Creator, for that of brutes, reptiles, and senseless images. They wandered from God, till all traces of true religion must have been lost, had not the revelation of the gospel prevented it. For whatever may be pretended, as to the sufficiency of man's reason to discover Divine truth and moral obligation, or to govern the practice aright, facts cannot be denied. And these plainly show that men have dishonoured God by the most absurd idolatries and superstitions; and have degraded themselves by the vilest affections and most abominable deeds.

Verses 26-32

In the horrid depravity of the heathen, the truth of our Lord's words was shown: "Light was come into the world, but men loved darkness rather than light, because their deeds were evil; for he that doeth evil hateth the light." The truth was not to their taste. And we all know how soon a man will contrive, against the strongest evidence, to reason himself out of the belief of what he dislikes. But a man cannot be brought to greater slavery than to be given up to his own lusts. As the Gentiles did not like to keep God in their knowledge, they committed crimes wholly against reason and their own welfare. The nature of man, whether pagan or Christian, is still the same; and the charges of the apostle apply more or less to the state and character of men at all times, till they are brought to full submission to the faith of Christ, and renewed by Divine power. There never yet was a man, who had not reason to lament his strong corruptions, and his secret dislike to the will of God. Therefore this chapter is a call to self-examination, the end of which should be, a deep conviction of sin, and of the necessity of deliverance from a state of condemnation.

Chapter 2

Chapter Outline

The Jews could not be justified by the law of Moses, any more than the Gentiles by the law of nature. (1–16)

The sins of the Jews confuted all their vain confidence in their outward privileges. (17–29)

Verses 1-16

The Jews thought themselves a holy people, entitled to their privileges by right, while they were unthankful, rebellious, and unrighteous. But all who act thus, of every nation, age, and description, must be reminded that the judgment of God will be according to their real character. The case is so plain, that we may appeal to the sinner's own thoughts. In every wilful sin, there is contempt of the goodness of God. And though the branches of man's disobedience are very various, all spring from the same root. But in true repentance, there must be hatred of former sinfulness, from a change wrought in the state of the mind, which disposes it to choose the good and to refuse the evil. It shows also a sense of inward wretchedness. Such is the great change wrought in repentance, it is conversion, and is needed by every human being. The ruin of sinners is their walking after a hard and impenitent heart. Their sinful doings are expressed by the strong words, "treasuring up wrath." In the description of the just man, notice the full demand of the law. It demands that the motives shall be pure, and rejects all actions from earthly ambition or ends. In the description of the unrighteous, contention is held forth as the principle of all evil. The human will is in a state of enmity against God. Even Gentiles, who had not the written law, had that within, which directed them what to do by the light of nature. Conscience is a witness, and first or last will bear witness. As they nature. Conscience is a witness, and first or last will bear witness. As they kept or broke these natural laws and dictates, their consciences either acquitted or condemned them. Nothing speaks more terror to sinners, and more comfort to saints, than that Christ shall be the Judge. Secret services shall be rewarded, secret sins shall be then punished, and brought to light.

Verses 17-24

The apostle directs his discourse to the Jews, and shows of what sins they were guilty, notwithstanding their profession and vain pretensions. A believing, humble, thankful glorying in God, is the root and sum of all religion. But proud, vain-glorious boasting in God, and in the outward profession of his name, is the root and sum of all hypocrisy. Spiritual pride is the most dangerous of all kinds of pride. A great evil of the sins professors is, the dishonour done to God and religion, by their not living according to their profession. Many despise their more ignorant neighbours who rest in a dead form of godliness; yet themselves trust in a form of knowledge, equally void of life and power, while some glory in the gospel, whose unholy lives dishonour God, and cause his name to be blasphemed.

Verses 25-29

No forms, ordinances, or notions can profit, without regenerating grace, which will always lead to seeking an interest in the righteousness of God by faith. For he is no more a Christian now, than he was really a Jew of old, who is only one outwardly: neither is that baptism, which is outward in the flesh: but he is the real Christian, who is inwardly a true believer, with an obedient faith. And the true baptism is that of the heart, by the washing of regeneration and the renewal of the Holy Ghost; bringing a spiritual frame of mind, and a willing following of truth in its holy ways. Let us pray that we may be made real Christians, not outwardly, but inwardly; in the heart and spirit, not in the letter; baptized, not with water only, but with the Holy Ghost; and let our praise be, not of men, but of God.

Chapter 3

Chapter Outline

Objections answered. (1–8)

All mankind are sinners. (9–18)

Both Jews and Gentiles cannot be justified by their own deeds. (19, 20)

It is owing to the free grace of God, through faith in the righteousness of Christ, yet the law is not done away. (21–31)

Verses 1-8

The law could not save in or from sins, yet it gave the Jews advantages for obtaining salvation. Their stated ordinances, education in the knowledge of the true God and his service, and many favours shown to the children of Abraham, all were means of grace, and doubtless were made useful to the conversion of many. But especially the Scriptures were committed to them. Enjoyment of God's word and ordinances, is the chief happiness of a people. But God's promises are made only to believers; therefore the unbelief of some, or of many professors, cannot make this faithfulness of no effect. He will fulfil his promises to his people, and bring his threatened vengeance upon unbelievers. God's judging the world, should for ever silence all doubtings and reflections upon his justice. The wickedness and obstinate unbelief of the Jews, proved man's need of the righteousness of God by faith, and also his justice in punishing for sin. Let us do evil, that good may come, is oftener in the heart than in the mouth of sinners; for few thus justify themselves in their wicked ways. The believer knows that duty belongs to him, and events to God; and that he must not commit any sin, or speak one falsehood, upon the hope, or even assurance, that God may thereby glorify himself. If any speak and act thus, their condemnation is just.

Verses 9-18

Here again is shown that all mankind are under the guilt of sin, as a burden; and under the government and dominion of sin, as enslaved to it, to work wickedness. This is made plain by several passages of Scripture from the Old Testament, which describe the corrupt and depraved state of all men, till grace restrain or change them. Great as our advantages are, these texts describe multitudes who call themselves Christians. Their principles and conduct prove that there is no fear of God before their eyes. And where no fear of God is, no good is to be looked for.

Verses 19, 20

It is in vain to seek for justification by the works of the law. All must plead guilty. Guilty before God, is a dreadful word; but no man can be justified by a law which condemns him for breaking it. The corruption in our nature, will for ever stop any justification by our own works.

Verses 21-26

Must guilty man remain under wrath? Is the wound for ever incurable? No; blessed be God, there is another way laid open for us. This is the righteousness of God; righteousness of his ordaining, and providing, and accepting. It is by that faith which has Jesus Christ for its object; an anointed Saviour, so Jesus Christ signifies. Justifying faith respects Christ as a Saviour, in all his three anointed offices, as Prophet, Priest, and King; trusting in him, accepting him, and cleaving to him: in all these, Jews and Gentiles are alike welcome to God through Christ. There is no difference, his righteousness is upon all that believe; not only offered to them, but put upon them as a crown, as a robe. It is free grace, mere mercy; there is nothing in us to deserve such favours. It comes freely unto us, but Christ bought it, and paid the price. And faith has special regard to the blood of Christ, as that which made the atonement. God, in all this, declares his righteousness. It is plain that he hates sin, when nothing less than the blood of Christ would satisfy for it. And it would not agree with his justice to demand the debt, when the Surety has paid it, and he has accepted that payment in full satisfaction.

Verses 27-31

God will have the great work of the justification and salvation of sinners carried on from first to last, so as to shut out boasting. Now, if we were saved by our own works, boasting would not be excluded. But the way of justification by faith for ever shuts out boasting. Yet believers are not left to be lawless; faith is a law, it is a working grace, wherever it is in truth. By faith, not in this matter an act of obedience, or a good work, but forming the relation between Christ and the sinner, which renders it proper that the believer should be pardoned and justified for the sake of the Saviour, and that the unbeliever who is not thus united or related to him, should remain under condemnation. The law is still of use to convince us of what is past, and to direct us for the future. Though we cannot be saved by it as a covenant, yet we own and submit to it, as a rule in the hand of the Mediator.

Chapter 4

Chapter Outline

The doctrine of justification by faith is shown by the case of Abraham.	(1–12)
He received the promise through the righteousness of faith.	(13–22)
And we are justified in the same way of believing.	(23–25)

Verses 1-12

To meet the views of the Jews, the apostle first refers to the example of Abraham, in whom the Jews gloried as their most renowned forefather. However exalted in various respects, he had nothing to boast in the presence of God, being saved by grace, through faith, even as others. Without noticing the years which passed before his call, and the failures at times in his obedience, and even in his faith, it was expressly stated in Scripture that "he believed God, and it was counted to him for righteousness," Ge 15:6. From this example it is observed, that if any man could work the full measure required by the law, the reward must be reckoned as a debt, which evidently was not the case even of Abraham, seeing faith was reckoned to him for righteousness. When believers are justified by faith, "their faith being counted for righteousness," their faith does not justify them as a part, small or great, of their righteousness; but as the appointed means of uniting them to Him who has chosen as the name whereby he shall be called, "the Lord our Righteousness." Pardoned people are the only blessed people. It clearly appears from the Scripture, that Abraham was justified several years before his circumcision. It is, therefore, plain that this rite was not necessary in order to justification. It was a sign of the original corruption of human nature. And it was such a sign as was also an outward seal, appointed not only to confirm God's promises to him and to his seed, and their obligation to be the Lord's, but likewise to assure him of his being already a real partaker of the righteousness of faith. Thus Abraham was the spiritual forefather of all believers, who walked after the example of his obedient faith. The seal of the Holy Spirit in our sanctification, making us new creatures, is the inward evidence of the righteousness of faith.

Verses 13-22

The promise was made to Abraham long before the law. It points at Christ, and it refers to the promise, Ge 12:3. In Thee shall all families of the earth be blessed. The law worketh wrath, by showing that every transgressor is exposed to the Divine displeasure. As God intended to give men a title to the promised blessings, so he appointed it to be by faith, that it might be wholly of grace, to make it sure to all who were of the like precious faith with Abraham, whether Jews or Gentiles, in all ages. The justification and salvation of sinners, the taking to himself the Gentiles who had not been a people, were a gracious calling of things which are not, as though they were; and this giving a being to things that were not, proves the almighty power of God. The nature and power of Abraham's faith are shown. He believed God's testimony, and looked for the performance of his promise, firmly hoping when the case seemed hopeless. It is weakness of faith, that makes a man lie poring on the difficulties in the way of a promise. Abraham took it not for a point that would admit of argument or debate. Unbelief is at the bottom of all our staggerings at God's promises. The strength of faith appeared in its victory over fears. God honours faith; and great faith honours God. It was imputed to him for righteousness. Faith is a grace that of all others gives glory to God. Faith clearly is the instrument by which we receive the righteousness of God, the redemption which is by Christ; and that which is the instrument whereby we take or receive it, cannot be the thing itself, nor can it be the gift thereby taken and received. Abraham's faith did not justify him by its own merit or value, but as giving him a part in Christ.

Verses 23-25

The history of Abraham, and of his justification, was recorded to teach men of after-ages; those especially to whom the gospel was then made known. It is plain, that we are not justified by the merit of our own works, but by faith in Jesus Christ and his righteousness; which is the truth urged in this and the foregoing chapter, as the great spring and foundation of all comfort. Christ did meritoriously work our justification and salvation by his death and passion, but the power and perfection thereof, with respect to us, depend on his resurrection. By his death he paid our debt, in his resurrection he received our acquittance, Isa 53:8. When he was discharged, we, in Him and together with Him, received the discharge from the guilt and punishment of all our sins. This last verse is an abridgement or summary of the whole gospel.

Chapter 5

Chapter Outline

Verses 1-5

A blessed change takes place in the sinner's state, when he becomes a true believer, whatever he has been. Being justified by faith he has peace with God. The holy, righteous God, cannot be at peace with a sinner, while under the guilt of sin. Justification takes away the guilt, and so makes way for peace. This is through our Lord Jesus Christ; through him as the great Peace-maker, the Mediator between God and man. The saints' happy state is a state of grace. Into this grace we are brought, which teaches that we were not born in this state. We could not have got into it of ourselves, but we are led into it, as pardoned offenders. Therein we stand, a posture that denotes perseverance; we stand firm and safe, upheld by the power of the enemy. And those who have hope for the glory of God hereafter, have enough to rejoice in now. Tribulation worketh patience, not in and of itself, but the powerful grace of God working in and with the tribulation. Patient sufferers have most of the Divine consolations, which abound as afflictions abound. It works needful experience of ourselves. This hope will not disappoint, because it is sealed with the Holy Spirit as a Spirit of love. It is the gracious work of the blessed Spirit to shed abroad the love of God in the hearts of all the saints. A right sense of God's love to us, will make us not ashamed, either of our hope, or of our sufferings for him.

Verses 6-11

Christ died for sinners; not only such as were useless, but such as were guilty and hateful; such that their everlasting destruction would be to the glory of God's justice. Christ died to save us, not in our sins, but from our sins; and we were yet sinners when he died for us. Nay, the carnal mind is not only an enemy to God, but enmity itself, chap. 8:7; Col 1:21. But God designed to deliver from sin, and to work a great change. While the sinful state continues, God loathes the sinner, and the sinner loathes God, Zec 11:8. And that for such as these Christ should die, is a mystery; no other such an instance of love is known, so that it may well be the employment of eternity to adore and wonder at it. Again; what idea had the apostle when he supposed the case of some one dying for a righteous man? And yet he only put it as a thing that might be. Was it not the undergoing this suffering, that the person intended to be benefitted might be released therefrom? But from what are believers in Christ released by his death? Not from bodily death; for that they all do and must endure. The evil, from which the deliverance could be effected only in this astonishing manner, must be more dreadful than natural death. There is no evil, to which the argument can be applied, except that which the apostle actually affirms, sin, and wrath, the punishment of sin, determined by the unerring justice of God. And if, by Divine grace, they were thus brought to repent, and to believe in Christ, and thus were justified by the price of his bloodshedding, and by faith in that atonement, much more through Him who died for them and rose again, would they be kept from falling under the power of sin and Satan, or departing finally from him. The living Lord of all, will complete the purpose of his dying love, by saving all true believers to the uttermost. Having such a pledge of salvation in the love of God through Christ, the apostle declared that believers not only rejoiced in the hope of heaven, and even in their tribulations for Christ's sake, but they gloried in God also, as their unchangeable Friend and all-sufficient Portion, through Christ only.

Verses 12-14

The design of what follows is plain. It is to exalt our views respecting the blessings Christ has procured for us, by comparing them with the evil which followed upon the fall of our first father; and by showing that these blessings not only extend to the removal of these evils, but far beyond. Adam sinning, his nature became guilty and corrupted, and so came to his children. Thus in him all have sinned. And death is by sin; for death is the wages of sin. Then entered all that misery which is the due desert of sin; temporal, spiritual, eternal death. If Adam had not sinned, he had not died; but a sentence of death was passed, as upon a criminal; it passed through all men, as an infectious disease that none escape. In proof of our union with Adam, and our part in his first transgression, observe, that sin prevailed in the world, for many ages before the giving of the law by Moses. And death reigned in that long time, not only over adults who wilfully sinned, but also over multitudes of infants, which shows that they had fallen in Adam under condemnation, and that the sin of Adam extended to all his posterity. He was a figure or type of Him that was to come as Surety of a new covenant, for all who are related to Him.

Verses 15-19

Through one man's offence, all mankind are exposed to eternal condemnation. But the grace and mercy of God, and the free gift of righteousness and salvation, are through Jesus Christ, as man: yet the Lord from heaven has brought the multitude of believers into a more safe and exalted state than that from which they fell in Adam. This free gift did not place them anew in a state of trial, but fixed them in a state of justification, as Adam would have been placed, had he stood. Notwithstanding the differences, there is a striking similarity. As by the offence of one, sin and death prevailed to the condemnation of all men, so by the righteousness of one, grace prevailed to the justification of all related to Christ by faith. Through the grace of God, the gift by grace has abounded to many through Christ; yet multitudes choose to remain under the dominion of sin and death, rather than to apply for the blessings of the reign of grace. But Christ will in nowise cast out any who are willing to come to him.

Verses 20, 21

By Christ and his righteousness, we have more and greater privileges than we lost by the offence of Adam. The moral law showed that many thoughts, tempers, words, and actions, were sinful, thus transgressions were multiplied. Not making sin to abound the more, but discovering the sinfulness of it, even as the letting in a clearer light into a room, discovers the dust and filth which were there before, but were not seen. The sin of Adam, and the effect of corruption in us, are the abounding of that offence which appeared on the entrance of the law. And the terrors of the law make gospel comforts the more sweet. Thus God the Holy Spirit has, by the blessed apostle, delivered to us a most important truth, full of consolation, suited to our need as sinners. Whatever one may have above another, every man is a sinner against God, stands condemned by the law, and needs pardon. A righteousness that is to justify cannot be made up of a mixture of sin and holiness. There can be no title to an eternal reward without a pure and spotless righteousness: let us look for it, even to the righteousness of Christ.

Chapter 6

Chapter Outline

Believers must die to sin, and live to God.	(1, 2)
This is urged by their Christian baptism and union with Christ.	(3–10)
They are made alive to God.	(11–15)
And are freed from the dominion of sin.	(16–20)
The end of sin is death, and of holiness everlasting life.	(21–23)

Verses 1, 2

The apostle is very full in pressing the necessity of holiness. He does not explain away the free grace of the gospel, but he shows that connexion between justification and holiness are inseparable. Let the thought be abhorred, of continuing in sin that grace may abound. True believers are dead to sin, therefore they ought not to follow it. No man can at the same time be both dead and alive. He is a fool who, desiring to be dead unto sin, thinks he may live in it.

Verses 3-10

Baptism teaches the necessity of dying to sin, and being as it were buried from all ungodly and unholy pursuits, and of rising to walk with God in newness of life. Unholy professors may have had the outward sign of a death unto sin, and a new birth unto righteousness, but they never passed from the family of Satan to that of God. The corrupt nature, called the old man, because derived from our first father Adam, is crucified with Christ, in every true believer, by the grace derived from the cross. It is weakened and in a dying state, though it yet struggles for life, and even for victory. But the whole body of sin, whatever is not according to the holy law of God, must be done away, so that the believer may no more be the slave of sin, but live to God, and find happiness in his service.

Verses 11-15

The strongest motives against sin, and to enforce holiness, are here stated. Being made free from the reign of sin, alive unto God, and having the prospect of eternal life, it becomes believers to be greatly concerned to advance thereto. But, as unholy lusts are not quite rooted out in this life, it must be the care of the Christian to resist their motions, earnestly striving, that, through Divine grace, they may not prevail in this mortal state. Let the thought that this state will soon be at an end, encourage the true Christian, as to the motions of lusts, which so often perplex and distress him. Let us present all our powers to God, as weapons or tools ready for the warfare, and work of righteousness, in his service. There is strength in the covenant of grace for us. Sin shall not have dominion. God's promises to us are more powerful and effectual for mortifying sin, than our promises to God. Sin may struggle in a real believer, and create him a great deal of trouble, but it shall not have dominion; it may vex him, but it shall not rule over him. Shall any take occasion from this encouraging doctrine to allow themselves in the practice of any sin? Far be such abominable thoughts, so contrary to the perfections of God, and the design of his gospel, so opposed to being under grace. What can be a stronger motive against sin than the love of Christ? Shall we sin against so much goodness, and such love?

Verses 16-20

Every man is the servant of the master to whose commands he yields himself; whether it be the sinful dispositions of his heart, in actions which lead to death, or the new and spiritual obedience implanted by regeneration. The apostle rejoiced now they obeyed from the heart the gospel, into which they were delivered as into a mould. As the same metal becomes a new vessel, when melted and recast in another mould, so the believer has become a new creature. And there is great difference in the liberty of mind and spirit, so opposite to the state of slavery, which the true Christian has in the service of his rightful Lord, whom he is enabled to consider as his Father, and himself as his son and heir, by the adoption of grace. The dominion of sin consists in being willingly slaves thereto, not in being harassed by it as a hated power, struggling for victory. Those who now are the servants of God, once were the slaves of sin.

Verses 21-23

The pleasure and profit of sin do not deserve to be called fruit. Sinners are but ploughing iniquity, sowing vanity, and reaping the same. Shame came into the world with sin, and is still the certain effect of it. The end of sin is death. Though the way may seem pleasant and inviting, yet it will be bitterness in the latter end. From this condemnation the believer is set at liberty, when made free from sin. If the fruit is unto holiness, if there is an active principle of true and growing grace, the end will be everlasting life; a very happy end! Though the way is up-hill, though it is narrow, thorny, and beset, yet everlasting life at the end of it is sure. The gift of God is eternal life. And this gift is through Jesus Christ our Lord. Christ purchased it, prepared it, prepares us for it, preserves us to it; he is the All in all in our salvation.

Chapter 7

Chapter Outline

Verses 1-6

So long as a man continues under the law as a covenant, and seeks justification by his own obedience, he continues the slave of sin in some form. Nothing but the Spirit of life in Christ Jesus, can make any sinner free from the law of sin and death. Believers are delivered from that power of the law, which condemns for the sins committed by them. And they are delivered from that power of the law which stirs up and provokes the sin that dwells in them. Understand this not of the law as a rule, but as a covenant of works. In profession and privilege, we are under a covenant of grace, and not under a covenant of works; under the gospel of Christ, not under the law of Moses. The difference is spoken of under the similitude or figure of being married to a new husband. The second marriage is to Christ. By death we are freed from obligation to the law as a covenant, as the wife is from her vows to her husband. In our believing powerfully and effectually, we are dead to the law, and have no more to do with it than the dead servant, who is freed from his master, has to do with his master's yoke. The day of our believing, is the day of being united to the Lord Jesus. We enter upon a life of dependence on him, and duty to him. Good works are from union with Christ; as the fruitfulness of the vine is the product of its being united to its roots; there is no fruit to God, till we are united to Christ. The law, and the greatest efforts of one under the law, still in the flesh, under the power of corrupt principles, cannot set the heart right with regard to the love of God, overcome worldly lusts, or give truth and sincerity in the inward parts, or any thing that comes by the special sanctifying influences of the Holy Spirit. Nothing more than a formal obedience to the outward letter of any precept, can be performed by us, without the renewing, new-creating grace of the new covenant.

Verses 7-13

There is no way of coming to that knowledge of sin, which is necessary to repentance, and therefore to peace and pardon, but by trying our hearts and lives by the law. In his own case the apostle would not have known the sinfulness of his thoughts, motives, and actions, but by the law. That perfect standard showed how wrong his heart and life were, proving his sins to be more numerous than he had before thought, but it did not contain any provision of mercy or grace for his relief. He is ignorant of human nature and the perverseness of his own heart, who does not perceive in himself a readiness to fancy there is something desirable in what is out of reach. We may perceive this in our children, though self-love makes us blind to it in ourselves. The more humble and spiritual any Christian is, the more clearly will he perceive that the apostle describes the true believer, from his first convictions of sin to his greatest progress in grace, during this present imperfect state. St. Paul was once a Pharisee, ignorant of the spirituality of the law, having some correctness of character, without knowing his inward depravity. When the commandment came to his conscience by the convictions of the Holy Spirit, and he saw what it demanded, he found his sinful mind rise against it. He felt at the same time the evil of sin, his own sinful state, that he was unable to fulfil the law, and was like a criminal when condemned. But though the evil principle in the human heart produces sinful motions, and the more by taking occasion of the commandment; yet the law is holy, and the commandment holy, just, and good. It is not favourable to sin, which it pursues into the heart, and discovers and reproves in the inward motions thereof. Nothing is so good but a corrupt and vicious nature will pervert it. The same heat that softens wax, hardens clay. Food or medicine when taken wrong, may cause death, though its nature is to nourish or to heal. The law may cause death through man's depravity, but sin is the poison that brings death. Not the law, but sin discovered by the law, was made death to the apostle. The ruinous nature of sin, and the sinfulness of the human heart, are here clearly shown.

Verses 14-17

Compared with the holy rule of conduct in the law of God, the apostle found himself so very far short of perfection, that he seemed to be carnal; like a man who is sold against his will to a hated master, from whom he cannot set himself at liberty. A real Christian unwillingly serves this hated master, yet cannot shake off the galling chain, till his powerful and gracious Friend above, rescues him. The remaining evil of his heart is a real and humbling hinderance to his serving God as angels do and the spirits of just made perfect. This strong language was the result of St. Paul's great advance in holiness, and the depth of his self-abasement and hatred of sin. If we do not understand this language, it is because we are so far beneath him in holiness, knowledge of the spirituality of God's law, and the evil of our own hearts, and hatred of moral evil. And many believers have adopted the apostle's language, showing that it is suitable to their deep feelings of abhorrence of sin, and self-abasement. The apostle enlarges on the conflict he daily maintained with the remainder of his original depravity. He was frequently led into tempers, words, or actions, which he did not approve or allow in his renewed judgement and affections. By distinguishing his real self, his spiritual part, from the self, or flesh, in which sin dwelt, and by observing that the evil actions were done, not by him, but by sin dwelling in him, the apostle did not mean that men are not accountable for their sins, but he teaches the evil of their sins, by showing that they are all done against reason and conscience. Sin dwelling in a man, does not prove its ruling, or having dominion over him. If a man dwells in a city, or in a country, still he may not rule there.

Verses 18-22

The more pure and holy the heart is, it will have the more quick feeling as to the sin that remains in it. The believer sees more of the beauty of holiness and the excellence of the law. His earnest desires to obey, increase as he grows in grace. But the whole good on which his will is fully bent, he does not do; sin ever springing up in him, through remaining corruption, he often does evil, though against the fixed determination of his will. The motions of sin within grieved the apostle. If by the striving of the flesh against the Spirit, was meant that he could not do or perform as the Spirit suggested, so also, by the effectual opposition of the Spirit, he could not do what the flesh prompted him to do. How different this case from that of those who make themselves easy with regard to the inward motions of the flesh prompting them to evil; who, against the light and warning of conscience, go on, even in outward practice, to do evil, and thus, with forethought, go on in the road to perdition! For as the believer is under grace, and his will is for the way of holiness, he sincerely delights in the law of God, and in the holiness which it demands, according to his inward man; that new man in him, which after God is created in true holiness.

Verses 23-25

This passage does not represent the apostle as one that walked after the flesh, but as one that had it greatly at heart, not to walk so. And if there are those who abuse this passage, as they also do the other Scriptures, to their own destruction, yet serious Christians find cause to bless God for having thus provided for their support and comfort. We are not, because of the abuse of such as are blinded by their own lusts, to find fault with the scripture, or any just and well warranted interpretation of it. And no man who is not engaged in this conflict, can clearly understand the meaning of these words, or rightly judge concerning this painful conflict, which led the apostle to bemoan himself as a wretched man, constrained to what he abhorred. He could not deliver himself; and this made him the more fervently thank God for the way of salvation revealed through Jesus Christ, which promised him, in the end, deliverance from this enemy. So then, says he, I myself, with my mind, my prevailing judgement, affections, and purposes, as a regenerate man, by Divine grace, serve and obey the law of God; but with the flesh, the carnal nature, the remains of depravity, I serve the law of sin, which wars against the law of my mind. Not serving it so as to live in it, or to allow it, but as unable to free himself from it, even in his very best state, and needing to look for help and deliverance out of himself. It is evident that he thanks God for Christ, as our deliverer, as our atonement and righteousness in himself, and not because of any holiness wrought in us. He knew of no such salvation, and disowned any such title to it. He was willing to act in all points agreeable to the law, in his mind and conscience, but was hindered by indwelling sin, and never attained the perfection the law requires. What can be deliverance for a man always sinful, but the free grace of God, as offered in Christ Jesus? The power of Divine grace, and of the Holy Spirit, could root out sin from our hearts even in this life, if Divine wisdom had not otherwise thought fit. But it is suffered, that Christians might constantly feel, and understand thoroughly, the wretched state from which Divine grace saves them; might be kept from trusting in themselves; and might ever hold all their consolation and hope, from the rich and free grace of God in Christ.

Chapter 8

Chapter Outline

Verses 1-9

Believers may be chastened of the Lord, but will not be condemned with the world. By their union with Christ through faith, they are thus secured. What is the principle of their walk; the flesh or the Spirit, the old or the new nature, corruption or grace? For which of these do we make provision, by which are we governed? The unrenewed will is unable to keep any commandment fully. And the law, besides outward duties, requires inward obedience. God showed abhorrence of sin by the sufferings of his Son in the flesh, that the believer's person might be pardoned and justified. Thus satisfaction was made to Divine justice, and the way of salvation opened for the sinner. By the Spirit the law of love is written upon the heart, and though the righteousness of the law is not fulfilled by us, yet, blessed be God, it is fulfilled in us; there is that in all true believers, which answers the intention of the law. The favour of God, the welfare of the soul, the concerns of eternity, are the things of the Spirit, which those that are after the Spirit do mind. Which way do our thoughts move with most pleasure? Which way go our plans and contrivances? Are we most wise for the world, or for our souls? Those that live in pleasure are dead, 1Ti 5:6. A sanctified soul is a living soul; and that life is peace. The carnal mind is not only an enemy to God, but enmity itself. The carnal man may, by the power of Divine grace, be made subject to the law of God, but the carnal mind never can; that must be broken and driven out. We may know our real state and character by inquiring whether we have the Spirit of God and Christ, or not, ver. 9. Ye are not in the flesh, but in the Spirit. Having the Spirit of Christ, means having a turn of mind in some degree like the mind that was in Christ Jesus, and is to be shown by a life and conversation suitable to his precepts and example.

Verses 10-17

If the Spirit be in us, Christ is in us. He dwells in the heart by faith. Grace in the soul is its new nature; the soul is alive to God, and has begun its holy happiness which shall endure for ever. The righteousness of Christ imputed, secures the soul, the better part, from death. From hence we see how much it is our duty to walk, not after the flesh, but after the Spirit. If any habitually live according to corrupt lustings, they will certainly perish in their sins, whatever they profess. And what can a worldly life present, worthy for a moment to be put against this noble prize of our high calling? Let us then, by the Spirit, endeavour more and more to mortify the flesh. Regeneration by the Holy Spirit brings a new and Divine life to the soul, though in a feeble state. And the sons of God have the Spirit to work in them the disposition of children; they have not the spirit of bondage, which the Old Testament church was under, through the darkness of that dispensation. The Spirit of adoption was not then plentifully poured out. Also it refers to that spirit of bondage, under which many saints were at their conversion. Many speak peace to themselves, to whom God does not speak peace. But those who are sanctified, have God's Spirit witnessing with their spirits, in and by his speaking peace to the soul. Though we may now seem to be losers for Christ, we shall not, we cannot, be losers by him in the end.

Verses 18-25

The sufferings of the saints strike no deeper than the things of time, last no longer than the present time, are light afflictions, and but for a moment. How vastly different are the sentence of the word and the sentiment of the world, concerning the sufferings of this present time! Indeed the whole creation seems to wait with earnest expectation for the period when the children of God shall be manifested in the glory prepared for them. There is an impurity, deformity, and infirmity, which has come upon the creature by the fall of man. There is an enmity of one creature to another. And they are used, or abused rather, by men as instruments of sin. Yet this deplorable state of the creation is in hope. God will deliver it from thus being held in bondage to man's depravity. The miseries of the human race, through their own and each other's wickedness, declare that the world is not always to continue as it is. Our having received the first-fruits of the Spirit, quickens our desires, encourages our hopes, and raises our expectations. Sin has been, and is, the guilty cause of all the suffering that exists in the creation of God. It has brought on the woes of earth; it has kindled the flames of hell. As to man, not a tear has been shed, not a groan has been uttered, not a pang has been felt, in body or mind, that has not come from sin. This is not all; sin is to be looked at as it affects the glory of God. Of this how fearfully regardless are the bulk of mankind! Believers have been brought into a state of safety; but their comfort consists rather in hope than in enjoyment. From this hope they cannot be turned by the vain expectation of finding satisfaction in the things of time and sense. We need patience, our way is rough and long; but He that shall come, will come, though he seems to tarry.

Verses 26, 27

Though the infirmities of Christians are many and great, so that they would be overpowered if left to themselves, yet the Holy Spirit supports them. The Spirit, as an enlightening Spirit, teaches us what to pray for; as a sanctifying Spirit, works and stirs up praying graces; as a comforting Spirit, silences our fears, and helps us over all discouragements. The Holy Spirit is the spring of all desires toward God, which are often more than words can utter. The Spirit who searches the hearts, can perceive the mind and will of the spirit, the renewed mind, and advocates his cause. The Spirit makes intercession to God, and the enemy prevails not.

Verses 28-31

That is good for the saints which does their souls good. Every providence tends to the spiritual good of those that love God; in breaking them off from sin, bringing them nearer to God, weaning them from the world, and fitting them for heaven. When the saints act out of character, corrections will be employed to bring them back again. And here is the order of the causes of our salvation, a golden chain, one which cannot be broken. 1. Whom he did foreknow, he also did predestinate to be conformed to the image of his Son. All that God designed for glory and happiness as the end, he decreed to grace and holiness as the way. The whole human race deserved destruction; but for reasons not perfectly known to us, God determined to recover some by regeneration and the power of his grace. He predestinated, or before decreed, that they should be conformed to the image of his Son. In this life they are in part renewed, and walk in his steps. 2. Whom he did predestinate, them he also called. It is an effectual call, from self and earth to God, and Christ, and heaven, as our end; from sin and vanity to grace and holiness, as our way. This is the gospel call. The love of God, ruling in the hearts of those who once were enemies to him, proves that they have been called according to his purpose. 3. Whom he called, them he also justified. None are thus justified but those that are effectually called. Those who stand out against the gospel call, abide under guilt and wrath. 4. Whom he justified, them he also glorified. The power of corruption being broken in effectual calling, and the guilt of sin removed in justification, nothing can come between that soul and glory. This encourages our faith and hope; for, as for God, his way, his work, is perfect. The apostle speaks as one amazed, and swallowed up in admiration, wondering at the height and depth, and length and breadth, of the love of Christ, which passeth knowledge. The more we know of other things, the less we wonder; but the further we are led into gospel mysteries, the more we are affected by them. While God is for us, and we keep in his love, we may with holy boldness defy all the powers of darkness.

Verses 32-39

All things whatever, in heaven and earth, are not so great a display of God's free love, as the gift of his coequal Son to be the atonement on the cross for the sin of man; and all the rest follows upon union with him, and interest in him. All things, all which can be the causes or means of any real good to the faithful Christian. He that has prepared a crown and a kingdom for us, will give us what we need in the way to it. Men may justify themselves, though the accusations are in full force against them; but if God justifies, that answers all. By Christ we are thus secured. By the merit of his death he paid our debt. Yea, rather that is risen again. This is convincing evidence that Divine justice was satisfied. We have such a Friend at the right hand of God; all power is given to him. He is there, making intercession. Believer! does your soul say within you, Oh that he were mine! and oh that I were his; that I could please him and live to him! Then do not toss your spirit and perplex your thoughts in fruitless, endless doubtings, but as you are convinced of ungodliness, believe on Him who justifies the ungodly. You are condemned, yet Christ is dead and risen. Flee to Him as such. God having manifested his love in giving his own Son for us, can we think that any thing should turn aside or do away that love? Troubles neither cause nor show any abatement of his love. Whatever believers may be separated from, enough remains. None can take Christ from the believer: none can take the believer from Him; and that is enough. All other hazards signify nothing. Alas, poor sinners! though you abound with the possessions of this world, what vain things are they! Can you say of any of them, Who shall separate us? You may be removed from pleasant dwellings, and friends, and estates. You may even live to see and seek your parting. At last you must part, for you must die. Then farewell, all this world accounts most valuable. And what hast thou left, poor soul, who hast not Christ, but that which thou wouldest gladly part with, and canst not; the condemning guilt of all thy sins! But the soul that is in Christ, when other things are pulled away, cleaves to Christ, and these separations pain him not. Yea, when death comes, that breaks all other unions, even that of the soul and body, it carries the believer's soul into the nearest union with its beloved Lord Jesus, and the full enjoyment of him for ever.

Chapter 9

Chapter Outline

The apostle's concern that his countrymen were strangers to the gospel.	(1–5)
The promises are made good to the spiritual seed of Abraham.	(6–13)
Answers to objections against God's sovereign conduct, in exercising mercy and justice.	(14–24)
This sovereignty is in God's dealing both with Jews and Gentiles.	(25–29)
The falling short of the Jews is owing to their seeking justification, not by faith, but by the works of the law.	(30–33)

Verses 1-5

Being about to discuss the rejection of the Jews and the calling of the Gentiles, and to show that the whole agrees with the sovereign electing love of God, the apostle expresses strongly his affection for his people. He solemnly appeals to Christ; and his conscience, enlightened and directed by the Holy Spirit, bore witness to his sincerity. He would submit to be treated as "accursed," to be disgraced, crucified; and even for a time be in the deepest horror and distress; if he could rescue his nation from the destruction about to come upon them for their obstinate unbelief. To be insensible to the eternal condition of our fellow-creatures, is contrary both to the love required by the law, and the mercy of the gospel. They had long been professed worshippers of Jehovah. The law, and the national covenant which was grounded thereon, belonged to them. The temple worship was typical of salvation by the Messiah, and the means of communion with God. All the promises concerning Christ and his salvation were given to them. He is not only over all, as Mediator, but he is God blessed for ever.

Verses 6-13

The rejection of the Jews by the gospel dispensation, did not break God's promise to the patriarchs. The promises and threatenings shall be fulfilled. Grace does not run in the blood; nor are saving benefits always found with outward church privileges. Not only some of Abraham's seed were chosen, and others not, but God therein wrought according to the counsel of his own will. God foresaw both Esau and Jacob as born in sin, by nature children of wrath even as others. If left to themselves they would have continued in sin through life; but for wise and holy reasons, not made known to us, he purposed to change Jacob's heart, and to leave Esau to his perverseness. This instance of Esau and Jacob throws light upon the Divine conduct to the fallen race of man. The whole Scripture shows the difference between the professed Christian and the real believer. Outward privileges are bestowed on many who are not the children of God. There is, however, full encouragement to diligent use of the means of grace which God has appointed.

Verses 14-24

Whatever God does, must be just. Wherein the holy, happy people of God differ from others, God's grace alone makes them differ. In this preventing, effectual, distinguishing grace, he acts as a benefactor, whose grace is his own. None have deserved it; so that those who are saved, must thank God only; and those who perish, must blame themselves only, Hos 13:9. God is bound no further than he has been pleased to bind himself by his own covenant and promise, which is his revealed will. And this is, that he will receive, and not cast out, those that come to Christ; but the drawing of souls in order to that coming, is an anticipating, distinguishing favour to whom he will. Why does he yet find fault? This is not an objection to be made by the creature against his Creator, by man against God. The truth, as it is in Jesus, abases man as nothing, as less than nothing, and advances God as sovereign Lord of all. Who art thou that art so foolish, so feeble, so unable to judge the Divine counsels? It becomes us to submit to him, not to reply against him. Would not men allow the infinite God the same sovereign right to manage the affairs of the creation, as the potter exercises in disposing of his clay, when of the same lump he makes one vessel to a more honourable, and one to a meaner use? God could do no wrong, however it might appear to men. God will make it appear that he hates sin. Also, he formed vessels filled with mercy. Sanctification is the preparation of the soul for glory. This is God's work. Sinners fit themselves for hell, but it is God who prepares saints for heaven; and all whom God designs for heaven hereafter, he fits for heaven now. Would we know who these vessels of mercy are? Those whom God has called; and these not of the Jews only, but of the Gentiles. Surely there can be no unrighteousness in any of these Divine dispensations. Nor in God's exercising long-suffering, patience, and forbearance towards sinners under increasing guilt, before he brings utter destruction upon them. The fault is in the hardened sinner himself. As to all who love and fear God, however such truths appear beyond their reason to fathom, yet they should keep silence before him. It is the Lord alone who made us to differ; we should adore his pardoning mercy and new-creating grace, and give diligence to make our calling and election sure.

Verses 25-29

The rejecting of the Jews, and the taking in the Gentiles, were foretold in the Old Testament. It tends very much to the clearing of a truth, to observe how the Scripture is fulfilled in it. It is a wonder of Divine power and mercy that there are any saved: for even those left to be a seed, if God had dealt with them according to their sins, had perished with the rest. This great truth this Scripture teaches us. Even among the vast number of professing Christians it is to be feared that only a remnant will be saved.

Verses 30-33

The Gentiles knew not their guilt and misery, therefore were not careful to procure a remedy. Yet they attained to righteousness by faith. Not by becoming proselytes to the Jewish religion, and submitting to the ceremonial law; but by embracing Christ, and believing in him, and submitting to the gospel. The Jews talked much of justification and holiness, and seemed very ambitious to be the favourites of God. They sought, but not in the right way, not in the humbling way, not in the appointed way. Not by faith, not by embracing Christ, depending upon Christ, and submitting to the gospel. They expected justification by observing the precepts and ceremonies of the law of Moses. The unbelieving Jews had a fair offer of righteousness, life, and salvation, made them upon gospel terms, which they did not like, and would not accept. Have we sought to know how we may be justified before God, seeking that blessing in the way here pointed out, by faith in Christ, as the Lord our Righteousness? Then we shall not be ashamed in that awful day, when all refuges of lies shall be swept away, and the Divine wrath shall overflow every hiding-place but that which God hath prepared in his own Son.

Chapter 10

Chapter Outline

The apostle's earnest desire for the salvation of the Jews.	(1–4)
The difference between the righteousness of the law, and the righteousness of faith.	(5–11)
The Gentiles stand on a level with the Jews, in justification and salvation.	(12–17)
The Jews might know this from Old Testament prophecies.	(18–21)

Verses 1-4

The Jews built on a false foundation, and refused to come to Christ for free salvation by faith, and numbers in every age do the same in various ways. The strictness of the law showed men their need of salvation by grace, through faith. And the ceremonies shadowed forth Christ as fulfilling the righteousness, and bearing the curse of the law. So that even under the law, all who were justified before God, obtained that blessing by faith, whereby they were made partakers of the perfect righteousness of the promised Redeemer. The law is not destroyed, nor the intention of the Lawgiver disappointed; but full satisfaction being made by the death of Christ for our breach of the law, the end is gained. That is, Christ has fulfilled the whole law, therefore whoever believeth in him, is counted just before God, as much as though he had fulfilled the whole law himself. Sinners never could go on in vain fancies of their own righteousness, if they knew the justice of God as a Governor, or his righteousness as a Saviour.

Verses 5-11

The self-condemned sinner need not perplex himself how this righteousness may be found. When we speak of looking upon Christ, and receiving, and feeding upon him, it is not Christ in heaven, nor Christ in the deep, that we mean; but Christ in the promise, Christ offered in the word. Justification by faith in Christ is a plain doctrine. It is brought before the mind and heart of every one, thus leaving him without excuse for unbelief. If a man confessed faith in Jesus, as the Lord and Saviour of lost sinners, and really believed in his heart that God had raised him from the dead, thus showing that he had accepted the atonement, he should be saved by the righteousness of Christ, imputed to him through faith. But no faith is justifying which is not powerful in sanctifying the heart, and regulating all its affections by the love of Christ. We must devote and give up to God our souls and our bodies: our souls in believing with the heart, and our bodies in confessing with the mouth. The believer shall never have cause to repent his confident trust in the Lord Jesus. Of such faith no sinner shall be ashamed before God; and he ought to glory in it before men.

Verses 12-17

There is not one God to the Jews, more kind, and another to the Gentiles, who is less kind; the Lord is a Father to all men. The promise is the same to all, who call on the name of the Lord Jesus as the Son of God, as God manifest in the flesh. All believers thus call upon the Lord Jesus, and none else will do so humbly or sincerely. But how should any call on the Lord Jesus, the Divine Saviour, who had not heard of him? And what is the life of a Christian but a life of prayer? It shows that we feel our dependence on him, and are ready to give up ourselves to him, and have a believing expectation of our all from him. It was necessary that the gospel should be preached to the Gentiles. Somebody must show them what they are to believe. How welcome the gospel ought to be to those to whom it was preached! The gospel is given, not only to be known and believed, but to be obeyed. It is not a system of notions, but a rule of practice. The beginning, progress, and strength of faith is by hearing. But it is only hearing the word, as the word of God that will strengthen faith.

Verses 18-21

Did not the Jews know that the Gentiles were to be called in? They might have known it from Moses and Isaiah. Isaiah speaks plainly of the grace and favour of God, as going before in the receiving of the Gentiles. Was not this our own case? Did not God begin in love, and make himself known to us when we did not ask after him? The patience of God towards provoking sinners is wonderful. The time of God's patience is called a day, light as day, and fit for work and business; but limited as a day, and there is a night at the end of it. God's patience makes man's disobedience worse, and renders that the more sinful. We may wonder at the mercy of God, that his goodness is not overcome by man's badness; we may wonder at the wickedness of man, that his badness is not overcome by God's goodness. And it is a matter of joy to think that God has sent the message of grace to so many millions, by the wide spread of his gospel.

Chapter 11

Chapter Outline

The rejection of the Jews is not universal.	(1–10)
God overruled their unbelief for making the Gentiles partakers of gospel privileges.	(11–21)
The Gentiles cautioned against pride and unbelief, The Jews shall be called as a nation, and brought into God's visible covenant again.	(22–32)
A solemn adoring of the wisdom, goodness, and justice of God.	(33–36)

Verses 1-10

There was a chosen remnant of believing Jews, who had righteousness and life by faith in Jesus Christ. These were kept according to the election of grace. If then this election was of grace, it could not be of works, either performed or foreseen. Every truly good disposition in a fallen creature must be the effect, therefore it cannot be the cause, of the grace of God bestowed on him. Salvation from the first to the last must be either of grace or of debt. These things are so directly contrary to each other that they cannot be blended together. God glorifies his grace by changing the hearts and tempers of the rebellious. How then should they wonder and praise him! The Jewish nation were as in a deep sleep, without knowledge of their danger, or concern about it; having no sense of their need of the Saviour, or of their being upon the borders of eternal ruin. David, having by the Spirit foretold the sufferings of Christ from his own people, the Jews, foretells the dreadful judgments of God upon them for it, Ps 69. This teaches us how to understand other prayers of David against his enemies; they are prophecies of the judgments of God, not expressions of his own anger. Divine curses will work long; and we have our eyes darkened, if we are bowed down in worldly-mindedness.

Verses 11-21

The gospel is the greatest riches of every place where it is. As therefore the righteous rejection of the unbelieving Jews, was the occasion of so large a multitude of the Gentiles being reconciled to God, and at peace with him; the future receiving of the Jews into the church would be such a change, as would resemble a general resurrection of the dead in sin to a life of righteousness. Abraham was as the root of the church. The Jews continued branches of this tree till, as a nation, they rejected the Messiah; after that, their relation to Abraham and to God was, as it were, cut off. The Gentiles were grafted into this tree in their room; being admitted into the church of God. Multitudes were made heirs of Abraham's faith, holiness and blessedness. It is the natural state of every one of us, to be wild by nature. Conversion is as the grafting in of wild branches into the good olive. The wild olive was often ingrafted into the fruitful one when it began to decay, and this not only brought forth fruit, but caused the decaying olive to revive and flourish. The Gentiles, of free grace, had been grafted in to share advantages. They ought therefore to beware of self-confidence, and every kind of pride or ambition; lest, having only a dead faith, and an empty profession, they should turn from God, and forfeit their privileges. If we stand at all, it is by faith; we are guilty and helpless in ourselves, and are to be humble, watchful, afraid of self-deception, or of being overcome by temptation. Not only are we at first justified by faith, but kept to the end in that justified state by faith only; yet, by a faith which is not alone, but which worketh by love to God and man.

Verses 22-32

Of all judgments, spiritual judgments are the sorest; of these the apostle is here speaking. The restoration of the Jews is, in the course of things, far less improbable than the call of the Gentiles to be the children of Abraham; and though others now possess these privileges, it will not hinder their being admitted again. By rejecting the gospel, and by their indignation at its being preached to the Gentiles, the Jews were become enemies to God; yet they are still to be favoured for the sake of their pious fathers. Though at present they are enemies to the gospel, for their hatred to the Gentiles; yet, when God's time is come, that will no longer exist, and God's love to their fathers will be remembered. True grace seeks not to confine God's favour. Those who find mercy themselves, should endeavour that through their mercy others also may obtain mercy. Not that the Jews will be restored to have their priesthood, and temple, and ceremonies again; an end is put to all these; but they are to be brought to believe in Christ, the true become one sheep-fold with the Gentiles, under Christ the Great Shepherd. The captivities of Israel, their dispersion, and their being shut out from the church, are emblems of the believer's corrections for doing wrong; and the continued care of the Lord towards that people, and the final mercy and blessed restoration intended for them, show the patience and love of God.

Verses 33-36

The apostle Paul knew the mysteries of the kingdom of God as well as ever any man; yet he confesses himself at a loss; and despairing to find the bottom, he humbly sits down at the brink, and adores the depth. Those who know most in this imperfect state, feel their own weakness most. There is not only depth in the Divine counsels, but riches; abundance of that which is precious and valuable. The Divine counsels are complete; they have not only depth and height, but breadth and length, Eph 3:18, and that passing knowledge. There is that vast distance and disproportion between God and man, between the Creator and the creature, which for ever shuts us from knowledge of his ways. What man shall teach God how to govern the world? The apostle adores the sovereignty of the Divine counsels. All things in heaven and earth, especially those which relate to our salvation, that belong to our peace, are all of him by way of creation, through him by way of providence, that they may be to him in their end. Of God, as the Spring and Fountain of all; through Christ, to God, as the end. These include all God's relations to his creatures; if all are of Him, and through Him, all should be to Him, and for Him. Whatever begins, let God's glory be the end: especially let us adore him when we talk of the Divine counsels and actings. The saints in heaven never dispute, but always praise.

Chapter 12

Chapter Outline

Believers are to dedicate themselves to God.	(1, 2)
To be humble, and faithfully to use their spiritual gifts, in their respective stations.	(3–8)
Exhortations to various duties.	(9–16)
And to peaceable conduct towards all men, with forbearance and benevolence.	(17–21)

Verses 1, 2

The apostle having closed the part of his epistle wherein he argues and proves various doctrines which are practically applied, here urges important duties from gospel principles. He entreated the Romans, as his brethren in Christ, by the mercies of God, to present their bodies as a living sacrifice to Him. This is a powerful appeal. We receive from the Lord every day the fruits of his mercy. Let us render ourselves; all we are, all we have, all we can do: and after all, what return is it for such very rich receivings? It is acceptable to God: a reasonable service, which we are able and ready to give a reason for, and which we understand. Conversion and sanctification are the renewing of the mind; a change, not of the substance, but of the qualities of the soul. The progress of sanctification, dying to sin more and more, and living to righteousness more and more, is the carrying on this renewing work, till it is perfected in glory. The great enemy to this renewal is, conformity to this world. Take heed of forming plans for happiness, as though it lay in the things of this world, which soon pass away. Do not fall in with the customs of those who walk in the lusts of the flesh, and mind earthly things. The work of the Holy Ghost first begins in the understanding, and is carried on to the will, affections, and conversation, till there is a change of the whole man into the likeness of God, in knowledge, righteousness, and true holiness. Thus, to be godly, is to give up ourselves to God.

Verses 3-8

Pride is a sin in us by nature; we need to be cautioned and armed against it. All the saints make up one body in Christ, who is the Head of the body, and the common Centre of their unity. In the spiritual body, some are fitted for and called to one sort of work; others for another sort of work. We are to do all the good we can, one to another, and for the common benefit. If we duly thought about the powers we have, and how far we fail properly to improve them, it would humble us. But as we must not be proud of our talents, so we must take heed lest, under a pretence of humility and self-denial, we are slothful in laying out ourselves for the good of others. We must not say, I am nothing, therefore I will sit still, and do nothing; but, I am nothing in myself, and therefore I will lay out myself to the utmost, in the strength of the grace of Christ. Whatever our gifts or situations may be, let us try to employ ourselves humbly, diligently, cheerfully, and in simplicity; not seeking our own credit or profit, but the good of many, for this world and that which is to come.

Verses 9-16

The professed love of Christians to each other should be sincere, free from deceit, and unmeaning and deceitful compliments. Depending on Divine grace, they must detest and dread all evil, and love and delight in whatever is kind and useful. We must not only do that which is good, but we must cleave to it. All our duty towards one another is summed up in one word, love. This denotes the love of parents to their children; which is more tender and natural than any other; unforced, unconstrained. And love to God and man, with zeal for the gospel, will make the wise Christian diligent in all his wordly business, and in gaining superior skill. God must be served with the spirit, under the influences of the Holy Spirit. He is honoured by our hope and trust in him, especially when we rejoice in that hope. He is served, not only by working for him, but by sitting still quietly, when he calls us to suffer. Patience for God's sake, is true piety. Those that rejoice in hope, are likely to be patient in tribulation. We should not be cold in the duty of prayer, nor soon weary of it. Not only must there be kindness to friends and brethren, but Christians must not harbour anger against enemies. It is but mock love, which rests in words of kindness, while our brethren need real supplies, and it is in our power to furnish them. Be ready to entertain those who do good: as there is occasion, we must welcome strangers. Bless, and curse not. It means thorough good will; not, bless them when at prayer, and curse them at other times; but bless them always, and curse not at all. True Christian love will make us take part in the sorrows and joys of each other. Labour as much as you can to agree in the same spiritual truths; and when you come short of that, yet agree in affection. Look upon worldly pomp and dignity with holy contempt. Do not mind it; be not in love with it. Be reconciled to the place God in his providence puts you in, whatever it be. Nothing is below us, but sin. We shall never find in our hearts to condescend to others, while we indulge conceit of ourselves; therefore that must be mortified.

Verses 17-21

Since men became enemies to God, they have been very ready to be enemies one to another. And those that embrace religion, must expect to meet with enemies in a world whose smiles seldom agree with Christ's. Recompense to no man evil for evil. That is a brutish recompence, befitting only animals, which are not conscious of any being above them, or of any existence hereafter. And not only do, but study and take care to do, that which is amiable and creditable, and recommends religion to all with whom you converse. Study the things that make for peace; if it be possible, without offending God and wounding conscience. Avenge not yourselves. This is a hard lesson to corrupt nature, therefore a remedy against it is added. Give place unto wrath. When a man's passion is up, and the stream is strong, let it pass off; lest it be made to rage the more against us. The line of our duty is clearly marked out, and if our enemies are not melted by persevering kindness, we are not to seek vengeance; they will be consumed by the fiery wrath of that God to whom vengeance belongeth. The last verse suggests what is not easily understood by the world; that in all strife and contention, those that revenge are conquered, and those that forgive are conquerors. Be not overcome of evil. Learn to defeat ill designs against you, either to change them, or to preserve your own peace. He that has this rule over his spirit, is better than the mighty. God's children may be asked whether it is not more sweet unto them than all earthly good, that God so enables them by his Spirit, thus to feel and act.

Chapter 13

Chapter Outline

Verses 1-7

The grace of the gospel teaches us submission and quiet, where pride and the carnal mind only see causes for murmuring and discontent. Whatever the persons in authority over us themselves may be, yet the just power they have, must be submitted to and obeyed. In the general course of human affairs, rulers are not a terror to honest, quiet, and good subjects, but to evil-doers. Such is the power of sin and corruption, that many will be kept back from crimes only by the fear of punishment. Thou hast the benefit of the government, therefore do what thou canst to preserve it, and nothing to disturb it. This directs private persons to behave quietly and peaceably where God has set them, 1Ti 2:1, 2. Christians must not use any trick or fraud. All smuggling, dealing in contraband goods, withholding or evading duties, is rebellion against the express command of God. Thus honest neighbours are robbed, who will have to pay the more; and the crimes of smugglers, and others who join with them, are abetted. It is painful that some professors of the gospel should countenance such dishonest practices. The lesson here taught it becomes all Christians to learn and practise, that the godly in the land will always be found the quiet and the peaceable in the land, whatever others are.

Verses 8-10

Christians must avoid useless expense, and be careful not to contract any debts they have not the power to discharge. They are also to stand aloof from all venturesome speculations and rash engagements, and whatever may expose them to the danger of not rendering to all their due. Do not keep in any one's debt. Give every one his own. Do not spend that on yourselves, which you owe to others. But many who are very sensible of the trouble, think little of the sin, of being in debt. Love to others includes all the duties of the second table. The last five of the ten commandments are all summed up in this royal law, Thou shalt love thy neighbour as thyself; with the same sincerity that thou lovest thyself, though not in the same measure and degree. He that loves his neighbour as himself, will desire the welfare of his neighbour. On this is built that golden rule, of doing as we would be done by. Love is a living, active principle of obedience to the whole law. Let us not only avoid injuries to the persons, connexions, property, and characters of men; but do no kind or degree of evil to any man, and study to be useful in every station of life.

Verses 11-14

Four things are here taught, as a Christian's directory for his day's work. When to awake; Now; and to awake out of the sleep of carnal security, sloth, and negligence; out of the sleep of spiritual death, and out of the sleep of spiritual deadness. Considering the time; a busy time; a perilous time. Also the salvation nigh at hand. Let us mind our way, and mend our pace, we are nearer our journey's end. Also to make ourselves ready. The night is far spent, the day is at hand; therefore it is time to dress ourselves. Observe what we must put off; clothes worn in the night. Cast off the sinful works of darkness. Observe what we must put on; how we should dress our souls. Put on the armour of light. A Christian must reckon himself undressed, if unarmed. The graces of the Spirit are this armour, to secure the soul from Satan's temptations, and the assaults of this present evil world. Put on Christ; that includes all. Put on righteousness of Christ, for justification. Put on the Spirit and grace of Christ, for sanctification. The Lord Jesus Christ must be put on as Lord to rule you as Jesus to save you; and in both, as Christ anointed and appointed by the Father to this ruling, saving work. And how to walk. When we are up and ready, we are not to sit still, but to appear abroad; let us walk. Christianity teaches us how to walk so as to please God, who ever sees us. Walk honestly as in the day; avoiding the works of darkness. Where there are riot and drunkenness, there usually are chambering and wantonness, and strife and envy. Solomon puts these all together, Pr 23:29–35. See what provision to make. Our great care must be to provide for our souls: but must we take no care about our bodies? Yes; but two things are forbidden. Perplexing ourselves with anxious, encumbering care; and indulging ourselves in irregular desires. Natural wants are to be answered, but evil appetites must be checked and denied. To ask meat for our necessities, is our duty, we are taught to pray for daily bread; but to ask meat for our lusts, is provoking God, Ps 78:18.

Chapter 14

Chapter Outline

The Jewish converts cautioned against judging, and Gentile believers against despising one the other.   (1–13)

And the Gentiles exhorted to take heed of giving offence in their use of indifferent things.   (14–23)

Verses 1-6

Differences of opinion prevailed even among the immediate followers of Christ and their disciples. Nor did St. Paul attempt to end them. Compelled assent to any doctrine, or conformity to outward observances without being convinced, would be hypocritical and of no avail. Attempts for producing absolute oneness of mind among Christians would be useless. Let not Christian fellowship be disturbed with strifes of words. It will be good for us to ask ourselves, when tempted to disdain and blame our brethren; Has not God owned them? and if he has, dare I disown them? Let not the Christian who uses his liberty, despise his weak brother as ignorant and superstitious. Let not the scrupulous believer find fault with his brother, for God accepted him, without regarding the distinctions of meats. We usurp the place of God, when we take upon us thus to judge the thoughts and intentions of others, which are out of our view. The case as to the observance of days was much the same. Those who knew that all these things were done away by Christ's coming, took no notice of the festivals of the Jews. But it is not enough that our consciences consent to what we do; it is necessary that it be certified from the word of God. Take heed of acting against a doubting conscience. We are all apt to make our own views the standard of truth, to deem things certain which to others appear doubtful. Thus Christians often despise or condemn each other, about doubtful matters of no moment. A thankful regard to God, the Author and Giver of all our mercies, sanctifies and sweetens them.

Verses 7-13

Though some are weak, and others are strong, yet all must agree not to live to themselves. No one who has given up his name to Christ, is allowedly a self-seeker; that is against true Christianity. The business of our lives is not to please ourselves, but to please God. That is true Christianity, which makes Christ all in all. Though Christians are of different strength, capacities, and practices in lesser things, yet they are all the Lord's; all are looking and serving, and approving themselves to Christ. He is Lord of those that are living, to rule them; of those that are dead, to revive them, and raise them up. Christians should not judge or despise one another, because both the one and the other must shortly give an account. A believing regard to the judgment of the great day, would silence rash judgings. Let every man search his own heart and life; he that is strict in judging and humbling himself, will not be apt to judge and despise his brother. We must take heed of saying or doing things which may cause others to stumble or to fall. The one signifies a lesser, the other a greater degree of offence; that which may be an occasion of grief or of guilt to our brother.

Verses 14-18

Christ deals gently with those who have true grace, though they are weak in it. Consider the design of Christ's death: also that drawing a soul to sin, threatens the destruction of that soul. Did Christ deny himself for our brethren, so as to die for them, and shall not we deny ourselves for them, so as to keep from any indulgence? We cannot hinder ungoverned tongues from speaking evil; but we must not give them any occasion. We must deny ourselves in many cases what we may lawfully do, when our doing it may hurt our good name. Our good often comes to be evil spoken of, because we use lawful things in an uncharitable and selfish manner. As we value the reputation of the good we profess and practise, let us seek that it may not be evil-spoken of. Righteousness, peace, and joy, are words that mean a great deal. As to God, our great concern is to appear before him justified by Christ's death, sanctified by the Spirit of his grace; for the righteous Lord loveth righteousness. As to our brethren, it is to live in peace, and love, and charity with them; following peace with all men. As to ourselves, it is joy in the Holy Ghost; that spiritual joy wrought by the blessed Spirit in the hearts of believers, which respects God as their reconciled Father, and heaven as their expected home. Regard to Christ in doing our duties, alone can make them acceptable. Those are most pleasing to God that are best pleased with him; and they abound most in peace and joy in the Holy Ghost. They are approved by wise and good men; and the opinion of others is not to be regarded.

Verses 19-23

Many wish for peace, and talk loudly for it, who do not follow the things that make for peace. Meekness, humility, self-denial, and love, make for peace. We cannot edify one another, while quarrelling and contending. Many, for meat and drink, destroy the work of God in themselves; nothing more destroys the soul than pampering and pleasing the flesh, and fulfilling the lusts of it; so others are hurt, by wilful offence given. Lawful things may be done unlawfully, by giving offence to brethren. This takes in all indifferent things, whereby a brother is drawn into sin or trouble; or has his graces, his comforts, or his resolutions weakened. Hast thou faith? It is meant of knowledge and clearness as to our Christian liberty. Enjoy the comfort of it, but do not trouble others by a wrong use of it. Nor may we act against a doubting conscience. How excellent are the blessings of Christ's kingdom, which consists not in outward rites and ceremonies, but in righteousness, peace, and joy in the Holy Ghost! How preferable is the service of God to all other services! and in serving him we are not called to live and die to ourselves, but unto Christ, whose we are, and whom we ought to serve.

Chapter 15

Chapter Outline

Verses 1-7

Christian liberty was allowed, not for our pleasure, but for the glory of God, and the good of others. We must please our neighbour, for the good of his soul; not by serving his wicked will, and humouring him in a sinful way; if we thus seek to please men, we are not the servants of Christ. Christ's whole life was a self-denying, self-displeasing life. And he is the most advanced Christian, who is the most conformed to Christ. Considering his spotless purity and holiness, nothing could be more contrary to him, than to be made sin and a curse for us, and to have the reproaches of God fall upon him; the just for the unjust. He bore the guilt of sin, and the curse for it; we are only called to bear a little of the trouble of it. He bore the presumptuous sins of the wicked; we are called only to bear the failings of the weak. And should not we be humble, self-denying, and ready to consider one another, who are members one of another? The Scriptures are written for our use and benefit, as much as for those to whom they were first given. Those are most learned who are most mighty in the Scriptures. That comfort which springs from the word of God, is the surest and sweetest, and the greatest stay to hope. The Spirit as a Comforter, is the earnest of our inheritance. This like-mindedness must be according to the precept of Christ, according to his pattern and example. It is the gift of God; and a precious gift it is, for which we must earnestly seek unto him. Our Divine Master invites his disciples, and encourages them by showing himself as meek and lowly in spirit. The same disposition ought to mark the conduct of his servants, especially of the strong towards the weak. The great end in all our actions must be, that God may be glorified; nothing more forwards this, than the mutual love and kindness of those who profess religion. Those that agree in Christ may well agree among themselves.

Verses 8-13

Christ fulfilled the prophecies and promises relating to the Jews, and the Gentile converts could have no excuse for despising them. The Gentiles, being brought into the church, are companions in patience and tribulation. They should praise God. Calling upon all the nations to praise the Lord, shows that they shall have knowledge of him. We shall never seek to Christ till we trust in him. And the whole plan of redemption is suited to reconcile us to one another, as well as to our gracious God, so that an abiding hope of eternal life, through the sanctifying and comforting power of the Holy Spirit, may be attained. Our own power will never reach this; therefore where this hope is, and is abounding, the blessed Spirit must have all the glory. "All joy and peace;" all sorts of true joy and peace, so as to suppress doubts and fears, through the powerful working of the Holy Spirit.

Verses 14-21

The apostle was persuaded that the Roman Christians were filled with a kind and affectionate spirit, as well as with knowledge. He had written to remind them of their duties and their dangers, because God had appointed him the minister of Christ to the Gentiles. Paul preached to them; but what made them sacrifices to God, was, their sanctification; not his work, but the work of the Holy Ghost: unholy things can never be pleasing to the holy God. The conversion of souls pertains unto God; therefore it is the matter of Paul's glorying, not the things of the flesh. But though a great preacher, he could not make one soul obedient, further than the Spirit of God accompanied his labours. He principally sought the good of those that sat in darkness. Whatever good we do, it is Christ who does it by us.

Verses 22-29

The apostle sought the things of Christ more than his own will, and would not leave his work of planting churches to go to Rome. It concerns all to do that first which is most needful. We must not take it ill if our friends prefer work which is pleasing to God, before visits and compliments, which may please us. It is justly expected from all Christians, that they should promote every good work, especially that blessed work, the conversion of souls. Christian society is a heaven upon earth, an earnest of our gathering together unto Christ at the great day. Yet it is but partial, compared with our communion with Christ; for that only will satisfy the soul. The apostle was going to Jerusalem, as the messenger of charity. God loves a cheerful giver. Every thing that passes between Christians should be a proof and instance of the union they have in Jesus Christ. The Gentiles received the gospel of salvation from the Jews; therefore were bound to minister to them in what was needed for the body. Concerning what he expected from them he speaks doubtfully; but concerning what he expected from God he speaks confidently. We cannot expect too little from man, nor too much from God. And how delightful and advantageous it is to have the gospel with the fulness of its blessings! What wonderful and happy effects does it produce, when attended with the power of the Spirit!

Verses 30-33

Let us learn to value the effectual fervent prayers of the righteous. How careful should we be, lest we forfeit our interest in the love and prayers of God's praying people! If we have experienced the Spirit's love, let us not be wanting in this office of kindness for others. Those that would prevail in prayer, must strive in prayer. Those who beg the prayers of others, must not neglect to pray for themselves. And though Christ knows our state and wants perfectly, he will know them from us. As God must be sought, for restraining the ill-will of our enemies, so also for preserving and increasing the good-will of our friends. All our joy depends upon the will of God. Let us be earnest in prayer with and for each other, that for Christ's sake, and by the love of the Holy Spirit, great blessings may come upon the souls of Christians, and the labours of ministers.

Chapter 16

Chapter Outline

Verses 1-16

Paul recommends Phebe to the Christians at Rome. It becomes Christians to help one another in their affairs, especially strangers; we know not what help we may need ourselves. Paul asks help for one that had been helpful to many; he that watereth shall be watered also himself. Though the care of all the churches came upon him daily, yet he could remember many persons, and send salutations to each, with particular characters of them, and express concern for them. Lest any should feel themselves hurt, as if Paul had forgotten them, he sends his remembrances to the rest, as brethren and saints, though not named. He adds, in the close, a general salutation to them all, in the name of the churches of Christ.

Verses 17-20

How earnest, how endearing are these exhortations! Whatever differs from the sound doctrine of the Scriptures, opens a door to divisions and offences. If truth be forsaken, unity and peace will not last long. Many call Christ, Master and Lord, who are far from serving him. But they serve their carnal, sensual, worldly interests. They corrupt the head by deceiving the heart; perverting the judgments by winding themselves into the affections. We have great need to keep our hearts with all diligence. It has been the common policy of seducers to set upon those who are softened by convictions. A pliable temper is good when under good guidance, otherwise it may be easily led astray. Be so wise as not to be deceived, yet so simple as not to be deceivers. The blessing the apostle expects from God, is victory over Satan. This includes all designs and devices of Satan against souls, to defile, disturb, and destroy them; all his attempts to keep us from the peace of heaven here, and the possession of heaven hereafter. When Satan seems to prevail, and we are ready to give up all as lost, then will the God of peace interpose in our behalf. Hold out therefore, faith and patience, yet a little while. If the grace of Christ be with us, who can prevail against us?

Verses 21-24

The apostle adds affectionate remembrances from persons with him, known to the Roman Christians. It is a great comfort to see the holiness and usefulness of our kindred. Not many mighty, not many noble are called, but some are. It is lawful for believers to bear civil offices; and it were to be wished that all offices in Christian states, and in the church, were bestowed upon prudent and steady Christians.

Verses 25-27

That which establishes souls, is, the plain preaching of Jesus Christ. Our redemption and salvation by our Lord Jesus Christ, are, without controversy, a great mystery of godliness. And yet, blessed be God, there is as much of this mystery made plain as will bring us to heaven, if we do not wilfully neglect so great salvation. Life and immortality are brought to light by the gospel, and the Sun of Righteousness is risen on the world. The Scriptures of the prophets, what they left in writing, is not only made plain in itself, but by it this mystery is made known to all nations. Christ is salvation to all nations. And the gospel is revealed, not to be talked of and disputed about, but to be submitted to. The obedience of faith is that obedience which is paid to the word of faith, and which comes by the grace of faith. All the glory that passes from fallen man to God, so as to be accepted of him, must go through the Lord Jesus, in whom alone our persons and doings are, or can be, pleasing to God. Of his righteousness we must make mention, even of his only; who, as he is the Mediator of all our prayers, so he is, and will be, to eternity, the Mediator of all our praises. Remembering that we are called to the obedience of faith, and that every degree of wisdom is from the only wise God, we should, by word and deed, render glory to him through Jesus Christ; that so the grace of our Lord Jesus Christ may be with us for ever.

1 Corinthians

The Corinthian church contained some Jews, but more Gentiles, and the apostle had to contend with the superstition of the one, and the sinful conduct of the other. The peace of this church was disturbed by false teachers, who undermined the influence of the apostle. Two parties were the result; one contending earnestly for the Jewish ceremonies, the other indulging in excesses contrary to the gospel, to which they were especially led by the luxury and the sins which prevailed around them. This epistle was written to rebuke some disorderly conduct, of which the apostle had been apprized, and to give advice as to some points whereon his judgment was requested by the Corinthians. Thus the scope was twofold. 1. To apply suitable remedies to the disorders and abuses which prevailed among them. 2. To give satisfactory answers on all the points upon which his advice had been desired. The address, and Christian mildness, yet firmness, with which the apostle writes, and goes on from general truths directly to oppose the errors and evil conduct of the Corinthians, is very remarkable. He states the truth and the will of God, as to various matters, with great force of argument and animation of style.

Chapter 1

Chapter Outline

A salutation and thanksgiving.	(1–9)
Exhortation to brotherly love, and reproof for divisions.	(10–16)
The doctrine of a crucified Saviour, as advancing the glory of God,	(17–25)
and humbling the creature before him.	(26–31)

Verses 1-9

All Christians are by baptism dedicated and devoted to Christ, and are under strict obligations to be holy. But in the true church of God are all who are sanctified in Christ Jesus, called to be saints, and who call upon him as God manifest in the flesh, for all the blessings of salvation; who acknowledge and obey him as their Lord, and as Lord of all; it includes no other persons. Christians are distinguished from the profane and atheists, that they dare not live without prayer; and they are distinguished from Jews and pagans, that they call on the name of Christ. Observe how often in these verses the apostle repeats the words, Our Lord Jesus Christ. He feared not to make too frequent or too honourable mention of him. To all who called upon Christ, the apostle gave his usual salutation, desiring, in their behalf, the pardoning mercy, sanctifying grace, and comforting peace of God, through Jesus Christ. Sinners can have no peace with God, nor any from him, but through Christ. He gives thanks for their conversion to the faith of Christ; that grace was given them by Jesus Christ. They had been enriched by him with all spiritual gifts. He speaks of utterance and knowledge. And where God has given these two gifts, he has given great power for usefulness.

These were gifts of the Holy Ghost, by which God bore witness to the apostles. Those that wait for the coming of our Lord Jesus Christ, will be kept by him to the end; and those that are so, will be blameless in the day of Christ, made so by rich and free grace. How glorious are the hopes of such a privilege; to be kept by the power of Christ, from the power of our corruptions and Satan's temptations!

Verses 10-16

In the great things of religion be of one mind; and where there is not unity of sentiment, still let there be union of affection. Agreement in the greater things should extinguish divisions about the lesser. There will be perfect union in heaven, and the nearer we approach it on earth, the nearer we come to perfection. Paul and Apollos both were faithful ministers of Jesus Christ, and helpers of their faith and joy; but those disposed to be contentious, broke into parties. So liable are the best things to be corrupted, and the gospel and its institutions made engines of discord and contention. Satan has always endeavoured to stir up strife among Christians, as one of his chief devices against the gospel. The apostle left it to other ministers to baptize, while he preached the gospel, as a more useful work.

Verses 17-25

Paul had been bred up in Jewish learning; but the plain preaching of a crucified Jesus, was more powerful than all the oratory and philosophy of the heathen world. This is the sum and substance of the gospel. Christ crucified is the foundation of all our hopes, the fountain of all our joys. And by his death we live. The preaching of salvation for lost sinners by the sufferings and death of the Son of God, if explained and faithfully applied, appears foolishness to those in the way to destruction. The sensual, the covetous, the proud, and ambitious, alike see that the gospel opposes their favourite pursuits. But those who receive the gospel, and are enlightened by the Spirit of God, see more of God's wisdom and power in the doctrine of Christ crucified, than in all his other works. God left a great part of the world to follow the dictates of man's boasted reason, and the event has shown that human wisdom is folly, and is unable to find or retain the knowledge of God as the Creator. It pleased him, by the foolishness of preaching, to save them that believe. By the foolishness of preaching; not by what could justly be called foolish preaching. But the thing preached was foolishness to wordly-wise men. The gospel ever was, and ever will be, foolishness to all in the road to destruction. The message of Christ, plainly delivered, ever has been a sure touchstone by which men may learn what road they are travelling. But the despised doctrine of salvation by faith in a crucified Saviour, God in human nature, purchasing the church with his own blood, to save multitudes, even all that believe, from ignorance, delusion, and vice, has been blessed in every age. And the weakest instruments God uses, are stronger in their effects, than the strongest men can use. Not that there is foolishness or weakness in God, but what men consider as such, overcomes all their admired wisdom and strength.

Verses 26-31

God did not choose philosophers, nor orators, nor statesmen, nor men of wealth, and power, and interest in the world, to publish the gospel of grace and peace. He best judges what men and what measures serve the purposes of his glory. Though not many noble are usually called by Divine grace, there have been some such in every age, who have not been ashamed of the gospel of Christ; and persons of every rank stand in need of pardoning grace. Often, a humble Christian, though poor as to this world, has more true knowledge of the gospel, than those who have made the letter of Scripture the study of their lives, but who have studied it rather as the witness of men, than as the word of God. And even young children have gained such knowledge of Divine truth as to silence infidels. The reason is, they are taught of God; the design is, that no flesh should glory in his presence. That distinction, in which alone they might glory, was not of themselves. It was by the sovereign choice and regenerating grace of God, that they were in Jesus Christ by faith. He is made of God to us wisdom, righteousness, sanctification, and redemption; all we need, or can desire. And he is made wisdom to us, that by his word and Spirit, and from his fulness and treasures of wisdom and knowledge, we may receive all that will make us wise unto salvation, and fit for every service to which we are called. We are guilty, liable to just punishment; and he is made righteousness, our great atonement and sacrifice. We are depraved and corrupt, and he is made sanctification, that he may in the end be made complete redemption; may free the soul from the being of sin, and loose the body from the bonds of the grave. And this is, that all flesh, according to the prophecy by Jeremiah, Jer 9:23–24, may glory in the special favour, all-sufficient grace, and precious salvation of Jehovah.

Chapter 2

Chapter Outline

The plain manner in which the apostle preached Christ crucified.	(1–5)
The wisdom contained in this doctrine.	(6–9)
It cannot be duly known but by the Holy Spirit.	(10–16)

Verses 1-5

Christ, in his person, and offices, and sufferings, is the sum and substance of the gospel, and ought to be the great subject of a gospel minister's preaching, but not so as to leave out other parts of God's revealed truth and will. Paul preached the whole counsel of God. Few know the fear and trembling of faithful ministers, from a deep sense of their own weakness They know how insufficient they are, and are fearful for themselves. When nothing but Christ crucified is plainly preached, the success must be entirely from Divine power accompanying the word, and thus men are brought to believe, to the salvation of their souls.

Verses 6-9

Those who receive the doctrine of Christ as Divine, and, having been enlightened by the Holy Spirit, have looked well into it, see not only the plain history of Christ, and him crucified, but the deep and admirable designs of Divine wisdom therein. It is the mystery made manifest to the saints, Col 1:26, though formerly hid from the heathen world; it was only shown in dark types and distant prophecies, but now is revealed and made known by the Spirit of God. Jesus Christ is the Lord of glory; a title much too great for any creature. There are many things which people would not do, if they knew the wisdom of God in the great work of redemption. There are things God hath prepared for those that love him, and wait for him, which sense cannot discover, no teaching can convey to our ears, nor can it yet enter our hearts. We must take them as they stand in the Scriptures, as God hath been pleased to reveal them to us.

Verses 10-16

God has revealed true wisdom to us by his Spirit. Here is a proof of the Divine authority of the Holy Scriptures, 2Pe 1:21. In proof of the Divinity of the Holy Ghost, observe, that he knows all things, and he searches all things, even the deep things of God. No one can know the things of God, but his Holy Spirit, who is one with the Father and the Son, and who makes known Divine mysteries to his church. This is most clear testimony, both to the real Godhead and the distinct person of the Holy Spirit. The apostles were not guided by worldly principles. They had the revelation of these things from the Spirit of God, and the saving impression of them from the same Spirit. These things they declared in plain, simple language, taught by the Holy Spirit, totally different from the affected oratory or enticing words of man's wisdom. The natural man, the wise man of the world, receives not the things of the Spirit of God. The pride of carnal reasoning is really as much opposed to spirituality, as the basest sensuality. The sanctified mind discerns the real beauties of holiness, but the power of discerning and judging about common and natural things is not lost. But the carnal man is a stranger to the principles, and pleasures, and actings of the Divine life. The spiritual man only, is the person to whom God gives the knowledge of his will. How little have any known of the mind of God by natural power! And the apostles were enabled by his Spirit to make known his mind. In the Holy Scriptures, the mind of Christ, and the mind of God in Christ, are fully made known to us. It is the great privilege of Christians, that they have the mind of Christ revealed to them by his Spirit. They experience his sanctifying power in their hearts, and bring forth good fruits in their lives.

Chapter 3

Chapter Outline

The Corinthians reproved for their contentions.   (1–4)

Verses 1-4

The most simple truths of the gospel, as to man's sinfulness and God's mercy, repentance towards God, and faith in our Lord Jesus Christ, stated in the plainest language, suit the people better than deeper mysteries. Men may have much doctrinal knowledge, yet be mere beginners in the life of faith and experience. Contentions and quarrels about religion are sad evidences of carnality. True religion makes men peaceable, not contentious. But it is to be lamented, that many who should walk as Christians, live and act too much like other men. Many professors, and preachers also, show themselves to be yet carnal, by vain-glorious strife, eagerness for dispute, and readiness to despise and speak evil of others.

Verses 5-9

The ministers about whom the Corinthians contended, were only instruments used by God. We should not put ministers into the place of God. He that planteth and he that watereth are one, employed by one Master, trusted with the same revelation, busied in one work, and engaged in one design. They have their different gifts from one and the same Spirit, for the very same purposes; and should carry on the same design heartily. Those who work hardest shall fare best. Those who are most faithful shall have the greatest reward. They work together with God, in promoting the purposes of his glory, and the salvation of precious souls; and He who knows their work, will take care they do not labour in vain. They are employed in his husbandry and building; and He will carefully look over them.

Verses 10-15

The apostle was a wise master-builder; but the grace of God made him such. Spiritual pride is abominable; it is using the greatest favours of God, to feed our own vanity, and make idols of ourselves. But let every man take heed; there may be bad building on a good foundation. Nothing must be laid upon it, but what the foundation will bear, and what is of a piece with it. Let us not dare to join a merely human or a carnal life with a Divine faith, the corruption of sin with the profession of Christianity. Christ is a firm, abiding, and immovable Rock of ages, every way able to bear all the weight that God himself or the sinner can lay upon him; neither is there salvation in any other. Leave out the doctrine of his atonement, and there is no foundation for our hopes. But of those who rest on this foundation, there are two sorts. Some hold nothing but the truth as it is in Jesus, and preach nothing else. Others build on the good foundation what will not abide the test, when the day of trail comes. We may be mistaken in ourselves and others; but there is a day coming that will show our actions in the true light, without covering or disguise. Those who spread true and pure religion in all its branches, and whose work will abide in the great day, shall receive a reward. And how great! how much exceeding their deserts! There are others, whose corrupt opinions and doctrines, or vain inventions and usages in the worship of God, shall be made known, disowned, and rejected, in that day. This is plainly meant of a figurative fire, not of a real one; for what real fire can consume religious rites or doctrines? And it is to try every man's works, those of Paul and Apollos, as well as others. Let us consider the tendency of our undertakings, compare them with God's word, and judge ourselves, that we be not judged of the Lord.

Verses 16, 17

From other parts of the epistle, it appears that the false teachers among the Corinthians taught unholy doctrines. Such teaching tended to corrupt, to pollute, and destroy the building, which should be kept pure and holy for God. Those who spread loose principles, which render the church of God unholy, bring destruction upon themselves. Christ by his Spirit dwells in all true believers. Christians are holy by profession, and should be pure and clean, both in heart and conversation. He is deceived who deems himself the temple of the Holy Ghost, yet is unconcerned about personal holiness, or the peace and purity of the church.

Verses 18-23

To have a high opinion of our own wisdom, is but to flatter ourselves; and self-flattery is the next step to self-deceit. The wisdom that wordly men esteem, is foolishness with God. How justly does he despise, and how easily can he baffle and confound it! The thoughts of the wisest men in the world, have vanity, weakness, and folly in them. All this should teach us to be humble, and make us willing to be taught of God, so as not to be led away, by pretences to human wisdom and skill, from the simple truths revealed by Christ. Mankind are very apt to oppose the design of the mercies of God. Observe the spiritual riches of a true believer; "All are yours," even ministers and ordinances. Nay, the world itself is yours. Saints have as much of it as Infinite Wisdom sees fit for them, and they have it with the Divine blessing. Life is yours, that you may have a season and opportunity to prepare for the life of heaven; and death is yours, that you may go to the possession of it. It is the kind messenger to take you from sin and sorrow, and to guide you to your Father's house. Things present are yours, for your support on the road; things to come are yours, to delight you for ever at your journey's end. If we belong to Christ, and are true to him, all good belongs to us, and is sure to us. Believers are the subjects of his kingdom. He is Lord over us, we must own his dominion, and cheerfully submit to his command. God in Christ, reconciling a sinful world to himself, and pouring the riches of his grace on a reconciled world, is the sum and substance of the gospel.

Chapter 4

Chapter Outline

Verses 1-6

Apostles were no more than servants of Christ, but they were not to be undervalued. They had a great trust, and for that reason, had an honourable office. Paul had a just concern for his own reputation, but he knew that he who chiefly aimed to please men, would not prove himself a faithful servant of Christ. It is a comfort that men are not to be our final judges. And it is not judging well of ourselves, or justifying ourselves, that will prove us safe and happy. Our own judgment is not to be depended upon as to our faithfulness, any more than our own works for our justification. There is a day coming, that will bring men's secret sins into open day, and discover the secrets of their hearts. Then every slandered believer will be justified, and every faithful servant approved and rewarded. The word of God is the best rule by which to judge as to men. Pride commonly is at the bottom of quarrels. Self-conceit contributes to produce undue esteem of our teachers, as well as of ourselves. We shall not be puffed up for one against another, if we remember that all are instruments, employed by God, and endowed by him with various talents.

Verses 7-13

We have no reason to be proud; all we have, or are, or do, that is good, is owing to the free and rich grace of God. A sinner snatched from destruction by sovereign grace alone, must be very absurd and inconsistent, if proud of the free gifts of God. St. Paul sets forth his own circumstances, ver. 9 Allusion is made to the cruel spectacles in the Roman games; where men were forced to cut one another to pieces, to divert the people; and where the victor did not escape with his life, though he should destroy his adversary, but was only kept for another combat, and must be killed at last. The thought that many eyes are upon believers, when struggling with difficulties or temptations, should encourage constancy and patience. "We are weak, but ye are strong." All Christians are not alike exposed. Some suffer greater hardships than others. The apostle enters into particulars of their sufferings. And how glorious the charity and devotion that carried them through all these hardships! They suffered in their persons and characters as the worst and vilest of men; as the very dirt of the world, that was to be swept away: nay, as the offscouring of all things, the dross of all things. And every one who would be faithful in Christ Jesus, must be prepared for poverty and contempt. Whatever the disciples of Christ suffer from men, they must follow the example, and fulfil the will and precepts of their Lord. They must be content, with him and for him, to be despised and abused. It is much better to be rejected, despised, and ill used, as St. Paul was, than to have the good opinion and favour of the world. Though cast off by the world as vile, yet we may be precious to God, gathered up with his own hand, and placed upon his throne.

Verses 14-21

In reproving for sin, we should distinguish between sinners and their sins. Reproofs that kindly and affectionately warn, are likely to reform. Though the apostle spoke with authority as a parent, he would rather beseech them in love. And as ministers are to set an example, others must follow them, as far as they follow Christ in faith and practice. Christians may mistake and differ in their views, but Christ and Christian truth are the same yesterday, to-day, and for ever. Whenever the gospel is effectual, it comes not in word only, but also in power, by the Holy Spirit, quickening dead sinners, delivering persons from the slavery of sin and Satan, renewing them both inwardly and outwardly, and comforting, strengthening, and establishing the saints, which cannot be done by the persuasive language of men, but by the power of God. And it is a happy temper, to have the spirit of love and meekness bear the rule, yet to maintain just authority.

Chapter 5

Chapter Outline

The apostle blames the Corinthians for connivance at an incestuous person;	(1–8)
and directs their behaviour towards those guilty of scandalous crimes.	(9–13)

Verses 1-8

The apostle notices a flagrant abuse, winked at by the Corinthians. Party spirit, and a false notion of Christian liberty, seem to have saved the offender from censure. Grievous indeed is it that crimes should sometimes be committed by professors of the gospel, of which even heathens would be ashamed. Spiritual pride and false doctrines tend to bring in, and to spread such scandals. How dreadful the effects of sin! The devil reigns where Christ does not. And a man is in his kingdom, and under his power, when not in Christ. The bad example of a man of influence is very mischievous; it spreads far and wide. Corrupt principles and examples, if not corrected, would hurt the whole church. Believers must have new hearts, and lead new lives. Their common conversation and religious deeds must be holy. So far is the sacrifice of Christ our Passover for us, from rendering personal and public holiness unnecessary, that it furnishes powerful reasons and motives for it. Without holiness we can neither live by faith in him, nor join in his ordinances with comfort and profit.

Verses 9-13

Christians are to avoid familiar converse with all who disgrace the Christian name. Such are only fit companions for their brethren in sin, and to such company they should be left, whenever it is possible to do so. Alas, that there are many called Christians, whose conversation is more dangerous than that of heathens!

Chapter 6

Chapter Outline

Cautions against going to law in heathen courts.   (1–8)

Sins which, if lived and died in, shut out from the kingdom of God.   (9–11)

Our bodies, which are the members of Christ, and temples of the Holy Ghost, must not be defiled.   (12–20)

Verses 1-8

Christians should not contend with one another, for they are brethren. This, if duly attended to, would prevent many law-suits, and end many quarrels and disputes. In matters of great damage to ourselves or families, we may use lawful means to right ourselves, but Christians should be of a forgiving temper. Refer the matters in dispute, rather than go to law about them. They are trifles, and may easily be settled, if you first conquer your own spirits. Bear and forbear, and the men of least skill among you may end your quarrels. It is a shame that little quarrels should grow to such a head among Christians, that they cannot be determined by the brethren. The peace of a man's own mind, and the calm of his neighbourhood, are worth more than victory. Lawsuits could not take place among brethren, unless there were faults among them.

Verses 9-11

The Corinthians are warned against many great evils, of which they had formerly been guilty. There is much force in these inquiries, when we consider that they were addressed to a people puffed up with a fancy of their being above others in wisdom and knowledge. All unrighteousness is sin; all reigning sin, nay, every actual sin, committed with design, and not repented of, shuts out of the kingdom of heaven. Be not deceived. Men are very much inclined to flatter themselves that they may live in sin, yet die in Christ, and go to heaven. But we cannot hope to sow to the flesh, and reap everlasting life. They are reminded what a change the gospel and grace of God had made in them. The blood of Christ, and the washing of regeneration, can take away all guilt. Our justification is owing to the suffering and merit of Christ; our sanctification to the working of the Holy Spirit; but both go together. All who are made righteous in the sight of God, are made holy by the grace of God.

Verses 12-20

Some among the Corinthians seem to have been ready to say, All things are lawful for me. This dangerous conceit St. Paul opposes. There is a liberty wherewith Christ has made us free, in which we must stand fast. But surely a Christian would never put himself into the power of any bodily appetite. The body is for the Lord; is to be an instrument of righteousness to holiness, therefore is never to be made an instrument of sin. It is an honour to the body, that Jesus Christ was raised from the dead; and it will be an honour to our bodies, that they will be raised. The hope of a resurrection to glory, should keep Christians from dishonouring their bodies by fleshly lusts. And if the soul be united to Christ by faith, the whole man is become a member of his spiritual body. Other vices may be conquered in fight; that here cautioned against, only by flight. And vast multitudes are cut off by this vice in its various forms and consequences. Its effects fall not only directly upon the body, but often upon the mind. Our bodies have been redeemed from deserved condemnation and hopeless slavery by the atoning sacrifice of Christ. We are to be clean, as vessels fitted for our Master's use. Being united to Christ as one spirit, and bought with a price of unspeakable value, the believer should consider himself as wholly the Lord's, by the strongest ties. May we make it our business, to the latest day and hour of our lives, to glorify God with our bodies, and with our spirits which are his.

Chapter 7

Chapter Outline

The apostle answers several questions about marriage.	(1–9)
Married Christians should not seek to part from their unbelieving consorts.	(10–16)
Persons, in any fixed station, should usually abide in that.	(17–24)
It was most desirable, on account of the then perilous days, for people to sit loose to this world.	(25–35)
Great prudence be used in marriage; it should be only in the Lord.	(36–40)

Verses 1-9

The apostle tells the Corinthians that it was good, in that juncture of time, for Christians to keep themselves single. Yet he says that marriage, and the comforts of that state, are settled by Divine wisdom. Though none may break the law of God, yet that perfect rule leaves men at liberty to serve him in the way most suited to their powers and circumstances, of which others often are very unfit judges. All must determine for themselves, seeking counsel from God how they ought to act.

Verses 10-16

Man and wife must not separate for any other cause than what Christ allows. Divorce, at that time, was very common among both Jews and Gentiles, on very slight pretexts. Marriage is a Divine institution; and is an engagement for life, by God's appointment. We are bound, as much as in us lies, to live peaceably with all men, Ro 12:18, therefore to promote the peace and comfort of our nearest relatives, though unbelievers. It should be the labour and study of those who are married, to make each other as easy and happy as possible. Should a Christian desert a husband or wife, when there is opportunity to give the greatest proof of love? Stay, and labour heartily for the conversion of thy relative. In every state and relation the Lord has called us to peace; and every thing should be done to promote harmony, as far as truth and holiness will permit.

Verses 17-24

The rules of Christianity reach every condition; and in every state a man may live so as to be a credit to it. It is the duty of every Christian to be content with his lot, and to conduct himself in his rank and place as becomes a Christian. Our comfort and happiness depend on what we are to Christ, not what we are in the world. No man should think to make his faith or religion, an argument to break through any natural or civil obligations. He should quietly and contentedly abide in the condition in which he is placed by Divine Providence.

Verses 25-35

Considering the distress of those times, the unmarried state was best. Notwithstanding, the apostle does not condemn marriage. How opposite are those to the apostle Paul who forbid many to marry, and entangle them with vows to remain single, whether they ought to do so or not! He exhorts all Christians to holy indifference toward the world. As to relations; they must not set their hearts on the comforts of the state. As to afflictions; they must not indulge the sorrow of the world: even in sorrow the heart may be joyful. As to worldly enjoyments; here is not their rest. As to worldly employment; those that prosper in trade, and increase in wealth, should hold their possessions as though they held them not. As to all worldly concerns; they must keep the world out of their hearts, that they may not abuse it when they have it in their hands. All worldly things are show; nothing solid. All will be quickly gone. Wise concern about worldly interests is a duty; but to be full of care, to have anxious and perplexing care, is a sin. By this maxim the apostle solves the case whether it were advisable to marry. That condition of life is best for every man, which is best for his soul, and keeps him most clear of the cares and snares of the world. Let us reflect on the advantages and snares of our own condition in life; that we may improve the one, and escape as far as possible all injury from the other. And whatever cares press upon the mind, let time still be kept for the things of the Lord.

Verses 36-40

The apostle is thought to give advice here about the disposal of children in marriage. In this view, the general meaning is plain. Children should seek and follow the directions of their parents as to marriage. And parents should consult their children's wishes; and not reckon they have power to do with them, and dictate just as they please, without reason. The whole is closed with advice to widows. Second marriages are not unlawful, so that it is kept in mind, to marry in the Lord. In our choice of relations, and change of conditions, we should always be guided by the fear of God, and the laws of God, and act in dependence on the providence of God. Change of condition ought only to be made after careful consideration, and on probable grounds, that it will be to advantage in our spiritual concerns.

Chapter 8

Chapter Outline

The danger of having a high conceit of knowledge.	(1–6)
The mischief of offending weak brethren.	(7–13)

Verses 1-6

There is no proof of ignorance more common than conceit of knowledge. Much may be known, when nothing is known to good purpose. And those who think they know any thing, and grow vain thereon, are the least likely to make good use of their knowledge. Satan hurts some as much by tempting them to be proud of mental powers, as others, by alluring to sensuality. Knowledge which puffs up the possessor, and renders him confident, is as dangerous as self-righteous pride, though what he knows may be right. Without holy affections all human knowledge is worthless. The heathens had gods of higher and lower degree; gods many, and lords many; so called, but not such in truth. Christians know better. One God made all, and has power over all. The one God, even the Father, signifies the Godhead as the sole object of all religious worship; and the Lord Jesus Christ denotes the person of Emmanuel, God manifest in the flesh, One with the Father, and with us; the appointed Mediator, and Lord of all; through whom we come to the Father, and through whom the Father sends all blessings to us, by the influence and working of the Holy Spirit. While we refuse all worship to the many who are called gods and lords, and to saints and angels, let us try whether we really come to God by faith in Christ.

Verses 7-13

Eating one kind of food, and abstaining from another, have nothing in them to recommend a person to God. But the apostle cautions against putting a stumbling-block in the way of the weak;

lest they be made bold to eat what was offered to the idol, not as common food, but as a sacrifice, and thereby be guilty of idolatry. He who has the Spirit of Christ in him, will love those whom Christ loved so as to die for them. Injuries done to Christians, are done to Christ; but most of all, the entangling them in guilt: wounding their consciences, is wounding him. We should be very tender of doing any thing that may occasion stumbling to others, though it may be innocent in itself. And if we must not endanger other men's souls, how much should we take care not to destroy our own! Let Christians beware of approaching the brink of evil, or the appearance of it, though many do this in public matters, for which perhaps they plead plausibly. Men cannot thus sin against their brethren, without offending Christ, and endangering their own souls.

Chapter 9

Chapter Outline

The apostle shows his authority, and asserts his right to be maintained.	(1–14)
He waved this part of his Christian liberty, for the good of others.	(15–23)
He did all this, with care and diligence, in view of an unfading crown.	(24–27)

Verses 1-14

It is not new for a minister to meet with unkind returns for good-will to a people, and diligent and successful services among them. To the cavils of some, the apostle answers, so as to set forth himself as an example of self-denial, for the good of others. He had a right to marry as well as other apostles, and to claim what was needful for his wife, and his children if he had any, from the churches, without labouring with his own hands to get it. Those who seek to do our souls good, should have food provided for them. But he renounced his right, rather than hinder his success by claiming it. It is the people's duty to maintain their minister. He may wave his right, as Paul did; but those transgress a precept of Christ, who deny or withhold due support.

Verses 15-23

It is the glory of a minister to deny himself, that he may serve Christ and save souls. But when a minister gives up his right for the sake of the gospel, he does more than his charge and office demands. By preaching the gospel, freely, the apostle showed that he acted from principles of zeal and love, and thus enjoyed much comfort and hope in his soul. And though he looked on the ceremonial law as a yoke taken off by Christ, yet he submitted to it, that he might work upon the Jews, do away their prejudices, prevail with them to hear the gospel, and win them over to Christ. Though he would transgress no laws of Christ, to please any man, yet he would accommodate himself to all men, where he might do it lawfully, to gain some. Doing good was the study and business of his life; and, that he might reach this end, he did not stand on privileges. We must carefully watch against extremes, and against relying on any thing but trust in Christ alone. We must not allow errors or faults, so as to hurt others, or disgrace the gospel.

Verses 24-27

The apostle compares himself to the racers and combatants in the Isthmian games, well known by the Corinthians. But in the Christian race all may run so as to obtain. There is the greatest encouragement, therefore, to persevere with all our strength, in this course. Those who ran in these games were kept to a spare diet. They used themselves to hardships. They practised the exercises. And those who pursue the interests of their souls, must combat hard with fleshly lusts. The body must not be suffered to rule. The apostle presses this advice on the Corinthians. He sets before himself and them the danger of yielding to fleshly desires, pampering the body, and its lusts and appetites. Holy fear of himself was needed to keep an apostle faithful: how much more is it needful for our preservation! Let us learn from hence humility and caution, and to watch against dangers which surround us while in the body.

Chapter 10

Chapter Outline

The great privileges, and yet terrible overthrow of the Israelites in the wilderness.	(1–5)
Cautions against all idolatrous, and other sinful practices.	(6–14)
The partaking in idolatry cannot exist with having communion with Christ.	(15–22)
All we do to be to the glory of God, and without offence to the consciences of others.	(23–33)

Verses 1-5

To dissuade the Corinthians from communion with idolaters, and security in any sinful course, the apostle sets before them the example of the Jewish nation of old. They were, by a miracle, led through the Red Sea, where the pursuing Egyptians were drowned. It was to them a typical baptism. The manna on which they fed was a type of Christ crucified, the Bread which came down from heaven, which whoso eateth shall live for ever. Christ is the Rock on which the Christian church is built; and of the streams that issue therefrom, all believers drink, and are refreshed. It typified the sacred influences of the Holy Spirit, as given to believers through Christ. But let none presume upon their great privileges, or profession of the truth; these will not secure heavenly happiness.

Verses 6-14

Carnal desires gain strength by indulgence, therefore should be checked in their first rise. Let us fear the sins of Israel, if we would shun their plagues. And it is but just to fear, that such as tempt Christ, will be left by him in the power of the old serpent. Murmuring against God's disposals and commands, greatly provokes him. Nothing in Scripture is written in vain; and it is our wisdom and duty to learn from it. Others have fallen, and so may we. The Christian's security against sin is distrust of himself. God has not promised to keep us from falling, if we do not look to ourselves. To this word of caution, a word of comfort is added. Others have the like burdens, and the like temptations: what they bear up under, and break through, we may also. God is wise as well as faithful, and will make our burdens according to our strength. He knows what we can bear. He will make a way to escape; he will deliver either from the trial itself, or at least the mischief of it. We have full encouragement to flee from sin, and to be faithful to God. We cannot fall by temptation, if we cleave fast to him. Whether the world smiles or frowns, it is an enemy; but believers shall be strengthened to overcome it, with all its terrors and enticements. The fear of the Lord, put into their hearts, will be the great means of safety.

Verses 15-22

Did not the joining in the Lord's supper show a profession of faith in Christ crucified, and of adoring gratitude to him for his salvation ? Christians, by this ordinance, and the faith therein professed, were united as the grains of wheat in one loaf of bread, or as the members in the human body, seeing they were all united to Christ, and had fellowship with him and one another. This is confirmed from the Jewish worship and customs in sacrifice. The apostle applies this to feasting with idolaters. Eating food as part of a heathen sacrifice, was worshipping the idol to whom it was made, and having fellowship or communion with it; just as he who eats the Lord's supper, is accounted to partake in the Christian sacrifice, or as they who ate the Jewish sacrifices partook of what was offered on their altar. It was denying Christianity; for communion with Christ, and communion with devils, could never be had at once. If Christians venture into places, and join in sacrifices to the lust of the flesh, the lust of the eye, and the pride of life, they will provoke God.

Verses 23-33

There were cases wherein Christians might eat what had been offered to idols, without sin. Such as when the flesh was sold in the market as common food, for the priest to whom it had been given. But a Christian must not merely consider what is lawful, but what is expedient, and to edify others. Christianity by no means forbids the common offices of kindness, or allows uncourteous behaviour to any, however they may differ from us in religious sentiments or practices. But this is not to be understood of religious festivals, partaking in idolatrous worship. According to this advice of the apostle, Christians should take care not to use their liberty to the hurt of others, or to their own reproach. In eating and drinking, and in all we do, we should aim at the glory of God, at pleasing and honouring him. This is the great end of all religion, and directs us where express rules are wanting. A holy, peaceable, and benevolent spirit, will disarm the greatest enemies.

Chapter 11

Chapter Outline

Verse 1

The first verse of this chapter seems properly to be the close to the last. The apostle not only preached such doctrine as they ought to believe, but led such a life as they ought to live. Yet Christ being our perfect example, the actions and conduct of men, as related in the Scriptures, should be followed only so far as they are like to his.

Verses 2-16

Here begin particulars respecting the public assemblies, ch. 1Co 14. In the abundance of spiritual gifts bestowed on the Corinthians, some abuses had crept in; but as Christ did the will, and sought the honour of God, so the Christian should avow his subjection to Christ, doing his will and seeking his glory. We should, even in our dress and habit, avoid every thing that may dishonour Christ. The woman was made subject to man, because made for his help and comfort. And she should do nothing, in Christian assemblies, which looked like a claim of being equal. She ought to have "power," that is, a veil, on her head, because of the angels. Their presence should keep Christians from all that is wrong while in the worship of God. Nevertheless, the man and the woman were made for one another. They were to be mutual comforts and blessings, not one a slave, and the other a tyrant. God has so settled matters, both in the kingdom of providence and that of grace, that the authority and subjection of each party should be for mutual help and benefit. It was the common usage of the churches, for women to appear in public assemblies, and join in public worship, veiled; and it was right that they should do so. The Christian religion sanctions national customs wherever these are not against the great principles of truth and holiness; affected singularities receive no countenance from any thing in the Bible.

Verses 17-22

The apostle rebukes the disorders in their partaking of the Lord's supper. The ordinances of Christ, if they do not make us better, will be apt to make us worse. If the use of them does not mend, it will harden. Upon coming together, they fell into divisions, schisms. Christians may separate from each other's communion, yet be charitable one towards another; they may continue in the same communion, yet be uncharitable. This last is schism, rather than the former. There is a careless and irregular eating of the Lord's supper, which adds to guilt. Many rich Corinthians seem to have acted very wrong at the Lord's table, or at the love-feasts, which took place at the same time as the supper. The rich despised the poor, and ate and drank up the provisions they brought, before the poor were allowed to partake; thus some wanted, while others had more than enough. What should have been a bond of mutual love and affection, was made an instrument of discord and disunion. We should be careful that nothing in our behaviour at the Lord's table, appears to make light of that sacred institution. The Lord's supper is not now made an occasion for gluttony or revelling, but is it not often made the support of self-righteous pride, or a cloak for hypocrisy? Let us never rest in the outward forms of worship; but look to our hearts.

Verses 23-34

The apostle describes the sacred ordinance, of which he had the knowledge by revelation from Christ. As to the visible signs, these are the bread and wine. What is eaten is called bread, though at the same time it is said to be the body of the Lord, plainly showing that the apostle did not mean that the bread was changed into flesh. St. Matthew tells us, our Lord bid them all drink of the cup, ch. Mt 26:27, as if he would, by this expression, provide against any believer being deprived of the cup. The things signified by these outward signs, are Christ's body and blood, his body broken, his blood shed, together with all the benefits which flow from his death and sacrifice. Our Saviour's actions were, taking the bread and cup, giving thanks, breaking the bread, and giving both the one and the other. The actions of the communicants were, to take the bread and eat, to take the cup and drink, and to do both in remembrance of Christ. But the outward acts are not the whole, or the principal part, of what is to be done at this holy ordinance. Those who partake of it, are to take him as their Lord and Life, yield themselves up to him, and live upon him. Here is an account of the ends of this ordinance. It is to be done in remembrance of Christ, to keep fresh in our minds his dying for us, as well as to remember Christ pleading for us, in virtue of his death, at God's right hand. It is not merely in remembrance of Christ, of what he has done and suffered; but to celebrate his grace in our redemption. We declare his death to be our life, the spring of all our comforts and hopes. And we glory in such a declaration; we show forth his death, and plead it as our accepted sacrifice and ransom. The Lord's supper is not an ordinance to be observed merely for a time, but to be continued. The apostle lays before the Corinthians the danger of receiving it with an unsuitable temper of mind; or keeping up the covenant with sin and death, while professing to renew and confirm the covenant with God. No doubt such incur great guilt, and so render themselves liable to spiritual judgements. But fearful believers should not be discouraged from attending at this holy ordinance. The Holy Spirit never caused this scripture to be written to deter serious Christians from their duty, though the devil has often made this use of it. The apostle was addressing Christians, and warning them to beware of the temporal judgements with which God chastised his offending servants. And in the midst of judgement, God remembers mercy: he many times punishes those whom he loves. It is better to bear trouble in this world, than to be miserable for ever. The apostle points our the duty of those who come to the Lord's table. Self-examination is necessary to right attendance at this holy ordinance. If we would thoroughly search ourselves, to condemn and set right what we find wrong, we should stop Divine judgements. The apostle closes all with a caution against the irregularities of which the Corinthians were guilty at the Lord's table. Let all look to it, that they do not come together to God's worship, so as to provoke him, and bring down vengeance on themselves.

Chapter 12

Chapter Outline

The variety of use of spiritual gifts are shown.	(1–11)
In the human body every member has its place and use.	(12–26)
This is applied to the church of Christ.	(27–30)
And there is something more excellent than spiritual gifts.	(31)

Verses 1-11

Spiritual gifts were extraordinary powers bestowed in the first ages, to convince unbelievers, and to spread the gospel. Gifts and graces greatly differ. Both were freely given of God. But where grace is given, it is for the salvation of those who have it. Gifts are for the advantage and salvation of others; and there may be great gifts where there is no grace. The extraordinary gifts of the Holy Spirit were chiefly exercised in the public assemblies, where the Corinthians seem to have made displays of them, wanting in the spirit of piety, and of Christian love. While heathens, they had not been influenced by the Spirit of Christ. No man can call Christ Lord, with believing dependence upon him, unless that faith is wrought by the Holy Ghost. No man could believe with his heart, or prove by a miracle, that Jesus was Christ, unless by the Holy Ghost. There are various gifts, and various offices to perform, but all proceed from one God, one Lord, one Spirit; that is, from the Father, Son, and Holy Ghost, the origin of all spiritual blessings. No man has them merely for himself. The more he profits others, the more will they turn to his own account. The gifts mentioned appear to mean exact understanding, and uttering the doctrines of the Christian religion; the knowledge of mysteries, and skill to give advice and counsel. Also the gift of healing the sick, the working of miracles, and to explain Scripture by a peculiar gift of the Spirit, and ability to speak and interpret languages. If we have any knowledge of the truth, or any power to make it known, we must give all the glory of God. The greater the gifts are, the more the possessor is exposed to temptations, and the larger is the measure of grace needed to keep him humble and spiritual; and he will meet with more painful experiences and humbling dispensations. We have little cause to glory in any gifts bestowed on us, or to despise those who have them not. (1Co 12:12-26)

Verses 12-26

Christ and his church form one body, as Head and members. Christians become members of this body by baptism. The outward rite is of Divine institution; it is a sign of the new birth, and is called therefore the washing of regeneration, Tit 3:5. But it is by the Spirit, only by the renewing of the Holy Ghost, that we are made members of Christ's body. And by communion with Christ at the Lord's supper, we are strengthened, not by drinking the wine, but by drinking into one Spirit. Each member has its form, place, and use. The meanest makes a part of the body. There must be a distinction of members in the body. So Christ's members have different powers and different places. We should do the duties of our own place, and not murmur, or quarrel with others. All the members of the body are useful and necessary to each other. Nor is there a member of the body of Christ, but may and ought to be useful to fellow-members. As in the natural body of man, the members should be closely united by the strongest bonds of love; the good of the whole should be the object of all. All Christians are dependent one upon another; each is to expect and receive help from the rest. Let us then have more of the spirit of union in our religion.

Verses 27-31

Contempt, hatred, envy, and strife, are very unnatural in Christians. It is like the members of the same body being without concern for one another, or quarrelling with each other. The proud, contentious spirit that prevailed, as to spiritual gifts, was thus condemned. The offices and gifts, or favours, dispensed by the Holy Spirit, are noticed. Chief ministers; persons enabled to interpret Scripture; those who laboured in word and doctrine; those who had power to heal diseases; such as helped the sick and weak; such as disposed of the money given in charity by the church, and managed the affairs of the church; and such as could speak divers languages. What holds the last and lowest rank in this list, is the power to speak languages; how vain, if a man does so merely to amuse or to exalt himself! See the distribution of these gifts, not to every one alike, ver. #(29, 30). This were to make the church all one, as if the body were all ear, or all eye. The Spirit distributes to every one as he will. We must be content though we are lower and less than others. We must not despise others, if we have greater gifts. How blessed the Christian church, if all the members did their duty! Instead of coveting the highest stations, or the most splendid gifts, let us leave the appointment of his instruments to God, and those in whom he works by his providence. Remember, those will not be approved hereafter who seek the chief places, but those who are most faithful to the trust placed in them, and most diligent in their Master's work.

Chapter 13

Chapter Outline

The necessity and advantage of the grace of   (1–3)
love.

Its excellency represented by its properties   (4–7)
and effects;

and by its abiding, and its superiority.   (8–13)

Verses 1-3

The excellent way had in view in the close of the former chapter, is not what is meant by charity in our common use of the word, almsgiving, but love in its fullest meaning; true love to God and man. Without this, the most glorious gifts are of no account to us, of no esteem in the sight of God. A clear head and a deep understanding, are of no value without a benevolent and charitable heart. There may be an open and lavish hand, where there is not a liberal and charitable heart. Doing good to others will do none to us, if it be not done from love to God, and good-will to men. If we give away all we have, while we withhold the heart from God, it will not profit. Nor even the most painful sufferings. How are those deluded who look for acceptance and reward for their good works, which are as scanty and defective as they are corrupt and selfish!

Verses 4-7

Some of the effects of charity are stated, that we may know whether we have this grace; and that if we have not, we may not rest till we have it. This love is a clear proof of regeneration, and is a touchstone of our professed faith in Christ. In this beautiful description of the nature and effects of love, it is meant to show the Corinthians that their conduct had, in many respects, been a contrast to it. Charity is an utter enemy to selfishness; it does not desire or seek its own praise, or honour, or profit, or pleasure. Not that charity destroys all regard to ourselves, or that the charitable man should neglect himself and all his interests. But charity never seeks its own to the hurt of others, or to neglect others. It ever prefers the welfare of others to its private advantage. How good-natured and amiable is Christian charity! How excellent would Christianity appear to the world, if those who profess it were more under this Divine principle, and paid due regard to the command on which its blessed Author laid the chief stress! Let us ask whether this Divine love dwells in our hearts. Has this principle guided us into becoming behaviour to all men? Are we willing to lay aside selfish objects and aims? Here is a call to watchfulness, diligence, and prayer.

Verses 8-13

Charity is much to be preferred to the gifts on which the Corinthians prided themselves. From its longer continuance. It is a grace, lasting as eternity. The present state is a state of childhood, the future that of manhood. Such is the difference between earth and heaven. What narrow views, what confused notions of things, have children when compared with grown men! Thus shall we think of our most valued gifts of this world, when we come to heaven. All things are dark and confused now, compared with what they will be hereafter. They can only be seen as by the reflection in a mirror, or in the description of a riddle; but hereafter our knowledge will be free from all obscurity and error. It is the light of heaven only, that will remove all clouds and darkness that hide the face of God from us. To sum up the excellences of charity, it is preferred not only to gifts, but to other graces, to faith and hope. Faith fixes on the Divine revelation, and assents thereto, relying on the

Divine Redeemer. Hope fastens on future happiness, and waits for that; but in heaven, faith will be swallowed up in actual sight, and hope in enjoyment. There is no room to believe and hope, when we see and enjoy. But there, love will be made perfect. There we shall perfectly love God. And there we shall perfectly love one another. Blessed state! how much surpassing the best below! God is love, 1Jo 4:8, 16. Where God is to be seen as he is, and face to face, there charity is in its greatest height; there only will it be perfected.

Chapter 14

Chapter Outline

Prophecy preferred to the gift of tongues.	(1–5)
The unprofitableness of speaking in unknown languages.	(6–14)
Exhortations to worship that can be understood.	(15–25)
Disorders from vain display of gifts;	(26–33)
and from women speaking in the church.	(34–40)

Verses 1-5

Prophesying, that is, explaining Scripture, is compared with speaking with tongues. This drew attention, more than the plain interpretation of Scripture; it gratified pride more, but promoted the purposes of Christian charity less; it would not equally do good to the souls of men. What cannot be understood, never can edify. No advantage can be reaped from the most excellent discourses, if delivered in language such as the hearers cannot speak or understand. Every ability or possession is valuable in proportion to its usefulness. Even fervent, spiritual affection must be governed by the exercise of the understanding, else men will disgrace the truths they profess to promote.

Verses 6-14

Even an apostle could not edify, unless he spoke so as to be understood by his hearers. To speak words that have no meaning to those who hear them, is but speaking into the air. That cannot answer the end of speaking, which has no meaning; in this case, speaker and hearers are barbarians to each other. All religious services should be so performed in Christian assemblies, that all may join in, and profit by them. Language plain and easy to be understood, is the most proper for public worship, and other religious exercises. Every true follower of Christ will rather desire to do good to others, than to get a name for learning or fine speaking.

Verses 15-25

There can be no assent to prayers that are not understood. A truly Christian minister will seek much more to do spiritual good to men's souls, than to get the greatest applause to himself. This is proving himself the servant of Christ. Children are apt to be struck with novelty; but do not act like them. Christians should be like children, void of guile and malice; yet they should not be unskilful as to the word of righteousness, but only as to the arts of mischief. It is a proof that a people are forsaken of God, when he gives them up to the rule of those who teach them to worship in another language. They can never be benefitted by such teaching. Yet thus the preachers did who delivered their instructions in an unknown tongue. Would it not make Christianity ridiculous to a heathen, to hear the ministers pray or preach in a language which neither he nor the assembly understood? But if those who minister, plainly interpret Scripture, or preach the great truths and rules of the gospel, a heathen or unlearned person might become a convert to Christianity. His conscience might be touched, the secrets of his heart might be revealed to him, and so he might be brought to confess his guilt, and to own that God was present in the assembly. Scripture truth, plainly and duly taught, has a wonderful power to awaken the conscience and touch the heart.

Verses 26–33

Religious exercises in public assemblies should have this view; Let all be done to edifying. As to the speaking in an unknown tongue, if another were present who could interpret, two miraculous gifts might be exercised at once, and thereby the church be edified, and the faith of the hearers confirmed at the same time. As to prophesying, two or three only should speak at one meeting, and this one after the other, not all at once. The man who is inspired by the Spirit of God will observe order and decency in delivering his revelations. God never teaches men to neglect their duties, or to act in any way unbecoming their age or station.

Verses 34–40

When the apostle exhorts Christian women to seek information on religious subjects from their husbands at home, it shows that believing families ought to assemble for promoting spiritual knowledge. The Spirit of Christ can never contradict itself; and if their revelations are against those of the apostle, they do not come from the same Spirit. The way to keep peace, truth, and order in the church, is to seek that which is good for it, to bear with that which is not hurtful to its welfare, and to keep up good behaviour, order, and decency.

Chapter 15

Chapter Outline

Verses 1-11

The word resurrection, usually points out our existence beyond the grave. Of the apostle's doctrine not a trace can be found in all the teaching of philosophers. The doctrine of Christ's death and resurrection, is the foundation of Christianity. Remove this, and all our hopes for eternity sink at once. And it is by holding this truth firm, that Christians stand in the day of trial, and are kept faithful to God. We believe in vain, unless we keep in the faith of the gospel. This truth is confirmed by Old Testament prophecies; and many saw Christ after he was risen. This apostle was highly favoured, but he always had a low opinion of himself, and expressed it. When sinners are, by Divine grace, turned into saints, God causes the remembrance of former sins to make them humble, diligent, and faithful. He ascribes to Divine grace all that was valuable in him. True believers, though not ignorant of what the Lord has done for, in, and by them, yet when they look at their whole conduct and their obligations, they are led to feel that none are so worthless as they are. All true Christians believe that Jesus Christ, and him crucified, and then risen from the dead, is the sun and substance of Christianity. All the apostles agreed in this testimony; by this faith they lived, and in this faith they died.

Verses 12-19

Having shown that Christ was risen, the apostle answers those who said there would be no resurrection. There had been no justification, or salvation, if Christ had not risen. And must not faith in Christ be vain, and of no use, if he is still among the dead? The proof of the resurrection of the body is the resurrection of our Lord. Even those who died in the faith, had perished in their sins, if Christ had not risen. All who believe in Christ, have hope in him, as a Redeemer; hope for redemption and salvation by him; but if there is no resurrection, or future recompence, their hope in him can only be as to this life. And they must be in a worse condition than the rest of mankind, especially at the time, and under the circumstances, in which the apostles wrote; for then Christians were hated and persecuted by all men. But it is not so; they, of all men, enjoy solid comforts amidst all their difficulties and trials, even in the times of the sharpest persecution.

Verses 20-34

All that are by faith united to Christ, are by his resurrection assured of their own. As through the sin of the first Adam, all men became mortal, because all had from him the same sinful nature, so, through the resurrection of Christ, shall all who are made to partake of the Spirit, and the spiritual nature, revive, and live for ever. There will be an order in the resurrection. Christ himself has been the first-fruits; at his coming, his redeemed people will be raised before others; at the last the wicked will rise also. Then will be the end of this present state of things. Would we triumph in that solemn and important season, we must now submit to his rule, accept his salvation, and live to his glory. Then shall we rejoice in the completion of his undertaking, that God may receive the whole glory of our salvation, that we may for ever serve him, and enjoy his favour. What shall those do, who are baptized for the dead, if the dead rise not at all? Perhaps baptism is used here in a figure, for afflictions, sufferings, and martyrdom, as Mt 20:22, 23. What is, or will become of those who have suffered many and great injuries, and have even lost their lives, for this doctrine of the resurrection, if the dead rise not at all? Whatever the meaning may be, doubtless the apostle's argument was understood by the Corinthians. And it is as plain to us that Christianity would be a foolish profession, if it proposed advantage to themselves by their faithfulness to God; and to have our fruit to holiness, that our end may be everlasting life. But we must not live like beasts, as we do not die like them. It must be ignorance of God that leads any to disbelieve the resurrection and future life. Those who own a God and a providence, and observe how unequal things are in the present life, how frequently the best men fare worst, cannot doubt as to an after-state, where every thing will be set to rights. Let us not be joined with ungodly men; but warn all around us, especially children and young persons, to shun them as a pestilence. Let us awake to righteousness, and not sin.

Verses 35-50

1. How are the dead raised up? that is, by what means? How can they be raised? 2. As to the bodies which shall rise. Will it be with the like shape, and form, and stature, and members, and qualities? The former objection is that of those who opposed the doctrine, the latter of curious doubters. To the first the answer is, This was to be brought about by Divine power; that power which all may see does somewhat like it, year after year, in the death and revival of the corn. It is foolish to question the Almighty power of God to raise the dead, when we see it every day quickening and reviving things that are dead. To the second inquiry; The grain undergoes a great change; and so will the dead, when they rise and live again. The seed dies, though a part of it springs into new life, though how it is we cannot fully understand. The works of creation and providence daily teach us to be humble, as well as to admire the Creator's wisdom and goodness. There is a great variety among other bodies, as there is among plants. There is a variety of glory among heavenly bodies. The bodies of the dead, when they rise, will be fitted for the heavenly bodies. The bodies of the dead, when they rise, will be fitted for the heavenly state; and there will be a variety of glories among them. Burying the dead, is like committing seed to the earth, that it may spring out of it again. Nothing is more loathsome than a dead body. But believers shall at the resurrection have bodies, made fit to be for ever united with spirits made perfect. To God all things are possible. He is the Author and Source of spiritual life and holiness, unto all his people, by the supply of his Holy Spirit to the soul; and he will also quicken and change the body by his Spirit. The dead in Christ shall not only rise, but shall rise thus gloriously changed. The bodies of the saints, when they rise again, will be changed. They will be then glorious and spiritual bodies, fitted to the heavenly world and state, where they are ever afterwards to dwell. The human body in its present form, and with its wants and weaknesses, cannot enter or enjoy the kingdom of God. Then let us not sow to the flesh, of which we can only reap corruption. And the body follows the state of the soul. He, therefore,

who neglects the life of the soul, casts away his present good; he who refuses to live to God, squanders all he has.

Verses 51-58

All the saints should not die, but all would be changed. In the gospel, many truths, before hidden in mystery, are made known. Death never shall appear in the regions to which our Lord will bear his risen saints. Therefore let us seek the full assurance of faith and hope, that in the midst of pain, and in the prospect of death, we may think calmly on the horrors of the tomb; assured that our bodies will there sleep, and in the mean time our souls will be present with the Redeemer. Sin gives death all its hurtful power. The sting of death is sin; but Christ, by dying, has taken out this sting; he has made atonement for sin, he has obtained remission of it. The strength of sin is the law. None can answer its demands, endure its curse, or do away his own transgressions. Hence terror and anguish. And hence death is terrible to the unbelieving and the impenitent. Death may seize a believer, but it cannot hold him in its power. How many springs of joy to the saints, and of thanksgiving to God, are opened by the death and resurrection, the sufferings and conquests of the Redeemer! In verse #(58), we have an exhortation, that believers should be stedfast, firm in the faith of that gospel which the apostle preached, and they received. Also, to be unmovable in their hope and expectation of this great privilege, of being raised incorruptible and immortal. And to abound in the work of the Lord, always doing the Lord's service, and obeying the Lord's commands. May Christ give us faith, and increase our faith, that we may not only be safe, but joyful and triumphant.

Chapter 16

Chapter Outline

A collection for the poor at Jerusalem.	(1–9)
Timothy and Apollos commended.	(10–12)
Exhortation to watchfulness in faith and love.	(13–18)
Christian salutations.	(19–24)

Verses 1-9

The good examples of other Christians and churches should rouse us. It is good to lay up in store for good uses. Those who are rich in this world, should be rich in good works, 1Ti 6:17, 18. The diligent hand will not make rich, without the Divine blessing, Pr 10:4, 22. And what more proper to stir us up to charity to the people and children of God, than to look at all we have as his gift? Works of mercy are real fruits of true love to God, and are therefore proper services on his own day. Ministers are doing their proper business, when putting forward, or helping works of charity. The heart of a Christian minister must be towards the people among whom he has laboured long, and with success. All our purposes must be made with submission to the Divine providence, Jas 4:15. Adversaries and opposition do not break the spirits of faithful and successful ministers, but warm their zeal, and inspire them with fresh courage. A faithful minister is more discouraged by the hardness of his hearers' hearts, and the backslidings of professors, than by the enemies' attempts.

Verses 10-12

Timothy came to do the work of the Lord. Therefore to vex his spirit, would be to grieve the Holy Spirit; to despise him, would be to despise Him that sent him. Those who work the work of the Lord, should be treated with tenderness and respect. Faithful ministers will not be jealous of each other. It becomes the ministers of the gospel to show concern for each other's reputation and usefulness.

Verses 13-18

A Christian is always in danger, therefore should ever be on the watch. He should be fixed in the faith of the gospel, and never desert or give it up. By this faith alone he will be able to keep his ground in an hour of temptation. Christians should be careful that charity not only reigns in their hearts, but shines in their lives. There is a great difference between Christian firmness and feverish warmth and transport. The apostle gave particular directions as to some who served the cause of Christ among them. Those who serve the saints, those who desire the honour of the churches, and to remove reproaches from them, are to be thought much of, and loved. They should willingly acknowledge the worth of such, and all who laboured with or helped the apostle.

Verses 19-24

Christianity by no means destroys civility. Religion should promote a courteous and obliging temper towards all. Those give a false idea of religion, and reproach it, who would take encouragement from it to be sour and morose. And Christian salutations are not mere empty compliments; but are real expressions of good-will to others, and commend them to the Divine grace and blessing. Every Christian family should be as a Christian church. Wherever two or three are gathered together in the name of Christ, and he is among them, there is a church. Here is a solemn warning. Many who have Christ's name much in their mouths, have no true love to him in their hearts. None love him in truth, who do not love his laws, and keep his commandments. Many are Christians in name, who do not love Christ Jesus the Lord in sincerity. Such are separated from the people of God, and the favour of God. Those who love not the Lord Jesus Christ, must perish without remedy. Let us not rest in any religious profession where there is not the love of Christ, earnest desires for his salvation, gratitude for his mercies, and obedience to his commandments. The grace of our Lord Jesus Christ has in it all that is good, for time and for eternity. To wish that our friends may have this grace with them, is wishing them the utmost good. And this we should wish all our friends and brethren in Christ. We can wish them nothing greater, and we should wish them nothing less. True Christianity makes us wish those whom we love, the blessings of both worlds; this is meant in wishing the grace of Christ to be with them. The apostle had dealt plainly with the Corinthians, and told them of their faults with just severity; but he parts in love, and with a solemn profession of his love to them for Christ's sake. May our love be with all who are in Christ Jesus. Let us try whether all things appear worthless to us, when compared with Christ and his righteousness. Do we allow ourselves in any known sin, or in the neglect of any known duty? By such inquiries, faithfully made, we may judge of the state of our souls.

2 Corinthians

The second epistle to the Corinthians probably was written about a year after the first. Its contents are closely connected with those of the former epistle. The manner in which the letter St. Paul formerly wrote had been received, is particularly noticed; this was such as to fill his heart with gratitude to God, who enabled him fully to discharge his duty towards them. Many had shown marks of repentance, and amended their conduct, but others still followed their false teachers; and as the apostle delayed his visit, from his unwillingness to treat them with severity, they charged him with levity and change of conduct. Also, with pride, vain-glory, and severity, and they spake of him with contempt. In this epistle we find the same ardent affection towards the disciples at Corinth, as in the former, the same zeal for the honour of the gospel, and the same boldness in giving Christian reproof. The first six chapters are chiefly practical: the rest have more reference to the state of the Corinthian church, but they contain many rules of general application.

Chapter 1

Chapter Outline

The apostle blesses God for comfort in, and deliverance out of troubles.	(1–11)
He professes his own and his fellow-labourers' integrity.	(12–14)
Gives reasons for his not coming to them.	(15–24)

Verses 1-11

We are encouraged to come boldly to the throne of grace, that we may obtain mercy, and find grace to help in time of need. The Lord is able to give peace to the troubled conscience, and to calm the raging passions of the soul. These blessings are given by him, as the Father of his redeemed family. It is our Saviour who says, Let not your heart be troubled. All comforts come from God, and our sweetest comforts are in him. He speaks peace to souls by granting the free remission of sins; and he comforts them by the enlivening influences of the Holy Spirit, and by the rich mercies of his grace. He is able to bind up the broken-hearted, to heal the most painful wounds, and also to give hope and joy under the heaviest sorrows. The favours God bestows on us, are not only to make us cheerful, but also that we may be useful to others. He sends comforts enough to support such as simply trust in and serve him. If we should be brought so low as to despair even of life, yet we may then trust God, who can bring back even from death. Their hope and trust were not in vain; nor shall any be ashamed who trust in the Lord. Past experiences encourage faith and hope, and lay us under obligation to trust in God for time to come. And it is our duty, not only to help one another with prayer, but in praise and thanksgiving, and thereby to make suitable returns for benefits received. Thus both trials and mercies will end in good to ourselves and others.

Verses 12-14

Though, as a sinner, the apostle could only rejoice and glory in Christ Jesus, yet, as a believer, he might rejoice and glory in being really what he professed. Conscience witnesses concerning the steady course and tenor of the life. Thereby we may judge ourselves, and not by this or by that single act. Our conversation will be well ordered, when we live and act under such a gracious principle in the heart. Having this, we may leave our characters in the Lord's hands, but using proper means to clear them, when the credit of the gospel, or our usefulness, calls for it.

Verses 15-24

The apostle clears himself from the charge of levity and inconstancy, in not coming to Corinth. Good men should be careful to keep the reputation of sincerity and constancy; they should not resolve, but on careful thought; and they will not change unless for weighty reasons. Nothing can render God's promises more certain: his giving them through Christ, assures us they are his promises; as the wonders God wrought in the life, resurrection, and ascension of his Son, confirm faith. The Holy Spirit makes Christians firm in the faith of the gospel: the quickening of the Spirit is an earnest of everlasting life; and the comforts of the Spirit are an earnest of everlasting joy. The apostle desired to spare the blame he feared would be unavoidable, if he had gone to Corinth before he learned what effect his former letter produced. Our strength and ability are owing to faith; and our comfort and joy must flow from faith. The holy tempers and gracious fruits which attend faith, secure from delusion in so important a matter.

Chapter 2

Chapter Outline

Reasons for the apostle not coming to Corinth.	(1–4)
Directions about restoring the repentant offender.	(5–11)
An account of his labours and success in spreading the gospel of Christ.	(12–17)

Verses 1-4

The apostle desired to have a cheerful meeting with them; and he had written in confidence of their doing what was to their benefit and his comfort; and that therefore they would be glad to remove every cause of disquiet from him. We should always give pain unwillingly, even when duty requires that it must be given.

Verses 5-11

The apostle desires them to receive the person who had done wrong, again into their communion; for he was aware of his fault, and much afflicted under his punishment. Even sorrow for sin should not unfit for other duties, and drive to despair. Not only was there danger last Satan should get advantage, by tempting the penitent to hard thoughts of God and religion, and so drive him to despair; but against the churches and the ministers of Christ, by bringing an evil report upon Christians as unforgiving; thus making divisions, and hindering the success of the ministry. In this, as in other things, wisdom is to be used, that the ministry may not be blamed for indulging sin on the one hand, or for too great severity towards sinners on the other hand. Satan has many plans to deceive, and knows how to make a bad use of our mistakes.

Verses 12-17

A believer's triumphs are all in Christ. To him be the praise and glory of all, while the success of the gospel is a good reason for a Christian's joy and rejoicing. In ancient triumphs, abundance of perfumes and sweet odours were used; so the name and salvation of Jesus, as ointment poured out, was a sweet savour diffused in every place. Unto some, the gospel is a savour of death unto death. They reject it to their ruin. Unto others, the gospel is a savour of life unto life: as it quickened them at first when they were dead in trespasses and sins, so it makes them more lively, and will end in eternal life. Observe the awful impressions this matter made upon the apostle, and should also make upon us. The work is great, and of ourselves we have no strength at all; all our sufficiency is of God. But what we do in religion, unless it is done in sincerity, as in the sight of God, is not of God, does not come from him, and will not reach to him. May we carefully watch ourselves in this matter; and seek the testimony of our consciences, under the teaching of the Holy Spirit, that as of sincerity, so speak we in Christ and of Christ.

Chapter 3

Chapter Outline

The preference of the gospel to the law given by Moses.	(1–11)
The preaching of the apostle was suitable to the excellency and evidence of the gospel, through the power of the Holy Ghost.	(12–18)

Verses 1-11

Even the appearance of self-praise and courting human applause, is painful to the humble and spiritual mind. Nothing is more delightful to faithful ministers, or more to their praise, than the success of their ministry, as shown in the spirits and lives of those among whom they labour. The law of Christ was written in their hearts, and the love of Christ shed abroad there. Nor was it written in tables of stone, as the law of God given to Moses, but on the fleshy (not fleshly, as fleshliness denotes sensuality) tables of the heart, Eze 36:26. Their hearts were humbled and softened to receive this impression, by the new-creating power of the Holy Spirit. He ascribes all the glory to God. And remember, as our whole dependence is upon the Lord, so the whole glory belongs to him alone. The letter killeth: the letter of the law is the ministration of death; and if we rest only in the letter of the gospel, we shall not be the better for so doing: but the Holy Spirit gives life spiritual, and life eternal. The Old Testament dispensation was the ministration of death, but the New Testament of life. The law made known sin, and the wrath and curse of God; it showed us a God above us, and a God against us; but the gospel makes known grace, and Emmanuel, God with us. Therein the righteousness of God by faith is revealed; and this shows us that the just shall live by his faith; this makes known the grace and mercy of God through Jesus Christ, for obtaining the forgiveness of sins and eternal life. The gospel so much exceeds the law in glory, that it eclipses the glory of the legal dispensation. But even the New Testament will be a killing letter, if shown as a mere system or form, and without dependence on God the Holy Spirit, to give it a quickening power.

Verses 12-18

It is the duty of the ministers of the gospel to use great plainness, or clearness, of speech. The Old Testament believers had only cloudy and passing glimpses of that glorious Saviour, and unbelievers looked no further than to the outward institution. But the great precepts of the gospel, believe, love, obey, are truths stated as clearly as possible. And the whole doctrine of Christ crucified, is made as plain as human language can make it. Those who lived under the law, had a veil upon their hearts. This veil is taken away by the doctrines of the Bible about Christ. When any person is converted to God, then the veil of ignorance is taken away. The condition of those who enjoy and believe the gospel is happy, for the heart is set at liberty to run the ways of God's commandments. They have light, and with open face they behold the glory of the Lord. Christians should prize and improve these privileges. We should not rest contented without knowing the transforming power of the gospel, by the working of the Spirit, bringing us to seek to be like the temper and tendency of the glorious gospel of our Lord and Saviour Jesus Christ, and into union with Him. We behold Christ, as in the glass of his word; and as the reflection from a mirror causes the face to shine, the faces of Christians shine also.

Chapter 4

Chapter Outline

The apostles laboured with much diligence,   (1–7)
sincerity, and faithfulness.

| Their sufferings for the gospel were great, yet with rich supports. | (8–12) |
| Prospects of eternal glory keep believers from fainting under troubles. | (13–18) |

Verses 1-7

The best of men would faint, if they did not receive mercy from God. And that mercy which has helped us out, and helped us on, hitherto, we may rely upon to help us even to the end. The apostles had no base and wicked designs, covered with fair and specious pretences. They did not try to make their ministry serve a turn. Sincerity or uprightness will keep the favourable opinion of wise and good men. Christ by his gospel makes a glorious discovery to the minds of men. But the design of the devil is, to keep men in ignorance; and when he cannot keep the light of the gospel of Christ out of the world, he spares no pains to keep men from the gospel, or to set them against it. The rejection of the gospel is here traced to the wilful blindness and wickedness of the human heart. Self was not the matter or the end of the apostles' preaching; they preached Christ as Jesus, the Saviour and Deliverer, who saves to the uttermost all that come to God through him. Ministers are servants to the souls of men; they must avoid becoming servants to the humours or the lusts of men. It is pleasant to behold the sun in the firmament; but it is more pleasant and profitable for the gospel to shine in the heart. As light was the beginning of the first creation; so, in the new creation, the light of the Spirit is his first work upon the soul. The treasure of gospel light and grace is put into earthen vessels. The ministers of the gospel are subject to the same passions and weaknesses as other men. God could have sent angels to make known the glorious doctrine of the gospel, or could have sent the most admired sons of men to teach the nations, but he chose humbler, weaker vessels, that his power might be more glorified in upholding them, and in the blessed change wrought by their ministry.

Verses 8-12

The apostles were great sufferers, yet they met with wonderful support. Believers may be forsaken of their friends, as well as persecuted by enemies; but their God will never leave them nor forsake them. There may be fears within, as well as fightings without; yet we are not destroyed. The apostle speaks of their sufferings as a counterpart of the sufferings of Christ, that people might see the power of Christ's resurrection, and of grace in and from the living Jesus. In comparison with them, other Christians were, even at that time, in prosperous circumstances.

Verses 13-18

The grace of faith is an effectual remedy against fainting in times of trouble. They knew that Christ was raised, and that his resurrection was an earnest and assurance of theirs. The hope of this resurrection will encourage in a suffering day, and set us above the fear of death. Also, their sufferings were for the advantage of the church, and to God's glory. The sufferings of Christ's ministers, as well as their preaching and conversation, are for the good of the church and the glory of God. The prospect of eternal life and happiness was their support and comfort. What sense was ready to pronounce heavy and long, grievous and tedious, faith perceived to be light and short, and but for a moment. The weight of all temporal afflictions was lightness itself, while the glory to come was a substance, weighty, and lasting beyond description. If the apostle could call his heavy and long-continued trials light, and but for a moment, what must our trifling difficulties be! Faith enables to make this right judgment of things. There are unseen things, as well as things that are seen. And there is this vast difference between them; unseen things are eternal, seen things but temporal, or temporary only. Let us then look off from the things which are seen; let us cease to seek for worldly advantages, or to fear present distresses. Let us give diligence to make our future happiness sure.

Chapter 5

Chapter Outline

The apostle's hope and desire of heavenly glory.	(1–8)
This excited to diligence. The reasons of his being affected with zeal for the Corinthians.	(9–15)
The necessity of regeneration, and of reconciliation with God through Christ.	(16–21)

Verses 1-8

The believer not only is well assured by faith that there is another and a happy life after this is ended, but he has good hope, through grace, of heaven as a dwelling-place, a resting-place, a hiding-place. In our Father's house there are many mansions, whose Builder and Maker is God. The happiness of the future state is what God has prepared for those that love him: everlasting habitations, not like the earthly tabernacles, the poor cottages of clay, in which our souls now dwell; that are mouldering and decaying, whose foundations are in the dust. The body of flesh is a heavy burden, the calamities of life are a heavy load. But believers groan, being burdened with a body of sin, and because of the many corruptions remaining and raging within them. Death will strip us of the clothing of flesh, and all the comforts of life, as well as end all our troubles here below. But believing souls shall be clothed with garments of praise, with robes of righteousness and glory. The present graces and comforts of the Spirit are earnests of everlasting grace and comfort. And though God is with us here, by his Spirit, and in his ordinances, yet we are not with him as we hope to be. Faith is for this world, and sight is for the other world. It is our duty, and it will be our interest, to walk by faith, till we live by sight. This shows clearly the happiness to be enjoyed by the souls of believers when absent from the body, and where Jesus makes known his glorious presence. We are related to the body and to the Lord; each claims a part in us. But how much more powerfully the Lord pleads for having the soul of the believer closely united with himself! Thou art one of the souls I have loved and chosen; one of those given to me. What is death, as an object of fear, compared with being absent from the Lord!

Verses 9-15

The apostle quickens himself and others to acts of duty. Well-grounded hopes of heaven will not encourage sloth and sinful security. Let all consider the judgment to come, which is called, The terror of the Lord. Knowing what terrible vengeance the Lord would execute upon the workers of iniquity, the apostle and his brethren used every argument and persuasion, to lead men to believe in the Lord Jesus, and to act as his disciples. Their zeal and diligence were for the glory of God and the good of the church. Christ's love to us will have a like effect upon us, if duly considered and rightly judged. All were lost and undone, dead and ruined, slaves to sin, having no power to deliver themselves, and must have remained thus miserable for ever, if Christ had not died. We should not make ourselves, but Christ, the end of our living and actions. A Christian's life should be devoted to Christ. Alas, how many show the worthlessness of their professed faith and love, by living to themselves and to the world!

Verses 16-21

The renewed man acts upon new principles, by new rules, with new ends, and in new company. The believer is created anew; his heart is not merely set right, but a new heart is given him. He is the workmanship of God, created in Christ Jesus unto good works. Though the same as a man, he is changed in his character and conduct. These words must and do mean more than an outward reformation. The man who formerly saw no beauty in the Saviour that he should desire him, now loves him above all things. The heart of the unregenerate is filled with enmity against God, and God is justly offended with him. Yet there may be reconciliation. Our offended God has reconciled us to himself by Jesus Christ. By the inspiration of God, the Scriptures were written, which are the word of reconciliation; showing that peace has been made by the cross, and how we may be interested therein. Though God cannot lose by the quarrel, nor gain by the peace, yet he beseeches sinners to lay aside their enmity, and accept the salvation he offers. Christ knew no sin. He was made Sin; not a sinner, but Sin, a Sin-offering, a Sacrifice for sin. The end and design of all this was, that we might be made the righteousness of God in him, might be justified freely by the grace of God through the redemption which is in Christ Jesus. Can any lose, labour, or suffer too much for Him, who gave his beloved Son to be the Sacrifice for their sins, that they might be made the righteousness of God in him?

Chapter 6

Chapter Outline

The apostle, with others, proved themselves faithful ministers of Christ, by their unblamable life and behaviour. (1–10)

By affection for them, And by earnest concern, that they might have no fellowship with unbelievers and idolaters. (11–18)

Verses 1-10

The gospel is a word of grace sounding in our ears. The gospel day is a day of salvation, the means of grace the means of salvation, the offers of the gospel the offers of salvation, and the present time the proper time to accept these offers. The morrow is none of ours: we know not what will be on the morrow, nor where we shall be. We now enjoy a day of grace; then let all be careful not to neglect it. Ministers of the gospel should look upon themselves as God's servants, and act in every thing suitably to that character. The apostle did so, by much patience in afflictions, by acting from good principles, and by due temper and behaviour. Believers, in this world, need the grace of God, to arm them against temptations, so as to bear the good report of men without pride; and so as to bear their reproaches with patience. They have nothing in themselves, but possess all things in Christ. Of such differences is a Christian's life made up, and through such a variety of conditions and reports, is our way to heaven; and we should be careful in all things to approve ourselves to God. The gospel, when faithfully preached, and fully received, betters the condition even of the poorest. They save what before they riotously spent, and diligently employ their time to useful purposes. They save and gain by religion, and thus are made rich, both for the world to come and for this, when compared with their sinful, profligate state, before they received the gospel.

Verses 11-18

It is wrong for believers to join with the wicked and profane. The word unbeliever applies to all destitute of true faith. True pastors will caution their beloved children in the gospel, not to be unequally yoked. The fatal effects of neglecting Scripture precepts as to marriages clearly appear. Instead of a help meet, the union brings a snare. Those whose cross it is to be unequally united, without their wilful fault, may expect consolation under it; but when believers enter into such unions, against the express warnings of God's word, they must expect must distress. The caution also extends to common conversation. We should not join in friendship and acquaintance with wicked men and unbelievers. Though we cannot wholly avoid seeing and hearing, and being with such, yet we should never choose them for friends. We must not defile ourselves by converse with those who defile themselves with sin. Come out from the workers of iniquity, and separate from their vain and sinful pleasures and pursuits; from all conformity to the corruptions of this present evil world. If it be an envied privilege to be the son or daughter of an earthly prince, who can express the dignity and happiness of being sons and daughters of the Almighty?

Chapter 7

Chapter Outline

Verses 1-4

The promises of God are strong reasons for us to follow after holiness; we must cleanse ourselves from all filthiness of flesh and spirit. If we hope in God as our Father, we must seek to be holy as he is holy, and perfect as our Father in heaven. His grace, by the influences of his Spirit, alone can purify, but holiness should be the object of our constant prayers. If the ministers of the gospel are thought contemptible, there is danger lest the gospel itself be despised also; and though ministers must flatter none, yet they must be gentle towards all. Ministers may look for esteem and favour, when they can safely appeal to the people, that they have corrupted no man by false doctrines or flattering speeches; that they have defrauded no man; nor sought to promote their own interests so as to hurt any. It was affection to them made the apostle speak so freely to them, and caused him to glory of them, in all places, and upon all occasions.

Verses 5-11

There were fightings without, or continual contentions with, and opposition from Jews and Gentiles; and there were fears within, and great concern for such as had embraced the Christian faith. But God comforts those who are cast down. We should look above and beyond all means and instruments, to God, as the author of all the consolation and good we enjoy. Sorrow according to the will of God, tending to the glory of God, and wrought by the Spirit of God, renders the heart humble, contrite, submissive, disposed to mortify every sin, and to walk in newness of life. And this repentance is connected with saving faith in Christ, and an interest in his atonement. There is a great difference between this sorrow of a godly sort, and the sorrow of the world. The happy fruits of true repentance are mentioned. Where the heart is changed, the life and actions will be changed. It wrought indignation at sin, at themselves, at the tempter and his instruments. It wrought a fear of watchfulness, and a cautious fear of sin. It wrought desire to be reconciled with God. It wrought zeal for duty, and against sin. It wrought revenge against sin and their own folly, by endeavours to make satisfaction for injuries done thereby. Deep humility before God, hatred of all sin, with faith in Christ, a new heart and a new life, make repentance unto salvation. May the Lord bestow it on every one of us.

Verses 12-16

The apostle was not disappointed concerning them, which he signified to Titus; and he could with joy declare the confidence he had in them for the time to come. Here see the duties of a pastor and of his flock; the latter must lighten the troubles of the pastoral office, by respect and obedience; the former make a due return by his care of them, and cherish the flock by testimonies of satisfaction, joy, and tenderness.

Chapter 8

Chapter Outline

The apostle reminds them of charitable contributions for the poor saints.	(1–6)
Enforces this by their gifts, and by the love and grace of Christ.	(7–9)
By the willingness they had shown to this good work.	(10–15)
He recommends Titus to them.	(16–24)

Verses 1-6

The grace of God must be owned as the root and fountain of all the good in us, or done by us, at any time. It is great grace and favour from God, if we are made useful to others, and forward to any good work. He commends the charity of the Macedonians. So far from needing that Paul should urge them, they prayed him to receive the gift. Whatever we use or lay out for God, it is only giving him what is his own. All we give for charitable uses, will not be accepted of God, nor turn to our advantage, unless we first give ourselves to the Lord. By ascribing all really good works to the grace of God, we not only give the glory to him whose due it is, but also show men where their strength is. Abundant spiritual joy enlarges men's hearts in the work and labour of love. How different this from the conduct of those who will not join in any good work, unless urged into it!

Verses 7-9

Faith is the root; and as without faith it is not possible to please God, Heb 11:6, so those who abound in faith, will abound in other graces and good works also; and this will work and show itself by love. Great talkers are not always the best doers; but these Corinthians were diligent to do, as well as to know and talk well. To all these good things the apostle desires them to add this grace also, to abound in charity to the poor. The best arguments for Christian duties, are drawn from the grace and love of Christ. Though he was rich, as being God, equal in power and glory with the Father, yet he not only became man for us, but became poor also. At length he emptied himself, as it were, to ransom their souls by his sacrifice on the cross. From what riches, blessed Lord, to what poverty didst thou descend for our sakes! and to what riches hast thou advanced us through thy poverty! It is our happiness to be wholly at thy disposal.

Verses 10-15

Good purposes are like buds and blossoms, pleasant to behold, and give hopes of good fruit; but they are lost, and signify nothing without good deeds. Good beginnings are well; but we lose the benefit, unless there is perseverance. When men purpose that which is good, and endeavour, according to their ability, to perform also, God will not reject them for what it is not in their power to do. But this scripture will not justify those who think good meanings are enough, or that good purposes, and the mere profession of a willing mind, are enough to save. Providence gives to some more of the good things of this world, and to some less, that those who have abundance might supply others who are in want. It is the will of God, that by our mutual supplying one another, there should be some sort of equality; not such a levelling as would destroy property, for in such a case there could be no exercise of charity. All should think themselves concerned to relieve those in want. This is shown from the gathering and giving out the manna in the wilderness, Ex 16:18. Those who have most of this world, have no more than food and raiment; and those who have but little of this world, seldom are quite without them.

Verses 16-24

The apostle commends the brethren sent to collect their charity, that it might be known who they were, and how safely they might be trusted. It is the duty of all Christians to act prudently; to hinder, as far as we can, all unjust suspicions. It is needful, in the first place, to act uprightly in the sight of God, but things honest in the sight of men should also be attended to. A clear character, as well as a pure conscience, is requisite for usefulness. They brought glory to Christ as instruments, and had obtained honour from Christ to be counted faithful, and employed in his service. The good opinion others have of us, should be an argument with us to do well.

Chapter 9

Chapter Outline

Verses 1-5

When we would have others do good, we must act toward them prudently and tenderly, and give them time. Christians should consider what is for the credit of their profession, and endeavour to adorn the doctrine of God their Saviour in all things. The duty of ministering to the saints is so plain, that there would seem no need to exhort Christians to it; yet self-love contends so powerfully against the love of Christ, that it is often necessary to stir up their minds by way of remembrance.

Verses 6-15

Money bestowed in charity, may to the carnal mind seem thrown away, but when given from proper principles, it is seed sown, from which a valuable increase may be expected. It should be given carefully. Works of charity, like other good works, should be done with thought and design. Due thought, as to our circumstances, and those we are about to relieve, will direct our gifts for charitable uses. Help should be given freely, be it more or less; not grudgingly, but cheerfully. While some scatter, and yet increase; others withhold more than is meet, and it tends to poverty. If we had more faith and love, we should waste less on ourselves, and sow more in hope of a plentiful increase. Can a man lose by doing that with which God is pleased? He is able to make all grace abound towards us, and to abound in us; to give a large increase of spiritual and of temporal good things. He can make us to have enough in all things; and to be content with what we have. God gives not only enough for ourselves, but that also wherewith we may supply the wants of others, and this should be as seed to be sown. We must show the reality of our subjection to the gospel, by works of charity. This will be for the credit of our profession, and to the praise and glory of God. Let us endeavour to copy the example of Christ, being unwearied in doing good, and deeming it more blessed to give than to receive. Blessed be God for the unspeakable gift of his grace, whereby he enables and inclines some of his people to bestow upon others, and others to be grateful for it; and blessed be his glorious name to all eternity, for Jesus Christ, that inestimable gift of his love, through whom this and every other good thing, pertaining to life and godliness, are freely given unto us, beyond all expression, measure, or bounds.

Chapter 10

Chapter Outline

The apostle states his authority with meekness and humility.	(1–6)
Reasons with the Corinthians.	(7–11)
Seeks the glory of God, and to be approved of him.	(12–18)

Verses 1-6

While others thought meanly, and spake scornfully of the apostle, he had low thoughts, and spake humbly of himself. We should be aware of our own infirmities, and think humbly of ourselves, even when men reproach us. The work of the ministry is a spiritual warfare with spiritual enemies, and for spiritual purposes. Outward force is not the method of the gospel, but strong persuasions, by the power of truth and the meekness of wisdom. Conscience is accountable to God only; and people must be persuaded to God and their duty, not driven by force. Thus the weapons of our warfare are very powerful; the evidence of truth is convincing. What opposition is made against the gospel, by the powers of sin and Satan in the hearts of men! But observe the conquest the word of God gains. The appointed means, however feeble they appear to some, will be mighty through God. And the preaching of the cross, by men of faith and prayer, has always been fatal to idolatry, impiety, and wickedness.

Verses 7-11

In outward appearance, Paul was mean and despised in the eyes of some, but this was a false rule to judge by. We must not think that none outward appearance, as if the want of such things proved a man not to be a real Christian, or an able, faithful minister of the lowly Saviour.

Verses 12-18

If we would compare ourselves with others who excel us, this would be a good method to keep us humble. The apostle fixes a good rule for his conduct; namely, not to boast of things without his measure, which was the measure God had distributed to him. There is not a more fruitful source of error, than to judge of persons and opinions by our own prejudices. How common is it for persons to judge of their own religious character, by the opinions and maxims of the world around them! But how different is the rule of God's word! And of all flattery, self-flattery is the worst. Therefore, instead of praising ourselves, we should strive to approve ourselves to God. In a word, let us glory in the Lord our salvation, and in all other things only as evidences of his love, or means of promoting his glory. Instead of praising ourselves, or seeking the praise of men, let us desire that honour which cometh from God only.

Chapter 11

Chapter Outline

Explains what he was going to add in   (16–21)
defence of his own character.

He gives an account of his labours, cares,   (22–33)
sufferings, dangers, and deliverances.

Verses 1-4

The apostle desired to preserve the Corinthians from being corrupted by the false apostles. There is but one Jesus, one Spirit, and one gospel, to be preached to them, and received by them; and why should any be prejudiced, by the devices of an adversary, against him who first taught them in faith? They should not listen to men, who, without cause, would draw them away from those who were the means of their conversion.

Verses 5-15

It is far better to be plain in speech, yet walking openly and consistently with the gospel, than to be admired by thousands, and be lifted up in pride, so as to disgrace the gospel by evil tempers and unholy lives. The apostle would not give room for any to accuse him of worldly designs in preaching the gospel, that others who opposed him at Corinth, might not in this respect gain advantage against him. Hypocrisy may be looked for, especially when we consider the great power which Satan, who rules in the hearts of the children of disobedience, has upon the minds of many. And as there are temptations to evil conduct, so there is equal danger on the other side. It serves Satan's purposes as well, to set up good works against the atonement of Christ, and salvation by faith and grace. But the end will discover those who are deceitful workers; their work will end in ruin. Satan will allow his ministers to preach either the law or the gospel separately; but the law as established by faith in Christ's righteousness and atonement, and the partaking of his Spirit, is the test of every false system.

Verses 16-21

It is the duty and practice of Christians to humble themselves, in obedience to the command and example of the Lord; yet prudence must direct in what it is needful to do things which we may do lawfully, even the speaking of what God has wrought for us, and in us, and by us. Doubtless here is reference to facts in which the character of the false apostles had been shown. It is astonishing to see how such men bring their followers into bondage, and how they take from them and insult them.

Verses 22-33

The apostle gives an account of his labours and sufferings; not out of pride or vain-glory, but to the honour of God, who enabled him to do and suffer so much for the cause of Christ; and shows wherein he excelled the false apostles, who tried to lessen his character and usefulness. It astonishes us to reflect on this account of his dangers, hardships, and sufferings, and to observe his patience, perseverance, diligence, cheerfulness, and usefulness, in the midst of all these trials. See what little reason we have to love the pomp and plenty of this world, when this blessed apostle felt so much hardship in it. Our utmost diligence and services appear unworthy of notice when compared with his, and our difficulties and trials scarcely can be perceived. It may well lead us to inquire whether or not we really are followers of Christ. Here we may study patience, courage, and firm trust in God. Here we may learn to think less of ourselves; and we should ever strictly keep to truth, as in God's presence; and should refer all to his glory, as the Father of our Lord Jesus Christ, who is blessed for evermore.

Chapter 12

Chapter Outline

The apostle's revelations.	(1–6)
Which were improved to his spiritual advantage.	(7–10)
The signs of an apostle were in him, His purpose of making them a visit; but he expresses his fear lest he should have to be severe with some.	(11–21)

Verses 1-6

There can be no doubt the apostle speaks of himself. Whether heavenly things were brought down to him, while his body was in a trance, as in the case of ancient prophets; or whether his soul was dislodged from the body for a time, and taken up into heaven, or whether he was taken up, body and soul together, he knew not. We are not capable, nor is it fit we should yet know, the particulars of that glorious place and state. He did not attempt to publish to the world what he had heard there, but he set forth the doctrine of Christ. On that foundation the church is built, and on that we must build our faith and hope. And while this teaches us to enlarge our expectations of the glory that shall be revealed, it should render us contented with the usual methods of learning the truth and will of God.

Verses 7-10

The apostle gives an account of the method God took to keep him humble, and to prevent his being lifted up above measure, on account of the visions and revelations he had. We are not told what this thorn in the flesh was, whether some great trouble, or some great temptation. But God often brings this good out of evil, that the reproaches of our enemies help to hide pride from us. If God loves us, he will keep us from being exalted above measure; and spiritual burdens are ordered to cure spiritual pride. This thorn in the flesh is said to be a messenger of Satan which he sent for evil; but God designed it, and overruled it for good. Prayer is a salve for every sore, a remedy for every malady; and when we are afflicted with thorns in the flesh, we should give ourselves to prayer. If an answer be not given to the first prayer, nor to the second, we are to continue praying. Troubles are sent to teach us to pray; and are continued, to teach us to continue instant in prayer. Though God accepts the prayer of faith, yet he does not always give what is asked for: as he sometimes grants in wrath, so he sometimes denies in love. When God does not take away our troubles and temptations, yet, if he gives grace enough for us, we have no reason to complain. Grace signifies the good-will of God towards us, and that is enough to enlighten and enliven us, sufficient to strengthen and comfort in all afflictions and distresses. His strength is made perfect in our weakness. Thus his grace is manifested and magnified. When we are weak in ourselves, then we are strong in the grace of our Lord Jesus Christ; when we feel that we are weak in ourselves, then we go to Christ, receive strength from him, and enjoy most the supplies of Divine strength and grace.

Verses 11-21

We owe it to good men, to stand up in the defence of their reputation; and we are under special obligations to those from whom we have received benefit, especially spiritual benefit, to own them as instruments in God's hand of good to us. Here is an account of the apostle's behaviour and kind intentions; in which see the character of a faithful minister of the gospel. This was his great aim and design, to do good. Here are noticed several sins commonly found among professors of religion. Falls and misdeeds are humbling to a minister; and God sometimes takes this way to humble those who might be tempted to be lifted up. These vast verses show to what excesses the false teachers had drawn aside their deluded followers. How grievous it is that such evils should be found among professors of the gospel! Yet thus it is, and has been too often, and it was so even in the days of the apostles.

Chapter 13

Chapter Outline

Verses 1-6

Though it is God's gracious method to bear long with sinners, yet he will not bear always; at length he will come, and will not spare those who remain obstinate and impenitent. Christ at his crucifixion, appeared as only a weak and helpless man, but his resurrection and life showed his Divine power. So the apostles, how mean and contemptible soever they appeared to the world, yet, as instruments, they manifested the power of God. Let them prove their tempers, conduct, and experience, as gold is assayed or proved by the touchstone. If they could prove themselves not to be reprobates, not to be rejected of Christ, he trusted they would know that he was not a reprobate, not disowned by Christ. They ought to know if Christ Jesus was in them, by the influences, graces, and indwelling of his Spirit, by his kingdom set up in their hearts. Let us question our own souls; either we are true Christians, or we are deceivers. Unless Christ be in us by his Spirit, and power of his love, our faith is dead, and we are yet disapproved by our Judge.

Verses 7-10

The most desirable thing we can ask of God, for ourselves and our friends, is to be kept from sin, that we and they may not do evil. We have far more need to pray that we may not do evil, than that we may not suffer evil. The apostle not only desired that they might be kept from sin, but also that they might grow in grace, and increase in holiness. We are earnestly to pray to God for those we caution, that they may cease to do evil, and learn to do well; and we should be glad for others to be strong in the grace of Christ, though it may be the means of showing our own weakness. let us also pray that we may be enabled to make a proper use of all our talents.

Verses 11-14

Here are several good exhortations. God is the Author of peace and Lover of concord; he hath loved us, and is willing to be at peace with us. And let it be our constant aim so to walk, that separation from our friends may be only for a time, and that we may meet in that happy world where parting will be unknown. He wishes that they may partake all the benefits which Christ of his free grace and favour has purchased; the Father out of his free love has purposed; and the Holy Ghost applies and bestows.

Galatians

The churches in Galatia were formed partly of converted Jews, and partly of Gentile converts, as was generally the case. St. Paul asserts his apostolic character and the doctrines he taught, that he might confirm the Galatian churches in the faith of Christ, especially with respect to the important point of justification by faith alone. Thus the subject is mainly the same as that which is discussed in the epistle to the Romans, that is, justification by faith alone. In this epistle, however, attention is particularly directed to the point, that men are justified by faith without the works of the law of Moses. Of the importance of the doctrines prominently set forth in this epistle, Luther thus speaks: "We have to fear as the greatest and nearest danger, lest Satan take from us this doctrine of faith, and bring into the church again the doctrine of works and of men's traditions. Wherefore it is very necessary that this doctrine be kept in continual practice and public exercise, both of reading and hearing. If this doctrine be lost, then is also the doctrine of truth, life and salvation, lost and gone."

Chapter 1

Chapter Outline

The apostle Paul asserts his apostolic character against such as lessened it.	(1–5)
He reproves the Galatians for revolting from the gospel of Christ under the influence of evil teachers.	(6–9)
He proves the Divine authority of his doctrine and mission; and declares what he was before his conversion and calling.	(10–14)
And how he proceeded after it.	(15–24)

Verses 1-5

St. Paul was an apostle of Jesus Christ; he was expressly appointed by him, consequently by God the Father, who is one with him in respect of his Divine nature, and who appointed Christ as Mediator. Grace, includes God's good-will towards us, and his good work upon us; and peace, all that inward comfort, or outward prosperity, which is really needful for us. They come from God the Father, as the Fountain, through Jesus Christ. But observe, first grace, and then peace; there can be no true peace without grace. Christ gave himself for our sins, to make atonement for us: this the justice of God required, and to this he freely submitted. Here is to be observed the infinite greatness of the price bestowed, and then it will appear plainly, that the power of sin is so great, that it could by no means be put away except the Son of God be given for it. He that considers these things well, understands that sin is a thing the most horrible that can be expressed; which ought to move us, and make us afraid indeed. Especially mark well the words, "for our sins." For here our weak nature starts back, and would first be made worthy by her own works. It would bring him that is whole, and not him that has need of a physician. Not only to redeem us from the wrath of God, and the curse of the law; but also to recover us from wicked practices and customs, to which we are naturally enslaved. But it is in vain for those who are not delivered from this present evil world by the sanctification of the Spirit, to expect that they are freed from its condemnation by the blood of Jesus.

Verses 6-9

Those who would establish any other way to heaven than what the gospel of Christ reveals, will find themselves wretchedly mistaken. The apostle presses upon the Galatians a due sense of their guilt in forsaking the gospel way of justification; yet he reproves with tenderness, and represents them as drawn into it by the arts of some that troubled them. In reproving others, we should be faithful, and yet endeavour to restore them in the spirit of meekness. Some would set up the works of the law in the place of Christ's righteousness, and thus they corrupted Christianity. The apostle solemnly denounces, as accursed, every one who attempts to lay so false a foundation. All other gospels than that of the grace of Christ, whether more flattering to self-righteous pride, or more favourable to worldly lusts, are devices of Satan. And while we declare that to reject the moral law as a rule of life, tends to dishonour Christ, and destroy true religion, we must also declare, that all dependence for justification on good works, whether real or supposed, is as fatal to those who persist in it. While we are zealous for good works, let us be careful not to put them in the place of Christ's righteousness, and not to advance any thing which may betray others into so dreadful a delusion.

Verses 10-14

In preaching the gospel, the apostle sought to bring persons to the obedience, not of men, but of God. But Paul would not attempt to alter the doctrine of Christ, either to gain their favour, or to avoid their fury. In so important a matter we must not fear the frowns of men, nor seek their favour, by using words of men's wisdom. Concerning the manner wherein he received the gospel, he had it by revelation from Heaven. He was not led to Christianity, as many are, merely by education.

Verses 15-24

St. Paul was wonderfully brought to the knowledge and faith of Christ. All who are savingly converted, are called by the grace of God; their conversion is wrought by his power and grace working in them. It will but little avail us to have Christ revealed to us, if he is not also revealed in us. He instantly prepared to obey, without hesitating as to his worldly interest, credit, ease, or life itself. And what matter of thanksgiving and joy is it to the churches of Christ, when they hear of such instances to the praise of the glory of his grace, whether they have ever seen them or not! They glorify God for his power and mercy in saving such persons, and for all the service to his people and cause that is done, and may be further expected from them.

Chapter 2

Chapter Outline

The apostle declares his being owned as an   (1–10)
apostle of the Gentiles.

He had publicly opposed Peter for judaizing.   (11–14)

And from thence he enters upon the doctrine   (15–21)
of justification by faith in Christ, without the
works of the law.

Verses 1-10

Observe the apostle's faithfulness in giving a full account of the doctrine he had preached among the Gentiles, and was still resolved to preach, that of Christianity, free from all mixture of Judaism. This doctrine would be ungrateful to many, yet he was not afraid to own it. His care was, lest the success of his past labours should be lessened, or his future usefulness be hindered. While we simply depend upon God for success to our labours, we should use every proper caution to remove mistakes, and against opposers. There are things which may lawfully be complied with, yet, when they cannot be done without betraying the truth, they ought to be refused. We must not give place to any conduct, whereby the truth of the gospel would be reflected upon. Though Paul conversed with the other apostles, yet he did not receive any addition to his knowledge, or authority, from them. Perceiving the grace given to him, they gave unto him and Barnabas the right hand of fellowship, whereby they acknowledged that he was designed to the honour and office of an apostle as well as themselves. They agreed that these two should go to the heathen, while they continued to preach to the Jews; judging it agreeable to the mind of Christ, so to divide their work. Here we learn that the gospel is not ours, but God's; and that men are but the keepers of it; for this we are to praise God. The apostle showed his charitable disposition, and how ready he was to own the Jewish converts as brethren, though many would scarcely allow the like favour to the converted Gentiles; but mere difference of opinion was no reason to him why he should not help them. Herein is a pattern of Christian charity, which we should extend to all the disciples of Christ.

Verses 11-14

Notwithstanding Peter's character, yet, when Paul saw him acting so as to hurt the truth of the gospel and the peace of the church, he was not afraid to reprove him. When he saw that Peter and the others did not live up to that principle which the gospel taught, and which they professed, namely, That by the death of Christ the partition wall between Jew and Gentile was taken down, and the observance of the law of Moses was no longer in force; as Peter's offence was public, he publicly reproved him. There is a very great difference between the prudence of St. Paul, who bore with, and used for a time, the ceremonies of the law as not sinful, and the timid conduct of St. Peter, who, by withdrawing from the Gentiles, led others to think that these ceremonies were necessary.

Verses 15-19

Paul, having thus shown he was not inferior to any apostle, not to Peter himself, speaks of the great foundation doctrine of the gospel. For what did we believe in Christ? Was it not that we might be justified by the faith of Christ? If so, is it not foolish to go back to the law, and to expect to be justified by the merit of moral works, or sacrifices, or ceremonies? The occasion of this declaration doubtless arose from the ceremonial law; but the argument is quite as strong against all dependence upon the works of the moral law, as respects justification. To give the greater weight to this, it is added, But if, while we seek to be justified by Christ, we ourselves also are found sinners, is Christ the minister of sin? This would be very dishonourable to Christ, and also very hurtful to them. By considering the law itself, he saw that justification was not to be expected by the works of it, and that there was now no further need of the sacrifices and cleansings of it, since they were done away in Christ, by his offering up himself a sacrifice for us. He did not hope or fear any thing from it; any more than a dead man from enemies. But the effect was not a careless, lawless life. It was necessary, that he might live to God, and be devoted to him through the motives and grace of the gospel. It is no new prejudice, though a most unjust one, that the doctrine of justification by faith alone, tends to encourage people in sin. Not so, for to take occasion from free grace, or the doctrine of it, to live in sin, is to try to make Christ the minister of sin, at any thought of which all Christian hearts would shudder.

Verses 20, 21

Here, in his own person, the apostle describes the spiritual or hidden life of a believer. The old man is crucified, Ro 6:6, but the new man is living; sin is mortified, and grace is quickened. He has the comforts and the triumphs of grace; yet that grace is not from himself, but from another. Believers see themselves living in a state of dependence on Christ. Hence it is, that though he lives in the flesh, yet he does not live after the flesh. Those who have true faith, live by that faith; and faith fastens upon Christ's giving himself for us. He loved me, and gave himself for me. As if the apostle said, The Lord saw me fleeing from him more and more. Such wickedness, error, and ignorance were in my will and understanding, that it was not possible for me to be ransomed by any other means than by such a price. Consider well this price. Here notice the false faith of many. And their profession is accordingly; they have the form of godliness without the power of it. They think they believe the articles of faith aright, but they are deceived. For to believe in Christ crucified, is not only to believe that he was crucified, but also to believe that I am crucified with him. And this is to know Christ crucified. Hence we learn what is the nature of grace. God's grace cannot stand with man's merit. Grace is no grace unless it is freely given every way. The more simply the believer relies on Christ for every thing, the more devotedly does he walk before Him in all his ordinances and commandments. Christ lives and reigns in him, and he lives here on earth by faith in the Son of God, which works by love, causes obedience, and changes into his holy image. Thus he neither abuses the grace of God, nor makes it in vain.

Chapter 3

Chapter Outline

Verses 1-5

Several things made the folly of the Galatian Christians worse. They had the doctrine of the cross preached, and the Lord's supper administered among them, in both which Christ crucified, and the nature of his sufferings, had been fully and clearly set forth. Had they been made partakers of the Holy Spirit, by the ministration of the law, or on account of any works done by them in obedience thereto? Was it not by their hearing and embracing the doctrine of faith in Christ alone for justification? Which of these had God owned with tokens of his favour and acceptance? It was not by the first, but the last. And those must be very unwise, who suffer themselves to be turned away from the ministry and doctrine which have been blessed to their spiritual advantage. Alas, that men should turn from the all-important doctrine of Christ crucified, to listen to useless distinctions, mere moral preaching, or wild fancies! The god of this world, by various men and means, has blinded men's eyes, lest they should learn to trust in a crucified Saviour. We may boldly demand where the fruits of the Holy Spirit are most evidently brought forth? whether among those who preach justification by the works of the law, or those who preach the doctrine of faith? Assuredly among the latter.

Verses 6-14

The apostle proves the doctrine he had blamed the Galatians for rejecting; namely, that of justification by faith without the works of the law. This he does from the example of Abraham, whose faith fastened upon the word and promise of God, and upon his believing he was owned and accepted of God as a righteous man. The Scripture is said to foresee, because the Holy Spirit that indited the Scripture did foresee. Through faith in the promise of God he was blessed; and it is only in the same way that others obtain this privilege. Let us then study the object, nature, and effects of Abraham's faith; for who can in any other way escape the curse of the holy law? The curse is against all sinners, therefore against all men; for all have sinned, and are become guilty before God: and if, as transgressors of the law, we are under its curse, it must be vain to look for justification by it. Those only are just or righteous who are freed from death and wrath, and restored into a state of life in the favour of God; and it is only through faith that persons become righteous. Thus we see that justification by faith is no new doctrine, but was taught in the church of God, long before the times of the gospel. It is, in truth, the only way wherein any sinners ever were, or can be justified. Though deliverance is not to be expected from the law, there is a way open to escape the curse, and regain the favour of God, namely, through faith in Christ. Christ redeemed us from the curse of the law; being made sin, or a sin-offering, for us, he was made a curse for us; not separated from God, but laid for a time under the Divine punishment. The heavy sufferings of the Son of God, more loudly warn sinners to flee from the wrath to come, than all the curses of the law; for how can God spare any man who remains under sin, seeing that he spared not his own Son, when our sins were charged upon him? Yet at the same time, Christ, as from the cross, freely invites sinners to take refuge in him.

Verses 15-18

The covenant God made with Abraham, was not done away by the giving the law to Moses. The covenant was made with Abraham and his Seed. It is still in force; Christ abideth for ever in his person, and his spiritual seed, who are his by faith. By this we learn the difference between the promises of the law and those of the gospel. The promises of the law are made to the person of every man; the promises of the gospel are first made to Christ, then by him to those who are by faith ingrafted into Christ. Rightly to divide the word of truth, a great difference must be put between the promise and the law, as to the inward affections, and the whole practice of life. When the promise is mingled with the law, it is made nothing but the law. Let Christ be always before our eyes, as a sure argument for the defence of faith, against dependence on human righteousness.

Verses 19-22

If that promise was enough for salvation, wherefore then serveth the law? The Israelites, though chosen to be God's peculiar people, were sinners as well as others. The law was not intended to discover a way of justification, different from that made known by the promise, but to lead men to see their need of the promise, by showing the sinfulness of sin, and to point to Christ, through whom alone they could be pardoned and justified. The promise was given by God himself; the law was given by the ministry of angels, and the hand of a mediator, even Moses. Hence the law could not be designed to set aside the promise. A mediator, as the very term signifies, is a friend that comes between two parties, and is not to act merely with and for one of them. The great design of the law was, that the promise by faith of Jesus Christ, might be given to those that believe; that, being convinced of their guilt, and the insufficiency of the law to effect a righteousness for them, they might be persuaded to believe on Christ, and so obtain the benefit of the promise. And it is not possible that the holy, just, and good law of God, the standard of duty to all, should be contrary to the gospel of Christ. It tends every way to promote it.

Verses 23-25

The law did not teach a living, saving knowledge; but, by its rites and ceremonies, especially by its sacrifices, it pointed to Christ, that they might be justified by faith. And thus it was, as the word properly signifies, a servant, to lead to Christ, as children are led to school by servants who have the care of them, that they might be more fully taught by Him the true way of justification and salvation, which is only by faith in Christ. And the vastly greater advantage of the gospel state is shown, under which we enjoy a clearer discovery of Divine grace and mercy than the Jews of old. Most men continue shut up as in a dark dungeon, in love with their sins, being blinded and lulled asleep by Satan, through wordly pleasures, interests, and pursuits. But the awakened sinner discovers his dreadful condition. Then he feels that the mercy and grace of God form his only hope. And the terrors of the law are often used by the convincing Spirit, to show the sinner his need of Christ, to bring him to rely on his sufferings and merits, that he may be justified by faith. Then the law, by the teaching of the Holy Spirit, becomes his loved rule of duty, and his standard for daily self-examination. In this use of it he learns to depend more simply on the Saviour.

Verses 26-29

Real Christians enjoy great privileges under the gospel; and are no longer accounted servants, but sons; not now kept at such a distance, and under such restraints as the Jews were. Having accepted Christ Jesus as their Lord and Saviour, and relying on him alone for justification and salvation, they become the sons of God. But no outward forms or profession can secure these blessings; for if any man have not the Spirit of Christ, he is none of his. In baptism we put on Christ; therein we profess to be his disciples. Being baptized into Christ, we are baptized into his death, that as he died and rose again, so we should die unto sin, and walk in newness and holiness of life. The putting on of Christ according to the gospel, consists not in outward imitation, but in a new birth, an entire change. He who makes believers to be heirs, will provide for them. Therefore our care must be to do the duties that belong to us, and all other cares we must cast upon God. And our special care must be for heaven; the things of this life are but trifles. The city of God in heaven, is the portion or child's part. Seek to be sure of that above all things.

Chapter 4

Chapter Outline

He expresses his earnest concern for them. (19, 20)

And then explains the difference between what is to be expected from the law, and from the gospel. (21–31)

Verses 1-7

The apostle deals plainly with those who urged the law of Moses together with the gospel of Christ, and endeavoured to bring believers under its bondage. They could not fully understand the meaning of the law as given by Moses. And as that was a dispensation of darkness, so of bondage; they were tied to many burdensome rites and observances, by which they were taught and kept subject like a child under tutors and governors. We learn the happier state of Christians under the gospel dispensation. From these verses see the wonders of Divine love and mercy; particularly of God the Father, in sending his Son into the world to redeem and save us; of the Son of God, in submitting so low, and suffering so much for us; and of the Holy Spirit, in condescending to dwell in the hearts of believers, for such gracious purposes. Also, the advantages Christians enjoy under the gospel. Although by nature children of wrath and disobedience, they become by grace children of love, and partake of the nature of the children of God; for he will have all his children resemble him. Among men the eldest son is heir; but all God's children shall have the inheritance of eldest sons. May the temper and conduct of sons ever show our adoption; and may the Holy Spirit witness with our spirits that we are children and heirs of God.

Verses 8-11

The happy change whereby the Galatians were turned from idols to the living God, and through Christ had received the adoption of sons, was the effect of his free and rich grace; they were laid under the greater obligation to keep to the liberty wherewith he had made them free. All our knowledge of God begins on his part; we know him because we are known of him. Though our religion forbids idolatry, yet many practise spiritual idolatry in their hearts. For what a man loves most, and cares most for, that is his god: some have their riches for their god, some their pleasures, and some their lusts. And many ignorantly worship a god of their own making; a god made all of mercy and no justice. For they persuade themselves that there is mercy for them with God, though they repent not, but go on in their sins. It is possible for those who have made great professions of religion, to be afterwards drawn aside from purity and simplicity. And the more mercy God has shown, in bringing any to know the gospel, and the liberties and privileges of it, the greater their sin and folly in suffering themselves to be deprived of them. Hence all who are members of the outward church should learn to fear and to suspect themselves. We must not be content because we have some good things in ourselves. Paul fears lest his labour is in vain, yet he still labours; and thus to do, whatever follows, is true wisdom and the fear of God. This every man must remember in his place and calling.

Verses 12-18

The apostle desires that they would be of one mind with him respecting the law of Moses, as well as united with him in love. In reproving others, we should take care to convince them that our reproofs are from sincere regard to the honour of God and religion and their welfare. The apostle reminds the Galatians of the difficulty under which he laboured when he first came among them. But he notices, that he was a welcome messenger to them. Yet how very uncertain are the favour and respect of men! Let us labour to be accepted of God. You once thought yourselves happy in receiving the gospel; have you now reason to think otherwise? Christians must not forbear speaking the truth, for fear of offending others. The false teachers who drew the Galatians from the truth of the gospel were designing men. They pretended affection, but they were not sincere and upright. An excellent rule is given. It is good to be zealous always in a good thing; not for a time only, or now and then, but always. Happy would it be for the church of Christ, if this zeal was better maintained.

Verses 19, 20

The Galatians were ready to account the apostle their enemy, but he assures them he was their friend; he had the feelings of a parent toward them. He was in doubt as to their state, and was anxious to know the result of their present delusions. Nothing is so sure a proof that a sinner has passed into a state of justification, as Christ being formed in him by the renewal of the Holy Spirit; but this cannot be hoped for, while men depend on the law for acceptance with God.

Verses 21-27

The difference between believers who rested in Christ only, and those who trusted in the law, is explained by the histories of Isaac and Ishmael. These things are an allegory, wherein, beside the literal and historical sense of the words, the Spirit of God points out something further. Hagar and Sarah were apt emblems of the two different dispensations of the covenant. The heavenly Jerusalem, the true church from above, represented by Sarah, is in a state of freedom, and is the mother of all believers, who are born of the Holy Spirit. They were by regeneration and true faith, made a part of the true seed of Abraham, according to the promise made to him.

Verses 28-31

The history thus explained is applied. So then, brethren, we are not children of the bond-woman, but of the free. If the privileges of all believers were so great, according to the new covenant, how absurd for the Gentile converts to be under that law, which could not deliver the unbelieving Jews from bondage or condemnation! We should not have found out this allegory in the history of Sarah and Hagar, if it had not been shown to us, yet we cannot doubt it was intended by the Holy Spirit. It is an explanation of the subject, not an argument in proof of it. The two covenants of works and grace, and legal and evangelical professors, are shadowed forth. Works and fruits brought forth in a man's own strength, are legal. But if arising from faith in Christ, they are evangelical. The first covenant spirit is of bondage unto sin and death. The second covenant spirit is of liberty and freedom; not liberty to sin, but in and unto duty. The first is a spirit of persecution; the second is a spirit of love. Let those professors look to it, who have a violent, harsh, imposing spirit, towards the people of God. Yet as Abraham turned aside to Hagar, so it is possible a believer may turn aside in some things to the covenant of works, when through unbelief and neglect of the promise he acts according to the law, in his own strength; or in a way of violence, not of love, towards the brethren. Yet it is not his way, not his spirit to do so; hence he is never at rest, till he returns to his dependence on Christ again. Let us rest our souls on the Scriptures, and by a gospel hope and cheerful obedience, show that our conversation and treasure are indeed in heaven.

Chapter 5

Chapter Outline

An earnest exhortation to stand fast in the liberty of the gospel.	(1–12)
To take heed of indulging a sinful temper.	(13–15)
And to walk in the Spirit, and not to fulfil the lusts of the flesh: the works of both are described.	(16–26)

Verses 1-6

Christ will not be the Saviour of any who will not own and rely upon him as their only Saviour. Let us take heed to the warnings and persuasions of the apostle to stedfastness in the doctrine and liberty of the gospel. All true Christians, being taught by the Holy Spirit, wait for eternal life, the reward of righteousness, and the object of their hope, as the gift of God by faith in Christ; and not for the sake of their own works. The Jewish convert might observe the ceremonies or assert his liberty, the Gentile might disregard them or might attend to them, provided he did not depend upon them. No outward privileges or profession will avail to acceptance with God, without sincere faith in our Lord Jesus. True faith is a working grace; it works by love to God, and to our brethren. May we be of the number of those who, through the Spirit, wait for the hope of righteousness by faith. The danger of old was not in things of no consequence in themselves, as many forms and observances now are. But without faith working by love, all else is worthless, and compared with it other things are of small value.

Verses 7-12

The life of a Christian is a race, wherein he must run, and hold on, if he would obtain the prize. It is not enough that we profess Christianity, but we must run well, by living up to that profession. Many who set out fairly in religion, are hindered in their progress, or turn out of the way. It concerns those who begin to turn out of the way, or to tire in it, seriously to inquire what hinders them. The opinion or persuasion, ver. #(8), was, no doubt, that of mixing the works of the law with faith in Christ in justification. The apostle leaves them to judge whence it must arise, but sufficiently shows that it could be owing to none but Satan. It is dangerous for Christian churches to encourage those who follow, but especially who spread, destructive errors. And in reproving sin and error, we should always distinguish between the leaders and the led. The Jews were offended, because Christ was preached as the only salvation for sinners. If Paul and others would have admitted that the observance of the law of Moses was to be joined with faith in Christ, as necessary to salvation, then believers might have avoided many of the sufferings they underwent. The first beginnings of such leaven should be opposed. And assuredly those who persist in disturbing the church of Christ must bear their judgment.

Verses 13-15

The gospel is a doctrine according to godliness, 1Ti 6:3, and is so far from giving the least countenance to sin, that it lays us under the strongest obligation to avoid and subdue it. The apostle urges that all the law is fulfilled in one word, even in this, Thou shalt love thy neighbour as thyself. If Christians, who should help one another, and rejoice one another, quarrel, what can be expected but that the God of love should deny his grace, that the Spirit of love should depart, and the evil spirit, who seeks their destruction, should prevail? Happy would it be, if Christians, instead of biting and devouring one another on account of different opinions, would set themselves against sin in themselves, and in the places where they live.

Verses 16-26

If it be our care to act under the guidance and power of the blessed Spirit, though we may not be freed from the stirrings and oppositions of the corrupt nature which remains in us, it shall not have dominion over us. Believers are engaged in a conflict, in which they earnestly desire that grace may obtain full and speedy victory. And those who desire thus to give themselves up to be led by the Holy Spirit, are not under the law as a covenant of works, nor exposed to its awful curse. Their hatred of sin, and desires after holiness, show that they have a part in the salvation of the gospel. The works of the flesh are many and manifest. And these sins will shut men out of heaven. Yet what numbers, calling themselves Christians, live in these, and say they hope for heaven! The fruits of the Spirit, or of the renewed nature, which we are to do, are named. And as the apostle had chiefly named works of the flesh, not only hurtful to men themselves, but tending to make them so to one another, so here he chiefly notices the fruits of the Spirit, which tend to make Christians agreeable one to another, as well as to make them happy. The fruits of the Spirit plainly show, that such are led by the Spirit. By describing the works of the flesh and fruits of the Spirit, we are told what to avoid and oppose, and what we are to cherish and cultivate; and this is the sincere care and endeavour of all real Christians. Sin does not now reign in their mortal bodies, so that they obey it, Ro 6:12, for they seek to destroy it. Christ never will own those who yield themselves up to be the servants of sin. And it is not enough that we cease to do evil, but we must learn to do well. Our conversation will always be answerable to the principle which guides and governs us, Ro 8:5. We must set ourselves in earnest to mortify the deeds of the body, and to walk in newness of life. Not being desirous of vain-glory, or unduly wishing for the esteem and applause of men, not provoking or envying one another, but seeking to bring forth more abundantly those good fruits, which are, through Jesus Christ, to the praise and glory of God.

Chapter 6

Chapter Outline

Verses 1-5

We are to bear one another's burdens. So we shall fulfil the law of Christ. This obliges to mutual forbearance and compassion towards each other, agreeably to his example. It becomes us to bear one another's burdens, as fellow-travellers. It is very common for a man to look upon himself as wiser and better than other men, and as fit to dictate to them. Such a one deceives himself; by pretending to what he has not, he puts a cheat upon himself, and sooner or later will find the sad effects. This will never gain esteem, either with God or men. Every one is advised to prove his own work. The better we know our own hearts and ways, the less shall we despise others, and the more be disposed to help them under infirmities and afflictions. How light soever men's sins seem to them when committed, yet they will be found a heavy burden, when they come to reckon with God about them. No man can pay a ransom for his brother; and sin is a burden to the soul. It is a spiritual burden; and the less a man feels it to be such, the more cause has he to suspect himself. Most men are dead in their sins, and therefore have no sight or sense of the spiritual burden of sin. Feeling the weight and burden of our sins, we must seek to be eased thereof by the Saviour, and be warned against every sin.

Verses 6-11

Many excuse themselves from the work of religion, though they may make a show, and profess it. They may impose upon others, yet they deceive themselves if they think to impose upon God, who knows their hearts as well as actions; and as he cannot be deceived, so he will not be mocked. Our present time is seed time; in the other world we shall reap as we sow now. As there are two sorts of sowing, one to the flesh, and the other to the Spirit, so will the reckoning be hereafter. Those who live a carnal, sensual life, must expect no other fruit from such a course than misery and ruin. But those who, under the guidance and influences of the Holy Spirit, live a life of faith in Christ, and abound in Christian graces, shall of the Spirit reap life everlasting. We are all very apt to tire in duty, particularly in doing good. This we should carefully watch and guard against. Only to perseverance in well-doing is the reward promised. Here is an exhortation to all to do good in their places. We should take care to do good in our life-time, and make this the business of our lives. Especially when fresh occasions offer, and as far as our power reaches.

Verses 12-15

Proud, vain, and carnal hearts, are content with just so much religion as will help to keep up a fair show. But the apostle professes his own faith, hope, and joy; and that his principal glory was in the cross of Christ. By which is here meant, his sufferings and death on the cross, the doctrine of salvation by a crucified Redeemer. By Christ, or by the cross of Christ, the world is crucified to the believer, and he to the world. The more we consider the sufferings of the Redeemer from the world, the less likely shall we be to love the world. The apostle was as little affected by its charms, as a beholder would be by any thing which had been graceful in the face of a crucified person, when he beholds it blackened in the agonies of death. He was no more affected by the objects around him, than one who is expiring would be struck with any of the prospects his dying eyes might view from the cross on which he hung. And as to those who have truly believed in Christ Jesus, all things are counted as utterly worthless compared with him. There is a new creation; old things are passed away, and new views and dispositions are brought in under the regenerating influences of God the Holy Spirit. Believers are brought into a new world, and being created in Christ Jesus unto good works, are formed to a life of holiness. It is a change of mind and heart, whereby we are enabled to believe in the Lord Jesus, and to live to God; and where this inward, practical religion is wanting, outward professions, or names, will never stand in any stead.

Verses 16-18

A new creation to the image of Christ, as showing faith in him, is the greatest distinction between one man and another, and a blessing is declared on all who walk according to this rule. The blessings are, peace and mercy. Peace with God and our conscience, and all the comforts of this life, as far as they are needful. And mercy, an interest in the free love and favour of God in Christ, the spring and fountain of all other blessings. The written word of God is the rule we are to go by, both in its doctrines and precepts. May his grace ever be with our spirit, to sanctify, quicken, and cheer us, and may we always be ready to maintain the honour of that which is indeed our life. The apostle had in his body the marks of the Lord Jesus, the scars of wounds from persecuting enemies, for his cleaving to Christ, and the doctrine of the gospel. The apostle calls the Galatians his brethren, therein he shows his humility and his tender affection for them; and he takes his leave with a very serious prayer, that they might enjoy the favour of Christ Jesus, both in its effects and in its evidences. We need desire no more to make us happy than the grace of our Lord Jesus Christ. The apostle does not pray that the law of Moses, or the righteousness of works, but that the grace of Christ, might be with them; that it might be in their hearts and with their spirits, quickening, comforting, and strengthening them: to all which he sets his Amen; signifying his desire that so it might be, and his faith that so it would be.

Ephesians

This epistle was written when St. Paul was a prisoner at Rome. The design appears to be to strengthen the Ephesians in the faith of Christ, and to give exalted views of the love of God, and of the dignity and excellence of Christ, fortifying their minds against the scandal of the cross. He shows that they were saved by grace, and that however wretched they once were, they now had equal privileges with the Jews. He encourages them to persevere in their Christian calling, and urges them to walk in a manner becoming their profession, faithfully discharging the general and common duties of religion, and the special duties of particular relations.

Chapter 1

Chapter Outline

A salutation, and an account of saving blessings, as prepared in God's eternal election, as purchased by Christ's blood.	(1–8)
And as conveyed in effectual calling: this is applied to the believing Jews, and to the believing Gentiles.	(9–14)
The apostle thanks God for their faith and love, and prays for the continuance of their knowledge and hope, with respect to the heavenly inheritance, and to God's powerful working in them.	(15–23)

Verses 1, 2

All Christians must be saints; if they come not under that character on earth, they will never be saints in glory. Those are not saints, who are not faithful, believing in Christ, and true to the profession they make of relation to their Lord. By grace, understand the free and undeserved love and favour of God, and those graces of the Spirit which come from it; by peace, all other blessings, spiritual and temporal, the fruits of the former. No peace without grace. No peace, nor grace, but from God the Father, and from the Lord Jesus Christ; and the best saints need fresh supplies of the graces of the Spirit, and desire to grow.

Verses 3-8

Spiritual and heavenly blessings are the best blessings; with which we cannot be miserable, and without which we cannot but be so. This was from the choice of them in Christ, before the foundation of the world, that they should be made holy by separation from sin, being set apart to God, and sanctified by the Holy Spirit, in consequence of their election in Christ. All who are chosen to happiness as the end, are chosen to holiness as the means. In love they were predestinated, or fore-ordained, to be adopted as children of God by faith in Christ Jesus, and to be openly admitted to the privileges of that high relation to himself. The reconciled and adopted believer, the pardoned sinner, gives all the praise of his salvation to his gracious Father. His love appointed this method of redemption, spared not his own Son, and brought believers to hear and embrace this salvation. It was rich grace to provide such a surety as his own Son, and freely to deliver him up. This method of grace gives no encouragement to evil, but shows sin in all its hatefulness, and how it deserves vengeance. The believer's actions, as well as his words, declare the praises of Divine mercy.

Verses 9-14

Blessings were made known to believers, by the Lord's showing to them the mystery of his sovereign will, and the method of redemption and salvation. But these must have been for ever hidden from us, if God had not made them known by his written word, preached gospel, and Spirit of truth. Christ united the two differing parties, God and man, in his own person, and satisfied for that wrong which caused the separation. He wrought, by his Spirit, those graces of faith and love, whereby we are made one with God, and among ourselves. He dispenses all his blessings, according to his good pleasure. His Divine teaching led whom he pleased to see the glory of those truths, which others were left to blaspheme. What a gracious promise that is, which secures the gift of the Holy Ghost to those who ask him! The sanctifying and comforting influences of the Holy Spirit seal believers as the children of God, and heirs of heaven. These are the first-fruits of holy happiness. For this we were made, and for this we were redeemed; this is the great design of God in all that he has done for us; let all be ascribed unto the praise of his glory.

Verses 15-23

God has laid up spiritual blessings for us in his Son the Lord Jesus; but requires us to draw them out and fetch them in by prayer. Even the best Christians need to be prayed for: and while we hear of the welfare of Christian friends, we should pray for them. Even true believers greatly want heavenly wisdom. Are not the best of us unwilling to come under God's yoke, though there is no other way to find rest for the soul? Do we not for a little pleasure often part with our peace? And if we dispute less, and prayed more with and for each other, we should daily see more and more what is the hope of our calling, and the riches of the Divine glory in this inheritance. It is desirable to feel the mighty power of Divine grace, beginning and carrying on the work of faith in our souls. But it is difficult to bring a soul to believe fully in Christ, and to venture its all, and the hope of eternal life, upon his righteousness. Nothing less than Almighty power will work this in us. Here is signified that it is Christ the Saviour, who supplies all the necessities of those who trust in him, and gives them all blessings in the richest abundance. And by being partakers of Christ himself, we come to be filled with the fulness of grace and glory in him. How then do those forget themselves who seek for righteousness out of him! This teaches us to come to Christ. And did we know what we are called to, and what we might find in him, surely we should come and be suitors to him. When feeling our weakness and the power of our enemies, we most perceive the greatness of that mighty power which effects the conversion of the believer, and is engaged to perfect his salvation. Surely this will constrain us by love to live to our Redeemer's glory.

Chapter 2

Chapter Outline

Verses 1-10

Sin is the death of the soul. A man dead in trespasses and sins has no desire for spiritual pleasures. When we look upon a corpse, it gives an awful feeling. A never-dying spirit is now fled, and has left nothing but the ruins of a man. But if we viewed things aright, we should be far more affected by the thought of a dead soul, a lost, fallen spirit. A state of sin is a state of conformity to this world. Wicked men are slaves to Satan. Satan is the author of that proud, carnal disposition which there is in ungodly men; he rules in the hearts of men. From Scripture it is clear, that whether men have been most prone to sensual or to spiritual wickedness, all men, being naturally children of disobedience, are also by nature children of wrath. What reason have sinners, then, to seek earnestly for that grace which will make them, of children of wrath, children of God and heirs of glory! God's eternal love or good-will toward his creatures, is the fountain whence all his mercies flow to us; and that love of God is great love, and that mercy is rich mercy. And every converted sinner is a saved sinner; delivered from sin and wrath. The grace that saves is the free, undeserved goodness and favour of God; and he saves, not by the works of the law, but through faith in Christ Jesus. Grace in the soul is a new life in the soul. A regenerated sinner becomes a living soul; he lives a life of holiness, being born of God: he lives, being delivered from the guilt of sin, by pardoning and justifying grace. Sinners roll themselves in the dust; sanctified souls sit in heavenly places, are raised above this world, by Christ's grace. The goodness of God in converting and saving sinners heretofore, encourages others in after-time, to hope in his grace and mercy. Our faith, our conversion, and our eternal salvation, are not of works, lest any man should boast. These things are not brought to pass by any thing done by us, therefore all boasting is shut out. All is the free gift of God, and the effect of being quickened by his power. It was his purpose, to which he prepared us, by blessing us with the knowledge of his will, and his Holy Spirit producing such a change in us, that we should glorify God by our good conversation, and perseverance in holiness. None can from Scripture abuse this doctrine, or accuse it of any tendency to evil. All who do so, are without excuse.

Verses 11-13

Christ and his covenant are the foundation of all the Christian's hopes. A sad and terrible description is here; but who is able to remove himself out of it? Would that this were not a true description of many baptized in the name of Christ. Who can, without trembling, reflect upon the misery of a person, separated for ever from the people of God, cut off from the body of Christ, fallen from the covenant of promise, having no hope, no Saviour, and without any God but a God of vengeance, to all eternity? To have no part in Christ! What true Christian can hear this without horror? Salvation is far from the wicked; but God is a help at hand to his people; and this is by the sufferings and death of Christ.

Verses 14-18

Jesus Christ made peace by the sacrifice of himself; in every sense Christ was their Peace, the author, centre, and substance of their being at peace with God, and of their union with the Jewish believers in one church. Through the person, sacrifice, and mediation of Christ, sinners are allowed to draw near to God as a Father, and are brought with acceptance into his presence, with their worship and services, under the teaching of the Holy Spirit, as one with the Father and the Son. Christ purchased leave for us to come to God; and the Spirit gives a heart to come, and strength to come, and then grace to serve God acceptably.

Verses 19-22

The church is compared to a city, and every converted sinner is free of it. It is also compared to a house, and every converted sinner is one of the family; a servant, and a child in God's house. The church is also compared to a building, founded on the doctrine of Christ; delivered by the prophets of the Old Testament, and the apostles of the New. God dwells in all believers now; they become the temple of God through the working of the blessed Spirit. Let us then ask if our hopes are fixed on Christ, according to the doctrine of his word? Have we devoted ourselves as holy temples to God through him? Are we habitations of God by the Spirit, are we spiritually-minded, and do we bring forth the fruits of the Spirit? Let us take heed not to grieve the holy Comforter. Let us desire his gracious presence, and his influences upon our hearts. Let us seek to discharge the duties allotted to us, to the glory of God.

Chapter 3

Chapter Outline

The apostle sets forth his office, and his qualifications for it, and his call to it.	(1–7)
Also the noble purposes answered by it.	(8–12)
He prays for the Ephesians.	(13–19)
And adds a thanksgiving.	(20, 21)

Verses 1-7

For having preached the doctrine of truth, the apostle was a prisoner, but a prisoner of Jesus Christ; the object of special protection and care, while thus suffering for him. All the gracious offers of the gospel, and the joyful tidings it contains, come from the rich grace of God; it is the great means by which the Spirit works grace in the souls of men. The mystery, is that secret, hidden purpose of salvation through Christ. This was not so fully and clearly shown in the ages before Christ, as unto the prophets of the New Testament. This was the great truth made known to the apostle, that God would call the Gentiles to salvation by faith in Christ. An effectual working of Divine power attends the gifts of Divine grace. As God appointed Paul to the office, so he qualified him for it.

Verses 8-12

Those whom God advances to honourable employments, he makes low in their own eyes; and where God gives grace to be humble, there he gives all other needful grace. How highly he speaks of Jesus Christ; the unsearchable riches of Christ! Though many are not enriched with these riches; yet how great a favour to have them preached among us, and to have an offer of them! And if we are not enriched with them it is our own fault. The first creation, when God made all things out of nothing, and the new creation, whereby sinners are made new creatures by converting grace, are of God by Jesus Christ. His riches are as unsearchable and as sure as ever, yet while angels adore the wisdom of God in the redemption of his church, the ignorance of self-wise and carnal men deems the whole to be foolishness.

Verses 13-19

The apostle seems to be more anxious lest the believers should be discouraged and faint upon his tribulations, than for what he himself had to bear. He asks for spiritual blessings, which are the best blessings. Strength from the Spirit of God in the inner man; strength in the soul; the strength of faith, to serve God, and to do our duty. If the law of Christ is written in our hearts, and the love of Christ is shed abroad there, then Christ dwells there. Where his Spirit dwells, there he dwells. We should desire that good affections may be fixed in us. And how desirable to have a fixed sense of the love of God in Christ to our souls! How powerfully the apostle speaks of the love of Christ! The breadth shows its extent to all nations and ranks; the length, that it continues from everlasting to everlasting; the depth, its saving those who are sunk into the depths of sin and misery; the height, its raising them up to heavenly happiness and glory. Those who receive grace for grace from Christ's fulness, may be said to be filled with the fulness of God. Should not this satisfy man? Must he needs fill himself with a thousand trifles, fancying thereby to complete his happiness?

Verses 20, 21

It is proper always to end prayers with praises. Let us expect more, and ask for more, encouraged by what Christ has already done for our souls, being assured that the conversion of sinners, and the comfort of believers, will be to his glory, for ever and ever.

Chapter 4

Chapter Outline

Verses 1-6

Nothing is pressed more earnestly in the Scriptures, than to walk as becomes those called to Christ's kingdom and glory. By lowliness, understand humility, which is opposed to pride. By meekness, that excellent disposition of soul, which makes men unwilling to provoke, and not easily to be provoked or offended. We find much in ourselves for which we can hardly forgive ourselves; therefore we must not be surprised if we find in others that which we think it hard to forgive. There is one Christ in whom all believers hope, and one heaven they are all hoping for; therefore they should be of one heart. They had all one faith, as to its object, Author, nature, and power. They all believed the same as to the great truths of religion; they had all been admitted into the church by one baptism, with water, in the name of the Father, and of the Son, and of the Holy Ghost, as the sign of regeneration. In all believers God the Father dwells, as in his holy temple, by his Spirit and special grace.

Verses 7-16

Unto every believer is given some gift of grace, for their mutual help. All is given as seems best to Christ to bestow upon every one. He received for them, that he might give to them, a large measure of gifts and graces; particularly the gift of the Holy Ghost. Not a mere head knowledge, or bare acknowledging Christ to be the Son of God, but such as brings trust and obedience. There is a fulness in Christ, and a measure of that fulness given in the counsel of God to every believer; but we never come to the perfect measure till we come to heaven. God's children are growing, as long as they are in this world; and the Christian's growth tends to the glory of Christ. The more a man finds himself drawn out to improve in his station, and according to his measure, all that he has received, to the spiritual good of others, he may the more certainly believe that he has the grace of sincere love and charity rooted in his heart. (Eph 4:17-24)

Verses 17-24

The apostle charged the Ephesians in the name and by the authority of the Lord Jesus, that having professed the gospel, they should not be as the unconverted Gentiles, who walked in vain fancies and carnal affections. Do not men, on every side, walk in the vanity of their minds? Must not we then urge the distinction between real and nominal Christians? They were void of all saving knowledge; they sat in darkness, and loved it rather than light. They had a dislike and hatred to a life of holiness, which is not only the way of life God requires and approves, and by which we live to him, but which has some likeness to God himself in his purity, righteousness, truth, and goodness. The truth of Christ appears in its beauty and power, when it appears as in Jesus. The corrupt nature is called a man; like the human body, it is of divers parts, supporting and strengthening one another. Sinful desires are deceitful lusts; they promise men happiness, but render them more miserable; and bring them to destruction, if not subdued and mortified. These therefore must be put off, as an old garment, a filthy garment; they must be subdued and mortified. But it is not enough to shake off corrupt principles; we must have gracious ones. By the new man, is meant the new nature, the new creature, directed by a new principle, even regenerating grace, enabling a man to lead a new life of righteousness and holiness. This is created, or brought forth by God's almighty power.

Verses 25-28

Notice the particulars wherewith we should adorn our Christian profession. Take heed of every thing contrary to truth. No longer flatter or deceive others. God's people are children who will not lie, who dare not lie, who hate and abhor lying. Take heed of anger and ungoverned passions. If there is just occasion to express displeasure at what is wrong, and to reprove, see that it be without sin. We give place to the devil, when the first motions of sin are not grievous to our souls; when we consent to them; and when we repeat an evil deed. This teaches that as sin, if yielded unto, lets in the devil upon us, we are to resist it, keeping from all appearance of evil. Idleness makes thieves. Those who will not work, expose themselves to temptations to steal. Men ought to be industrious, that they may do some good, and that they may be kept from temptation. They must labour, not only that they may live honestly, but that they may have to give to the wants of others. What then must we think of those called Christians, who grow rich by fraud, oppression, and deceitful practices! Alms, to be accepted of God, must not be gained by unrighteousness and robbery, but by honesty and industry. God hates robbery for burnt-offerings.

Verses 29-32

Filthy words proceed from corruption in the speaker, and they corrupt the minds and manners of those who hear them: Christians should beware of all such discourse. It is the duty of Christians to seek, by the blessing of God, to bring persons to think seriously, and to encourage and warn believers by their conversation. Be ye kind one to another. This sets forth the principle of love in the heart, and the outward expression of it, in a humble, courteous behaviour. Mark how God's forgiveness causes us to forgive. God forgives us, though we had no cause to sin against him. We must forgive, as he has forgiven us. All lying, and corrupt communications, that stir up evil desires and lusts, grieve the Spirit of God. Corrupt passions of bitterness, wrath, anger, clamour, evil-speaking, and malice, grieve the Holy Spirit. Provoke not the holy, blessed Spirit of God to withdraw his presence and his gracious influences. The body will be redeemed from the power of the grave at the resurrection day. Wherever that blessed Spirit dwells as a Sanctifier, he is the earnest of all the joys and glories of that redemption day; and we should be undone, should God take away his Holy Spirit from us.

Chapter 5

Chapter Outline

Exhortation to brotherly love.	(1, 2)
Cautions against several sins.	(3–14)
Directions to a contrary behaviour, and to relative duties.	(15–21)
The duties of wives and husbands are enforced by the spiritual relation between Christ and the church.	(22–33)

Verses 1, 2

Because God, for Christ's sake, has forgiven you, therefore be ye followers of God, imitators of God. Resemble him especially in his love and pardoning goodness, as becomes those beloved by their heavenly Father. In Christ's sacrifice his love triumphs, and we are to consider it fully.

Verses 3-14

Filthy lusts must be rooted out. These sins must be dreaded and detested. Here are not only cautions against gross acts of sin, but against what some may make light of. But these things are so far from being profitable. that they pollute and poison the hearers. Our cheerfulness should show itself as becomes Christians, in what may tend to God's glory. A covetous man makes a god of his money; places that hope, confidence, and delight, in worldly good, which should be in God only. Those who allow themselves, either in the lusts of the flesh or the love of the world, belong not to the kingdom of grace, nor shall they come to the kingdom of glory. When the vilest transgressors repent and believe the gospel, they become children of obedience, from whom God's wrath is turned away. Dare we make light of that which brings down the wrath of God? Sinners, like men in the dark, are going they know not whither, and doing they know not what. But the grace of God wrought a mighty change in the souls of many. Walk as children of light, as having knowledge and holiness. These works of darkness are unfruitful, whatever profit they may boast; for they end in the destruction of the impenitent sinner. There are many ways of abetting, or taking part in the sins of others; by commendation, counsel, consent, or concealment. And if we share with others in their sins, we must expect to share in their plagues. If we do not reprove the sins of others, we have fellowship with them. A good man will be ashamed to speak of what many wicked men are not ashamed to do. We must have not only a sight and a knowledge that sin is sin, and in some measure shameful, but see it as a breach of God's holy law. After the example of prophets and apostles, we should call on those asleep and dead in sin, to awake and arise, that Christ may give them light.

Verses 15-21

Another remedy against sin, is care, or caution, it being impossible else to maintain purity of heart and life. Time is a talent given us by God, and it is misspent and lost when not employed according to his design. If we have lost our time heretofore, we must double our diligence for the future. Of that time which thousands on a dying bed would gladly redeem at the price of the whole world, how little do men think, and to what trifles they daily sacrifice it! People are very apt to complain of bad times; it were well if that stirred them more to redeem time. Be not unwise. Ignorance of our duty, and neglect of our souls, show the greatest folly. Drunkenness is a sin that never goes alone, but carries men into other evils; it is a sin very provoking to God. The drunkard holds out to his family and to the world the sad spectacle of a sinner hardened beyond what is common, and hastening to perdition. When afflicted or weary, let us not seek to raise our spirits by strong drink, which is hateful and hurtful, and only ends in making sorrows more felt. But by fervent prayer let us seek to be filled with the Spirit, and to avoid whatever may grieve our gracious Comforter. All God's people have reason to sing for joy. Though we are not always singing, we should be always giving thanks; we should never want disposition for this duty, as we never want matter for it, through the whole course of our lives. Always, even in trials and afflictions, and for all things; being satisfied of their loving intent, and good tendency. God keeps believers from sinning against him, and engages them to submit one to another in all he has commanded, to promote his glory, and to fulfil their duties to each other.

Verses 22-33

The duty of wives is, submission to their husbands in the Lord, which includes honouring and obeying them, from a principle of love to them. The duty of husbands is to love their wives. The love of Christ to the church is an example, which is sincere, pure, and constant, notwithstanding her failures. Christ gave himself for the church, that he might sanctify it in this world, and glorify it in the next, that he might bestow on all his members a principle of holiness, and deliver them from the guilt, the pollution, and the dominion of sin, by those influences of the Holy Spirit, of which baptismal water was the outward sign. The church and believers will not be without spot or wrinkle till they come to glory. But those only who are sanctified now, shall be glorified hereafter. The words of Adam, mentioned by the apostle, are spoken literally of marriage; but they have also a hidden sense in them, relating to the union between Christ and his church. It was a kind of type, as having resemblance. There will be failures and defects on both sides, in the present state of human nature, yet this does not alter the relation. All the duties of marriage are included in unity and love. And while we adore and rejoice in the condescending love of Christ, let husbands and wives learn hence their duties to each other. Thus the worst evils would be prevented, and many painful effects would be avoided.

Chapter 6

Chapter Outline

Verses 1-4

The great duty of children is, to obey their parents. That obedience includes inward reverence, as well as outward acts, and in every age prosperity has attended those distinguished for obedience to parents. The duty of parents. Be not impatient; use no unreasonable severities. Deal prudently and wisely with children; convince their judgements and work upon their reason. Bring them up well; under proper and compassionate correction; and in the knowledge of the duty God requires. Often is this duty neglected, even among professors of the gospel. Many set their children against religion; but this does not excuse the children's disobedience, though it may be awfully occasion it. God alone can change the heart, yet he gives his blessing to the good lessons and examples of parents, and answers their prayers. But those, whose chief anxiety is that their children should be rich and accomplished, whatever becomes of their souls, must not look for the blessing of God.

Verses 5-9

The duty of servants is summed up in one word, obedience. The servants of old were generally slaves. The apostles were to teach servants and masters their duties, in doing which evils would be lessened, till slavery should be rooted out by the influence of Christianity. Servants are to reverence those over them. They are to be sincere; not pretending obedience when they mean to disobey, but serving faithfully. And they must serve their masters not only when their master's eye is upon them; but must be strict in the discharge of their duty, when he is absent and out of the way. Steady regard to the Lord Jesus Christ will make men faithful and sincere in every station, not grudgingly or by constraint, but from a principle of love to the masters and their concerns. This makes service easy to them, pleasing to their masters, and acceptable to the Lord Christ. God will reward even the meanest drudgery done from a sense of duty, and with a view to glorify him. Here is the duty of masters. Act after the same manner. Be just to servants, as you expect they should be to you; show the like good-will and concern for them, and be careful herein to approve yourselves to God. Be not tyrannical and overbearing. You have a Master to obey, and you and they are but fellow-servants in respect to Christ Jesus. If masters and servants would consider their duties to God, and the account they must shortly give to him, they would be more mindful of their duty to each other, and thus families would be more orderly and happy.

Verses 10-18

Spiritual strength and courage are needed for our spiritual warfare and suffering. Those who would prove themselves to have true grace, must aim at all grace; and put on the whole armour of God, which he prepares and bestows. The Christian armour is made to be worn; and there is no putting off our armour till we have done our warfare, and finished our course. The combat is not against human enemies, nor against our own corrupt nature only; we have to do with an enemy who has a thousand ways of beguiling unstable souls. The devils assault us in the things that belong to our souls, and labour to deface the heavenly image in our hearts. We must resolve by God's grace, not to yield to Satan. Resist him, and he will flee. If we give way, he will get ground. If we distrust either our cause, or our Leader, or our armour, we give him advantage. The different parts of the armour of heavy-armed soldiers, who had to sustain the fiercest assaults of the enemy, are here described. There is none for the back; nothing to defend those who turn back in the Christian warfare. Truth, or sincerity, is the girdle. This girds on all the other pieces of our armour, and is first mentioned. There can be no religion without sincerity. The righteousness of Christ, imputed to us, is a breastplate against the arrows of Divine wrath. The righteousness of Christ implanted in us, fortifies the heart against the attacks of Satan. Resolution must be as greaves, or armour to our legs; and to stand their ground or to march forward in rugged paths, the feet must be shod with the preparation of the gospel of peace. Motives to obedience, amidst trials, must be drawn from a clear knowledge of the gospel. Faith is all in all in an hour of temptation. Faith, as relying on unseen objects, receiving Christ and the benefits of redemption, and so deriving grace from him, is like a shield, a defence every way. The devil is the wicked one. Violent temptations, by which the soul is set on fire of hell, are darts Satan shoots at us. Also, hard thoughts of God, and as to ourselves. Faith applying the word of God and the grace of Christ, quenches the darts of temptation. Salvation must be our helmet. A good hope of salvation, a Scriptural expectation of victory, will purify the soul, and keep it from being defiled by Satan. To the Christian armed for defense in battle, the apostle recommends only one weapon of attack; but it is enough, the sword of the Spirit, which is the word of God. It subdues and mortifies evil desires and blasphemous thoughts as they rise within; and answers unbelief and error as they assault from without. A single text, well understood, and rightly applied, at once destroys a temptation or an objection, and subdues the most formidable adversary. Prayer must fasten all the other parts of our Christian armour. There are other duties of religion, and of our stations in the world, but we must keep up times of prayer. Though set and solemn prayer may not be seasonable when other duties are to be done, yet short pious prayers darted out, always are so. We must use holy thoughts in our ordinary course. A vain heart will be vain in prayer. We must pray with all kinds of prayer, public, private, and secret; social and solitary; solemn and sudden: with all the parts of prayer; confession of sin, petition for mercy, and thanksgiving for favours received. And we must do it by the grace of God the Holy Spirit, in dependence on, and according to, his teaching. We must preserve in particular requests, notwithstanding discouragements. We must pray, not for ourselves only, but for all saints. Our enemies are mighty, and we are without strength, but our Redeemer is almighty, and in the power of his mighty we may overcome. Wherefore we must stir up ourselves. Have not we, when God has called, often neglected to answer? Let us think upon these things, and continue our prayers with patience. (Eph 6:19-24)

Verses 19-24

The gospel was a mystery till made known by Divine revelation; and it is the work of Christ's ministers to declare it. The best and most eminent ministers need the prayers of believers. Those particularly should be prayed for, who are exposed to great hardships and perils in their work. Peace be to the brethren, and love with faith. By peace, understand all manner of peace; peace with God, peace of conscience, peace among themselves. And the grace of the Spirit, producing faith and love, and every grace. These he desires for those in whom they were already begun. And all grace and blessings come to the saints from God, through Jesus Christ our Lord. Grace, that is, the favour of God; and all good, spiritual and temporal, which is from it, is and shall be with all those who thus love our Lord Jesus Christ in sincerity, and with them only.

Philippians

The Philippians felt a very deep interest for the apostle. The scope of the epistle is to confirm them in the faith, to encourage them to walk as becomes the gospel of Christ, to caution them against judaizing teachers, and to express gratitude for their Christian bounty. This epistle is the only one, among those written by St. Paul, in which no censures are implied or expressed. Full commendation and confidence are in every part, and the Philippians are addressed with a peculiar affection, which every serious reader will perceive.

Chapter 1

Chapter Outline

The apostle offers up thanksgivings and prayers, for the good work of grace in the Philippians.	(1–7)
He expresses affection, and prays for them.	(8–11)
Fortifies them against being cast down at his sufferings.	(12–20)
He stood prepared for glorifying Christ by life, or death.	(21–26)
Exhortations to zeal, and constancy in professing the gospel.	(27–30)

Verses 1-7

The highest honour of the most eminent ministers is, to be servants of Christ. And those who are not really saints on earth, never will be saints in heaven. Out of Christ, the best saints are sinners, and unable to stand before God. There is no peace without grace. Inward peace springs from a sense of Divine favour. And there is no grace and peace but from God our Father, the fountain and origin of all blessings. At Philippi the apostle was evil entreated, and saw little fruit of his labour; yet he remembers Philippi with joy. We must thank our God for the graces and comforts, gifts and usefulness of others, as we receive the benefit, and God receives the glory. The work of grace will never be perfected till the day of Jesus Christ, the day of his appearance. But we may always be confident God will perform his good work, in every soul wherein he has really begun it by regeneration; though we must not trust in outward appearances, nor in any thing but a new creation to holiness. People are dear to their ministers, when they receive benefit by their ministry. Fellow-sufferers in the cause of God should be dear one to another.

Verses 8-11

Shall not we pity and love those souls whom Christ loves and pities? Those who abound in any grace, need to abound more. Try things which differ; that we may approve the things which are excellent. The truths and laws of Christ are excellent; and they recommend themselves as such to any attentive mind. Sincerity is that in which we should have our conversation in the world, and it is the glory of all our graces. Christians should not be apt to take offence, and should be very careful not to offend God or the brethren. The things which most honour God will most benefit us. Let us not leave it doubtful whether any good fruit is found in us or not. A small measure of Christian love, knowledge, and fruitfulness should not satisfy any.

Verses 12-20

The apostle was a prisoner at Rome; and to take off the offence of the cross, he shows the wisdom and goodness of God in his sufferings. These things made him known, where he would never have otherwise been known; and led some to inquire after the gospel. He suffered from false friends, as well as from enemies. How wretched the temper of those who preached Christ out of envy and contention, and to add affliction to the bonds that oppressed this best of men! The apostle was easy in the midst of all. Since our troubles may tend to the good of many, we ought to rejoice. Whatever turns to our salvation, is by the Spirit of Christ; and prayer is the appointed means of seeking for it. Our earnest expectation and hope should not be to be honoured of men, or to escape the cross, but to be upheld amidst temptation, contempt, and affliction. Let us leave it to Christ, which way he will make us serviceable to his glory, whether by labour or suffering, by diligence or patience, by living to his honour in working for him, or dying to his honour in suffering for him.

Verses 21-26

Death is a great loss to a carnal, worldly man, for he loses all his earthly comforts and all his hopes; but to a true believer it is gain, for it is the end of all his weakness and misery. It delivers him from all the evils of life, and brings him to possess the chief good. The apostle's difficulty was not between living in this world and living in heaven; between these two there is no comparison; but between serving Christ in this world and enjoying him in another. Not between two evil things, but between two good things; living to Christ and being with him. See the power of faith and of Divine grace; it can make us willing to die. In this world we are compassed with sin; but when with Christ, we shall escape sin and temptation, sorrow and death, for ever. But those who have most reason to desire to depart, should be willing to remain in the world as long as God has any work for them to do. And the more unexpected mercies are before they come, the more of God will be seen in them.

Verses 27-30

Those who profess the gospel of Christ, should live as becomes those who believe gospel truths, submit to gospel laws, and depend upon gospel promises. The original word "conversation" denotes the conduct of citizens who seek the credit, safety, peace, and prosperity of their city. There is that in the faith of the gospel, which is worth striving for; there is much opposition, and there is need of striving. A man may sleep and go to hell; but he who would go to heaven, must look about him and be diligent. There may be oneness of heart and affection among Christians, where there is diversity of judgment about many things. Faith is God's gift on the behalf of Christ; the ability and disposition to believe are from God. And if we suffer reproach and loss for Christ, we are to reckon them a gift, and prize them accordingly. Yet salvation must not be ascribed to bodily afflictions, as though afflictions and worldly persecutions deserved it; but from God only is salvation: faith and patience are his gifts.

Chapter 2

Chapter Outline

Exhortations to a kind, humble spirit and behaviour.	(1–4)
The example of Christ.	(5–11)
Diligence in the affairs of salvation, and to be examples to the world.	(12–18)
The apostle's purpose of visiting Philippi.	(19–30)

Verses 1-4

Here are further exhortations to Christian duties; to like-mindedness and lowly-mindedness, according to the example of the Lord Jesus. Kindness is the law of Christ's kingdom, the lesson of his school, the livery of his family. Several motives to brotherly love are mentioned. If you expect or experience the benefit of God's compassions to yourselves, be compassionate one to another. It is the joy of ministers to see people like-minded. Christ came to humble us, let there not be among us a spirit of pride. We must be severe upon our own faults, and quick in observing our own defects, but ready to make favourable allowances for others. We must kindly care for others, but not be busy-bodies in other men's matters. Neither inward nor outward peace can be enjoyed, without lowliness of mind.

Verses 5-11

The example of our Lord Jesus Christ is set before us. We must resemble him in his life, if we would have the benefit of his death. Notice the two natures of Christ; his Divine nature, and human nature. Who being in the form of God, partaking the Divine nature, as the eternal and only-begotten Son of God, Joh 1:1, had not thought it a robbery to be equal with God, and to receive Divine worship from men. His human nature; herein he became like us in all things except sin. Thus low, of his own will, he stooped from the glory he had with the Father before the world was. Christ's two states, of humiliation and exaltation, are noticed. Christ not only took upon him the likeness and fashion, or form of a man, but of one in a low state; not appearing in splendour. His whole life was a life of poverty and suffering. But the lowest step was his dying the death of the cross, the death of a malefactor and a slave; exposed to public hatred and scorn. The exaltation was of Christ's human nature, in union with the Divine. At the name of Jesus, not the mere sound of the word, but the authority of Jesus, all should pay solemn homage. It is to the glory of God the Father, to confess that Jesus Christ is Lord; for it is his will, that all men should honour the Son as they honour the Father, Joh 5:23. Here we see such motives to self-denying love as nothing else can supply. Do we thus love and obey the Son of God?

Verses 12-18

We must be diligent in the use of all the means which lead to our salvation, persevering therein to the end. With great care, lest, with all our advantages, we should come short. Work out your salvation, for it is God who worketh in you. This encourages us to do our utmost, because our labour shall not be in vain: we must still depend on the grace of God. The working of God's grace in us, is to quicken and engage our endeavours. God's good-will to us, is the cause of his good work in us. Do your duty without murmurings. Do it, and do not find fault with it. Mind your work, and do not quarrel with it. By peaceableness; give no just occasion of offence. The children of God should differ from the sons of men. The more perverse others are, the more careful we should be to keep ourselves blameless and harmless. The doctrine and example of consistent believers will enlighten others, and direct their way to Christ and holiness, even as the light-house warns mariners to avoid rocks, and directs their course into the harbour. Let us try thus to shine. The gospel is the word of life, it makes known to us eternal life through Jesus Christ. Running, denotes earnestness and vigour, continual pressing forward; labouring, denotes constancy, and close application. It is the will of God that believers should be much in rejoicing; and those who are so happy as to have good ministers, have great reason to rejoice with them. (Php 2:19-30)

Verses 19-30

It is best with us, when our duty becomes natural to us. Naturally, that is, sincerely, and not in pretence only; with a willing heart and upright views. We are apt to prefer our own credit, ease, and safety, before truth, holiness, and duty; but Timothy did not so. Paul desired liberty, not that he might take pleasure, but that he might do good. Epaphroditus was willing to go to the Philippians, that he might be comforted with those who had sorrowed for him when he was sick. It seems, his illness was caused by the work of God. The apostle urges them to love him the more on that account. It is doubly pleasant to have our mercies restored by God, after great danger of their removal; and this should make them more valued. What is given in answer to prayer, should be received with great thankfulness and joy.

Chapter 3

Chapter Outline

The apostle cautions the Philippians against judaizing false teachers, and renounces his own former privileges.

(1–11)

Expresses earnest desire to be found in Christ; also his pressing on toward perfection; and recommends his own example to other believers.

(12–21)

Verses 1-11

Sincere Christians rejoice in Christ Jesus. The prophet calls the false prophets dumb dogs, Isa 56:10; to which the apostle seems to refer. Dogs, for their malice against faithful professors of the gospel of Christ, barking at them and biting them. They urged human works in opposition to the faith of Christ; but Paul calls them evil-workers. He calls them the concision; as they rent the church of Christ, and cut it to pieces. The work of religion is to no purpose, unless the heart is in it, and we must worship God in the strength and grace of the Divine Spirit. They rejoice in Christ Jesus, not in mere outward enjoyments and performances. Nor can we too earnestly guard against those who oppose or abuse the doctrine of free salvation. If the apostle would have gloried and trusted in the flesh, he had as much cause as any man. But the things which he counted gain while a Pharisee, and had reckoned up, those he counted loss for Christ. The apostle did not persuade them to do any thing but what he himself did; or to venture on any thing but that on which he himself ventured his never-dying soul. He deemed all these things to be but loss, compared with the knowledge of Christ, by faith in his person and salvation. He speaks of all worldly enjoyments and outward privileges which sought a place with Christ in his heart, or could pretend to any merit and desert, and counted them but loss; but it might be said, It is easy to say so; but what would he do when he came to the trial? He had suffered the loss of all for the privileges of a Christian. Nay, he not only counted them loss, but the vilest refuse, offals thrown to dogs; not only less valuable than Christ, but in the highest degree contemptible, when set up as against him. True knowledge of Christ alters and changes men, their judgments and manners, and makes them as if made again anew. The believer prefers Christ, knowing that it is better for us to be without all worldly riches, than without Christ and his word. Let us see what the apostle resolved to cleave to, and that was Christ and heaven. We are undone, without righteousness wherein to appear before God, for we are guilty. There is a righteousness provided for us in Jesus Christ, and it is a complete and perfect righteousness. None can have benefit by it, who trust in themselves. Faith is the appointed means of applying the saving benefit. It is by faith in Christ's blood. We are made conformable to Christ's death, when we die to sin, as he died for sin; and the world is crucified to us, and we to the world, by the cross of Christ. The apostle was willing to do or to suffer any thing, to attain the glorious resurrection of saints. This hope and prospect carried him through all difficulties in his work. He did not hope to attain it through his own merit and righteousness, but through the merit and righteousness of Jesus Christ. (Php 3:12-21)

Verses 12-21

This simple dependence and earnestness of soul, were not mentioned as if the apostle had gained the prize, or were already made perfect in the Saviour's likeness. He forgot the things which were behind, so as not to be content with past labours or present measures of grace. He reached forth, stretched himself forward towards his point; expressions showing great concern to become more and more like unto Christ. He who runs a race, must never stop short of the end, but press forward as fast as he can; so those who have heaven in their view, must still press forward to it, in holy desires and hopes, and constant endeavours. Eternal life is the gift of God, but it is in Christ Jesus; through his hand it must come to us, as it is procured for us by him. There is no getting to heaven as our home, but by Christ as our Way. True believers, in seeking this assurance, as well as to glorify him, will seek more nearly to resemble his sufferings and death, by dying to sin, and by crucifying the flesh with its affections and lusts. In these things there is a great difference among real Christians, but all know something of them. Believers make Christ all in all, and set their hearts upon another world. If they differ from one another, and are not of the same judgment in lesser matters, yet they must not judge one another; while they all meet now in Christ, and hope to meet shortly in heaven. Let them join in all the great things in which they are agreed, and wait for further light as to lesser things wherein they differ. The enemies of the cross of Christ mind nothing but their sensual appetites. Sin is the sinner's shame, especially when gloried in. The way of those who mind earthly things, may seem pleasant, but death and hell are at the end of it. If we choose their way, we shall share their end. The life of a Christian is in heaven, where his Head and his home are, and where he hopes to be shortly; he sets his affections upon things above; and where his heart is, there will his conversation be. There is glory kept for the bodies of the saints, in which they will appear at the resurrection. Then the body will be made glorious; not only raised again to life, but raised to great advantage. Observe the power by which this change will be wrought. May we be always prepared for the coming of our Judge; looking to have our vile bodies changed by his Almighty power, and applying to him daily to new-create our souls unto holiness; to deliver us from our enemies, and to employ our bodies and souls as instruments of righteousness in his service.

Chapter 4

Chapter Outline

Verse 1

The believing hope and prospect of eternal life, should make us steady and constant in our Christian course. There is difference of gifts and graces, yet, being renewed by the same Spirit, we are brethren. To stand fast in the Lord, is to stand fast in his strength, and by his grace.

Verses 2-9

Let believers be of one mind, and ready to help each other. As the apostle had found the benefit of their assistance, he knew how comfortable it would be to his fellow-labourers to have the help of others. Let us seek to give assurance that our names are written in the book of life. Joy in God is of great consequence in the Christian life; and Christians need to be again and again called to it. It more than outweighs all causes for sorrow. Let their enemies perceive how moderate they were as to outward things, and how composedly they suffered loss and hardships. The day of judgment will soon arrive, with full redemption to believers, and destruction to ungodly men. There is a care of diligence which is our duty, and agrees with a wise forecast and due concern; but there is a care of fear and distrust, which is sin and folly, and only perplexes and distracts the mind. As a remedy against perplexing care, constant prayer is recommended. Not only stated times for prayer, but in every thing by prayer. We must join thanksgivings with prayers and supplications; not only seek supplies of good, but own the mercies we have received. God needs not to be told our wants or desires; he knows them better than we do; but he will have us show that we value the mercy, and feel our dependence on him. The peace of God, the comfortable sense of being reconciled to God, and having a part in his favour, and the hope of the heavenly blessedness, are a greater good than can be fully expressed. This peace will keep our hearts and minds through Christ Jesus; it will keep us from sinning under troubles, and from sinking under them; keep us calm and with inward satisfaction. Believers are to get and to keep a good name; a name for good things with God and good men. We should walk in all the ways of virtue, and abide therein; then, whether our praise is of men or not, it will be of God. The apostle is for an example. His doctrine and life agreed together. The way to have the God of peace with us, is to keep close to our duty. All our privileges and salvation arise in the free mercy of God; yet the enjoyment of them depends on our sincere and holy conduct. These are works of God, pertaining to God, and to him only are they to be ascribed, and to no other, neither men, words, nor deeds.

Verses 10-19

It is a good work to succour and help a good minister in trouble. The nature of true Christian sympathy, is not only to feel concern for our friends in their troubles, but to do what we can to help them. The apostle was often in bonds, imprisonments, and necessities; but in all, he learned to be content, to bring his mind to his condition, and make the best of it. Pride, unbelief, vain hankering after something we have not got, and fickle disrelish of present things, make men discontented even under favourable circumstances. Let us pray for patient submission and hope when we are abased; for humility and a heavenly mind when exalted. It is a special grace to have an equal temper of mind always. And in a low state not to lose our comfort in God, nor distrust his providence, nor take any wrong course for our own supply. In a prosperous condition not to be proud, or secure, or worldly. This is a harder lesson than the other; for the temptations of fulness and prosperity are more than those of affliction and want. The apostle had no design to urge them to give more, but to encourage such kindness as will meet a glorious reward hereafter. Through Christ we have grace to do what is good, and through him we must expect the reward; and as we have all things by him, let us do all things for him, and to his glory.

Verses 20-23

The apostle ends with praises to God. We should look upon God, under all our weakness and fears, not as an enemy, but as a Father, disposed to pity us and help us. We must give glory to God as a Father. God's grace and favour, which reconciled souls enjoy, with the whole of the graces in us, which flow from it, are all purchased for us by Christ's merit, and applied by his pleading for us; and therefore are justly called the grace of our Lord Jesus Christ.

Colossians

This epistle was sent because of some difficulties which arose among the Colossians, probably from false teachers, in consequence of which they sent to the apostle. The scope of the epistle is to show, that all hope of man's redemption is founded on Christ, in whom alone are all complete fulness, perfections, and sufficiency. The Colossians are cautioned against the devices of judaizing teachers, and also against the notions of carnal wisdom, and human inventions and traditions, as not consistent with full reliance on Christ. In the first two chapters the apostle tells them what they must believe, and in the two last what they must do; the doctrine of faith, and the precepts of life for salvation.

Chapter 1

Chapter Outline

The apostle Paul salutes the Colossians, and blesses God for their faith, love, and hope.	(1–8)
Prays for their fruitfulness in spiritual knowledge.	(9–14)
Gives a glorious view of Christ.	(15–23)
And sets out his own character, as the apostle of the Gentiles.	(24–29)

Verses 1-8

All true Christians are brethren one to another. Faithfulness runs through every character and relation of the Christian life. Faith, hope, and love, are the three principal graces in the Christian life, and proper matter for prayer and thanksgiving. The more we fix our hopes on the reward in the other world, the more free shall we be in doing good with our earthly treasure. It was treasured up for them, no enemy could deprive them of it. The gospel is the word of truth, and we may safely venture our souls upon it. And all who hear the word of the gospel, ought to bring forth the fruit of the gospel, obey it, and have their principles and lives formed according to it. Worldly love arises, either from views of interest or from likeness in manners; carnal love, from the appetite for pleasure. To these, something corrupt, selfish, and base always cleaves. But Christian love arises from the Holy Spirit, and is full of holiness. (Col 1:9-14)

Verses 9-14

The apostle was constant in prayer, that the believers might be filled with the knowledge of God's will, in all wisdom. Good words will not do without good works. He who undertakes to give strength to his people, is a God of power, and of glorious power. The blessed Spirit is the author of this. In praying for spiritual strength, we are not straitened, or confined in the promises, and should not be so in our hopes and desires. The grace of God in the hearts of believers is the power of God; and there is glory in this power. The special use of this strength was for sufferings. There is work to be done, even when we are suffering. Amidst all their trials they gave thanks to the Father of our Lord Jesus, whose special grace fitted them to partake of the inheritance provided for the saints. To bring about this change, those were made willing subjects of Christ, who were slaves of Satan. All who are designed for heaven hereafter, are prepared for heaven now. Those who have the inheritance of sons, have the education of sons, and the disposition of sons. By faith in Christ they enjoyed this redemption, as the purchase of his atoning blood, whereby forgiveness of sins, and all other spiritual blessings were bestowed. Surely then we shall deem it a favour to be delivered from Satan's kingdom and brought into that of Christ, knowing that all trials will soon end, and that every believer will be found among those who come out of great tribulation.

Verses 15-23

Christ in his human nature, is the visible discovery of the invisible God, and he that hath seen Him hath seen the Father. Let us adore these mysteries in humble faith, and behold the glory of the Lord in Christ Jesus. He was born or begotten before all the creation, before any creature was made; which is the Scripture way of representing eternity, and by which the eternity of God is represented to us. All things being created by Him, were created for him; being made by his power, they were made according to his pleasure, and for his praise and glory. He not only created them all at first, but it is by the word of his power that they are upheld. Christ as Mediator is the Head of the body, the church; all grace and strength are from him; and the church is his body. All fulness dwells in him; a fulness of merit and righteousness, of strength and grace for us. God showed his justice in requiring full satisfaction. This mode of redeeming mankind by the death of Christ was most suitable. Here is presented to our view the method of being reconciled. And that, notwithstanding the hatred of sin on God's part, it pleased God to reconcile fallen man to himself. If convinced that we were enemies in our minds by wicked works, and that we are now reconciled to God by the sacrifice and death of Christ in our nature, we shall not attempt to explain away, nor yet think fully to comprehend these mysteries; but we shall see the glory of this plan of redemption, and rejoice in the hope set before us. If this be so, that God's love is so great to us, what shall we do now for God? Be frequent in prayer, and abound in holy duties; and live no more to yourselves, but to Christ. Christ died for us. But wherefore? That we should still live in sin? No; but that we should die to sin, and live henceforth not to ourselves, but to Him.

Verses 24-29

Both the sufferings of the Head and of the members are called the sufferings of Christ, and make up, as it were, one body of sufferings. But He suffered for the redemption of the church; we suffer on other accounts; for we do but slightly taste that cup of afflictions of which Christ first drank deeply. A Christian may be said to fill up that which remains of the sufferings of Christ, when he takes up his cross, and after the pattern of Christ, bears patiently the afflictions God allots to him. Let us be thankful that God has made known to us mysteries hidden from ages and generations, and has showed the riches of his glory among us. As Christ is preached among us, let us seriously inquire, whether he dwells and reigns in us; for this alone can warrant our assured hope of his glory. We must be faithful to death, through all trials, that we may receive the crown of life, and obtain the end of our faith, the salvation of our souls.

Chapter 2

Chapter Outline

The apostle expresses his love to, and joy in believers.	(1–7)
He cautions against the errors of heathen philosophy; also against Jewish traditions, and rites which had been fulfilled in Christ.	(8–17)
Against worshipping angels; and against legal ordinances.	(18–23)

Verses 1-7

The soul prospers when we have clear knowledge of the truth as it is in Jesus. When we not only believe with the heart, but are ready, when called, to make confession with the mouth. Knowledge and faith make a soul rich. The stronger our faith, and the warmer our love, the more will our comfort be. The treasures of wisdom are hid, not from us, but for us, in Christ. These were hid from proud unbelievers, but displayed in the person and redemption of Christ. See the danger of enticing words; how many are ruined by the false disguises and fair appearances of evil principles and wicked practices! Be aware and afraid of those who would entice to any evil; for they aim to spoil you. All Christians have, in profession at least, received Jesus Christ the Lord, consented to him, and taken him for theirs. We cannot be built up in Christ, or grow in him, unless we are first rooted in him, or founded upon him. Being established in the faith, we must abound therein, and improve in it more and more. God justly withdraws this benefit from those who do not receive it with thanksgiving; and gratitude for his mercies is justly required by God.

Verses 8-17

There is a philosophy which rightly exercises our reasonable faculties; a study of the works of God, which leads us to the knowledge of God, and confirms our faith in him. But there is a philosophy which is vain and deceitful; and while it pleases men's fancies, hinders their faith: such are curious speculations about things above us, or no concern to us. Those who walk in the way of the world, are turned from following Christ. We have in Him the substance of all the shadows of the ceremonial law. All the defects of it are made up in the gospel of Christ, by his complete sacrifice for sin, and by the revelation of the will of God. To be complete, is to be furnished with all things necessary for salvation. By this one word "complete," is shown that we have in Christ whatever is required. "In him," not when we look to Christ, as though he were distant from us, but we are in him, when, by the power of the Spirit, we have faith wrought in our hearts by the Spirit, and we are united to our Head. The circumcision of the heart, the crucifixion of the flesh, the death and burial to sin and to the world, and the resurrection to newness of life, set forth in baptism, and by faith wrought in our hearts, prove that our sins are forgiven, and that we are fully delivered from the curse of the law. Through Christ, we, who were dead in sins, are quickened. Christ's death was the death of our sins; Christ's resurrection is the quickening of our souls. The law of ordinances, which was a yoke to the Jews, and a partition-wall to the Gentiles, the Lord Jesus took out of the way. When the substance was come, the shadows fled. Since every mortal man is, through the hand-writing of the law, guilty of death, how very dreadful is the condition of the ungodly and unholy, who trample under foot that blood of the Son of God, whereby alone this deadly hand-writing can be blotted out! Let not any be troubled about bigoted judgments which related to meats, or the Jewish solemnities. The setting apart a portion of our time for the worship and service of God, is a moral and unchangeable duty, but had no necessary dependence upon the seventh day of the week, the sabbath of the Jews. The first day of the week, or the Lord's day, is the time kept holy by Christians, in remembrance of Christ's resurrection. All the Jewish rites were shadows of gospel blessings.

Verses 18-23

It looked like humility to apply to angels, as if men were conscious of their unworthiness to speak directly to God. But it is not warrantable; it is taking that honour which is due to Christ only, and giving it to a creature. There really was pride in this seeming humility. Those who worship angels, disclaim Christ, who is the only Mediator between God and man. It is an insult to Christ, who is the Head of the church, to use any intercessors but him. When men let go their hold of Christ, they catch at what will stand them in no stead. The body of Christ is a growing body. And true believers cannot live in the fashions of the world. True wisdom is, to keep close to the appointments of the gospel; in entire subjection to Christ, who is the only Head of his church. Self-imposed sufferings and fastings, might have a show of uncommon spirituality and willingness for suffering, but this was not "in any honour" to God. The whole tended, in a wrong manner, to satisfy the carnal mind, by gratifying self-will, self-wisdom, self-righteousness, and contempt of others. The things being such as carry not with them so much as the show of wisdom; or so faint a show that they do the soul no good, and provide not for the satisfying of the flesh. What the Lord has left indifferent, let us regard as such, and leave others to the like freedom; and remembering the passing nature of earthly things, let us seek to glorify God in the use of them.

Chapter 3

Chapter Outline

The Colossians exhorted to be heavenly-minded;   (1–4)

to mortify all corrupt affections;   (5–11)

to live in mutual love, forbearance, and   (12–17)
forgiveness;

and to practise the duties of wives and   (18–25)
husbands, children, parents, and servants.

Verses 1-4

As Christians are freed from the ceremonial law, they must walk the more closely with God in gospel obedience. As heaven and earth are contrary one to the other, both cannot be followed together; and affection to the one will weaken and abate affection to the other. Those that are born again are dead to sin, because its dominion is broken, its power gradually subdued by the operation of grace, and it shall at length be extinguished by the perfection of glory. To be dead, then, means this, that those who have the Holy Spirit, mortifying within them the lusts of the flesh, are able to despise earthly things, and to desire those that are heavenly. Christ is, at present, one whom we have not seen; but our comfort is, that our life is safe with him. The streams of this living water flow into the soul by the influences of the Holy Spirit, through faith. Christ lives in the believer by his Spirit, and the believer lives to him in all he does. At the second coming of Christ, there will be a general assembling of all the redeemed; and those whose life is now hid with Christ, shall then appear with him in his glory. Do we look for such happiness, and should we not set our affections upon that world, and live above this?

Verses 5-11

It is our duty to mortify our members which incline to the things of the world. Mortify them, kill them, suppress them, as weeds or vermin which spread and destroy all about them. Continual opposition must be made to all corrupt workings, and no provision made for carnal indulgences. Occasions of sin must be avoided: the lusts of the flesh, and the love of the world; and covetousness, which is idolatry; love of present good, and of outward enjoyments. It is necessary to mortify sins, because if we do not kill them, they will kill us. The gospel changes the higher as well as the lower powers of the soul, and supports the rule of right reason and conscience, over appetite and passion. There is now no difference from country, or conditions and circumstances of life. It is the duty of every one to be holy, because Christ is a Christian's All, his only Lord and Saviour, and all his hope and happiness.

Verses 12-17

We must not only do no hurt to any, but do what good we can to all. Those who are the elect of God, holy and beloved, ought to be lowly and compassionate towards all. While in this world, where there is so much corruption in our hearts, quarrels will sometimes arise. But it is our duty to forgive one another, imitating the forgiveness through which we are saved. Let the peace of God rule in your hearts; it is of his working in all who are his. Thanksgiving to God, helps to make us agreeable to all men. The gospel is the word of Christ. Many have the word, but it dwells in them poorly; it has no power over them. The soul prospers, when we are full of the Scriptures and of the grace of Christ. But when we sing psalms, we must be affected with what we sing. Whatever we are employed about, let us do every thing in the name of the Lord Jesus, and in believing dependence on him. Those who do all in Christ's name, will never want matter of thanksgiving to God, even the Father.

Verses 18-25

The epistles most taken up in displaying the glory of the Divine grace, and magnifying the Lord Jesus, are the most particular in pressing the duties of the Christian life. We must never separate the privileges and duties of the gospel. Submission is the duty of wives. But it is submission, not to a severe lord or stern tyrant, but to her own husband, who is engaged to affectionate duty. And husbands must love their wives with tender and faithful affection. Dutiful children are the most likely to prosper. And parents must be tender, as well as children obedient. Servants are to do their duty, and obey their masters' commands, in all things consistent with duty to God their heavenly Master. They must be both just and diligent; without selfish designs, or hypocrisy and disguise. Those who fear God, will be just and faithful when from under their master's eye, because they know they are under the eye of God. And do all with diligence, not idly and slothfully; cheerfully, not discontented at the providence of God which put them in that relation. And for servants' encouragement, let them know, that in serving their masters according to the command of Christ, they serve Christ, and he will give them a glorious reward at last. But, on the other hand, he who doeth wrong, shall receive for the wrong which he hath done. God will punish the unjust, as well as reward the faithful servant; and the same if masters wrong their servants. For the righteous Judge of the earth will deal justly between master and servant. Both will stand upon a level at his tribunal. How happy would true religion make the world, if it every where prevailed, influenced every state of things, and every relation of life! But the profession of those persons who are regardless of duties, and give just cause for complaint to those they are connected with, deceives themselves, as well as brings reproach on the gospel.

Chapter 4

Chapter Outline

Verse 1

The apostle proceeds with the duty of masters to their servants. Not only justice is required of them, but strict equity and kindness. Let them deal with servants as they expect God should deal with themselves.

Verses 2-6

No duties can be done aright, unless we persevere in fervent prayer, and watch therein with thanksgiving. The people are to pray particularly for their ministers. Believers are exhorted to right conduct towards unbelievers. Be careful in all converse with them, to do them good, and recommend religion by all fit means. Diligence in redeeming time, commends religion to the good opinion of others. Even what is only carelessness may cause a lasting prejudice against the truth. Let all discourse be discreet and seasonable, as becomes Christians. Though it be not always of grace, it must always be with grace. Though our discourse be of that which is common, yet it must be in a Christian manner. Grace is the salt which seasons our discourse, and keeps it from corrupting. It is not enough to answer what is asked, unless we answer aright also.

Verses 7-9

Ministers are servants to Christ, and fellow-servants to one another. They have one Lord, though they have different stations and powers for service. It is a great comfort under the troubles and difficulties of life, to have fellow Christians caring for us. Circumstances of life make no difference in the spiritual relation among sincere Christians; they partake of the same privileges, and are entitled to the same regards. What amazing changes Divine grace makes! Faithless servants become faithful and beloved brethren, and some who had done wrong, become fellow-workers of good.

Verses 10-18

Paul had differed with Barnabas, on the account of this Mark, yet he is not only reconciled, but recommends him to the churches; an example of a truly Christian and forgiving spirit. If men have been guilty of a fault, it must not always be remembered against them. We must forget as well as forgive. The apostle had comfort in the communion of saints and ministers. One is his fellow-servant, another his fellow-prisoner, and all his fellow-workers, working out their own salvation, and endeavouring to promote the salvation of others. The effectual, fervent prayer is the prevailing prayer, and availeth much. The smiles, flatteries, or frowns of the world, the spirit of error, or the working of self-love, leads many to a way of preaching and living which comes far short of fulfilling their ministry. But those who preach the same doctrine as Paul, and follow his example, may expect the Divine favour and blessing.

1 Thessalonians

This epistle is generally considered to have been the first of those written by St. Paul. The occasion seems to have been the good report of the stedfastness of the church at Thessalonica in the faith of the gospel. It is full of affection and confidence, and more consolatory and practical, and less doctrinal, than some of the other epistles.

Chapter 1

Chapter Outline

The faith, love, and patience of the Thessalonians, are evident tokens of their election which was manifested in the power with which the gospel came to them.   (1–5)

Its powerful and exemplary effects upon their hearts and lives.   (6–10)

Verses 1-5

As all good comes from God, so no good can be hoped for by sinners, but from God in Christ. And the best good may be expected from God, as our Father, for the sake of Christ. We should pray, not only for ourselves, but for others also; remembering them without ceasing. Wherever there is a true faith, it will work; it will affect both the heart and life. Faith works by love; it shows itself in love to God, and love to our neighbour. And wherever there is a well-grounded hope of eternal life, this will appear by the exercise of patience; and it is a sign of sincerity, when in all we do, we seek to approve ourselves to God. By this we may know our election, if we not only speak of the things of God with out lips, but feel their power in our hearts, mortifying our lusts, weaning us from the world, and raising us up to heavenly things. Unless the Spirit of God comes with the word of God, it will be to us a dead letter. Thus they entertained it by the power of the Holy Ghost. They were fully convinced of the truth of it, so as not to be shaken in mind by objections and doubts; and they were willing to leave all for Christ, and to venture their souls and everlasting condition upon the truth of the gospel revelation.

Verses 6-10

When careless, ignorant, and immoral persons are turned from their carnal pursuits and connexions, to believe in and obey the Lord Jesus, to live soberly, righteously, and godly, the matter speaks for itself. The believers under the Old Testament waited for the coming of the Messiah, and believers now wait for his second coming. He is yet to come. And God had raised him from the dead, which is a full assurance unto all men that he will come to judgment. He came to purchase salvation, and will, when he comes again, bring salvation with him, full and final deliverance from that wrath which is yet to come. Let all, without delay, flee from the wrath to come, and seek refuge in Christ and his salvation.

Chapter 2

Chapter Outline

The apostle reminds the Thessalonians of his preaching and behaviour.	(1–12)
And of their receiving the gospel as the word of God.	(13–16)
His joy on their account.	(17–20)

Verses 1-6

The apostle had no wordly design in his preaching. Suffering in a good cause should sharpen holy resolution. The gospel of Christ at first met with much opposition; and it was preached with contention, with striving in preaching, and against opposition. And as the matter of the apostle's exhortation was true and pure, the manner of his speaking was without guile. The gospel of Christ is designed for mortifying corrupt affections, and that men may be brought under the power of faith. This is the great motive to sincerity, to consider that God not only sees all we do, but knows our thoughts afar off, and searches the heart. And it is from this God who trieth our hearts, that we must receive our reward. The evidences of the apostle's sincerity were, that he avoided flattery and covetousness. He avoided ambition and vain-glory.

Verses 7-12

Mildness and tenderness greatly recommend religion, and are most conformable to God's gracious dealing with sinners, in and by the gospel. This is the way to win people. We should not only be faithful to our calling as Christians, but in our particular callings and relations. Our great gospel privilege is, that God has called us to his kingdom and glory. The great gospel duty is, that we walk worthy of God. We should live as becomes those called with such a high and holy calling. Our great business is to honour, serve, and please God, and to seek to be worthy of him.

Verses 13-16

We should receive the word of God with affections suitable to its holiness, wisdom, truth, and goodness. The words of men are frail and perishing, like themselves, and sometimes false, foolish, and fickle; but God's word is holy, wise, just, and faithful. Let us receive and regard it accordingly. The word wrought in them, to make them examples to others in faith and good works, and in patience under sufferings, and in trials for the sake of the gospel. Murder and persecution are hateful to God, and no zeal for any thing in religion can excuse it. Nothing tends more to any person or people's filling up the measure of their sins, than opposing the gospel, and hindering the salvation of souls. The pure gospel of Christ is abhorred by many, and the faithful preaching of it is hindered in many ways. But those who forbid the preaching it to sinners, to men dead in sin, do not by this please God. Those have cruel hearts, and are enemies to the glory of God, and to the salvation of his people, who deny them the Bible.

Verses 17-20

This world is not a place where we are to be always, or long together. In heaven holy souls shall meet, and never part more. And though the apostle could not come to them yet, and thought he might never be able to come, yet our Lord Jesus Christ will come; nothing shall hinder that. May God give faithful ministers to all who serve him with their spirit in the gospel of his Son, and send them to all who are in darkness

Chapter 3

Chapter Outline

The apostle sent Timothy to establish and   (1–5)
comfort the Thessalonians.

He rejoiced at the good tidings of their faith   (6–10)
and love.

And for their increase in grace.   (11–13)

Verses 1-5

The more we find pleasure in the ways of God, the more we shall desire to persevere therein. The apostle's design was to establish and comfort the Thessalonians as to the object of their faith, that Jesus Christ was the Saviour of the world; and as to the recompence of faith, which was more than enough to make up all their losses, and to reward all their labours. But he feared his labours would be in vain. If the devil cannot hinder ministers from labouring in the word and doctrine, he will, if possible, hinder the success of their labours. No one would willingly labour in vain. It is the will and purpose of God, that we enter into his kingdom through many afflictions. And the apostles, far from flattering people with the expectation of worldly prosperity in religion, told them plainly they must count upon trouble in the flesh. Herein they followed the example of their great Master, the Author of our faith. Christians were in danger, and they should be forewarned; they will thus be kept from being improved by any devices of the tempter.

Verses 6-10

Thankfulness to God is very imperfect in the present state; but one great end of the ministry of the word is to help faith forward. That which was the instrument to obtain faith, is also the means of increasing and confirming it, namely, the ordinances of God; and as faith cometh by hearing, so it is confirmed by hearing also.

Verses 11-13

Prayer is religious worship, and all religious worship is due unto God only. Prayer is to be offered to God as our Father. Prayer is not only to be offered in the name of Christ, but offered up to Christ himself, as our Lord and our Saviour. Let us acknowledge God in all our ways, and he will direct our paths. Mutual love is required of all Christians. And love is of God, and is fulfilling the gospel as well as the law. We need the Spirit's influences in order to our growth in grace; and the way to obtain them, is prayer. Holiness is required of all who would go to heaven; and we must act so that we do not contradict the profession we make of holiness. The Lord Jesus will certainly come in his glory; his saints will come with him. Then the excellence as well as the necessity of holiness will appear; and without this no hearts shall be established at that day, nor shall any avoid condemnation.

Chapter 4

Chapter Outline

Exhortations to purity and holiness.	(1–8)
To brotherly love, peaceable behaviour, and diligence.	(9–12)
Not to sorrow unduly for the death of godly relations and friends, considering the glorious resurrection of their bodies at Christ's second coming.	(13–18)

Verses 1-8

To abide in the faith of the gospel is not enough, we must abound in the work of faith. The rule according to which all ought to walk and act, is the commandments given by the Lord Jesus Christ. Sanctification, in the renewal of their souls under the influences of the Holy Spirit, and attention to appointed duties, constituted the will of God respecting them. In aspiring after this renewal of the soul unto holiness, strict restraint must be put upon the appetites and senses of the body, and on the thoughts and inclinations of the will, which lead to wrong uses of them. The Lord calls none into his family to live unholy lives, but that they may be taught and enabled to walk before him in holiness. Some make light of the precepts of holiness, because they hear them from men; but they are God's commands, and to break them is to despise God.

Verses 9-12

We should notice in others what is good, to their praise, that we may engage them to abound therein more and more. All who are savingly taught of God, are taught to love one another. The teaching of the Spirit exceeds the teachings of men; and men's teaching is vain and useless, unless God teach. Those remarkable for this or any other grace, need to increase therein, as well as to persevere to the end. It is very desirable to have a calm and quiet temper, and to be of a peaceable and quiet behaviour. Satan is busy to trouble us; and we have in our hearts what disposes us to be unquiet; therefore let us study to be quiet. Those who are busy-bodies, meddling in other men's matters, have little quiet in their own minds, and cause great disturbances among their neighbours. They seldom mind the other exhortation, to be diligent in their own calling, to work with their own hands. Christianity does not take us from the work and duty of our particular callings, but teaches us to be diligent therein. People often by slothfulness reduce themselves to great straits, and are liable to many wants; while such as are diligent in their own business, earn their own bread, and have great pleasure in so doing.

Verses 13-18

Here is comfort for the relations and friends of those who die in the Lord. Grief for the death of friends is lawful; we may weep for our own loss, though it may be their gain. Christianity does not forbid, and grace does not do away, our natural affections. Yet we must not be excessive in our sorrows; this is too much like those who have no hope of a better life. Death is an unknown thing, and we know little about the state after death; yet the doctrines of the resurrection and the second coming of Christ, are a remedy against the fear of death, and undue sorrow for the death of our Christian friends; and of these doctrines we have full assurance. It will be some happiness that all the saints shall meet, and remain together for ever; but the principal happiness of heaven is to be with the Lord, to see him, live with him, and enjoy him for ever. We should support one another in times sorrow; not deaden one another's spirits, or weaken one another's hands. And this may be done by the many lessons to be learned from the resurrection of the dead, and the second coming of Christ. What! comfort a man by telling him he is going to appear before the judgment-seat of God! Who can feel comfort from those words? That man alone with whose spirit the Spirit of God bears witness that his sins are blotted out, and the thoughts of whose heart are purified by the Holy Spirit, so that he can love God, and worthily magnify his name. We are not in a safe state unless it is thus with us, or we are desiring to be so.

Chapter 5

Chapter Outline

The apostle exhorts to be always ready for the coming of Christ to judgment, which will be with suddenness and surprise. (1–11)

He directs to several particular duties. (12–22)

And concludes with prayer, greetings, and a blessing.   (23–28)

Verses 1-5

It is needless or useless to ask about the particular time of Christ's coming. Christ did not reveal this to the apostles. There are times and seasons for us to work in, and these are our duty and interest to know and observe; but as to the time when we must give up our account, we know it not, nor is it needful that we should. The coming of Christ will be a great surprise to men. Our Lord himself said so. As the hour of death is the same to each person that the judgment will be to mankind in general, so the same remarks answer for both. Christ's coming will be terrible to the ungodly. Their destruction will overtake them while they dream of happiness, and please themselves with vain amusements. There will be no means to escape the terror or the punishment of that day. This day will be a happy day to the righteous. They are not in darkness; they are the children of the light. It is the happy condition of all true Christians. But how many are speaking peace and safety to themselves, over whose heads utter destruction is hovering! Let us endeavour to awaken ourselves and each other, and guard against our spiritual enemies.

Verses 6-11

Most of mankind do not consider the things of another world at all, because they are asleep; or they do not consider them aright, because they sleep and dream. Our moderation as to all earthly things should be known to all men. Shall Christians, who have the light of the blessed gospel shining in their faces, be careless about their souls, and unmindful of another world? We need the spiritual armour, or the three Christian graces, faith, love, and hope. Faith; if we believe that the eye of God is always upon us, that there is another world to prepare for, we shall see reason to watch and be sober. True and fervent love to God, and the things of God, will keep us watchful and sober. If we have hope of salvation, let us take heed of any thing that would shake our trust in the Lord. We have ground on which to build unshaken hope, when we consider, that salvation is by our Lord Jesus Christ, who died for us, to atone for our sins and to ransom our souls. We should join in prayer and praise one with another. We should set a good example one before another, and this is the best means to answer the end of society. Thus we shall learn how to live to Him, with whom we hope to live for ever.

Verses 12-15

The ministers of the gospel are described by the work of their office, which is to serve and honour the Lord. It is their duty not only to give good counsel, but also to warn the flock of dangers, and reprove for whatever may be amiss. The people should honour and love their ministers, because their business is the welfare of men's souls. And the people should be at peace among themselves, doing all they can to guard against any differences. But love of peace must not make us wink at sin. The fearful and sorrowful spirits, should be encouraged, and a kind word may do much good. We must bear and forbear. We must be long-suffering, and keep down anger, and this to all men. Whatever man do to us, we must do good to others.

Verses 16-22

We are to rejoice in creature-comforts, as if we rejoiced not, and must not expect to live many years, and rejoice in them all; but if we do rejoice in God, we may do that evermore. A truly religious life is a life of constant joy. And we should rejoice more, if we prayed more. Prayer will help forward all lawful business, and every good work. If we pray without ceasing, we shall not want matter for thanksgiving in every thing. We shall see cause to give thanks for sparing and preventing, for common and uncommon, past and present, temporal and spiritual mercies. Not only for prosperous and pleasing, but also for afflicting providences, for chastisements and corrections; for God designs all for our good, though we at present see not how they tend to it. Quench not the Spirit. Christians are said to be baptized with the Holy Ghost and with fire. He worketh as fire, by enlightening, enlivening, and purifying the souls of men. As fire is put out by taking away fuel, and as it is quenched by pouring water, or putting a great deal of earth upon it; so we must be careful not to quench the Holy Spirit, by indulging carnal lusts and affections, minding only earthly things. Believers often hinder their growth in grace, by not giving themselves up to the spiritual affections raised in their hearts by the Holy Spirit. By prophesyings, here understand the preaching of the word, the interpreting and applying the Scriptures. We must not despise preaching, though it is plain, and we are told no more than what we knew before. We must search the Scriptures. And proving all things must be to hold fast that which is good. We should abstain from sin, and whatever looks like sin, leads to it, and borders upon it. He who is not shy of the appearances of sin, who shuns not the occasions of it, and who avoids not the temptations and approaches to it, will not long keep from doing sin.

Verses 23-28

The apostle prays that they might be sanctified more perfectly, for the best are sanctified but in part while in this world; therefore we should pray for, and press toward, complete holiness. And as we must fall, if God did not carry on his good work in the soul, we should pray to God to perfect his work, till we are presented faultless before the throne of his glory. We should pray for one another; and brethren should thus express brotherly love. This epistle was to be read to all the brethren. Not only are the common people allowed to read the Scriptures, but it is their duty, and what they should be persuaded to do. The word of God should not be kept in an unknown tongue, but transplanted, that as all men are concerned to know the Scriptures, so they all may be able to read them. The Scriptures should be read in all public congregations, for the benefit of the unlearned especially. We need no more to make us happy, than to know the grace of our Lord Jesus Christ. He is an ever-flowing and an over-flowing fountain of grace to supply all our wants.

2 Thessalonians

The second epistle to the Thessalonians was written soon after the first. The apostle was told that, from some expressions in his first letter, many expected the second coming of Christ was at hand, and that the day of judgment would arrive in their time. Some of these neglected their worldly duties. St. Paul wrote again to correct their error, which hindered the spread of the gospel. He had written agreeably to the words of the prophets of the Old Testament; and he tells them there were many counsels of the Most High yet to be fulfilled, before that day of the Lord should come, though, because it is sure, he had spoken of it as near. The subject led to a remarkable foretelling, of some of the future events which were to take place in the after-ages of the Christian church, and which show the prophetic spirit the apostle possessed.

Chapter 1

Chapter Outline

The apostle blesses God for the growing state of the love and patience of the Thessalonians.	(1–4)
And encourages them to persevere under all their sufferings for Christ, considering his coming at the great day of account.	(5–12)

Verses 1-4

Where there is the truth of grace, there will be an increase of it. The path of the just is as the shining light, which shines more and more unto the perfect day. And where there is the increase of grace, God must have all the glory. Where faith grows, love will abound, for faith works by love. It shows faith and patience, such as may be proposed as a pattern for others, when trials from God, and persecutions from men, quicken the exercise of those graces; for the patience and faith of which the apostle gloried, bore them up, and enabled them to endure all their tribulations.

Verses 5-10

Religion, if worth anything, is worth every thing; and those have no religion, or none worth having, or know not how to value it, cannot find their hearts to suffer for it. We cannot by all our sufferings, any more than by our services, merit heaven; but by our patience under sufferings, we are prepared for the promised joy. Nothing more strongly marks a man for eternal ruin, than a spirit of persecution and enmity to the name and people of God. God will trouble those that trouble his people. And there is a rest for the people of God; a rest from sin and sorrow. The certainty of future recompence is proved by the righteousness of God. The thoughts of this should be terrible to wicked men, and support the righteous. Faith, looking to the great day, is enabled partly to understand the book of providence, which appears confused to unbelievers. The Lord Jesus will in that day appear from heaven. He will come in the glory and power of the upper world. His light will be piercing, and his power consuming, to all who in that day shall be found as chaff. This appearance will be terrible to those that know not God, especially to those who rebel against revelation, and obey not the gospel of our Lord Jesus Christ. This is the great crime of multitudes, the gospel is revealed, and they will not believe it; or if they pretend to believe, they will not obey it. Believing the truths of the gospel, is in order to our obeying the precepts of the gospel. Though sinners may be long spared, they will be punished at last. They did sin's work, and must receive sin's wages. Here God punishes sinners by creatures as instruments; but then, it will be destruction from the Almighty; and who knows the power of his anger? It will be a joyful day to some, to the saints, to those who believe and obey the gospel. In that bright and blessed day, Christ Jesus will be glorified and admired by his saints. And Christ will be glorified and admired in them. His grace and power will be shown, when it shall appear what he has purchased for, and wrought in, and bestowed upon those who believe in him. Lord, if the glory put upon thy saints shall be thus admired, how much more shalt thou be admired, as the Bestower of that glory! The glory of thy justice in the damnation of the wicked will be admired, but not as the glory of thy mercy in the salvation of believers. How will this strike the adoring angels with holy admiration, and transport thy admiring saints with eternal rapture! The meanest believer shall enjoy more than the most enlarged heart can imagine while we are here; Christ will be admired in all those that believe, the meanest believer not excepted.

Verses 11, 12

Believing thoughts and expectations of the second coming of Christ should lead us to pray to God more, for ourselves and others. If there is any good in us, it is owing to the good pleasure of his goodness, and therefore it is called grace. There are many purposes of grace and good-will in God toward his people, and the apostle prays that God would complete in them the work of faith with power. This is to their doing every other good work. The power of God not only begins, but carries on the work of faith. And this is the great end and design of the grace of our God and Lord Jesus Christ, which is made known to us, and wrought in us.

Chapter 2

Chapter Outline

Cautions against the error that the time of Christ's coming was just at hand. There would first be a general apostacy from the faith, and a revealing of the antichristian man of sin.	(1–4)
His destruction, and that of those who obey him.	(5–12)

The security of the Thessalonians from apostacy; an exhortation to stedfastness, and prayer for them.

(13–17)

Verses 1-4

If errors arise among Christians, we should set them right; and good men will be careful to suppress errors which rise from mistaking their words and actions. We have a cunning adversary, who watches to do mischief, and will promote errors, even by the words of Scripture. Whatever uncertainty we are in, or whatever mistakes may arise about the time of Christ's coming, that coming itself is certain. This has been the faith and hope of all Christians, in all ages of the church; it was the faith and hope of the Old Testament saints. All believers shall be gathered together to Christ, to be with him, and to be happy in his presence for ever. We should firmly believe the second coming of Christ; but there was danger lest the Thessalonians, being mistaken as to the time, should question the truth or certainty of the thing itself. False doctrines are like the winds that toss the water to and fro; and they unsettle the minds of men, which are as unstable as water. It is enough for us to know that our Lord will come, and will gather all his saints unto him. A reason why they should not expect the coming of Christ, as at hand, is given. There would be a general falling away first, such as would occasion the rise of antichrist, that man of sin. There have been great disputes who or what is intended by this man of sin and son of perdition. The man of sin not only practises wickedness, but also promotes and commands sin and wickedness in others; and is the son of perdition, because he is devoted to certain destruction, and is the instrument to destroy many others, both in soul and body. As God was in the temple of old, and worshipped there, and is in and with his church now; so the antichrist here mentioned, is a usurper of God's authority in the Christian church, who claims Divine honours.

Verses 5-12

Something hindered or withheld the man of sin. It is supposed to be the power of the Roman empire, which the apostle did not mention more plainly at that time. Corruption of doctrine and worship came in by degrees, and the usurping of power was gradual; thus the mystery of iniquity prevailed. Superstition and idolatry were advanced by pretended devotion, and bigotry and persecution were promoted by pretended zeal for God and his glory. This mystery of iniquity was even then begun; while the apostles were yet living, persons pretended zeal for Christ, but really opposed him. The fall or ruin of the antichristian state is declared. The pure word of God, with the Spirit of God, will discover this mystery of iniquity, and in due time it shall be destroyed by the brightness of Christ's coming. Signs and wonders, visions and miracles, are pretended; but they are false signs to support false doctrines; and lying wonders, or only pretended miracles, to cheat the people; and the diabolical deceits with which the antichristian state has been supported, are notorious. The persons are described, who are his willing subjects. Their sin is this; They did not love the truth, and therefore did not believe it; and they were pleased with false notions. God leaves them to themselves, then sin will follow of course, and spiritual judgments here, and eternal punishments hereafter. These prophecies have, in a great measure, come to pass, and confirm the truth of the Scriptures. This passage exactly agrees with the system of popery, as it prevails in the Romish church, and under the Romish popes. But though the son of perdition has been revealed, though he has opposed and exalted himself above all that is called God, or that is worshipped; and has spoken and acted as if he were a god upon earth, and has proclaimed his insolent pride, and supported his delusions, by lying miracles and all kinds of frauds; still the Lord has not yet fully destroyed him with the brightness of his coming; that and other prophecies remain to be fulfilled before the end shall come.

Verses 13-15

When we hear of the apostacy of many, it is a great comfort and joy, that there is a remnant according to the election of grace, which does and shall persevere; especially we should rejoice, if we have reason to hope that we are of that number. The preservation of the saints, is because God loved them with an everlasting love, from the beginning of the world. The end and the means must not be separated. Faith and holiness must be joined together as well as holiness and happiness. The outward call of God is by the gospel; and this is rendered effectual by the inward working of the Spirit. The belief of the truth brings the sinner to rely on Christ, and so to love and obey him; it is sealed by the Holy Spirit upon his heart. We have no certain proof of any thing having been delivered by the apostles, more than what we find contained in the Holy Scriptures. Let us then stand fast in the doctrines taught by the apostles, and reject all additions, and vain traditions.

Verses 16, 17

We may and should direct our prayers, not only to God the Father, through our Lord Jesus Christ, but also to our Lord Jesus Christ himself. And we should pray in his name unto God, not only as his Father, but as our Father in and through him. The love of God in Christ Jesus, is the spring and fountain of all the good we have or hope for. There is good reason for strong consolations, because the saints have good hope through grace. The free grace and mercy of God are what they hope for, and what their hopes are founded on, and not any worth or merit of their own. The more pleasure we take in the word, and works, and ways of God, the more likely we shall be to persevere therein. But, if we are wavering in faith, and of a doubtful mind, halting and faltering in our duty, no wonder that we are strangers to the joys of religion.

Chapter 3

Chapter Outline

And concludes with a prayer for them, and a greeting.

(16–18)

Verses 1-5

Those who are far apart still may meet together at the throne of grace; and those not able to do or receive any other kindness, may in this way do and receive real and very great kindness. Enemies to the preaching of the gospel, and persecutors of its faithful preachers, are unreasonable and wicked men. Many do not believe the gospel; and no wonder if such are restless and show malice in their endeavours to oppose it. The evil of sin is the greatest evil, but there are other evils we need to be preserved from, and we have encouragement to depend upon the grace of God. When once the promise is made, the performance is sure and certain. The apostle had confidence in them, but that was founded upon his confidence in God; for there is otherwise no confidence in man. He prays for them for spiritual blessings. It is our sin and our misery, that we place our affections upon wrong objects. There is not true love of God, without faith in Jesus Christ. If, by the special grace of God, we have that faith which multitudes have not, we should earnestly pray that we may be enabled, without reserve, to obey his commands, and that we may be enabled, without reserve, to the love of God, and the patience of Christ.

Verses 6-15

Those who have received the gospel, are to live according to the gospel. Such as could work, and would not, were not to be maintained in idleness. Christianity is not to countenance slothfulness, which would consume what is meant to encourage the industrious, and to support the sick and afflicted. Industry in our callings as men, is a duty required by our calling as Christians. But some expected to be maintained in idleness, and indulged a curious and conceited temper. They meddled with the concerns of others, and did much harm. It is a great error and abuse of religion, to make it a cloak for idleness or any other sin. The servant who waits for the coming of his Lord aright, must be working as his Lord has commanded. If we are idle, the devil and a corrupt heart will soon find us somewhat to do. The mind of man is a busy thing; if it is not employed in doing good, it will be doing evil. It is an excellent, but rare union, to be active in our own business, yet quiet as to other people's. If any refused to labour with quietness, they were to note him with censure, and to separate from his company, yet they were to seek his good by loving admonitions. The Lords is with you while you are with him. Hold on your way, and hold on to the end. We must never give over, or tire in our work. It will be time enough to rest when we come to heaven.

Verses 16-18

The apostle prays for the Thessalonians. And let us desire the same blessings for ourselves and our friends. Peace with God. This peace is desired for them always, or in every thing. Peace by all means; in every way; that, as they enjoyed the means of grace, they might use all methods to secure peace. We need nothing more to make us safe and happy, nor can we desire any thing better for ourselves and our friends, than to have God's gracious presence with us and them. No matter where we are, if God be with us; nor who is absent, if God be present. It is through the grace of our Lord

Jesus Christ, that we hope to have peace with God, and to enjoy the presence of God. This grace is all in all to make us happy; though we wish ever so much to others, there remains enough for ourselves.

1 Timothy

The design of the epistle appears to be, that Timothy having been left at Ephesus, St. Paul wrote to instruct him in the choice of proper officers in the church, as well as in the exercise of a regular ministry. Also, to caution against the influence of false teachers, who by subtle distinctions and endless disputes, corrupted the purity and simplicity of the gospel. He presses upon him constant regard to the greatest diligence, faithfulness, and zeal. These subjects occupy the first four chapters; the fifth chapter instructs respecting particular classes; in the latter part, controversies and disputes are condemned, the love of money blamed, and the rich exhorted to good works.

Chapter 1

Chapter Outline

The apostle salutes Timothy.	(1–4)
The design of the law as given by Moses.	(5–11)
Of his own conversion and call to the apostleship.	(12–17)
The obligation to maintain faith and a good conscience.	(18–20)

Verses 1-4

Jesus Christ is a Christian's hope; all our hopes of eternal life are built upon him; and Christ is in us the hope of glory. The apostle seems to have been the means of Timothy's conversion; who served with him in his ministry, as a dutiful son with a loving father. That which raises questions, is not for edifying; that which gives occasion for doubtful disputes, pulls down the church rather than builds it up. Godliness of heart and life can only be kept up and increased, by the exercise of faith in the truths and promises of God, through Jesus Christ.

Verses 5-11

Whatever tends to weaken love to God, or love to the brethren, tends to defeat the end of the commandment. The design of the gospel is answered, when sinners, through repentance towards God and faith in Jesus Christ, are brought to exercise Christian love. And as believers were righteous persons in God's appointed way, the law was not against them. But unless we are made righteous by faith in Christ, really repenting and forsaking sin, we are yet under the curse of the law, even according to the gospel of the blessed God, and are unfit to share the holy happiness of heaven.

Verses 12-17

The apostle knew that he would justly have perished, if the Lord had been extreme to mark what was amiss; and also if his grace and mercy had not been abundant to him when dead in sin, working faith and love to Christ in his heart. This is a faithful saying; these are true and faithful words, which may be depended on, That the Son of God came into the world, willingly and purposely to save sinners. No man, with Paul's example before him, can question the love and power of Christ to save him, if he really desires to trust in him as the Son of God, who once died on the cross, and now reigns upon the throne of glory, to save all that come to God through him. Let us then admire and praise the grace of God our Saviour; and ascribe to the Father, Son, and Holy Ghost, three Persons in the unity of the Godhead, the glory of all done in, by, and for us.

Verses 18-20

The ministry is a warfare against sin and Satan; carried on under the Lord Jesus, who is the Captain of our salvation. The good hopes others have had of us, should stir us up to duty. And let us be upright in our conduct in all things. The design of the highest censures in the primitive church, was, to prevent further sin, and to reclaim the sinner. May all who are tempted to put away a good conscience, and to abuse the gospel, remember that this is the way to make shipwreck of faith also.

Chapter 2

Chapter Outline

Prayer to be made for all persons, since the grace of the gospel makes no difference of ranks or stations.   (1–7)

How men and women ought to behave, both in their religious and common life.   (8–15)

Verses 1-7

The disciples of Christ must be praying people; all, without distinction of nation, sect, rank, or party. Our duty as Christians, is summed up in two words; godliness, that is, the right worshiping of God; and honesty, that is, good conduct toward all men. These must go together: we are not truly honest, if we are not godly, and do not render to God his due; and we are not truly godly, if not honest. What is acceptable in the sight of God our Saviour, we should abound in. There is one Mediator, and that Mediator gave himself a ransom for all. And this appointment has been made for the benefit of the Jews and the Gentiles of every nation; that all who are willing may come in this way, to the mercy-seat of a pardoning God, to seek reconciliation with him. Sin had made a quarrel between us and God; Jesus Christ is the Mediator who makes peace. He is a ransom that was to be known in due time. In the Old Testament times, his sufferings, and the glory that should follow, were spoken of as things to be revealed in the last times. Those who are saved must come to the knowledge of the truth, for that is God's appointed way to save sinners: if we do not know the truth, we cannot be ruled by it.

Verses 8-15

Under the gospel, prayer is not to be confined to any one particular house of prayer, but men must pray every where. We must pray in our closets, pray in our families, pray at our meals, pray when we are on journeys, and pray in the solemn assemblies, whether more public or private. We must pray in charity; without wrath, or malice, or anger at any person. We must pray in faith, without doubting, and without disputing. Women who profess the Christian religion, must be modest in apparel, not affecting gaudiness, gaiety, or costliness. Good works are the best ornament; these are, in the sight of God, of great price. Modesty and neatness are more to be consulted in garments than elegance and fashion. And it would be well if the professors of serious godliness were wholly free from vanity in dress. They should spend more time and money in relieving the sick and distressed, than in decorating themselves and their children. To do this in a manner unsuitable to their rank in life, and their profession of godliness, is sinful. These are not trifles, but Divine commands. The best ornaments for professors of godliness, are good works. According to St. Paul, women are not allowed to be public teachers in the church; for teaching is an office of authority. But good women may and ought to teach their children at home the principles of true religion. Also, women must not think themselves excused from learning what is necessary to salvation, though they must not usurp authority. As woman was last in the creation, which is one reason for her subjection, so she was first in the transgression. But there is a word of comfort; that those who continue in sobriety, shall be saved in child-bearing, or with child-bearing, by the Messiah, who was born of a woman. And the especial sorrow to which the female sex is subject, should cause men to exercise their authority with much gentleness, tenderness, and affection.

Chapter 3

Chapter Outline

The qualifications and behaviour of gospel bishops.	(1–7)
And of deacons and their wives.	(8–13)
The reason of writing about these, and other church affairs.	(14–16)

Verses 1-7

If a man desired the pastoral office, and from love to Christ, and the souls of men, was ready to deny himself, and undergo hardships by devoting himself to that service, he sought to be employed in a good work, and his desire should be approved, provided he was qualified for the office. A minister must give as little occasion for blame as can be, lest he bring reproach upon his office. He must be sober, temperate, moderate in all his actions, and in the use of all creature-comforts. Sobriety and watchfulness are put together in Scripture, they assist one the other. The families of ministers ought to be examples of good to all other families. We should take heed of pride; it is a sin that turned angels into devils. He must be of good repute among his neighbours, and under no reproach from his former life. To encourage all faithful ministers, we have Christ's gracious word of promise, Lo, I am with you alway, even unto the end of the world, Mt 28:20. And he will fit his ministers for their work, and carry them through difficulties with comfort, and reward their faithfulness.

Verses 8-13

The deacons were at first appointed to distribute the charity of the church, and to manage its concerns, yet pastors and evangelists were among them. The deacons had a great trust reposed in them. They must be grave, serious, prudent men. It is not fit that public trusts should be lodged in the hands of any, till they are found fit for the business with which they are to be trusted. All who are related to ministers, must take great care to walk as becomes the gospel of Christ.

Verses 14-16

The church is the house of God; he dwells there. The church holds forth the Scripture and the doctrine of Christ, as a pillar holds forth a proclamation. When a church ceases to be the pillar and ground of truth, we may and ought to forsake her; for our regard to truth should be first and greatest. The mystery of godliness is Christ. He is God, who was made flesh, and was manifest in the flesh. God was pleased to manifest himself to man, by his own Son taking the nature of man. Though reproached as a sinner, and put to death as a malefactor, Christ was raised again by the Spirit, and so was justified from all the false charges with which he was loaded. Angels ministered to him, for he is the Lord of angels. The Gentiles welcomed the gospel which the Jews rejected. Let us remember that God was manifest in the flesh, to take away our sins, to redeem us from all iniquity, and to purify unto himself a peculiar people, zealous of good works. These doctrines must be shown forth by the fruits of the Spirit in our lives.

Chapter 4

Chapter Outline

Verses 1-5

The Holy Spirit, both in the Old and the New Testament, spoke of a general turning from the faith of Christ, and the pure worship of God. This should come during the Christian dispensation, for those are called the latter days. False teachers forbid as evil what God has allowed, and command as a duty what he has left indifferent. We find exercise for watchfulness and self-denial, in attending to the requirements of God's law, without being tasked to imaginary duties, which reject what he has allowed. But nothing justifies an intemperate or improper use of things; and nothing will be good to us, unless we seek by prayer for the Lord's blessing upon it.

Verses 6-10

Outward acts of self-denial profit little. What will it avail us to mortify the body, if we do not mortify sin? No diligence in mere outward things could be of much use. The gain of godliness lies much in the promise; and the promises to godly people relate partly to the life that now is, but especially to the life which is to come: though we lose for Christ, we shall not lose by him. If Christ be thus the Saviour of all men, then much more will he be the Rewarder of those who seek and serve him; he will provide well for those whom he has made new creatures.

Verses 11-16

Men's youth will not be despised, if they keep from vanities and follies. Those who teach by their doctrine, must teach by their life. Their discourse must be edifying; their conversation must be holy; they must be examples of love to God and all good men, examples of spiritual-mindedness. Ministers must mind these things as their principal work and business. By this means their profiting will appear in all things, as well as to all persons; this is the way to profit in knowledge and grace, and also to profit others. The doctrine of a minister of Christ must be scriptural, clear, evangelical, and practical; well stated, explained, defended, and applied. But these duties leave no leisure for wordly pleasures, trifling visits, or idle conversation, and but little for what is mere amusement, and only ornamental. May every believer be enabled to let his profiting appear unto all men; seeking to experience the power of the gospel in his own soul, and to bring forth its fruits in his life.

Chapter 5

Chapter Outline

Verses 1, 2

Respect must be paid to the dignity of years and place. The younger, if faulty, must be rebuked, not as desirous to find fault with them, but as willing to make the best of them. There is need of much meekness and care in reproving those who deserve reproof.

Verses 3-8

Honour widows that are widows indeed, relieve them, and maintain them. It is the duty of children, if their parents are in need, and they are able to relieve them, to do it to the utmost of their power. Widowhood is a desolate state; but let widows trust in the Lord, and continue in prayer. All who live in pleasure, are dead while they live, spiritually dead, dead in trespasses and sins. Alas, what numbers there are of this description among nominal Christians, even to the latest period of life! If any men or women do not maintain their poor relations, they in effect deny the faith. If they spend upon their lusts and pleasures, what should maintain their families, they have denied the faith, and are worse than infidels. If professors of the gospel give way to any corrupt principle or conduct, they are worse than those who do not profess to believe the doctrines of grace.

Verses 9-16

Every one brought into any office in the church, should be free from just censure; and many are proper objects of charity, yet ought not to be employed in public services. Those who would find mercy when they are in distress, must show mercy when they are in prosperity; and those who show most readiness for every good work, are most likely to be faithful in whatever is trusted to them. Those who are idle, very seldom are only idle, they make mischief among neighbours, and sow discord among brethren. All believers are required to relieve those belonging to their families who are destitute, that the church may not be prevented from relieving such as are entirely destitute and friendless.

Verses 17-25

Care must be taken that ministers are maintained. And those who are laborious in this work are worthy of double honour and esteem. It is their just due, as much as the reward of the labourer. The apostle charges Timothy solemnly to guard against partiality. We have great need to watch at all times, that we do not partake of other men's sins. Keep thyself pure, not only from doing the like thyself, but from countenancing it, or any way helping to it in others. The apostle also charges Timothy to take care of his health. As we are not to make our bodies masters, so neither slaves; but to use them so that they may be most helpful to us in the service of God. There are secret, and there are open sins: some men's sins are open before-hand, and going before unto judgment; some they follow after. God will bring to light the hidden things of darkness, and make known the counsels of all hearts. Looking forward to the judgment-day, let us all attend to our proper offices, whether in higher or lower stations, studying that the name and doctrine of God may never be blasphemed on our account.

Chapter 6

Chapter Outline

Verses 1-5

Christians were not to suppose that religious knowledge, or Christian privileges, gave them any right to despise heathen masters, or to disobey lawful commands, or to expose their faults to others. And such as enjoyed the privilege of living with believing masters, were not to withhold due respect and reverence, because they were equal in respect to religious privileges, but were to serve with double diligence and cheerfulness, because of their faith in Christ, and as partakers of his free salvation. We are not to consent to any words as wholesome, except the words of our Lord Jesus Christ; to these we must give unfeigned consent. Commonly those are most proud who know least; for they do not know themselves. Hence come envy, strife, railings, evil-surmisings, disputes that are all subtlety, and of no solidity, between men of corrupt and carnal minds, ignorant of the truth and its sanctifying power, and seeking their worldly advantage. (1Ti 6:6-10)

Verses 6-10

Those that make a trade of Christianity to serve their turn for this world, will be disappointed; but those who mind it as their calling, will find it has the promise of the life that now is, as well as of that which is to come. He that is godly, is sure to be happy in another world; and if contented with his condition in this world, he has enough; and all truly godly people are content. When brought into the greatest straits, we cannot be poorer than when we came into this world; a shroud, a coffin, and a grave, are all that the richest man in the world can have from all his wealth. If nature should be content with a little, grace should be content with less. The necessaries of life bound a true Christian's desires, and with these he will endeavour to be content. We see here the evil of covetousness. It is not said, they that are rich, but they will be rich; who place their happiness in wealth, and are eager and determined in the pursuit. Those that are such, give to Satan the opportunity of tempting them, leading them to use dishonest means, and other bad practices, to add to their gains. Also, leading into so many employments, and such a hurry of business, as leave no time or inclination for spiritual religion; leading to connexions that draw into sin and folly. What sins will not men be drawn into by the love of money! People may have money, and yet not love it; but if they love it, this will push them on to all evil. Every sort of wickedness and vice, in one way or another, grows from the love of money. We cannot look around without perceiving many proofs of this, especially in a day of outward prosperity, great expenses, and loose profession.

Verses 11-16

It ill becomes any men, but especially men of God, to set their hearts upon the things of this world; men of God should be taken up with the things of God. There must be a conflict with corruption, and temptations, and the powers of darkness. Eternal life is the crown proposed for our encouragement. We are called to lay hold thereon. To the rich must especially be pointed out their dangers and duties, as to the proper use of wealth. But who can give such a charge, that is not himself above the love of things that wealth can buy? The appearing of Christ is certain, but it is not for us to know the time. Mortal eyes cannot bear the brightness of the Divine glory. None can approach him except as he is made known unto sinners in and by Christ. The Godhead is here adored without distinction of Persons, as all these things are properly spoken, whether of the Father, the Son, or the Holy Ghost. God is revealed to us, only in and through the human nature of Christ, as the only begotten Son of the Father.

Verses 17-21

Being rich in this world is wholly different from being rich towards God. Nothing is more uncertain than worldly wealth. Those who are rich, must see that God gives them their riches; and he only can give to enjoy them richly; for many have riches, but enjoy them poorly, not having a heart to use them. What is the best estate worth, more than as it gives opportunity of doing the more good? Showing faith in Christ by fruits of love, let us lay hold on eternal life, when the self-indulgent, covetous, and ungodly around, lift up their eyes in torment. That learning which opposes the truth of the gospel, is not true science, or real knowledge, or it would approve the gospel, and consent to it. Those who advance reason above faith, are in danger of leaving faith. Grace includes all that is good, and grace is an earnest, a beginning of glory; wherever God gives grace, he will give glory.

2 Timothy

The first design of this epistle seems to have been, to apprize Timothy of what had occurred during the imprisonment of the apostle, and to request him to come to Rome. But being uncertain whether he should be suffered to live to see him, Paul gives a variety of advices and encouragements, for the faithful discharge of his ministerial duties. As this was a private epistle written to St. Paul's most intimate friend, under the miseries of imprisonment, and in the near prospect of death, it shows the temper and character of the apostle, and contains convincing proofs that he sincerely believed the doctrines he preached.

Chapter 1

Chapter Outline

Paul expresses great affection for Timothy. (1–5)

Exhorts him to improve his spiritual gifts. (6–14)

Tells of many who basely deserted him; but speaks with affection of Onesiphorus. (15–18)

Verses 1-5

The promise of eternal life to believers in Christ Jesus, is the leading subject of ministers who are employed according to the will of God. The blessings here named, are the best we can ask for our beloved friends, that they may have peace with God the Father and Christ Jesus our Lord. Whatever good we do, God must have the glory. True believers have in every age the same religion as to substance. Their faith is unfeigned; it will stand the trial, and it dwells in them as a living principle. Thus pious women may take encouragement from the success of Lois and Eunice with Timothy, who proved so excellent and useful a minister. Some of the most worthy and valuable ministers the church of Christ has been favoured with, have had to bless God for early religious impressions made upon their minds by the teaching of their mothers or other female relatives.

Verses 6-14

God has not given us the spirit of fear, but the spirit of power, of courage and resolution, to meet difficulties and dangers; the spirit of love to him, which will carry us through opposition. And the spirit of a sound mind, quietness of mind. The Holy Spirit is not the author of a timid or cowardly disposition, or of slavish fears. We are likely to bear afflictions well, when we have strength and power from God to enable us to bear them. As is usual with Paul, when he mentions Christ and his redemption, he enlarges upon them; so full was he of that which is all our salvation, and ought to be all our desire. The call of the gospel is a holy call, making holy. Salvation is of free grace. This is said to be given us before the world began, that is, in the purpose of God from all eternity; in Christ Jesus, for all the gifts that come from God to sinful man, come in and through Christ Jesus alone. And as there is so clear a prospect of eternal happiness by faith in Him, who is the Resurrection and the Life, let us give more diligence in making his salvation sure to our souls. Those who cleave to the gospel, need not be ashamed, the cause will bear them out; but those who oppose it, shall be ashamed. The apostle had trusted his life, his soul, and eternal interests, to the Lord Jesus. No one else could deliver and secure his soul through the trials of life and death. There is a day coming, when our souls will be inquired after. Thou hadst a soul committed to thee; how was it employed? in the service of sin, or in the service of Christ? The hope of the lowest real Christian rests on the same foundation as that of the great apostle. He also has learned the value and the danger of his soul; he also has believed in Christ; and the change wrought in his soul, convinces the believer that the Lord Jesus will keep him to his heavenly kingdom. Paul exhorts Timothy to hold fast the Holy Scriptures, the substance of solid gospel truth in them. It is not enough to assent to the sound words, but we must love them. The Christian doctrine is a trust committed to us; it is of unspeakable value in itself, and will be of unspeakable advantage to us. It is committed to us, to be preserved pure and entire, yet we must not think to keep it by our own strength, but by the power of the Holy Spirit dwelling in us; and it will not be gained by those who trust in their own hearts, and lean to their own understandings. (2Ti 1:15-18)

Verses 15-18

The apostle mentions the constancy of Onesiphorus; he oft refreshed him with his letters, and counsels, and comforts, and was not ashamed of him. A good man will seek to do good. The day of death and judgment is an awful day. And if we would have mercy then, we must seek for it now of the Lord. The best we can ask, for ourselves or our friends, is, that the Lord will grant that we and they may find mercy of the Lord, when called to pass out of time into eternity, and to appear before the judgment seat of Christ.

Chapter 2

Chapter Outline

The apostle exhorts Timothy to persevere with diligence, like a soldier, a combatant, and a husbandman.	(1–7)
Encouraging him by assurances of a happy end of his faithfulness.	(8–13)
Warnings to shun vain babblings and dangerous errors.	(14–21)
Charges to flee youthful lusts, and to minister with zeal against error, but with meekness of spirit.	(22–26)

Verses 1-7

As our trials increase, we need to grow stronger in that which is good; our faith stronger, our resolution stronger, our love to God and Christ stronger. This is opposed to our being strong in our own strength. All Christians, but especially ministers, must be faithful to their Captain, and resolute in his cause. The great care of a Christian must be to please Christ. We are to strive to get the mastery of our lusts and corruptions, but we cannot expect the prize unless we observe the laws. We must take care that we do good in a right manner, that our good may not be spoken evil of. Some who are active, spend their zeal about outward forms and doubtful disputations. But those who strive lawfully shall be crowned at last. If we would partake the fruits, we must labour; if we would gain the prize, we must run the race. We must do the will of God, before we receive the promises, for which reason we have need of patience. Together with our prayers for others, that the Lord would give them understanding in all things, we must exhort and stir them up to consider what they hear or read.

Verses 8-13

Let suffering saints remember, and look to Jesus, the Author and Finisher of their faith, who for the joy that was set before him, endured the cross, despised the shame, and is now set down at the right hand of the throne of God. We must not think it strange if the best men meet with the worst treatment; but this is cheering, that the word of God is not bound. Here we see the real and true cause of the apostle's suffering trouble in, or for, the sake of the gospel. If we are dead to this world, its pleasures, profits, and honours, we shall be for ever with Christ in a better world. He is faithful to his threatenings, and faithful to his promises. This truth makes sure the unbeliever's condemnation, and the believer's salvation.

Verses 14-21

Those disposed to strive, commonly strive about matters of small moment. But strifes of words destroy the things of God. The apostle mentions some who erred. They did not deny the resurrection, but they corrupted that true doctrine. Yet nothing can be so foolish or erroneous, but it will overturn the temporary faith of some professors. This foundation has two writings on it. One speaks our comfort. None can overthrow the faith of any whom God hath chosen. The other speaks our duty. Those who would have the comfort of the privilege, must make conscience of the duty Christ gave himself for us, that he might redeem us from all iniquity, Tit 2:14. The church of Christ is like a dwelling: some furniture is of great value; some of smaller value, and put to meaner uses. Some professors of religion are like vessels of wood and earth. When the vessels of dishonour are cast out to be destroyed, the others will be filled with all the fulness of God. We must see to it that we are holy vessels. Every one in the church whom God approves, will be devoted to his Master's service, and thus fitted for his use.

Verses 22-26

The more we follow that which is good, the faster and the further we shall flee from that which is evil. The keeping up the communion of saints, will take us from fellowship with unfruitful works of darkness. See how often the apostle cautions against disputes in religion; which surely shows that religion consists more in believing and practising what God requires, than in subtle disputes. Those are unapt to teach, who are apt to strive, and are fierce and froward. Teaching, not persecution, is the Scripture method of dealing with those in error. The same God who gives the discovery of the truth, by his grace brings us to acknowledge it, otherwise our hearts would continue to rebel against it. There is no "peradventure," in respect of God's pardoning those who do repent; but we cannot tell that he will give repentance to those who oppose his will. Sinners are taken in a snare, and in the worst snare, because it is the devil's; they are slaves to him. And if any long for deliverance, let them remember they never can escape, except by repentance, which is the gift of God; and we must ask it of him by earnest, persevering prayer.

Chapter 3

Chapter Outline

Verses 1-9

Even in gospel times there would be perilous times; on account of persecution from without, still more on account of corruptions within. Men love to gratify their own lusts, more than to please God and do their duty. When every man is eager for what he can get, and anxious to keep what he has, this makes men dangerous to one another. When men do not fear God, they will not regard man. When children are disobedient to their parents, that makes the times perilous. Men are unholy and without the fear of God, because unthankful for the mercies of God. We abuse God's gifts, if we make them the food and fuel of our lusts. Times are perilous also, when parents are without natural affection to children. And when men have no rule over their own spirits, but despise that which is good and to be honoured. God is to be loved above all; but a carnal mind, full of enmity against him, prefers any thing before him, especially carnal pleasure. A form of godliness is very different from the power; from such as are found to be hypocrites, real Christians must withdraw. Such persons have been found within the outward church, in every place, and at all times. There ever have been artful men, who, by pretences and flatteries, creep into the favour and confidence of those who are too easy of belief, ignorant, and fanciful. All must be ever learning to know the Lord; but these follow every new notion, yet never seek the truth as it is in Jesus. Like the Egyptian magicians, these were men of corrupt minds, prejudiced against the truth, and found to be quite without faith. Yet though the spirit of error may be let loose for a time, Satan can deceive the nations and the churches no further, and no longer, than God will permit.

Verses 10-13

The more fully we know the doctrine of Christ, as taught by the apostles, the more closely we shall cleave to it. When we know the afflictions of believers only in part, they tempt us to decline the cause for which they suffer. A form of godliness, a profession of Christian faith without a godly life, often is allowed to pass, while open profession of the truth as it is in Jesus, and resolute attention to the duties of godliness, stir up the scorn and enmity of the world. As good men, by the grace of God, grow better, so bad men, through the craft of Satan, and the power of their own corruptions, grow worse. The way of sin is down-hill; such go on from bad to worse, deceiving and being deceived. Those who deceive others, deceive themselves, as they will find at last, to their cost. The history of the outward church, awfully shows that the apostle spake this as he was moved by the Holy Ghost.

Verses 14-17

Those who would learn the things of God, and be assured of them, must know the Holy Scriptures, for they are the Divine revelation. The age of children is the age to learn; and those who would get true learning, must get it out of the Scriptures. They must not lie by us neglected, seldom or never looked into. The Bible is a sure guide to eternal life. The prophets and apostles did not speak from themselves, but delivered what they received of God, 2Pe 1:21. It is profitable for all purposes of the Christian life. It is of use to all, for all need to be taught, corrected, and reproved. There is something in the Scriptures suitable for every case. Oh that we may love our Bibles more, and keep closer to them! then shall we find benefit, and at last gain the happiness therein promised by faith in our Lord Jesus Christ, who is the main subject of both Testaments. We best oppose error by promoting a solid knowledge of the word of truth; and the greatest kindness we can do to children, is to make them early to know the Bible.

Chapter 4

Chapter Outline

The apostle solemnly charges Timothy to be diligent, though many will not bear sound doctrine.	(1–5)
Enforces the charge from his own martyrdom, then at hand.	(6–8)
Desires him to come speedily.	(9–13)

He cautions, and complains of such as had deserted him; and expresses his faith as to his own preservation to the heavenly kingdom.

(14–18)

Friendly greetings and his usual blessing.

(19–22)

Verses 1-5

People will turn away from the truth, they will grow weary of the plain gospel of Christ, they will be greedy of fables, and take pleasure in them. People do so when they will not endure that preaching which is searching, plain, and to the purpose. Those who love souls must be ever watchful, must venture and bear all the painful effects of their faithfulness, and take all opportunities of making known the pure gospel.

Verses 6-8

The blood of the martyrs, though not a sacrifice of atonement, yet was a sacrifice of acknowledgment to the grace of God and his truth. Death to a good man, is his release from the imprisonment of this world, and his departure to the enjoyments of another world. As a Christian, and a minister, Paul had kept the faith, kept the doctrines of the gospel. What comfort will it afford, to be able to speak in this manner toward the end of our days! The crown of believers is a crown of righteousness, purchased by the righteousness of Christ. Believers have it not at present, yet it is sure, for it is laid up for them. The believer, amidst poverty, pain, sickness, and the agonies of death, may rejoice; but if the duties of a man's place and station are neglected, his evidence of interest in Christ will be darkened, and uncertainty and distress may be expected to cloud and harass his last hours.

Verses 9-13

The love of this world, is often the cause of turning back from the truths and ways of Jesus Christ. Paul was guided by Divine inspiration, yet he would have his books. As long as we live, we must still learn. The apostles did not neglect human means, in seeking the necessaries of life, or their own instruction. Let us thank the Divine goodness in having given us so many writings of wise and pious men in all ages; and let us seek that by reading them our profiting may appear to all.

Verses 14-18

There is as much danger from false brethren, as from open enemies. It is dangerous having to do with those who would be enemies to such a man as Paul. The Christians at Rome were forward to meet him, Ac 28, but when there seemed to be a danger of suffering with him, then all forsook him. God might justly be angry with them, but he prays God to forgive them. The apostle was delivered out of the mouth of the lion, that is, of Nero, or some of his judges. If the Lord stands by us, he will strengthen us in difficulties and dangers, and his presence will more than supply every one's absence.

Verses 19-22

We need no more to make us happy, than to have the Lord Jesus Christ with our spirits; for in him all spiritual blessings are summed up. It is the best prayer we can offer for our friends, that the Lord Jesus Christ may be with their spirits, to sanctify and save them, and at last to receive them to himself. Many who believed as Paul, are now before the throne, giving glory to their Lord: may we be followers of them.

Titus

This epistle chiefly contains directions to Titus concerning the elders of the Church, and the manner in which he should give instruction; and the latter part tells him to urge obedience to magistrates, to enforce good works, avoid foolish questions, and shun heresies. The instructions the apostle gave are all plain and simple. The Christian religion was not formed to answer worldly or selfish views, but it is the wisdom of God and the power of God.

Chapter 1

Chapter Outline

The apostle salutes Titus.	(1–4)
The qualifications of a faithful pastor.	(5–9)
The evil temper and practices of false teachers.	(10–16)

Verses 1-4

All are the servants of God who are not slaves of sin and Satan. All gospel truth is according to godliness, teaching the fear of God. The intent of the gospel is to raise up hope as well as faith; to take off the mind and heart from the world, and to raise them to heaven and the things above. How excellent then is the gospel, which was the matter of Divine promise so early, and what thanks are due for our privileges! Faith comes by hearing, and hearing by the word of God; and whoso is appointed and called, must preach the word. Grace is the free favour of God, and acceptance with him. Mercy, the fruits of the favour, in the pardon of sin, and freedom from all miseries both here and hereafter. And peace is the effect and fruit of mercy. Peace with God through Christ who is our Peace, and with the creatures and ourselves. Grace is the fountain of all blessings. Mercy, and peace, and all good, spring out of this.

Verses 5-9

The character and qualification of pastors, here called elders and bishops, agree with what the apostle wrote to Timothy. Being such bishops and overseers of the flock, to be examples to them, and God's stewards to take care of the affairs of his household, there is great reason that they should be blameless. What they are not to be, is plainly shown, as well as what they are to be, as servants of Christ, and able ministers of the letter and practice of the gospel. And here are described the spirit and practice becoming such as should be examples of good works.

Verses 10-16

False teachers are described. Faithful ministers must oppose such in good time, that their folly being made manifest, they may go no further They had a base end in what they did; serving a worldly interest under pretence of religion: for the love of money is the root of all evil. Such should be resisted, and put to shame, by sound doctrine from the Scriptures. Shameful actions, the reproach of heathens, should be far from Christians; falsehood and lying, envious craft and cruelty, brutal and sensual practices, and idleness and sloth, are sins condemned even by the light of nature. But Christian meekness is as far from cowardly passing over sin and error, as from anger and impatience. And though there may be national differences of character, yet the heart of man in every age and place is deceitful and desperately wicked. But the sharpest reproofs must aim at the good of the reproved; and soundness in the faith is most desirable and necessary. To those who are defiled and unbelieving, nothing is pure; they abuse, and turn things lawful and good into sin. Many profess to know God, yet in their lives deny and reject him. See the miserable state of hypocrites, such as have a form of godliness, but are without the power; yet let us not be so ready to fix this charge on others, as careful that it does not apply to ourselves.

Chapter 2

Chapter Outline

The duties which become sound doctrine.	(1–8)
Believing servants must be obedient.	(9, 10)
All is enforced from the holy design of the gospel, which concerns all believers.	(11–15)

Verses 1-8

Old disciples of Christ must behave in every thing agreeably to the Christian doctrine. That the aged men be sober; not thinking that the decays of nature will justify any excess; but seeking comfort from nearer communion with God, not from any undue indulgence. Faith works by, and must be seen in love, of God for himself, and of men for God's sake. Aged persons are apt to be peevish and fretful; therefore need to be on their guard. Though there is not express Scripture for every word, or look, yet there are general rules, according to which all must be ordered. Young women must be sober and discreet; for many expose themselves to fatal temptations by what at first might be only want of discretion. The reason is added, that the word of God may not be blasphemed. Failures in duties greatly reproach Christianity. Young men are apt to be eager and thoughtless, therefore must be earnestly called upon to be sober-minded: there are more young people ruined by pride than by any other sin. Every godly man's endeavour must be to stop the mouths of adversaries. Let thine own conscience answer for thine uprightness. What a glory is it for a Christian, when that mouth which would fain open itself against him, cannot find any evil in him to speak of!

Verses 9, 10

Servants must know and do their duty to their earthly masters, with a reference to their heavenly one. In serving an earthly master according to Christ's will, He is served; such shall be rewarded by him. Not giving disrespectful or provoking language; but to take a check or reproof with silence, not making confident or bold replies. When conscious of a fault, to excuse or justify it, doubles it. Never putting to their own use that which is their master's, nor wasting the goods they are trusted with. Showing all good fidelity to improve a master's goods, and promote his thriving. If ye have not been faithful in that which is another man's, who shall give you that which is your own? Lu 16:12. True religion is an honour to the professors of it; and they should adorn it in all things.

Verses 11-15

The doctrine of grace and salvation by the gospel, is for all ranks and conditions of men. It teaches to forsake sin; to have no more to do with it. An earthly, sensual conversation suits not a heavenly calling. It teaches to make conscience of that which is good. We must look to God in Christ, as the object of our hope and worship. A gospel conversation must be a godly conversation. See our duty in a very few words; denying ungodliness and worldly lusts, living soberly, righteously, and godly, notwithstanding all snares, temptations, corrupt examples, ill usage, and what remains of sin in the believer's heart, with all their hinderances. It teaches to look for the glories of another world. At, and in, the glorious appearing of Christ, the blessed hope of Christians will be complete: To bring us to holiness and happiness was the end of Christ's death. Jesus Christ, that great God and our Saviour, who saves not only as God, much less as Man alone; but as God-man, two natures in one person. He loved us, and gave himself for us; and what can we do less than love and give up ourselves to him! Redemption from sin and sanctification of the nature go together, and make a peculiar people unto God, free from guilt and condemnation, and purified by the Holy Spirit. All Scripture is profitable. Here is what will furnish for all parts of duty, and the right discharge of them. Let us inquire whether our whole dependence is placed upon that grace which saves the lost, pardons the guilty, and sanctifies the unclean. And the further we are removed from boasting of fancied good works, or trusting in them, so that we glory in Christ alone, the more zealous shall we be to abound in real good works.

Chapter 3

Chapter Outline

Verses 1-7

Spiritual privileges do not make void or weaken, but confirm civil duties. Mere good words and good meanings are not enough without good works. They were not to be quarrelsome, but to show meekness on all occasions, not toward friends only, but to all men, though with wisdom, Jas 3:13. And let this text teach us how wrong it is for a Christian to be churlish to the worst, weakest, and most abject. The servants of sin have many masters, their lusts hurry them different ways; pride commands one thing, covetousness another. Thus they are hateful, deserving to be hated. It is the misery of sinners, that they hate one another; and it is the duty and happiness of saints to love one another. And we are delivered out of our miserable condition, only by the mercy and free grace of God, the merit and sufferings of Christ, and the working of his Spirit. God the Father is God our Saviour. He is the fountain from which the Holy Spirit flows, to teach, regenerate, and save his fallen creatures; and this blessing comes to mankind through Christ. The spring and rise of it, is the kindness and love of God to man. Love and grace have, through the Spirit, great power to change and turn the heart to God. Works must be in the saved, but are not among the causes of their salvation. A new principle of grace and holiness is wrought, which sways, and governs, and makes the man a new creature. Most pretend they would have heaven at last, yet they care not for holiness now; they would have the end without the beginning. Here is the outward sign and seal thereof in baptism, called therefore the washing of regeneration. The work is inward and spiritual; this is outwardly signified and sealed in this ordinance. Slight not this outward sign and seal; yet rest not in the outward washing, but look to the answer of a good conscience, without which the outward washing will avail nothing. The worker therein is the Spirit of God; it is the renewing of the Holy Ghost. Through him we mortify sin, perform duty, walk in God's ways; all the working of the Divine life in us, and the fruits of righteousness without, are through this blessed and holy Spirit. The Spirit and his saving gifts and graces, come through Christ, as a Saviour, whose undertaking and work are to bring to grace and glory. Justification, in the gospel sense, is the free forgiveness of a sinner; accepting him as righteous through the righteousness of Christ received by faith. God, in justifying a sinner in the way of the gospel, is gracious to him, yet just to himself and his law. As forgiveness is through a perfect righteousness, and satisfaction is made to justice by Christ, it cannot be merited by the sinner himself. Eternal life is set before us in the promise; the Spirit works faith in us, and hope of that life; faith and hope bring it near, and fill with joy in expectation of it.

Verses 8-11

When the grace of God towards mankind has been declared, the necessity of good works is pressed. Those who believe in God, must make it their care to maintain good works, to seek opportunities for doing them, being influenced by love and gratitude. Trifling, foolish questions must be avoided, and subtle distinctions and vain inquiries; nor should people be eager after novelties, but love sound doctrine which tends most to edifying. Though we may now think some sins light and little, if the Lord awaken the conscience, we shall feel even the smallest sin heavy upon our souls.

Verses 12-15

Christianity is not a fruitless profession; and its professors must be filled with the fruits of righteousness, which are by Jesus Christ, to the glory and praise of God. They must be doing good, as well as keeping away from evil. Let "ours" follow some honest labour and employment, to provide for themselves and their families. Christianity obliges all to seek some honest work and calling, and therein to abide with God. The apostle concludes with expressions of kind regard and fervent prayer. Grace be with you all; the love and favour of God, with the fruits and effects thereof, according to need; and the increase and feeling of them more and more in your souls. This is the apostle's wish and prayer, showing his affection to them, and desire for their good, and would be a means of obtaining for them, and bringing down on them, the thing requested. Grace is the chief thing to be wished and prayed for, with respect to ourselves or others; it is "all good."

Philemon

Philemon was an inhabitant of Colosse, a person of some note and wealth, and a convert under the ministry of St. Paul. Onesimus was the slave of Philemon: having run away from his master, he went to Rome, where he was converted to the Christian faith, by the word as set forth by Paul, who kept him till his conduct proved the truth and sincerity of his conversion. He wished to repair the injury he had done to his master, but fearing the punishment his offence deserved might be inflicted, he entreated the apostle to write to Philemon. And St. Paul seems no where to reason more beautifully, or to entreat more forcibly, than in this epistle.

Chapter 1

Chapter Outline

The apostle's joy and praise for Philemon's steady faith in the Lord Jesus, and love to all the saints.	(1–7)
He recommends Onesimus as one who would make rich amends for the misconduct of which he had been guilty; and on behalf of whom the apostle promises to make up any loss Philemon had sustained.	(8–22)
Salutations and a blessing.	(23–25)

Verses 1-7

Faith in Christ, and love to him, should unite saints more closely than any outward relation can unite the people of the world. Paul in his private prayers was particular in remembering his friends. We must remember Christian friends much and often, as their cases may need, bearing them in our thoughts, and upon our hearts, before our God. Different sentiments and ways in what is not essential, must not make difference of affection, as to the truth. He inquired concerning his friends, as to the truth, growth, and fruitfulness of their graces, their faith in Christ, and love to him, and to all the saints. The good which Philemon did, was matter of joy and comfort to him and others, who therefore desired that he would continue and abound in good fruits, more and more, to God's honour.

Verses 8-14

It does not lower any one to condescend, and sometimes even to beseech, where, in strictness of right, we might command: the apostle argues from love, rather than authority, in behalf of one converted through his means; and this was Onesimus. In allusion to that name, which signifies "profitable," the apostle allows that in time past he had been unprofitable to Philemon, but hastens to mention the change by which he had become profitable. Unholy persons are unprofitable; they answer not the great end of their being. But what happy changes conversion makes! of evil, good; of unprofitable, useful. Religious servants are treasures in a family. Such will make conscience of their time and trusts, and manage all they can for the best. No prospect of usefulness should lead any to neglect their obligations, or to fail in obedience to superiors. One great evidence of true repentance consists in returning to practise the duties which have been neglected. In his unconverted state, Onesimus had withdrawn, to his master's injury; but now he had seen his sin and repented, he was willing and desirous to return to his duty. Little do men know for what purposes the Lord leaves some to change their situations, or engage in undertakings, perhaps from evil motives. Had not the Lord overruled some of our ungodly projects, we may reflect upon cases, in which our destruction must have been sure.

Verses 15-22

When we speak of the nature of any sin or offence against God, the evil of it is not to be lessened; but in a penitent sinner, as God covers it, so must we. Such changed characters often become a blessing to all among whom they reside. Christianity does not do away our duties to others, but directs to the right doing of them. True penitents will be open in owning their faults, as doubtless Onesimus had been to Paul, upon his being awakened and brought to repentance; especially in cases of injury done to others. The communion of saints does not destroy distinction of property. This passage is an instance of that being imputed to one, which is contracted by another; and of one becoming answerable for another, by a voluntary engagement, that he might be freed from the punishment due to his crimes, according to the doctrine that Christ of his own will bore the punishment of our sins, that we might receive the reward of his righteousness. Philemon was Paul's son in the faith, yet he entreated him as a brother. Onesimus was a poor slave, yet Paul besought for him as if seeking some great thing for himself. Christians should do what may give joy to the hearts of one another. From the world they expect trouble; they should find comfort and joy in one another. When any of our mercies are taken away, our trust and hope must be in God. We must diligently use the means, and if no other should be at hand, abound in prayer. Yet, though prayer prevails, it does not merit the things obtained. And if Christians do not meet on earth, still the grace of the Lord Jesus will be with their spirits, and they will soon meet before the throne to join for ever in admiring the riches of redeeming love. The example of Onesimus may encourage the vilest sinners to return to God, but it is shamefully prevented, if any are made bold thereby to persist in evil courses. Are not many taken away in their sins, while others become more hardened? Resist not present convictions, lest they return no more.

Verses 23-25

Never have believers found more enjoyment of God, than when suffering together for him. Grace is the best wish for ourselves and others; with this the apostle begins and ends. All grace is from Christ; he purchased, and he bestows it. What need we more to make us happy, than to have the grace of our Lord Jesus Christ with our spirit? Let us do that now, which we should do at the last breath. Then men are ready to renounce the world, and to prefer the least portion of grace and faith before a kingdom.

Hebrews

This epistle shows Christ as the end, foundation, body, and truth of the figures of the law, which of themselves were no virtue for the soul. The great truth set forth in this epistle is that Jesus of Nazareth is the true God. The unconverted Jews used many arguments to draw their converted brethren from the Christian faith. They represented the law of Moses as superior to the Christian dispensation, and spoke against every thing connected with the Saviour. The apostle, therefore, shows the superiority of Jesus of Nazareth, as the Son of God, and the benefits from his sufferings and death as the sacrifice for sin, so that the Christian religion is much more excellent and perfect than that of Moses. And the principal design seems to be, to bring the converted Hebrews forward in the knowledge of the gospel, and thus to establish them in the Christian faith, and to prevent their turning from it, against which they are earnestly warned. But while it contains many things suitable to the Hebrews of early times, it also contains many which can never cease to interest the church of God; for the knowledge of Jesus Christ is the very marrow and kernel of all the Scriptures. The ceremonial law is full of Christ, and all the gospel is full of Christ; the blessed lines of both Testaments meet in Him; and how they both agree and sweetly unite in Jesus Christ, is the chief object of the epistle to the Hebrews to discover.

Chapter 1

Chapter Outline

The surpassing dignity of the Son of God in his Divine person, and in his creating and mediatorial work. (1–3)

And in his superiority to all the holy angels. (4–14)

Verses 1-3

God spake to his ancient people at sundry times, through successive generations, and in divers manners, as he thought proper; sometimes by personal directions, sometimes by dreams, sometimes by visions, sometimes by Divine influences on the minds of the prophets. The gospel revelation is excellent above the former; in that it is a revelation which God has made by his Son. In beholding the power, wisdom, and goodness of the Lord Jesus Christ, we behold the power, wisdom, and goodness of the Father, Joh 14:7; the fulness of the Godhead dwells, not typically, or in a figure, but really, in him. When, on the fall of man, the world was breaking to pieces under the wrath and curse of God, the Son of God, undertaking the work of redemption, sustained it by his almighty power and goodness. From the glory of the person and office of Christ, we proceed to the glory of his grace. The glory of His person and nature, gave to his sufferings such merit as was a full satisfaction to the honour of God, who suffered an infinite injury and affront by the sins of men. We never can be thankful enough that God has in so many ways, and with such increasing clearness, spoken to us fallen sinners concerning salvation. That he should by himself cleanse us from our sins is a wonder of love beyond our utmost powers of admiration, gratitude, and praise.

Verses 4-14

Many Jews had a superstitious or idolatrous respect for angels, because they had received the law and other tidings of the Divine will by their ministry. They looked upon them as mediators between God and men, and some went so far as to pay them a kind of religious homage or worship. Thus it was necessary that the apostle should insist, not only on Christ's being the Creator of all things, and therefore of angels themselves, but as being the risen and exalted Messiah in human nature, to whom angels, authorities, and powers are made subject. To prove this, several passages are brought from the Old Testament. On comparing what God there says of the angels, with what he says to Christ, the inferiority of the angels to Christ plainly appears. Here is the office of the angels; they are God's ministers or servants, to do his pleasure. But, how much greater things are said of Christ by the Father! And let us own and honour him as God; for if he had not been God, he had never done the Mediator's work, and had never worn the Mediator's crown. It is declared how Christ was qualified for the office of Mediator, and how he was confirmed in it: he has the name Messiah from his being anointed. Only as Man he has his fellows, and as anointed with the Holy Spirit; but he is above all prophets, priests, and kings, that ever were employed in the service of God on earth. Another passage of Scripture, Ps 102:25–27, is recited, in which the Almighty power of the Lord Jesus Christ is declared, both in creating the world and in changing it. Christ will fold up this world as a garment, not to be abused any longer, not to be used as it has been. As a sovereign, when his garments of state are folded and put away, is a sovereign still, so our Lord, when he has laid aside the earth and heavens like a vesture, shall be still the same. Let us not then set our hearts upon that which is not what we take it to be, and will not be what it now is. Sin has made a great change in the world for the worse, and Christ will make a great change in it for the better. Let the thoughts of this make us watchful, diligent, and desirous of that better world. The Saviour has done much to make all men his friends, yet he has enemies. But they shall be made his footstool, by humble submission, or by utter destruction. Christ shall go on conquering and to conquer. The most exalted angels are but ministering spirits, mere servants of Christ, to execute his commands. The saints, at present, are heirs, not yet come into possession. The angels minister to them in opposing the malice and power of evil spirits, in protecting and keeping their bodies, instructing and comforting their souls, under Christ and the Holy Ghost. Angels shall gather all the saints together at the last day, when all whose hearts and hopes are set upon perishing treasures and fading glories, will be driven from Christ's presence into everlasting misery.

Chapter 2

Chapter Outline

The reason of his sufferings, and the fitness   (10–13)
of them.

Christ's taking the nature of man, and not   (14–18)
his taking the nature of angels, was necessary
to his priestly office.

Verses 1-4

Christ being proved to be superior to the angels, this doctrine is applied. Our minds and memories are like a leaky vessel, they do not, without much care, retain what is poured into them. This proceeds from the corruption of our nature, temptations, worldly cares, and pleasures. Sinning against the gospel is neglect of this great salvation; it is a contempt of the saving grace of God in Christ, making light of it, not caring for it, not regarding either the worth of gospel grace, or the want of it, and our undone state without it. The Lord's judgments under the gospel dispensation are chiefly spiritual, but are on that account the more to be dreaded. Here is an appeal to the consciences of sinners. Even partial neglects will not escape rebukes; they often bring darkness on the souls they do not finally ruin. The setting forth the gospel was continued and confirmed by those who heard Christ, by the evangelists and apostles, who were witnesses of what Jesus Christ began both to do and to teach; and by the gifts of the Holy Ghost, qualified for the work to which they were called. And all this according to God's own will. It was the will of God that we should have sure ground for our faith, and a strong foundation for our hope in receiving the gospel. Let us mind this one thing needful, and attend to the Holy Scriptures, written by those who heard the words of our gracious Lord, and were inspired by his Spirit; then we shall be blessed with the good part that cannot be taken away.

Verses 5-9

Neither the state in which the church is at present, nor its more completely restored state, when the prince of this world shall be cast out, and the kingdoms of the earth become the kingdom of Christ, is left to the government of the angels: Christ will take to him his great power, and will reign. And what is the moving cause of all the kindness God shows to men in giving Christ for them and to them? it is the grace of God. As a reward of Christ's humiliation in suffering death, he has unlimited dominion over all things; thus this ancient scripture was fulfilled in him. Thus God has done wonderful things for us in creation and providence, but for these we have made the basest returns.

Verses 10-13

Whatever the proud, carnal, and unbelieving may imagine or object, the spiritual mind will see peculiar glory in the cross of Christ, and be satisfied that it became Him, who in all things displays his own perfections in bringing many sons to glory, to make the Author of their salvation perfect through sufferings. His way to the crown was by the cross, and so must that of his people be. Christ sanctifies; he has purchased and sent the sanctifying Spirit: the Spirit sanctifies as the Spirit of Christ. True believers are sanctified, endowed with holy principles and powers, set apart to high and holy uses and purposes. Christ and believers are all of one heavenly Father, who is God. They are brought into relation with Christ. But the words, his not being ashamed to call them brethren, express the high superiority of Christ to the human nature. This is shown from three texts of Scripture. See Ps 22:22; 18:2; Isa 8:18.

Verses 14-18

The angels fell, and remained without hope or help. Christ never designed to be the Saviour of the fallen angels, therefore he did not take their nature; and the nature of angels could not be an atoning sacrifice for the sin of man. Here is a price paid, enough for all, and suitable to all, for it was in our nature. Here the wonderful love of God appeared, that, when Christ knew what he must suffer in our nature, and how he must die in it, yet he readily took it upon him. And this atonement made way for his people's deliverance from Satan's bondage, and for the pardon of their sins through faith. Let those who dread death, and strive to get the better of their terrors, no longer attempt to outbrave or to stifle them, no longer grow careless or wicked through despair. Let them not expect help from the world, or human devices; but let them seek pardon, peace, grace, and a lively hope of heaven, by faith in Him who died and rose again, that thus they may rise above the fear of death. The remembrance of his own sorrows and temptations, makes Christ mindful of the trials of his people, and ready to help them. He is ready and willing to succour those who are tempted, and seek him. He became man, and was tempted, that he might be every way qualified to succour his people, seeing that he had passed through the same temptations himself, but continued perfectly free from sin. Then let not the afflicted and tempted despond, or give place to Satan, as if temptations made it wrong for them to come to the Lord in prayer. Not soul ever perished under temptation, that cried unto the Lord from real alarm at its danger, with faith and expectation of relief. This is our duty upon our first being surprised by temptations, and would stop their progress, which is our wisdom.

Chapter 3

Chapter Outline

Verses 1-6

Christ is to be considered as the Apostle of our profession, the Messenger sent by God to men, the great Revealer of that faith which we profess to hold, and of that hope which we profess to have. As Christ, the Messiah, anointed for the office both of Apostle and High Priest. As Jesus, our

Saviour, our Healer, the great Physician of souls. Consider him thus. Consider what he is in himself, what he is to us, and what he will be to us hereafter and for ever. Close and serious thoughts of Christ bring us to know more of him. The Jews had a high opinion of the faithfulness of Moses, yet his faithfulness was but a type of Christ's. Christ was the Master of this house, of his church, his people, as well as their Maker. Moses was a faithful servant; Christ, as the eternal Son of God, is rightful Owner and Sovereign Ruler of the Church. There must not only be setting out well in the ways of Christ, but stedfastness and perseverance therein to the end. Every meditation on his person and his salvation, will suggest more wisdom, new motives to love, confidence, and obedience.

Verses 7-13

Days of temptation are often days of provocation. But to provoke God, when he is letting us see that we entirely depend and live upon him, is a provocation indeed. The hardening of the heart is the spring of all other sins. The sins of others, especially of our relations, should be warnings to us. All sin, especially sin committed by God's professing, privileged people, not only provokes God, but it grieves him. God is loth to destroy any in, or for their sin; he waits long to be gracious to them. But sin, long persisted in, will make God's wrath discover itself in destroying the impenitent; there is no resting under the wrath of God. "Take heed:" all who would get safe to heaven must look about them; if once we allow ourselves to distrust God, we may soon desert him. Let those that think they stand, take heed lest they fall. Since to-morrow is not ours, we must make the best improvement of this day. And there are none, even the strongest of the flock, who do not need help of other Christians. Neither are there any so low and despised, but the care of their standing in the faith, and of their safety, belongs to all. Sin has so many ways and colours, that we need more eyes than ours own. Sin appears fair, but is vile; it appears pleasant, but is destructive; it promises much, but performs nothing. The deceitfulness of sin hardens the soul; one sin allowed makes way for another; and every act of sin confirms the habit. Let every one beware of sin.

Verses 14-19

The saints' privilege is, they are made partakers of Christ, that is, of the Spirit, the nature, graces, righteousness, and life of Christ; they are interested in all Christ is, in all he has done, or will do. The same spirit with which Christians set out in the ways of God, they should maintain unto the end. Perseverance in faith is the best evidence of the sincerity of our faith. Hearing the word often is a means of salvation, yet, if not hearkened to, it will expose more to the Divine wrath. The happiness of being partakers of Christ and his complete salvation, and the fear of God's wrath and eternal misery, should stir us up to persevere in the life of obedient faith. Let us beware of trusting to outward privileges or professions, and pray to be numbered with the true believers who enter heaven, when all others fail because of unbelief. As our obedience follows according to the power of our faith, so our sins and want of care are according to the prevailing of unbelief in us.

Chapter 4

Chapter Outline

Humble, cautious fear is urged, lest any   (1–10)
should come short of the promised rest,
through unbelief.

Arguments and motives to faith and hope   (11–16)
in our approaches to God.

Verses 1-10

The privileges we have under the gospel, are greater than any had under the law of Moses, though the same gospel for substance was preached under both Testaments. There have been in all ages many unprofitable hearers; and unbelief is at the root of all unfruitfulness under the word. Faith in the hearer is the life of the word. But it is a painful consequence of partial neglect, and of a loose and wavering profession, that they often cause men to seem to come short. Let us then give diligence, that we may have a clear entrance into the kingdom of God. As God finished his work, and then rested from it, so he will cause those who believe, to finish their work, and then to enjoy their rest. It is evident, that there is a more spiritual and excellent sabbath remaining for the people of God, than that of the seventh day, or that into which Joshua led the Jews. This rest is, a rest of grace, and comfort, and holiness, in the gospel state. And a rest in glory, where the people of God shall enjoy the end of their faith, and the object of all their desires. The rest, or sabbatism, which is the subject of the apostle's reasoning, and as to which he concludes that it remains to be enjoyed, is undoubtedly the heavenly rest, which remains to the people of God, and is opposed to a state of labour and trouble in this world. It is the rest they shall obtain when the Lord Jesus shall appear from heaven. But those who do not believe, shall never enter into this spiritual rest, either of grace here or glory hereafter. God has always declared man's rest to be in him, and his love to be the only real happiness of the soul; and faith in his promises, through his Son, to be the only way of entering that rest.

Verses 11-16

Observe the end proposed: rest spiritual and eternal; the rest of grace here, and glory hereafter; in Christ on earth, with Christ in heaven. After due and diligent labour, sweet and satisfying rest shall follow; and labour now, will make that rest more pleasant when it comes. Let us labour, and quicken each other to be diligent in duty. The Holy Scriptures are the word of God. When God sets it home by his Spirit, it convinces powerfully, converts powerfully, and comforts powerfully. It makes a soul that has long been proud, to be humble; and a perverse spirit, to be meek and obedient. Sinful habits, that are become as it were natural to the soul, and rooted deeply in it, are separated and cut off by this sword. It will discover to men their thoughts and purposes, the vileness of many, the bad principles they are moved by, the sinful ends they act to. The word will show the sinner all that is in his heart. Let us hold fast the doctrines of Christian faith in our heads, its enlivening principles in our hearts, the open profession of it in our lips, and be subject to it in our lives. Christ executed one part of his priesthood on earth, in dying for us; the other he executes in heaven, pleading the cause, and presenting the offerings of his people. In the sight of Infinite Wisdom, it was needful that the Saviour of men should be one who has the fellow-feeling which no being but a fellow-creature could possibly have; and therefore it was necessary he should actual experience of all the effects of sin that could be separated from its actual guilt. God sent his own Son in the likeness of sinful flesh, Ro 8:3; but the more holy and pure he was, the more he must have been unwilling in his nature to sin, and must have had deeper impression of its evil; consequently the more must he be concerned to deliver his people from its guilt and power. We should encourage ourselves by the excellence of our High Priest, to come boldly to the throne of grace. Mercy and grace are the things we want; mercy to pardon all our sins, and grace to purify our souls. Besides our daily dependence upon God for present supplies, there are seasons for which we should provide in our prayers; times of temptation, either by adversity or prosperity, and especially our dying time. We are to come with reverence and godly fear, yet not as if dragged to the seat of justice, but as kindly invited to the mercy-seat, where grace reigns. We have boldness to enter into the holiest only by the blood of Jesus; he is our Advocate, and has purchased all our souls want or can desire.

Chapter 5

Chapter Outline

Verses 1-10

The High Priest must be a man, a partaker of our nature. This shows that man had sinned. For God would not suffer sinful man to come to him alone. But every one is welcome to God, that comes to him by this High Priest; and as we value acceptance with God, and pardon, we must apply by faith to this our great High Priest Christ Jesus, who can intercede for those that are out of the way of truth, duty, and happiness; one who has tenderness to lead them back from the by-paths of error, sin, and misery. Those only can expect assistance from God, and acceptance with him, and his presence and blessing on them and their services, that are called of God. This is applied to Christ. In the days of his flesh, Christ made himself subject to death: he hungered: he was a tempted, suffering, dying Jesus. Christ set an example, not only to pray, but to be fervent in prayer. How many dry prayers, how few wetted with tears, do we offer up to God! He was strengthened to support the immense weight of suffering laid upon him. There is no real deliverance from death but to be carried through it. He was raised and exalted, and to him was given the power of saving all sinners to the uttermost, who come unto God through him. Christ has left us an example that we should learn humble obedience to the will of God, by all our afflictions. We need affliction, to teach us submission. His obedience in our nature encourages our attempts to obey, and for us to expect support and comfort under all the temptations and sufferings to which we are exposed. Being made perfect for this great work, he is become the Author of eternal salvation to all that obey him. But are we of that number?

Verses 11-14

Dull hearers make the preaching of the gospel difficult, and even those who have some faith may be dull hearers, and slow to believe. Much is looked for from those to whom much is given. To be unskilful, denotes want of experience in the things of the gospel. Christian experience is a spiritual sense, taste, or relish of the goodness, sweetness, and excellence of the truths of the gospel. And no tongue can express the satisfaction which the soul receives, from a sense of Divine goodness, grace, and love to it in Christ.

Chapter 6

Chapter Outline

The Hebrews are urged to go forward in the doctrine of Christ, and the consequences of apostasy, or turning back, are described.	(1–8)
The apostle expresses satisfaction, as to the most of them.	(9, 10)
And encourages them to persevere in faith and holiness.	(11–20)

Verses 1-8

Every part of the truth and will of God should be set before all who profess the gospel, and be urged on their hearts and consciences. We should not be always speaking about outward things; these have their places and use, but often take up too much attention and time, which might be better employed. The humbled sinner who pleads guilty, and cries for mercy, can have no ground from this passage to be discouraged, whatever his conscience may accuse him of. Nor does it prove that any one who is made a new creature in Christ, ever becomes a final apostate from him. The apostle is not speaking of the falling away of mere professors, never convinced or influenced by the gospel. Such have nothing to fall away from, but an empty name, or hypocritical profession. Neither is he speaking of partial declinings or backslidings. Nor are such sins meant, as Christians fall into through the strength of temptations, or the power of some worldly or fleshly lust. But the falling away here mentioned, is an open and avowed renouncing of Christ, from enmity of heart against him, his cause, and people, by men approving in their minds the deeds of his murderers, and all this after they have received the knowledge of the truth, and tasted some of its comforts. Of these it is said, that it is impossible to renew them again unto repentance. Not because the blood of Christ is not sufficient to obtain pardon for this sin; but this sin, in its very nature, is opposite to repentance and every thing that leads to it. If those who through mistaken views of this passage, as well as of their own case, fear that there is no mercy for them, would attend to the account given of the nature of this sin, that it is a total and a willing renouncing of Christ, and his cause, and joining with his enemies, it would relieve them from wrong fears. We should ourselves beware, and caution others, of every approach near to a gulf so awful as apostacy; yet in doing this we should keep close to the word of God, and be careful not to wound and terrify the weak, or discourage the fallen and penitent. Believers not only taste of the word of God, but they drink it in. And this fruitful field or garden receives the blessing. But the merely nominal Christian, continuing unfruitful under the means of grace, or producing nothing but deceit and selfishness, was near the awful state above described; and everlasting misery was the end reserved for him. Let us watch with humble caution and prayer as to ourselves.

Verses 9, 10

There are things that are never separated from salvation; things that show the person to be in a state of salvation, and which will end in eternal salvation. And the things that accompany salvation, are better things than ever any dissembler or apostate enjoyed. The works of love, done for the glory of Christ, or done to his saints for Christ's sake, from time to time, as God gives occasion, are evident marks of a man's salvation; and more sure tokens of saving grace given, than the enlightenings and tastings spoken of before. No love is to be reckoned as love, but working love; and no works are right works, which flow not from love to Christ.

Verses 11-20

The hope here meant, is a sure looking for good things promised, through those promises, with love, desire, and valuing of them. Hope has its degrees, as faith also. The promise of blessedness God has made to believers, is from God's eternal purpose, settled between the eternal Father, Son, and Spirit. These promises of God may safely be depended upon; for here we have two things which cannot change, the counsel and the oath of God, in which it is not possible for God to lie; it would be contrary to his nature as well as to his will. And as He cannot lie; the destruction of the unbeliever, and the salvation of the believer, are alike certain. Here observe, those to whom God has given full security of happiness, have a title to the promises by inheritance. The consolations of God are strong enough to support his people under their heaviest trials. Here is a refuge for all sinners who flee to the mercy of God, through the redemption of Christ, according to the covenant of grace, laying aside all other confidences. We are in this world as a ship at sea, tossed up and down, and in danger of being cast away. We need an anchor to keep us sure and steady. Gospel hope is our anchor in the storms of this world. It is sure and stedfast, or it could not keep us so. The free grace of God, the merits and mediation of Christ, and the powerful influences of his Spirit, are the grounds of this hope, and so it is a stedfast hope. Christ is the object and ground of the believer's hope. Let us therefore set our affections on things above, and wait patiently for his appearance, when we shall certainly appear with him in glory.

Chapter 7

Chapter Outline

Verses 1-3

Melchizedec met Abraham when returning from the rescue of Lot. His name, "King of Righteousness," doubtless suitable to his character, marked him as a type of the Messiah and his kingdom. The name of his city signified "Peace;" and as king of peace he typified Christ, the Prince of Peace, the great Reconciler of God and man. Nothing is recorded as to the beginning or end of his life; thus he typically resembled the Son of God, whose existence is from everlasting to everlasting, who had no one that was before him, and will have no one come after him, in his priesthood. Every part of Scripture honours the great King of Righteousness and Peace, our glorious High Priest and Saviour; and the more we examine it, the more we shall be convinced, that the testimony of Jesus is the spirit of prophecy.

Verses 4-10

That High Priest who should afterward appear, of whom Melchizedec was a type, must be much superior to the Levitical priests. Observe Abraham's great dignity and happiness; that he had the promises. That man is rich and happy indeed, who has the promises, both of the life that now is, and of that which is to come. This honour have all those who receive the Lord Jesus. Let us go forth in our spiritual conflicts, trusting in his word and strength, ascribing our victories to his grace, and desiring to be met and blessed by him in all our ways.

Verses 11-25

The priesthood and law by which perfection could not come, are done away; a Priest is risen, and a dispensation now set up, by which true believers may be made perfect. That there is such a change is plain. The law which made the Levitical priesthood, showed that the priests were frail, dying creatures, not able to save their own lives, much less could they save the souls of those who came to them. But the High Priest of our profession holds his office by the power of endless life in himself; not only to keep himself alive, but to give spiritual and eternal life to all who rely upon his sacrifice and intercession. The better covenant, of which Jesus was the Surety, is not here contrasted with the covenant of works, by which every transgressor is shut up under the curse. It is distinguished from the Sinai covenant with Israel, and the legal dispensation under which the church so long remained. The better covenant brought the church and every believer into clearer light, more perfect liberty, and more abundant privileges. In the order of Aaron there was a multitude of priests, of high priests one after another; but in the priesthood of Christ there is only one and the same. This is the believer's safety and happiness, that this everlasting High Priest is able to save to the uttermost, in all times, in all cases. Surely then it becomes us to desire a spirituality and holiness, as much beyond those of the Old Testament believers, as our advantages exceed theirs.

Verses 26-28

Observe the description of the personal holiness of Christ. He is free from all habits or principles of sin, not having the least disposition to it in his nature. No sin dwells in him, not the least sinful inclination, though such dwells in the best of Christians. He is harmless, free from all actual transgression; he did no violence, nor was there any deceit in his mouth. He is undefiled. It is hard to keep ourselves pure, so as not to partake the guilt of other men's sins. But none need be dismayed who come to God in the name of his beloved Son. Let them be assured that he will deliver them in the time of trial and suffering, in the time of prosperity, in the hour of death, and in the day of judgment.

Chapter 8

Chapter Outline

The excellence of Christ's priesthood above that of Aaron is shown.	(1–6)
The great excellence of the new covenant above the former.	(7–13)

Verses 1-6

The substance, or summary, of what had been declared was, that Christians had such a High Priest as they needed. He took upon himself human nature, appeared on earth, and there gave himself as a sacrifice to God for the sins of his people. We must not dare to approach God, or to present any thing to him, but in and through Christ, depending upon his merits and mediation; for we are accepted only in the Beloved. In all obedience and worship, we should keep close to God's word, which is the only and perfect standard. Christ is the substance and end of the law of righteousness. But the covenant here referred to, was that made with Israel as a nation, securing temporal benefits to them. The promises of all spiritual blessings, and of eternal life, revealed in the gospel, and made sure through Christ, are of infinitely greater value. Let us bless God that we have a High Priest that suits our helpless condition.

Verses 7-13

The superior excellence of the priesthood of Christ, above that of Aaron, is shown from that covenant of grace, of which Christ was Mediator. The law not only made all subject to it, liable to be condemned for the guilt of sin, but also was unable to remove that guilt, and clear the conscience from the sense and terror of it. Whereas, by the blood of Christ, a full remission of sins was provided, so that God would remember them no more. God once wrote his laws to his people, now he will write his laws in them; he will give them understanding to know and to believe his laws; he will give them memories to retain them; he will give them hearts to love them, courage to profess them, and power to put them in practice. This is the foundation of the covenant; and when this is laid, duty will be done wisely, sincerely, readily, easily, resolutely, constantly, and with comfort. A plentiful outpouring of the Spirit of God will make the ministration of the gospel so effectual, that there shall be a mighty increase and spreading of Christian knowledge in persons of all sorts. Oh that this promise might be fulfilled in our days, that the hand of God may be with his ministers so that great numbers may believe, and be turned to the Lord! The pardon of sin will always be found to accompany the true knowledge of God. Notice the freeness of this pardon; its fulness; its fixedness. This pardoning mercy is connected with all other spiritual mercies: unpardoned sin hinders mercy, and pulls down judgments; but the pardon of sin prevents judgment, and opens a wide door to all spiritual blessings. Let us search whether we are taught by the Holy Spirit to know Christ, so as uprightly to love, fear, trust, and obey him. All worldly vanities, outward privileges, or mere notions of religion, will soon vanish away, and leave those who trust in them miserable for ever.

Chapter 9

Chapter Outline

Verses 1-5

The apostle shows to the Hebrews the typical reference of their ceremonies to Christ. The tabernacle was a movable temple, shadowing forth the unsettled state of the church upon earth, and the human nature of the Lord Jesus Christ, in whom the fulness of the Godhead dwelt bodily. The typical meaning of these things has been shown in former remarks, and the ordinances and articles of the Mosaic covenant point out Christ as our Light, and as the Bread of life to our souls; and remind us of his Divine Person, his holy priesthood, perfect righteousness, and all-prevailing intercession. Thus was the Lord Jesus Christ, all and in all, from the beginning. And as interpreted by the gospel, these things are a glorious representation of the wisdom of God, and confirm faith in Him who was prefigured by them.

Verses 6-10

The apostle goes on to speak of the Old Testament services. Christ, having undertaken to be our High Priest, could not enter into heaven till he had shed his blood for us; and none of us can enter, either into God's gracious presence here, or his glorious presence hereafter, but by the blood of Jesus. Sins are errors, great errors, both in judgment and practice; and who can understand all his errors? They leave guilt upon the conscience, not to be washed away but by the blood of Christ. We must plead this blood on earth, while he is pleading it for us in heaven. A few believers, under the Divine teaching, saw something of the way of access to God, of communion with him, and of admission into heaven through the promised Redeemer, but the Israelites in general looked no further than the outward forms. These could not take away the defilement or dominion of sin. They could neither discharge the debts, nor resolve the doubts, of him who did the service. Gospel times are, and should be, times of reformation, of clearer light as to all things needful to be known, and of greater love, causing us to bear ill-will to none, but good-will to all. We have greater freedom, both of spirit and speech, in the gospel, and greater obligations to a more holy living.

Verses 11-14

All good things past, present, and to come, were and are founded upon the priestly office of Christ, and come to us from thence. Our High Priest entered into heaven once for all, and has obtained eternal redemption. The Holy Ghost further signified and showed that the Old Testament sacrifices only freed the outward man from ceremonial uncleanness, and fitted him for some outward privileges. What gave such power to the blood of Christ? It was Christ's offering himself without any sinful stain in his nature or life. This cleanses the most guilty conscience from dead, or deadly, works to serve the living God; from sinful works, such as pollute the soul, as dead bodies did the persons of the Jews who touched them; while the grace that seals pardon, new-creates the polluted soul. Nothing more destroys the faith of the gospel, than by any means to weaken the direct power of the blood of Christ. The depth of the mystery of the sacrifice of Christ, we cannot dive into, the height we cannot comprehend. We cannot search out the greatness of it, or the wisdom, the love, the grace that is in it. But in considering the sacrifice of Christ, faith finds life, food, and refreshment.

Verses 15-22

The solemn transactions between God and man, are sometimes called a covenant, here a testament, which is a willing deed of a person, bestowing legacies on such persons as are described, and it only takes effect upon his death. Thus Christ died, not only to obtain the blessings of salvation for us, but to give power to the disposal of them. All, by sin, were become guilty before God, had forfeited every thing that is good; but God, willing to show the greatness of his mercy, proclaimed a covenant of grace. Nothing could be clean to a sinner, not even his religious duties; except as his guilt was done away by the death of a sacrifice, of value sufficient for that end, and unless he continually depended upon it. May we ascribe all real good works to the same all-procuring cause, and offer our spiritual sacrifices as sprinkled with Christ's blood, and so purified from their defilement.

Verses 23-28

It is evident that the sacrifices of Christ are infinitely better than those of the law, which could neither procure pardon for sin, nor impart power against it. Sin would still have been upon us, and have had dominion over us; but Jesus Christ, by one sacrifice, has destroyed the works of the devil, that believers may be made righteous, holy, and happy. As no wisdom, learning, virtue, wealth, or power, can keep one of the human race from death, so nothing can deliver a sinner from being condemned at the day of judgment, except the atoning sacrifice of Christ; nor will one be saved from eternal punishment who despises or neglects this great salvation. The believer knows that his Redeemer liveth, and that he shall see him. Here is the faith and patience of the church, of all sincere believers. Hence is their continual prayer as the fruit and expression of their faith, Even so come, Lord Jesus.

Chapter 10

Chapter Outline

The insufficiency of sacrifices for taking away sin, The necessity and power of the sacrifice of Christ for that purpose. (1–18)

An argument for holy boldness in the believer's access to God through Jesus Christ, And for steadfastness in faith, and mutual love and duty. (19–25)

The danger of apostasy. (26–31)

The sufferings of believers, and encouragement to maintain their holy profession. (32–39)

Verses 1-10

The apostle having shown that the tabernacle, and ordinances of the covenant of Sinai, were only emblems and types of the gospel, concludes that the sacrifices the high priests offered continually, could not make the worshippers perfect, with respect to pardon, and the purifying of their consciences. But when "God manifested in the flesh," became the sacrifice, and his death upon the accursed tree the ransom, then the Sufferer being of infinite worth, his free-will sufferings were of infinite value. The atoning sacrifice must be one capable of consenting, and must of his own will place himself in the sinner's stead: Christ did so. The fountain of all that Christ has done for his people, is the sovereign will and grace of God. The righteousness brought in, and the sacrifice once offered by Christ, are of eternal power, and his salvation shall never be done away. They are of power to make all the comers thereunto perfect; they derive from the atoning blood, strength and motives for obedience, and inward comfort.

Verses 11-18

Under the new covenant, or gospel dispensation, full and final pardon is to be had. This makes a vast difference between the new covenant and the old one. Under the old, sacrifices must be often repeated, and after all, only pardon as to this world was to be obtained by them. Under the new, one Sacrifice is enough to procure for all nations and ages, spiritual pardon, or being freed from punishment in the world to come. Well might this be called a new covenant. Let none suppose that human inventions can avail those who put them in the place of the sacrifice of the Son of God. What then remains, but that we seek an interest in this Sacrifice by faith; and the seal of it to our souls, by the sanctification of the Spirit unto obedience? So that by the law being written in our hearts, we may know that we are justified, and that God will no more remember our sins.

Verses 19-25

The apostle having closed the first part of the epistle, the doctrine is applied to practical purposes. As believers had an open way to the presence of God, it became them to use this privilege. The way and means by which Christians enjoy such privileges, is by the blood of Jesus, by the merit of that blood which he offered up as an atoning sacrifice. The agreement of infinite holiness with pardoning mercy, was not clearly understood till the human nature of Christ, the Son of God, was wounded and bruised for our sins. Our way to heaven is by a crucified Saviour; his death is to us the way of life, and to those who believe this, he will be precious. They must draw near to God; it would be contempt of Christ, still to keep at a distance. Their bodies were to be washed with pure water, alluding to the cleansings directed under the law: thus the use of water in baptism, was to remind Christians that their conduct should be pure and holy. While they derived comfort and grace from their reconciled Father to their own souls, they would adorn the doctrine of God their Saviour in all things. Believers are to consider how they can be of service to each other, especially stirring up each other to the more vigorous and abundant exercise of love, and the practice of good works. The communion of saints is a great help and privilege, and a means of stedfastness and perseverance. We should observe the coming of times of trial, and be thereby quickened to greater diligence. There is a trying day coming on all men, the day of our death.

Verses 26-31

The exhortations against apostacy and to perseverance, are urged by many strong reasons. The sin here mentioned is a total and final falling away, when men, with a full and fixed will and resolution, despise and reject Christ, the only Saviour; despise and resist the Spirit, the only Sanctifier; and despise and renounce the gospel, the only way of salvation, and the words of eternal life. Of this destruction God gives some notorious sinners, while on earth, a fearful foreboding in their consciences, with despair of being able to endure or to escape it. But what punishment can be sorer than to die without mercy? We answer, to die by mercy, by the mercy and grace which they have despised. How dreadful is the case, when not only the justice of God, but his abused grace and mercy call for vengeance! All this does not in the least mean that any souls who sorrow for sin will be shut out from mercy, or that any will be refused the benefit of Christ's sacrifice, who are willing to accept these blessings. Him that cometh unto Christ, he will in no wise cast out.

Verses 32-39

Many and various afflictions united against the early Christians, and they had a great conflict. The Christian spirit is not a selfish spirit; it puts us upon pitying others, visiting them, helping them, and pleading for them. All things here are but shadows. The happiness of the saints in heaven will last for ever; enemies can never take it away as earthly goods. This will make rich amends for all we may lose and suffer here. The greatest part of the saints' happiness, as yet, is in promise. It is a trial of the patience of Christians, to be content to live after their work is done, and to stay for their reward till God's time to give it is come. He will soon come to them at death, to end all their sufferings, and to give them a crown of life. The Christian's present conflict may be sharp, but will be soon over. God never is pleased with the formal profession and outward duties and services of such as do not persevere; but he beholds them with great displeasure. And those who have been kept faithful in great trails for the time past, have reason to hope for the same grace to help them still to live by faith, till they receive the end of their faith and patience, even the salvation of their souls. Living by faith, and dying in faith, our souls are safe for ever.

Chapter 11

Chapter Outline

The nature and power of faith described.	(1–3)
It is set forth by instances from Abel to Noah.	(4–7)
By Abraham and his descendants.	(8–19)
By Jacob, Joseph, Moses, the Israelites, and Rahab.	(20–31)
By other Old Testament believers.	(32–38)
The better state of believers under the gospel.	(39, 40)

Verses 1-3

Faith always has been the mark of God's servants, from the beginning of the world. Where the principle is planted by the regenerating Spirit of God, it will cause the truth to be received, concerning justification by the sufferings and merits of Christ. And the same things that are the object of our hope, are the object of our faith. It is a firm persuasion and expectation, that God will perform all he has promised to us in Christ. This persuasion gives the soul to enjoy those things now; it gives them a subsistence or reality in the soul, by the first-fruits and foretastes of them. Faith proves to the mind, the reality of things that cannot be seen by the bodily eye. It is a full approval of all God has revealed, as holy, just, and good. This view of faith is explained by many examples of persons in former times, who obtained a good report, or an honourable character in the word of God. Faith was the principle of their holy obedience, remarkable services, and patient sufferings. The Bible gives the most true and exact account of the origin of all things, and we are to believe it, and not to wrest the Scripture account of the creation, because it does not suit with the differing fancies of men. All that we see of the works of creation, were brought into being by the command of God.

Verses 4-7

Here follow some illustrious examples of faith from the Old Testament. Abel brought a sacrifice of atonement from the firstlings of the flock, acknowledging himself a sinner who deserved to die, and only hoping for mercy through the great Sacrifice. Cain's proud rage and enmity against the accepted worshipper of God, led to the awful effects the same principles have produced in every age; the cruel persecution, and even murder of believers. By faith Abel, being dead, yet speaketh; he left an instructive and speaking example. Enoch was translated, or removed, that he should not see death; God took him into heaven, as Christ will do the saints who shall be alive at his second coming. We cannot come to God, unless we believe that he is what he has revealed himself to be in the Scripture. Those who would find God, must seek him with all their heart. Noah's faith influenced his practice; it moved him to prepare an ark. His faith condemned the unbelief of others; and his obedience condemned their contempt and rebellion. Good examples either convert sinners or condemn them. This shows how believers, being warned of God to flee from the wrath to come, are moved with fear, take refuge in Christ, and become heirs of the righteousness of faith.

Verses 8-19

We are often called to leave worldly connexions, interests, and comforts. If heirs of Abraham's faith, we shall obey and go forth, though not knowing what may befall us; and we shall be found in the way of duty, looking for the performance of God's promises. The trial of Abraham's faith was, that he simply and fully obeyed the call of God. Sarah received the promise as the promise of God; being convinced of that, she truly judged that he both could and would perform it. Many, who have a part in the promises, do not soon receive the things promised. Faith can lay hold of blessings at a great distance; can make them present; can love them and rejoice in them, though strangers; as saints, whose home is heaven; as pilgrims, travelling toward their home. By faith, they overcome the terrors of death, and bid a cheerful farewell to this world, and to all the comforts and crosses of it. And those once truly and savingly called out of a sinful state, have no mind to return into it. All true believers desire the heavenly inheritance; and the stronger faith is, the more fervent those desires will be. Notwithstanding their meanness by nature, their vileness by sin, and the poverty of their outward condition, God is not ashamed to be called the God of all true believers; such is his mercy, such is his love to them. Let them never be ashamed of being called his people, nor of any of those who are truly so, how much soever despised in the world. Above all, let them take care that they are not a shame and reproach to their God. The greatest trial and act of faith upon record is, Abraham's offering up Isaac, Ge 22:2. There, every word shows a trial. It is our duty to reason down our doubts and fears, by looking, as Abraham did, to the Almighty power of God. The best way to enjoy our comforts is, to give them up to God; he will then again give them as shall be the best for us. Let us look how far our faith has caused the like obedience, when we have been called to lesser acts of self-denial, or to make smaller sacrifices to our duty. Have we given up what was called for, fully believing that the Lord would make up all our losses, and even bless us by the most afflicting dispensations?

Verses 20-31

Isaac blessed Jacob and Esau, concerning things to come. Things present are not the best things; no man knoweth love or hatred by having them or wanting them. Jacob lived by faith, and he died by faith, and in faith. Though the grace of faith is of use always through our whole lives, it is especially so when we come to die. Faith has a great work to do at last, to help the believer to die to the Lord, so as to honour him, by patience, hope, and joy. Joseph was tried by temptations to sin, by persecution for keeping his integrity; and he was tried by honours and power in the court of Pharaoh, yet his faith carried him through. It is a great mercy to be free from wicked laws and edicts; but when we are not so, we must use all lawful means for our security. In this faith of Moses' parents there was a mixture of unbelief, but God was pleased to overlook it. Faith gives strength against the sinful, slavish fear of men; it sets God before the soul, shows the vanity of the creature, and that all must give way to the will and power of God. The pleasures of sin are, and will be, but short; they must end either in speedy repentance or in speedy ruin. The pleasures of this world are for the most part the pleasures of sin; they are always so when we cannot enjoy them without deserting God and his people. Suffering is to be chosen rather than sin; there being more evil in the least sin, than there can be in the greatest suffering. God's people are, and always have been, a reproached people. Christ accounts himself reproached in their reproaches; and thus they become greater riches than the treasures of the richest empire in the world. Moses made his choice when ripe for judgment and enjoyment, able to know what he did, and why he did it. It is needful for persons to be seriously religious; to despise the world, when most capable of relishing and enjoying it. Believers may and ought to have respect to the recompence of reward. By faith we may be fully sure of God's providence, and of his gracious and powerful presence with us. Such a sight of God will enable believers to keep on to the end, whatever they may meet in the way. It is not owing to our own righteousness, or best performances, that we are saved from the wrath of God; but to the blood of Christ, and his imputed righteousness. True faith makes sin bitter to the soul, even while it receives the pardon and atonement. All our spiritual privileges on earth, should quicken us in our way to heaven. The Lord will make even Babylon fall before the faith of his people, and when he has some great thing to do for them, he raises up great and strong faith in them. A true believer is desirous, not only to be in covenant with God, but in communion with the people of God; and is willing to fare as they fare. By her works Rahab declared herself to be just. That she was not justified by her works appears plainly; because the work she did was faulty in the manner, and not perfectly good, therefore it could not be answerable to the perfect justice or righteousness of God.

Verses 32-38

After all our searches into the Scriptures, there is more to be learned from them. We should be pleased to think, how great the number of believers was under the Old Testament, and how strong their faith, though the objects of it were not then so fully made known as now. And we should lament that now, in gospel times, when the rule of faith is more clear and perfect, the number of believers should be so small, and their faith so weak. It is the excellence of the grace of faith, that, while it helps men to do great things, like Gideon, it keeps from high and great thoughts of themselves. Faith, like Barak's, has recourse unto God in all dangers and difficulties, and then makes grateful returns to God for all mercies and deliverances. By faith, the servants of God shall overcome even the roaring lion that goeth about seeking whom he may devour. The believer's faith endures to the end, and, in dying, gives him victory over death and all his deadly enemies, like Samson. The grace of God often fixes upon very undeserving and ill-deserving persons, to do great things for them and by them. But the grace of faith, wherever it is, will put men upon acknowledging God in all their ways, as Jephthah. It will make men bold and courageous in a good cause. Few ever met with greater trials, few ever showed more lively faith, than David, and he has left a testimony as to the trials and acts of faith, in the book of Psalms, which has been, and ever will be, of great value to the people of God. Those are likely to grow up to be distinguished for faith, who begin betimes, like Samuel, to exercise it. And faith will enable a man to serve God and his generation, in whatever way he may be employed. The interests and powers of kings and kingdoms, are often opposed to God and his people; but God can easily subdue all that set themselves against him. It is a greater honour and happiness to work righteousness than to work miracles. By faith we have comfort of the promises; and by faith we are prepared to wait for the promises, and in due time to receive them. And though we do not hope to have our dead relatives or friends restored to life in this world, yet faith will support under the loss of them, and direct to the hope of a better resurrection. Shall we be most amazed at the wickedness of human nature, that it is capable of such awful cruelties to fellow-creatures, or at the excellence of Divine grace, that is able to bear up the faithful under such cruelties, and to carry them safely through all? What a difference between God's judgement of a saint, and man's judgment! The world is not worthy of those scorned, persecuted saints, whom their persecutors reckon unworthy to live. They are not worthy of their company, example, counsel, or other benefits. For they know not what a saint is, nor the worth of a saint, nor how to use him; they hate, and drive such away, as they do the offer of Christ and his grace. (Heb 11:39)

Verses 39, 40

The world considers that the righteous are not worthy to live in the world, and God declares the world is not worthy of them. Though the righteous and the worldlings widely differ in their judgment, they agree in this, it is not fit that good men should have their rest in this world. Therefore God receives them out of it. The apostle tells the Hebrews, that God had provided some better things for them, therefore they might be sure that he expected as good things from them. As our advantages, with the better things God has provided for us, are so much beyond theirs, so should our obedience of faith, patience of hope, and labour of love, be greater. And unless we get true faith as these believers had, they will rise up to condemn us at the last day. Let us then pray continually for the increase of our faith, that we may follow these bright examples, and be, with them, at length made perfect in holiness and happiness, and shine like the sun in the kingdom of our Father for evermore.

Chapter 12

Chapter Outline

An exhortation to be constant and persevere, The example of Christ is set forth, and the gracious design of God in all the sufferings believers endured.   (1–11)

Peace and holiness are recommended, with cautions against despising spiritual blessings.   (12–17)

The New Testament dispensation shown to be much more excellent than the Old.   (18–29)

Verses 1-11

The persevering obedience of faith in Christ, was the race set before the Hebrews, wherein they must either win the crown of glory, or have everlasting misery for their portion; and it is set before us. By the sin that does so easily beset us, understand that sin to which we are most prone, or to which we are most exposed, from habit, age, or circumstances. This is a most important exhortation; for while a man's darling sin, be it what it will, remains unsubdued, it will hinder him from running the Christian race, as it takes from him every motive for running, and gives power to every discouragement. When weary and faint in their minds, let them recollect that the holy Jesus suffered, to save them from eternal misery. By stedfastly looking to Jesus, their thoughts would strengthen holy affections, and keep under their carnal desires. Let us then frequently consider him. What are our little trials to his agonies, or even to our deserts? What are they to the sufferings of many others? There is a proneness in believers to grow weary, and to faint under trials and afflictions; this is from the imperfection of grace and the remains of corruption. Christians should not faint under their trials. Though their enemies and persecutors may be instruments to inflict sufferings, yet they are Divine chastisements; their heavenly Father has his hand in all, and his wise end to answer by all. They must not make light of afflictions, and be without feeling under them, for they are the hand and rod of God, and are his rebukes for sin. They must not despond and sink under trials, nor fret and repine, but bear up with faith and patience. God may let others alone in their sins, but he will correct sin in his own children. In this he acts as becomes a father. Our earthly parents sometimes may chasten us, to gratify their passion, rather than to reform our manners. But the Father of our souls never willingly grieves nor afflicts his children. It is always for our profit. Our whole life here is a state of childhood, and imperfect as to spiritual things; therefore we must submit to the discipline of such a state. When we come to a perfect state, we shall be fully reconciled to all God's chastisement of us now. God's correction is not condemnation; the chastening may be borne with patience, and greatly promote holiness. Let us then learn to consider the afflictions brought on us by the malice of men, as corrections sent by our wise and gracious Father, for our spiritual good.

Verses 12-17

A burden of affliction is apt to make the Christian's hands hang down, and his knees grow feeble, to dispirit him and discourage him; but against this he must strive, that he may better run his spiritual race and course. Faith and patience enable believers to follow peace and holiness, as a man follows his calling constantly, diligently, and with pleasure. Peace with men, of all sects and parties, will be favourable to our pursuit of holiness. But peace and holiness go together; there can be not right peace without holiness. Where persons fail of having the true grace of God, corruption will prevail and break forth; beware lest any unmortified lust in the heart, which seems to be dead, should spring up, to trouble and disturb the whole body. Falling away from Christ is the fruit of preferring the delights of the flesh, to the blessing of God, and the heavenly inheritance, as Esau did. But sinners will not always have such mean thoughts of the Divine blessing and inheritance as they now have. It agrees with the profane man's disposition, to desire the blessing, yet to despise the means whereby the blessing is to be gained. But God will neither sever the means from the blessing, nor join the blessing with the satisfying of man's lusts. God's mercy and blessing were never sought carefully and not obtained.

Verses 18-29

Mount Sinai, on which the Jewish church state was formed, was a mount such as might be touched, though forbidden to be so, a place that could be felt; so the Mosaic dispensation was much in outward and earthly things. The gospel state is kind and condescending, suited to our weak frame. Under the gospel all may come with boldness to God's presence. But the most holy must despair, if judged by the holy law given from Sinai, without a Saviour. The gospel church is called Mount Zion; there believers have clearer views of heaven, and more heavenly tempers of soul. All the children of God are heirs, and every one has the privileges of the first-born. Let a soul be supposed to join that glorious assembly and church above, that is yet unacquainted with God, still carnally-minded, loving this present world and state of things, looking back to it with a lingering eye, full of pride and guile, filled with lusts; such a soul would seem to have mistaken its way, place, state, and company. It would be uneasy to itself and all about it. Christ is the Mediator of this new covenant, between God and man, to bring them together in this covenant; to keep them together; to plead with God for us, and to plead with us for God; and at length to bring God and his people together in heaven. This covenant is made firm by the blood of Christ sprinkled upon our consciences, as the blood of the sacrifice was sprinkled upon the altar and the victim. This blood of Christ speaks in behalf of sinners; it pleads not for vengeance, but for mercy. See then that you refuse not his gracious call and offered salvation. See that you do not refuse Him who speaketh from heaven, with infinite tenderness and love; for how can those escape, who turn from God in unbelief or apostasy, while he so graciously beseeches them to be reconciled, and to receive his everlasting favour! God's dealing with men under the gospel, in a way of grace, assures us, that he will deal with the despisers of the gospel, in a way of judgment. We cannot worship God acceptably, unless we worship him with reverence and godly fear. Only the grace of God enables us to worship God aright. God is the same just and righteous God under the gospel as under the law. The inheritance of believers is secured to them; and all things pertaining to salvation are freely given in answer to prayer. Let us seek for grace, that we may serve God with reverence and godly fear.

Chapter 13

Chapter Outline

Exhortations to various duties, and to be content with what Providence allots. (1–6)

To respect the instructions of faithful pastors, with cautions against being carried away by strange doctrines. (7–15)

Further exhortations to duties, that relate to God, to our neighbour, and to those set over us in the Lord. (16–21)

This epistle to be seriously considered. (22–25)

Verses 1-6

The design of Christ in giving himself for us, is, that he may purchase to himself a peculiar people, zealous of good works; and true religion is the strongest bond of friendship. Here are earnest exhortations to several Christian duties, especially contentment. The sin opposed to this grace and duty is covetousness, an over-eager desire for the wealth of this world, with envy of those who have more than ourselves. Having treasures in heaven, we may be content with mean things here. Those who cannot be so, would not be content though God raised their condition. Adam was in paradise, yet not contented; some angels in heaven were not contented; but the apostle Paul, though abased and empty, had learned in every state, in any state, to be content. Christians have reason to be contented with their present lot. This promise contains the sum and substance of all the promises; "I will never, no, never leave thee, no, never forsake thee." In the original there are no less than five negatives put together, to confirm the promise: the true believer shall have the gracious presence of God with him, in life, at death, and for ever. Men can do nothing against God, and God can make all that men do against his people, to turn to their good.

Verses 7-15

The instructions and examples of ministers, who honourably and comfortably closed their testimony, should be particularly remembered by survivors. And though their ministers were some dead, others dying, yet the great Head and High Priest of the church, the Bishop of their souls, ever lives, and is ever the same. Christ is the same in the Old Testament day. as in the gospel day, and will be so to his people for ever, equally merciful, powerful, and all-sufficient. Still he fills the hungry, encourages the trembling, and welcomes repenting sinners: still he rejects the proud and self-righteous, abhors mere profession, and teaches all whom he saves, to love righteousness, and to hate iniquity. Believers should seek to have their hearts established in simple dependence on free grace, by the Holy Spirit, which would comfort their hearts, and render them proof against delusion. Christ is both our Altar and our Sacrifice; he sanctifies the gift. The Lord's supper is the feast of the gospel passover. Having showed that keeping to the Levitical law would, according to its own rules, keep men from the Christian altar, the apostle adds, Let us go forth therefore unto him without the camp; go forth from the ceremonial law, from sin, from the world, and from ourselves. Living by faith in Christ, set apart to God through his blood, let us willingly separate from this evil world. Sin, sinners, nor death, will not suffer us to continue long here; therefore let us go forth now by faith and seek in Christ the rest and peace which this world cannot afford us. Let us bring our sacrifices to this altar, and to this our High Priest, and offer them up by him. The sacrifice of praise to God, we should offer always. In this are worship and prayer, as well as thanksgiving.

Verses 16-21

We must, according to our power, give to the necessities of the souls and bodies of men: God will accept these offerings with pleasure, and will accept and bless the offerers through Christ. The apostle then states what is their duty to living ministers; to obey and submit to them, so far as is agreeable to the mind and will of God, made known in his word. Christians must not think themselves too wise, too good, or too great, to learn. The people must search the Scriptures, and so far as the ministers teach according to that rule, they ought to receive their instructions as the word of God, which works in those that believe. It is the interest of hearers, that the account their ministers give of them may be with joy, and not with grief. Faithful ministers deliver their own souls, but the ruin of a fruitless and faithless people will be upon their own heads. The more earnestly the people pray for their ministers, the more benefit they may expect from their ministry. A good conscience has respect to all God's commands, and all our duty. Those who have this good conscience, yet need the prayers of others. When ministers come to a people who pray for them, they come with greater satisfaction to themselves, and success to the people. We should seek all our mercies by prayer. God is the God of peace, fully reconciled to believers; who has made a way for peace and reconciliation between himself and sinners, and who loves peace on earth, especially in his churches. He is the Author of spiritual peace in the hearts and consciences of his people. How firm a covenant is that which has its foundation in the blood of the Son of God! The perfecting of the saints in every good work, is the great thing desired by them, and for them; and that they may at length be fitted for the employment and happiness of heaven. There is no good thing wrought in us, but it is the work of God. And no good thing is wrought in us by God, but through Christ, for his sake and by his Spirit.

Verses 22-25

So bad are men, and even believers, through the remainders of their corruption, that when the most important, comfortable doctrine is delivered to them for their own good, and that with the most convincing evidence, there is need of earnest entreaty and exhortation that they would bear it, and not fall out with it, neglect it, or reject it. It is good to have the law of holy love and kindness written in the hearts of Christians, one towards another. Religion teaches men true civility and good breeding. It is not ill-tempered or uncourteous. Let the favour of God be toward you, and his grace continually working in you, and with you, bringing forth the fruits of holiness, as the first-fruits of glory.

James

This epistle of James is one of the most instructive writings in the New Testament. Being chiefly directed against particular errors at that time brought in among the Jewish Christians, it does not contain the same full doctrinal statements as the other epistles, but it presents an admirable summary of the practical duties of all believers. The leading truths of Christianity are set forth throughout; and on attentive consideration, it will be found entirely to agree with St. Paul's statements concerning grace and justification, while it abounds with earnest exhortations to the patience of hope and obedience of faith and love, interspersed with warnings, reproofs, and encouragements, according to the characters addressed. The truths laid down are very serious, and necessary to be maintained; and the rules for practice ought to be observed in all times. In Christ there are no dead and sapless branches, faith is not an idle grace; wherever it is, it brings forth fruit in works.

Chapter 1

Chapter Outline

How to apply to God under troubles, and how to behave in prosperous and in adverse circumstances.	(1–11)
To look upon all evil as proceeding from ourselves, and all good from God.	(12–18)
The duty of watching against a rash temper, and of receiving the word of God with meekness.	(19–21)
And of living according thereto.	(22–25)
The difference between vain pretences and real religion.	(26, 27)

Verses 1-11

Christianity teaches men to be joyful under troubles: such exercises are sent from God's love; and trials in the way of duty will brighten our graces now, and our crown at last. Let us take care, in times of trial, that patience, and not passion, is set to work in us: whatever is said or done, let patience have the saying and doing of it. When the work of patience is complete, it will furnish all that is necessary for our Christian race and warfare. We should not pray so much for the removal of affliction, as for wisdom to make a right use of it. And who does not want wisdom to guide him under trials, both in regulating his own spirit, and in managing his affairs? Here is something in answer to every discouraging turn of the mind, when we go to God under a sense of our own weakness and folly. If, after all, any should say, This may be the case with some, but I fear I shall not succeed, the promise is, To any that asketh, it shall be given. A mind that has single and prevailing regard to its spiritual and eternal interest, and that keeps steady in its purposes for God, will grow wise by afflictions, will continue fervent in devotion, and rise above trials and oppositions. When our faith and spirits rise and fall with second causes, there will be unsteadiness in our words and actions. This may not always expose men to contempt in the world, but such ways cannot please God. No condition of life is such as to hinder rejoicing in God. Those of low degree may rejoice, if they are exalted to be rich in faith and heirs of the kingdom of God; and the rich may rejoice in humbling providences, that lead to a humble and lowly disposition of mind. Worldly wealth is a withering thing. Then, let him that is rich rejoice in the grace of God, which makes and keeps him humble; and in the trials and exercises which teach him to seek happiness in and from God, not from perishing enjoyments.

Verses 12-18

It is not every man who suffers, that is blessed; but he who with patience and constancy goes through all difficulties in the way of duty. Afflictions cannot make us miserable, if it be not our own fault. The tried Christian shall be a crowned one. The crown of life is promised to all who have the love of God reigning in their hearts. Every soul that truly loves God, shall have its trials in this world fully recompensed in that world above, where love is made perfect. The commands of God, and the dealings of his providence, try men's hearts, and show the dispositions which prevail in them. But nothing sinful in the heart or conduct can be ascribed to God. He is not the author of the dross, though his fiery trial exposes it. Those who lay the blame of sin, either upon their constitution, or upon their condition in the world, or pretend they cannot keep from sinning, wrong God as if he were the author of sin. Afflictions, as sent by God, are designed to draw out our graces, but not our corruptions. The origin of evil and temptation is in our own hearts. Stop the beginnings of sin, or all the evils that follow must be wholly charged upon us. God has no pleasure in the death of men, as he has no hand in their sin; but both sin and misery are owing to themselves. As the sun is the same in nature and influences, though the earth and clouds, often coming between, make it seem to us to vary, so God is unchangeable, and our changes and shadows are not from any changes or alterations in him. What the sun is in nature, God is in grace, providence, and glory; and infinitely more. As every good gift is from God, so particularly our being born again, and all its holy, happy consequences come from him. A true Christian becomes as different a person from what he was before the renewing influences of Divine grace, as if he were formed over again. We should devote all our faculties to God's service, that we may be a kind of first-fruits of his creatures.

Verses 19-21

Instead of blaming God under our trials, let us open our ears and hearts to learn what he teaches by them. And if men would govern their tongues, they must govern their passions. The worst thing we can bring to any dispute, is anger. Here is an exhortation to lay apart, and to cast off as a filthy garment, all sinful practices. This must reach to sins of thought and affection, as well as of speech and practice; to every thing corrupt and sinful. We must yield ourselves to the word of God, with humble and teachable minds. Being willing to hear of our faults, taking it not only patiently, but thankfully. It is the design of the word of God to make us wise to salvation; and those who propose any mean or low ends in attending upon it, dishonour the gospel, and disappoint their own souls.

Verses 22-25

If we heard a sermon every day of the week, and an angel from heaven were the preacher, yet, if we rested in hearing only, it would never bring us to heaven. Mere hearers are self-deceivers; and self-deceit will be found the worst deceit at last. If we flatter ourselves, it is our own fault; the truth, as it is in Jesus, flatters no man. Let the word of truth be carefully attended to, and it will set before us the corruption of our nature, the disorders of our hearts and lives; and it will tell us plainly what we are. Our sins are the spots the law discovers: Christ's blood is the laver the gospel shows. But in vain do we hear God's word, and look into the gospel glass, if we go away, and forget our spots, instead of washing them off; and forget our remedy, instead of applying to it. This is the case with those who do not hear the word as they ought. In hearing the word, we look into it for counsel and direction, and when we study it, it turns to our spiritual life. Those who keep in the law and word of God, are, and shall be, blessed in all their ways. His gracious recompence hereafter, would be connected with his present peace and comfort. Every part of Divine revelation has its use, in bringing the sinner to Christ for salvation, and in directing and encouraging him to walk at liberty, by the Spirit of adoption, according to the holy commands of God. And mark the distinctness, it is not for his deeds, that any man is blessed, but in his deed. It is not talking, but walking, that will bring us to heaven. Christ will become more precious to the believer's soul, which by his grace will become more fitted for the inheritance of the saints in light.

Verses 26, 27

When men take more pains to seem religious than really to be so, it is a sign their religion is in vain. The not bridling the tongue, readiness to speak of the faults of others, or to lessen their wisdom and piety, are signs of a vain religion. The man who has a slandering tongue, cannot have a truly humble, gracious heart. False religious may be known by their impurity and uncharitableness. True religion teaches us to do every thing as in the presence of God. An unspotted life must go with unfeigned love and charity. Our true religion is equal to the measure in which these things have place in our hearts and conduct. And let us remember, that nothing avails in Christ Jesus, but faith that worketh by love, purifies the heart, subdues carnal lusts, and obeys God's commands.

Chapter 2

Chapter Outline

All professions of faith are vain, if not producing love and justice to others. (1–13)

The necessity of good works to prove the sincerity of faith, which otherwise will be of no more advantage than the faith of devils. (14–26)

Verses 1-13

Those who profess faith in Christ as the Lord of glory, must not respect persons on account of mere outward circumstances and appearances, in a manner not agreeing with their profession of being disciples of the lowly Jesus. St. James does not here encourage rudeness or disorder: civil respect must be paid; but never such as to influence the proceedings of Christians in disposing of the offices of the church of Christ, or in passing the censures of the church, or in any matter of religion. Questioning ourselves is of great use in every part of the holy life. Let us be more frequent in this, and in every thing take occasion to discourse with our souls. As places of worship cannot be built or maintained without expense, it may be proper that those who contribute thereto should be accommodated accordingly; but were all persons more spiritually-minded, the poor would be treated with more attention that usually is the case in worshipping congregations. A lowly state is most favourable for inward peace and for growth in holiness. God would give to all believers riches and honours of this world, if these would do them good, seeing that he has chosen them to be rich in faith, and made them heirs of his kingdom, which he promised to bestow on all who love him. Consider how often riches lead to vice and mischief, and what great reproaches are thrown upon God and religion, by men of wealth, power, and worldly greatness; and it will make this sin appear very sinful and foolish. The Scripture gives as a law, to love our neighbour as ourselves. This law is a royal law, it comes from the King of kings; and if Christians act unjustly, they are convicted by the law as transgressors. To think that our good deeds will atone for our bad deeds, plainly puts us upon looking for another atonement. According to the covenant of works, one breach of any one command brings a man under condemnation, from which no obedience, past, present, or future, can deliver him. This shows us the happiness of those that are in Christ. We may serve him without slavish fear. God's restraints are not a bondage, but our own corruptions are so. The doom passed upon impenitent sinners at last, will be judgment without mercy. But God deems it his glory and joy, to pardon and bless those who might justly be condemned at his tribunal; and his grace teaches those who partake of his mercy, to copy it in their conduct.

Verses 14-26

Those are wrong who put a mere notional belief of the gospel for the whole of evangelical religion, as many now do. No doubt, true faith alone, whereby men have part in Christ's righteousness, atonement, and grace, saves their souls; but it produces holy fruits, and is shown to be real by its effect on their works; while mere assent to any form of doctrine, or mere historical belief of any facts, wholly differs from this saving faith. A bare profession may gain the good opinion of pious people; and it may procure, in some cases, worldly good things; but what profit will it be, for any to gain the whole world, and to lose their souls? Can this faith save him? All things should be accounted profitable or unprofitable to us, as they tend to forward or hinder the salvation of our souls. This place of Scripture plainly shows that an opinion, or assent to the gospel, without works, is not faith. There is no way to show we really believe in Christ, but by being diligent in good works, from gospel motives, and for gospel purposes. Men may boast to others, and be conceited of that which they really have not. There is not only to be assent in faith, but consent; not only an assent to the truth of the word, but a consent to take Christ. True believing is not an act of the understanding only, but a work of the whole heart. That a justifying faith cannot be without works, is shown from two examples, Abraham and Rahab. Abraham believed God, and it was reckoned unto him for righteousness. Faith, producing such works, advanced him to peculiar favours. We see then, ver. #(24), how that by works a man is justified, not by a bare opinion or profession, or believing without obeying; but by having such faith as produces good works. And to have to deny his own reason, affections, and interests, is an action fit to try a believer. Observe here, the wonderful power of faith in changing sinners. Rahab's conduct proved her faith to be living, or having power; it showed that she believed with her heart, not merely by an assent of the understanding. Let us then take heed, for the best works, without faith, are dead; they want root and principle. By faith any thing we do is really good; as done in obedience to God, and aiming at his acceptance: the root is as though it were dead, when there is no fruit. Faith is the root, good works are the fruits; and we must see to it that we have both. This is the grace of God wherein we stand, and we should stand to it. There is no middle state. Every one must either live God's friend, or God's enemy. Living to God, as it is the consequence of faith, which justifies and will save, obliges us to do nothing against him, but every thing for him and to him.

Chapter 3

Chapter Outline

Cautions against proud behaviour, and the mischief of an unruly tongue.	(1–12)
The excellence of heavenly wisdom, in opposition to that which is worldly.	(13–18)

Verses 1-12

We are taught to dread an unruly tongue, as one of the greatest evils. The affairs of mankind are thrown into confusion by the tongues of men. Every age of the world, and every condition of life, private or public, affords examples of this. Hell has more to do in promoting the fire of the tongue than men generally think; and whenever men's tongues are employed in sinful ways, they are set on fire of hell. No man can tame the tongue without Divine grace and assistance. The apostle does not represent it as impossible, but as extremely difficult. Other sins decay with age, this many times gets worse; we grow more froward and fretful, as natural strength decays, and the days come on in which we have no pleasure. When other sins are tamed and subdued by the infirmities of age, the spirit often grows more tart, nature being drawn down to the dregs, and the words used become more passionate. That man's tongue confutes itself, which at one time pretends to adore the perfections of God, and to refer all things to him; and at another time condemns even good men, if they do not use the same words and expressions. True religion will not admit of contradictions: how many sins would be prevented, if men would always be consistent! Pious and edifying language is the genuine produce of a sanctified heart; and none who understand Christianity, expect to hear curses, lies, boastings, and revilings from a true believer's mouth, any more than they look for the fruit of one tree from another. But facts prove that more professors succeed in bridling their senses and appetites, than in duly restraining their tongues. Then, depending on Divine grace, let us take heed to bless and curse not; and let us aim to be consistent in our words and actions.

Verses 13-18

These verses show the difference between men's pretending to be wise, and their being really so. He who thinks well, or he who talks well, is not wise in the sense of the Scripture, if he does not live and act well. True wisdom may be know by the meekness of the spirit and temper. Those who live in malice, envy, and contention, live in confusion; and are liable to be provoked and hurried to any evil work. Such wisdom comes not down from above, but springs up from earthly principles, acts on earthly motives, and is intent on serving earthly purposes. Those who are lifted up with such wisdom, described by the apostle James, is near to the Christian love, described by the apostle Paul; and both are so described that every man may fully prove the reality of his attainments in them. It has no disguise or deceit. It cannot fall in with those managements the world counts wise, which are crafty and guileful; but it is sincere, and open, and steady, and uniform, and consistent with itself. May the purity, peace, gentleness, teachableness, and mercy shown in all our actions, and the fruits of righteousness abounding in our lives, prove that God has bestowed upon us this excellent gift.

Chapter 4

Chapter Outline

Here are cautions against corrupt affections, and love of this world, which is enmity to God.	(1–10)
Exhortations to undertake no affairs of life, without constant regard to the will and providence of God.	(11–17)

Verses 1-10

Since all wars and fightings come from the corruptions of our own hearts, it is right to mortify those lusts that war in the members. Wordly and fleshly lusts are distempers, which will not allow content or satisfaction. Sinful desires and affections stop prayer, and the working of our desires toward God. And let us beware that we do not abuse or misuse the mercies received, by the disposition of the heart when prayers are granted When men ask of God prosperity, they often ask with wrong aims and intentions. If we thus seek the things of this world, it is just in God to deny them. Unbelieving and cold desires beg denials; and we may be sure that when prayers are rather the language of lusts than of graces, they will return empty. Here is a decided warning to avoid all criminal friendships with this world. Worldly-mindedness is enmity to God. An enemy may be reconciled, but "enmity" never can be reconciled. A man may have a large portion in things of this life, and yet be kept in the love of God; but he who sets his heart upon the world, who will conform to it rather than lose its friendship, is an enemy to God. So that any one who resolves at all events to be upon friendly terms with the world, must be the enemy of God. Did then the Jews, or the loose professors of Christianity, think the Scripture spake in vain against this worldly-mindedness? or does the Holy Spirit who dwells in all Christians, or the new nature which he creates, produce such fruit? Natural corruption shows itself by envying. The spirit of the world teaches us to lay up, or lay out for ourselves, according to our own fancies; God the Holy Spirit teaches us to be willing to do good to all about us, as we are able. The grace of God will correct and cure the spirit by nature in us; and where he gives grace, he gives another spirit than that of the world. The proud resist God: in their understanding they resist the truths of God; in their will they resist the laws of God; in their passions they resist the providence of God; therefore, no wonder that God resists the proud. How wretched the state of those who make God their enemy! God will give more grace to the humble, because they see their need of it, pray for it are thankful for it, and such shall have it. Submit to God, ver. #(7). Submit your understanding to the truth of God; submit your wills to the will of his precept, the will of his providence. Submit yourselves to God, for he is ready to do you good. If we yield to temptations, the devil will continually follow us; but if we put on the whole armour of God, and stand out against him, he will leave us. Let sinners then submit to God, and seek his grace and favour; resisting the devil. All sin must be wept over; here, in godly sorrow, or, hereafter, in eternal misery. And the Lord will not refuse to comfort one who really mourns for sin, or to exalt one who humbles himself before him.

Verses 11-17

Our lips must be governed by the law of kindness, as well as truth and justice. Christians are brethren. And to break God's commands, is to speak evil of them, and to judge them, as if they laid too great a restraint upon us. We have the law of God, which is a rule to all; let us not presume to set up our own notions and opinions as a rule to those about us, and let us be careful that we be not condemned of the Lord. "Go to now," is a call to any one to consider his conduct as being wrong. How apt worldly and contriving men are to leave God out of their plans! How vain it is to look for any thing good without God's blessing and guidance! The frailty, shortness, and uncertainty of life, ought to check the vanity and presumptuous confidence of all projects for futurity. We can fix the hour and minute of the sun's rising and setting to-morrow, but we cannot fix the certain time of a vapour being scattered. So short, unreal, and fading is human life, and all the prosperity or enjoyment that attends it; though bliss or woe for ever must be according to our conduct during this fleeting moment. We are always to depend on the will of God. Our times are not in our own hands, but at the disposal of God. Our heads may be filled with cares and contrivances for ourselves, or our families, or our friends; but Providence often throws our plans into confusion. All we design, and all we do, should be with submissive dependence on God. It is foolish, and it is hurtful, to boast of worldly things and aspiring projects; it will bring great disappointment, and will prove destruction in the end. Omissions are sins which will be brought into judgment, as well as commissions. He that does not the good he knows should be done, as well as he who does the evil he knows should not be done, will be condemned. Oh that we were as careful not to omit prayer, and not to neglect to meditate and examine our consciences, as we are not to commit gross outward vices against light!

Chapter 5

Chapter Outline

Verses 1-6

Public troubles are most grievous to those who live in pleasure, and are secure and sensual, though all ranks suffer deeply at such times. All idolized treasures will soon perish, except as they will rise up in judgment against their possessors. Take heed of defrauding and oppressing; and avoid the very appearance of it. God does not forbid us to use lawful pleasures; but to live in pleasure, especially sinful pleasure, is a provoking sin. Is it no harm for people to unfit themselves for minding the concerns of their souls, by indulging bodily appetites? The just may be condemned and killed; but when such suffer by oppressors, this is marked by God. Above all their other crimes, the Jews had condemned and crucified that Just One who had come among them, even Jesus Christ the righteous.

Verses 7-11

Consider him that waits for a crop of corn; and will not you wait for a crown of glory? If you should be called to wait longer than the husbandman, is not there something more worth waiting for? In every sense the coming of the Lord drew nigh, and all his people's losses, hardships, and sufferings, would be repaid. Men count time long, because they measure it by their own lives; but all time is as nothing to God; it is as a moment. To short-lived creatures a few years seem an age; but Scripture, measuring all things by the existence of God, reckons thousands of years but so many days. God brought about things in Job's case, so as plainly to prove that he is very pitiful and of tender mercy. This did not appear during his troubles, but was seen in the event, and believers now will find a happy end to their trials. Let us serve our God, and bear our trials, as those who believe that the end will crown all. Our eternal happiness is safe if we trust to him: all else is mere vanity, which soon will be done with for ever.

Verses 12-18

The sin of swearing is condemned; but how many make light of common profane swearing! Such swearing expressly throws contempt upon God's name and authority. This sin brings neither gain, nor pleasure, nor reputation, but is showing enmity to God without occasion and without advantage It shows a man to be an enemy to God, however he pretends to call himself by his name, or sometimes joins in acts of worship. But the Lord will not hold him guiltless that taketh his name in vain. In a day of affliction nothing is more seasonable than prayer. The spirit is then most humble, and the heart is broken and tender. It is necessary to exercise faith and hope under afflictions; and prayer is the appointed means for obtaining and increasing these graces. Observe, that the saving of the sick is not ascribed to the anointing with oil, but to prayer. In a time of sickness it is not cold and formal prayer that is effectual, but the prayer of faith. The great thing we should beg of God for ourselves and others in the time of sickness is, the pardon of sin. Let nothing be done to encourage any to delay, under the mistaken fancy that a confession, a prayer, a minister's absolution and exhortation, or the sacrament, will set all right at last, where the duties of a godly life have been disregarded. To acknowledge our faults to each other, will tend greatly to peace and brotherly love. And when a righteous person, a true believer, justified in Christ, and by his grace walking before God in holy obedience, presents an effectual fervent prayer, wrought in his heart by the power of the Holy Spirit, raising holy affections and believing expectations and so leading earnestly to plead the promises of God at his mercy-seat, it avails much. The power of prayer is proved from the history of Elijah. In prayer we must not look to the merit of man, but to the grace of God. It is not enough to say a prayer, but we must pray in prayer. Thoughts must be fixed, desires must be firm and ardent, and graces exercised. This instance of the power of prayer, encourages every Christian to be earnest in prayer. God never says to any of the seed of Jacob, Seek my face in vain. Where there may not be so much of miracle in God's answering our prayers, yet there may be as much of grace.

Verses 19, 20

It is no mark of a wise or holy man, to boast of being free from error, or to refuse to acknowledge an error. And there is some doctrinal mistake at the bottom of every practical mistake. There is no one habitually bad, but upon some bad principle. This is conversion; to turn a sinner from the error of his ways, not merely from one party to another, or from one notion and way of thinking to another. There is no way effectually and finally to hide sin, but forsaking it. Many sins are hindered in the party converted; many also may be so in others whom he may influence. The salvation of one soul is of infinitely greater importance than preserving the lives of multitudes, or promoting the welfare of a whole people. Let us in our several stations keep these things in mind, sparing no pains in God's service, and the event will prove that our labour is not in vain in the Lord. For six thousand years He has been multiplying pardons, and yet his free grace is not tired nor grown weary. Certainly Divine mercy is an ocean that is ever full and ever flowing. May the Lord give us a part in this abundant mercy, through the blood of Christ, and the sanctification of the Spirit.

1 Peter

The same great doctrines, as in St. Paul's epistles, are here applied to same practical purposes. And this epistle is remarkable for the sweetness, gentleness, and humble love, with which it is written. It gives a short, and yet a very clear summary, both of the consolations and the instructions needful for the encouragement and direction of a Christian in his journey to heaven, raising his thoughts and desires to that happiness, and strengthening him against all opposition in the way, both from corruption within, and temptations and afflictions without.

Chapter 1

Chapter Outline

The apostle blesses God for his special benefits through Christ.	(1–9)
Salvation by Christ foretold in ancient prophecy.	(10–12)
All are exhorted to holy conversation.	(13–16)
Such as is suitable to their principles, privileges, and obligations.	(17–25)

Verses 1-9

This epistle is addressed to believers in general, who are strangers in every city or country where they live, and are scattered through the nations. These are to ascribe their salvation to the electing love of the Father, the redemption of the Son, and the sanctification of the Holy Ghost; and so to give glory to one God in three Persons, into whose name they had been baptized. Hope, in the world's phrase, refers only to an uncertain good, for all worldly hopes are tottering, built upon sand, and the worldling's hopes of heaven are blind and groundless conjectures. But the hope of the sons of the living God is a living hope; not only as to its object, but as to its effect also. It enlivens and comforts in all distresses, enables to meet and get over all difficulties. Mercy is the spring of all this; yea, great mercy and manifold mercy. And this well-grounded hope of salvation, is an active and living principle of obedience in the soul of the believer. The matter of a Christian's joy, is the remembrance of the happiness laid up for him. It is incorruptible, it cannot come to nothing, it is an estate that cannot be spent. Also undefiled; this signifies its purity and perfection. And it fadeth not; is not sometimes more or less pleasant, but ever the same, still like itself. All possessions here are stained with defects and failings; still something is wanting: fair houses have sad cares flying about the gilded and ceiled roofs; soft beds and full tables, are often with sick bodies and uneasy stomachs. All possessions are stained with sin, either in getting or in using them. How ready we are to turn the things we possess into occasions and instruments of sin, and to think there is no liberty or delight in their use, without abusing them! Worldly possessions are uncertain and soon pass away, like the flowers and plants of the field. That must be of the greatest worth, which is laid up in the highest and best place, in heaven. Happy are those whose hearts the Holy Spirit sets on this inheritance. God not only gives his people grace, but preserves them unto glory. Every believer has always something wherein he may greatly rejoice; it should show itself in the countenance and conduct. The Lord does not willingly afflict, yet his wise love often appoints sharp trials, to show his people their hearts, and to do them good at the latter end. Gold does not increase by trial in the fire, it becomes less; but faith is made firm, and multiplied, by troubles and afflictions. Gold must perish at last, and can only purchase perishing things, while the trial of faith will be found to praise, and honour, and glory. Let this reconcile us to present afflictions. Seek then to believe Christ's excellence in himself, and his love to us; this will kindle such a fire in the heart as will make it rise up in a sacrifice of love to him. And the glory of God and our own happiness are so united, that if we sincerely seek the one now, we shall attain the other when the soul shall no more be subject to evil. The certainty of this hope is as if believers had already received it.

Verses 10-12

Jesus Christ was the main subject of the prophets' studies. Their inquiry into the sufferings of Christ and the glories that should follow, would lead to a view of the whole gospel, the sum whereof is, That Christ Jesus was delivered for our offences, and raised again for our justification. God is pleased to answer our necessities rather than our requests. The doctrine of the prophets, and that of the apostles, exactly agree, as coming from the same Spirit of God. The gospel is the ministration of the Spirit; its success depends upon his operation and blessing. Let us then search diligently those Scriptures which contain the doctrines of salvation.

Verses 13-16

As the traveller, the racer, the warrior, and the labourer, gathered in their long and loose garments, that they might be ready in their business, so let Christians do by their minds and affections. Be sober, be watchful against all spiritual dangers and enemies, and be temperate in all behaviour. Be sober-minded in opinion, as well as in practice, and humble in your judgment of yourselves. A strong and perfect trust in the grace of God, is agreeable with best endeavours in our duty. Holiness is the desire and duty of every Christian. It must be in all affairs, in every condition, and towards all people. We must especially watch and pray against the sins to which we are inclined. The written word of God is the surest rule of a Christian's life, and by this rule we are commanded to be holy every way. God makes those holy whom he saves.

Verses 17-25

Holy confidence in God as a Father, and awful fear of him as a Judge, agree together; and to regard God always as a Judge, makes him dear to us as a Father. If believers do evil, God will visit them with corrections. Then, let Christians not doubt God's faithfulness to his promises, nor give way to enslaving dread of his wrath, but let them reverence his holiness. The fearless professor is defenceless, and Satan takes him captive at his will; the desponding professor has no heart to avail himself of his advantages, and is easily brought to surrender. The price paid for man's redemption was the precious blood of Christ. Not only openly wicked, but unprofitable conversation is highly dangerous, though it may plead custom. It is folly to resolve, I will live and die in such a way, because my forefathers did so. God had purposes of special favour toward his people, long before he made manifest such grace unto them. But the clearness of light, the supports of faith, the power of ordinances, are all much greater since Christ came upon earth, than they were before. The comfort is, that being by faith made one with Christ, his present glory is an assurance that where he is we shall be also, Joh 14:3. The soul must be purified, before it can give up its own desires and indulgences. And the word of God planted in the heart by the Holy Ghost, is a means of spiritual life, stirring up to our duty, working a total change in the dispositions and affections of the soul, till it brings to eternal life. In contrast with the excellence of the renewed spiritual man, as born again, observe the vanity of the natural man. In his life, and in his fall, he is like grass, the flower of grass, which soon withers and dies away. We should hear, and thus receive and love, the holy, living word, and rather hazard all than lose it; and we must banish all other things from the place due to it. We should lodge it in our hearts as our only treasures here, and the certain pledge of the treasure of glory laid up for believers in heaven.

Chapter 2

Chapter Outline

Verses 1-10

Evil-speaking is a sign of malice and guile in the heart; and hinders our profiting by the word of God. A new life needs suitable food. Infants desire milk, and make the best endeavours for it which they are able to do; such must be a Christian's desires after the word of God. Our Lord Jesus Christ is very merciful to us miserable sinners; and he has a fulness of grace. But even the best of God's servants, in this life, have only a taste of the consolations of God. Christ is called a Stone, to teach his servants that he is their protection and security, the foundation on which they are built. He is precious in the excellence of his nature, the dignity of his office, and the glory of his services. All true believers are a holy priesthood; sacred to God, serviceable to others, endowed with heavenly gifts and graces. But the most spiritual sacrifices of the best in prayer and praise are not acceptable, except through Jesus Christ. Christ is the chief Corner-stone, that unites the whole number of believers into one everlasting temple, and bears the weight of the whole fabric. Elected, or chosen, for a foundation that is everlasting. Precious beyond compare, by all that can give worth. To be built on Christ means, to believe in him; but in this many deceive themselves, they consider not what it is, nor the necessity of it, to partake of the salvation he has wrought. Though the frame of the world were falling to pieces, that man who is built on this foundation may hear it without fear. He shall not be confounded. The believing soul makes haste to Christ, but it never finds cause to hasten from him. All true Christians are a chosen generation; they make one family, a people distinct from the world: of another spirit, principle, and practice; which they could never be, if they were not chosen in Christ to be such, and sanctified by his Spirit. Their first state is a state of gross darkness, but they are called out of darkness into a state of joy, pleasure, and prosperity; that they should show forth the praises of the Lord by their profession of his truth, and their good conduct. How vast their obligations to Him who has made them his people, and has shown mercy to them! To be without this mercy is a woful state, though a man have all worldly enjoyments. And there is nothing that so kindly works repentance, as right thoughts of the mercy and love of God. Let us not dare to abuse and affront the free grace of God, if we mean to be saved by it; but let all who would be found among those who obtain mercy, walk as his people.

Verses 11, 12

Even the best of men, the chosen generation, the people of God, need to be exhorted to keep from the worst sins. And fleshly lusts are most destructive to man's soul. It is a sore judgment to be given up to them. There is a day of visitation coming, wherein God may call to repentance by his word and his grace; then many will glorify God, and the holy lives of his people will have promoted the happy change.

Verses 13-17

A Christian conversation must be honest; which it cannot be, if there is not a just and careful discharge of all relative duties: the apostle here treats of these distinctly. Regard to those duties is the will of God, consequently, the Christian's duty, and the way to silence the base slanders of ignorant and foolish men. Christians must endeavour, in all relations, to behave aright, that they do not make their liberty a cloak or covering for any wickedness, or for the neglect of duty; but they must remember that they are servants of God.

Verses 18-25

Servants in those days generally were slaves, and had heathen masters, who often used them cruelly; yet the apostle directs them to be subject to the masters placed over them by Providence, with a fear to dishonour or offend God. And not only to those pleased with reasonable service, but to the severe, and those angry without cause. The sinful misconduct of one relation, does not justify sinful behaviour in the other; the servant is bound to do his duty, though the master may be sinfully froward and perverse. But masters should be meek and gentle to their servants and inferiors. What glory or distinction could it be, for professed Christians to be patient when corrected for their faults? But if when they behaved well they were ill treated by proud and passionate heathen masters, yet bore it without peevish complaints, or purposes of revenge, and persevered in their duty, this would be acceptable to God as a distinguishing effect of his grace, and would be rewarded by him. Christ's death was designed not only for an example of patience under sufferings, but he bore our sins; he bore the punishment of them, and thereby satisfied Divine justice. Hereby he takes them away from us. The fruits of Christ's sufferings are the death of sin, and a new holy life of righteousness; for both which we have an example, and powerful motives, and ability to perform also, from the death and resurrection of Christ. And our justification; Christ was bruised and crucified as a sacrifice for our sins, and by his stripes the diseases of our souls are cured. Here is man's sin; he goes astray; it is his own act. His misery; he goes astray from the pasture, from the Shepherd, and from the flock, and so exposes himself to dangers without number. Here is the recovery by conversion; they are now returned as the effect of Divine grace. This return is, from all their errors and wanderings, to Christ. Sinners, before their conversion, are always going astray; their life is a continued error.

Chapter 3

Chapter Outline

Verses 1-7

The wife must discharge her duty to her own husband, though he obey not the word. We daily see how narrowly evil men watch the ways and lives of professors of religion. Putting on of apparel is not forbidden, but vanity and costliness in ornament. Religious people should take care that all their behaviour answers to their profession. But how few know the right measure and bounds of those two necessaries of life, food and raiment! Unless poverty is our carver, and cuts us short, there is scarcely any one who does not desire something beyond what is good for us. Far more are beholden to the lowliness of their state, than the lowliness of their mind; and many will not be so bounded, but lavish their time and money upon trifles. The apostle directs Christian females to put on something not corruptible, that beautifies the soul, even the graces of God's Holy Spirit. A true Christian's chief care lies in right ordering his own spirit. This will do more to fix the affections, and excite the esteem of a husband, than studied ornaments or fashionable apparel, attended by a froward and quarrelsome temper. Christians ought to do their duty to one another, from a willing mind, and in obedience to the command of God. Wives should be subject to their husbands, not from dread and amazement, but from desire to do well, and please God. The husband's duty to the wife implies giving due respect unto her, and maintaining her authority, protecting her, and placing trust in her. They are heirs together of all the blessings of this life and that which is to come, and should live peaceably one with another. Prayer sweetens their converse. And it is not enough that they pray with the family, but husband and wife together by themselves, and with their children. Those who are acquainted with prayer, find such unspeakable sweetness in it, that they will not be hindered therein. That you may pray much, live holily; and that you may live holily, be much in prayer.

Verses 8-13

Though Christians cannot always be exactly of the same mind, yet they should have compassion one of another, and love as brethren. If any man desires to live comfortably on earth, or to possess eternal life in heaven, he must bridle his tongue from wicked, abusive, or deceitful words. He must forsake and keep far from evil actions, do all the good he can, and seek peace with all men. For God, all-wise and every where present, watches over the righteous, and takes care of them. None could or should harm those who copied the example of Christ, who is perfect goodness, and did good to others as his followers.

Verses 14-22

We sanctify God before others, when our conduct invites and encourages them to glorify and honour him. What was the ground and reason of their hope? We should be able to defend our religion with meekness, in the fear of God. There is no room for any other fears where this great fear is; it disturbs not. The conscience is good, when it does its office well. That person is in a sad condition on whom sin and suffering meet: sin makes suffering extreme, comfortless, and destructive. Surely it is better to suffer for well-doing than for evil-doing, whatever our natural impatience at times may suggest. The example of Christ is an argument for patience under sufferings. In the case of our Lord's suffering, he that knew no sin, suffered instead of those who knew no righteousness. The blessed end and design of our Lord's sufferings were, to reconcile us to God, and to bring us to eternal glory. He was put to death in respect of his human nature, but was quickened and raised by the power of the Holy Spirit. If Christ could not be freed from sufferings, why should Christians think to be so? God takes exact notice of the means and advantages people in all ages have had. As to the old world, Christ sent his Spirit; gave warning by Noah. But though the patience of God waits long, it will cease at last. And the spirits of disobedient sinners, as soon as they are out of their bodies, are committed to the prison of hell, where those that despised Noah's warning now are, and from whence there is no redemption. Noah's salvation in the ark upon the water, which carried him above the floods, set forth the salvation of all true believers. That temporal salvation by the ark was a type of the eternal salvation of believers by baptism of the Holy Spirit. To prevent mistakes, the apostle declares what he means by saving baptism; not the outward ceremony of washing with water, which, in itself, does no more than put away the filth of the flesh, but that baptism, of which the baptismal water formed the sign. Not the outward ordinance, but when a man, by the regeneration of the Spirit, was enabled to repent and profess faith, and purpose a new life, uprightly, and as in the presence of God. Let us beware that we rest not upon outward forms. Let us learn to look on the ordinances of God spiritually, and to inquire after the spiritual effect and working of them on our consciences. We would willingly have all religion reduced to outward things. But many who were baptized, and constantly attended the ordinances, have remained without

Christ, died in their sins, and are now past recovery. Rest not then till thou art cleansed by the Spirit of Christ and the blood of Christ. His resurrection from the dead is that whereby we are assured of purifying and peace.

Chapter 4

Chapter Outline

The consideration of Christ's sufferings is urged for purity and holiness.   (1–6)

And the approaching end of the Jewish state, as a reason for sobriety, watchfulness, and prayer.   (7–11)

Believers encouraged to rejoice and glory in reproaches and sufferings for Christ, and to commit their souls to the care of a faithful God.   (12–19)

Verses 1-6

The strongest and best arguments against sin, are taken from the sufferings of Christ. He died to destroy sin; and though he cheerfully submitted to the worst sufferings, yet he never gave way to the least sin. Temptations could not prevail, were it not for man's own corruption; but true Christians make the will of God, not their own lust or desires, the rule of their lives and actions. And true conversion makes a marvellous change in the heart and life. It alters the mind, judgment, affections, and conversation. When a man is truly converted, it is very grievous to him to think how the time past of his life has been spent. One sin draws on another. Six sins are here mentioned which have dependence one upon another. It is a Christian's duty, not only to keep from gross wickedness, but also from things that lead to sin, or appear evil. The gospel had been preached to those since dead, who by the proud and carnal judgment of wicked men were condemned as evildoers, some even suffering death. But being quickened to Divine life by the Holy Spirit, they lived to God as his devoted servants. Let not believers care, though the world scorns and reproaches them.

Verses 7-11

The destruction of the Jewish church and nation, foretold by our Saviour, was very near. And the speedy approach of death and judgment concerns all, to which these words naturally lead our minds. Our approaching end, is a powerful argument to make us sober in all worldly matters, and earnest in religion. There are so many things amiss in all, that unless love covers, excuses, and forgives in others, the mistakes and faults for which every one needs the forbearance of others, Satan will prevail to stir up divisions and discords. But we are not to suppose that charity will cover or make amends for the sins of those who exercise it, so as to induce God to forgive them. The nature of a Christian's work, which is high work and hard work, the goodness of the Master, and the excellence of the reward, all require that our endeavours should be serious and earnest. And in all the duties and services of life, we should aim at the glory of God as our chief end. He is a miserable, unsettled wretch, who cleaves to himself, and forgets God; is only perplexed about his credit, and gain, and base ends, which are often broken, and which, when he attains, both he and they must shortly perish together. But he who has given up himself and his all to God, may say confidently that the Lord is his portion; and nothing but glory through Christ Jesus, is solid and lasting; that abideth for ever.

Verses 12-19

By patience and fortitude in suffering, by dependence on the promises of God, and keeping to the word the Holy Spirit hath revealed, the Holy Spirit is glorified; but by the contempt and reproaches cast upon believers, he is evil spoken of, and is blasphemed. One would think such cautions as these were needless to Christians. But their enemies falsely charged them with foul crimes. And even the best of men need to be warned against the worst of sins. There is no comfort in sufferings, when we bring them upon ourselves by our own sin and folly. A time of universal calamity was at hand, as foretold by our Saviour, Mt 24:9, 10. And if such things befall in this life, how awful will the day of judgment be! It is true that the righteous are scarcely saved; even those who endeavour to walk uprightly in the ways of God. This does not mean that the purpose and performance of God are uncertain, but only the great difficulties and hard encounters in the way; that they go through so many temptations and tribulations, so many fightings without and fears within. Yet all outward difficulties would be as nothing, were it not for lusts and corruptions within. These are the worst clogs and troubles. And if the way of the righteous be so hard, then how hard shall be the end of the ungodly sinner, who walks in sin with delight, and thinks the righteous is a fool for all his pains! The only way to keep the soul well, is, to commit it to God by prayer, and patient perseverance in well-doing. He will overrule all to the final advantage of the believer.

Chapter 5

Chapter Outline

Elders exhorted and encouraged.   (1–4)

Younger Christians are to submit to their elders, and to yield with humility and patience to God, and to be sober, watchful, and stedfast in faith.   (5–9)

Prayers for their growth and establishment.   (10–14)

Verses 1-4

The apostle Peter does not command, but exhorts. He does not claim power to rule over all pastors and churches. It was the peculiar honour of Peter and a few more, to be witnesses of Christ's sufferings; but it is the privilege of all true Christians to partake of the glory that shall be revealed. These poor, dispersed, suffering Christians, were the flock of God, redeemed to God by the great Shepherd, living in holy love and communion, according to the will of God. They are also dignified with the title of God's heritage or clergy; his peculiar lot, chosen for his own people, to enjoy his special favour, and to do him special service. Christ is the chief Shepherd of the whole flock and heritage of God. And all faithful ministers will receive a crown of unfading glory, infinitely better and more honourable than all the authority, wealth, and pleasure of the world.

Verses 5-9

Humility preserves peace and order in all Christian churches and societies; pride disturbs them. Where God gives grace to be humble, he will give wisdom, faith, and holiness. To be humble, and subject to our reconciled God, will bring greater comfort to the soul than the gratification of pride and ambition. But it is to be in due time; not in thy fancied time, but God's own wisely appointed time. Does he wait, and wilt not thou? What difficulties will not the firm belief of his wisdom, power, and goodness get over! Then be humble under his hand. Cast "all you care;" personal cares, family cares, cares for the present, and cares for the future, for yourselves, for others, for the church, on God. These are burdensome, and often very sinful, when they arise from unbelief and distrust, when they torture and distract the mind, unfit us for duties, and hinder our delight in the service of God. The remedy is, to cast our care upon God, and leave every event to his wise and gracious disposal. Firm belief that the Divine will and counsels are right, calms the spirit of a man. Truly the godly too often forget this, and fret themselves to no purpose. Refer all to God's disposal. The golden mines of all spiritual comfort and good are wholly his, and the Spirit itself. Then, will he not furnish what is fit for us, if we humbly attend on him, and lay the care of providing for us, upon his wisdom and love? The whole design of Satan is to devour and destroy souls. He always is contriving whom he may insnare to eternal ruin. Our duty plainly is, to be sober; to govern both the outward and the inward man by the rules of temperance. To be vigilant; suspicious of constant danger from this spiritual enemy, watchful and diligent to prevent his designs. Be stedfast, or solid, by faith. A man cannot fight upon a quagmire, there is no standing without firm ground to tread upon; this faith alone furnishes. It lifts the soul to the firm advanced ground of the promises, and fixes it there. The consideration of what others suffer, is proper to encourage us to bear our share in any affliction; and in whatever form Satan assaults us, or by whatever means, we may know that our brethren experience the same.

Verses 10-14

In conclusion, the apostle prays to God for them, as the God of all grace. Perfect implies their progress towards perfection. Stablish imports the curing of our natural lightness and inconstancy. Strengthen has respect to the growth of graces, especially where weakest and lowest. Settle signifies to fix upon a sure foundation, and may refer to Him who is the Foundation and Strength of believers. These expressions show that perseverance and progress in grace are first to be sought after by every Christian. The power of these doctrines on the hearts, and the fruits in the lives, showed who are partakers of the grace of God. The cherishing and increase of Christian love, and of affection one to another, is no matter of empty compliment, but the stamp and badge of Jesus Christ on his followers. Others may have a false peace for a time, and wicked men may wish for it to themselves and to one another; but theirs is a vain hope, and will come to nought. All solid peace is founded on Christ, and flows from him.

2 Peter

This epistle clearly is connected with the former epistle of Peter. The apostle having stated the blessings to which God has called Christians, exhorts those who had received these precious gifts, to endeavour to improve in graces and virtues. They are urged to this from the wickedness of false teachers. They are guarded against impostors and scoffers, by disproving their false assertions, ch. 3:1–7, and by showing why the great day of Christ's coming was delayed, with a description of its awful circumstances and consequences; and suitable exhortations to diligence and holiness are given.

Chapter 1

Chapter Outline

Exhortations to add the exercise of various other graces to faith. (1–11)

The apostle looks forward to his approaching decease. (12–15)

And confirms the truth of the gospel, relating to Christ's appearing to judgment. (16–21)

Verses 1-11

Faith unites the weak believer to Christ, as really as it does the strong one, and purifies the heart of one as truly as of another; and every sincere believer is by his faith justified in the sight of God. Faith worketh godliness, and produces effects which no other grace in the soul can do. In Christ all fulness dwells, and pardon, peace, grace, and knowledge, and new principles, are thus given through the Holy Spirit. The promises to those who are partakers of a Divine nature, will cause us to inquire whether we are really renewed in the spirit of our minds; let us turn all these promises into prayers for the transforming and purifying grace of the Holy Spirit. The believer must add knowledge to his virtue, increasing acquaintance with the whole truth and will of God. We must add temperance to knowledge; moderation about worldly things; and add to temperance, patience, or cheerful submission to the will of God. Tribulation worketh patience, whereby we bear all calamities and crosses with silence and submission. To patience we must add godliness: this includes the holy affections and dispositions found in the true worshipper of God; with tender affection to all fellow Christians, who are children of the same Father, servants of the same Master, members of the same family, travellers to the same country, heirs of the same inheritance. Wherefore let Christians labour to attain assurance of their calling, and of their election, by believing and well-doing; and thus carefully to endeavour, is a firm argument of the grace and mercy of God, upholding them so that they shall not utterly fall. Those who are diligent in the work of religion, shall have a triumphant entrance into that everlasting kingdom where Christ reigns, and they shall reign with him for ever and ever; and it is in the practice of every good work that we are to expect entrance to heaven.

Verses 12-15

We must be established in the belief of the truth, that we may not be shaken by every wind of doctrine; and especially in the truth necessary for us to know in our day, what belongs to our peace, and what is opposed in our time. The body is but a tabernacle, or tent, of the soul. It is a mean and movable dwelling. The nearness of death makes the apostle diligent in the business of life. Nothing can so give composure in the prospect, or in the hour, of death, as to know that we have faithfully and simply followed the Lord Jesus, and sought his glory. Those who fear the Lord, talk of his loving-kindness. This is the way to spread the knowledge of the Lord; and by the written word, they are enabled to do this.

Verses 16-21

The gospel is no weak thing, but comes in power, Ro 1:16. The law sets before us our wretched state by sin, but there it leaves us. It discovers our disease, but does not make known the cure. It is the sight of Jesus crucified, in the gospel, that heals the soul. Try to dissuade the covetous worldling from his greediness, one ounce of gold weighs down all reasons. Offer to stay a furious man from anger by arguments, he has not patience to hear them. Try to detain the licentious, one smile is stronger with him than all reason. But come with the gospel, and urge them with the precious blood of Jesus Christ, shed to save their souls from hell, and to satisfy for their sins, and this is that powerful pleading which makes good men confess that their hearts burn within them, and bad men, even an Agrippa, to say they are almost persuaded to be Christians, Ac 26:28. God is well pleased with Christ, and with us in him. This is the Messiah who was promised, through whom all who believe in him shall be accepted and saved. The truth and reality of the gospel also are foretold by the prophets and penmen of the Old Testament, who spake and wrote under influence, and according to the direction of the Spirit of God. How firm and sure should our faith be, who have such a firm and sure word to rest upon! When the light of the Scripture is darted into the blind mind and dark understanding, by the Holy Spirit of God, it is like the day-break that advances, and diffuses itself through the whole soul, till it makes perfect day. As the Scripture is the revelation of the mind and will of God, every man ought to search it, to understand the sense and meaning. The Christian knows that book to be the word of God, in which he tastes a sweetness, and feels a power, and sees a glory, truly divine. And the prophecies already fulfilled in the person and salvation of Christ, and in the great concerns of the church and the world, form an unanswerable proof of the truth of Christianity. The Holy Ghost inspired holy men to speak and write. He so assisted and directed them in delivering what they had received from him, that they clearly expressed what they made known. So that the Scriptures are to be accounted the words of the Holy Ghost, and all the plainness and simplicity, all the power and all the propriety of the words and expressions, come from God. Mix faith with what you find in the Scriptures, and esteem and reverence the Bible as a book written by holy men, taught by the Holy Ghost.

Chapter 2

Chapter Outline

Believers are cautioned against false teachers, and the certainty of their punishment shown from examples.

An account of these seducers, as exceedingly wicked.

But as making high pretences to liberty and purity.

Verses 1-9

Though the way of error is a hurtful way, many are always ready to walk therein. Let us take care we give no occasion to the enemy to blaspheme the holy name whereby we are called, or to speak evil of the way of salvation by Jesus Christ, who is the Way, the Truth, and the Life. These seducers used feigned words, they deceived the hearts of their followers. Such are condemned already, and the wrath of God abides upon them. God's usual method of proceeding is shown by examples. Angels were cast down from all their glory and dignity, for their disobedience. If creatures sin, even in heaven, they must suffer in hell. Sin is the work of darkness, and darkness is the wages of sin. See how God dealt with the old world. The number of offenders no more procures favour, than their quality. If the sin be universal, the punishment shall likewise extend to all. If in a fruitful soil the people abound in sin, God can at once turn a fruitful land into barrenness, and a well-watered country into ashes. No plans or politics can keep off judgments from a sinful people. He who keeps fire and water from hurting his people, Isa 43:2, can make either destroy his enemies; they are never safe. When God sends destruction on the ungodly, he commands deliverance for the righteous. In bad company we cannot but get either guilt or grief. Let the sins of others be troubles to us. Yet it is possible for the children of the Lord, living among the most profane, to retain their integrity; there being more power in the grace of Christ, and his dwelling in them, than in the temptations of Satan, or the example of the wicked, with all their terrors or allurements. In our intentions and inclinations to commit sin, we meet with strange hinderances, if we mark them When we intend mischief, God sends many stops to hinder us, as if to say, Take heed what you do. His wisdom and power will surely effect the purposes of his love, and the engagements of his truth; while wicked men often escape suffering here, because they are kept to the day of judgment, to be punished with the devil and his angels.

Verses 10-16

Impure seducers and their abandoned followers, give themselves up to their own fleshly minds. Refusing to bring every thought to the obedience of Christ, they act against God's righteous precepts. They walk after the flesh, they go on in sinful courses, and increase to greater degrees of impurity and wickedness. They also despise those whom God has set in authority over them, and requires them to honour. Outward temporal good things are the wages sinners expect and promise themselves. And none have more cause to tremble, than those who are bold to gratify their sinful lusts, by presuming on the Divine grace and mercy. Many such there have been, and are, who speak lightly of the restraints of God's law, and deem themselves freed from obligations to obey it. Let Christians stand at a distance from such.

Verses 17-22

The word of truth is the water of life, which refreshes the souls that receive it; but deceivers spread and promote error, and are set forth as empty, because there is no truth in them. As clouds hinder the light of the sun, so do these darken counsel by words wherein there is no truth. Seeing that these men increase darkness in this world, it is very just that the mist of darkness should be their portion in the next. In the midst of their talk of liberty, these men are the vilest slaves; their own lusts gain a complete victory over them, and they are actually in bondage. When men are entangled, they are easily overcome; therefore Christians should keep close to the word of God, and watch against all who seek to bewilder them. A state of apostacy is worse than a state of ignorance. To bring an evil report upon the good way of God, and a false charge against the way of truth, must expose to the heaviest condemnation. How dreadful is the state here described! Yet though such a case is deplorable, it is not utterly hopeless; the leper may be made clean, and even the dead may be raised. Is thy backsliding a grief to thee? Believe in the Lord Jesus, and thou shalt be saved.

Chapter 3

Chapter Outline

The design here is to remind of Christ's final coming to judgement.	(1–4)
He will appear unexpectedly, when the present frame of nature will be dissolved by fire.	(5–10)
From thence is inferred the need for holiness, and stedfastness in the faith.	(11–18)

Verses 1-4

The purified minds of Christians are to be stirred up, that they may be active and lively in the work of holiness. There will be scoffers in the last days, under the gospel, men who make light of sin, and mock at salvation by Jesus Christ. One very principal article of our faith refers to what only has a promise to rest upon, and scoffers will attack it till our Lord is come. They will not believe that he will come. Because they see no changes, therefore they fear not God, Ps 55:19. What he never has done, they fancy he never can do, or never will do.

Verses 5-10

Had these scoffers considered the dreadful vengeance with which God swept away a whole world of ungodly men at once, surely they would not have scoffed at his threatening an equally terrible judgment. The heavens and the earth which now are, by the same word, it is declared, will be destroyed by fire. This is as sure to come, as the truth and the power of God can make it. Christians are here taught and established in the truth of the coming of the Lord. Though, in the account of men, there is a vast difference between one day and a thousand years, yet, in the account of God, there is no difference. All things past, present, and future, are ever before him: the delay of a thousand years cannot be so much to him, as putting off any thing for a day or for an hour is to us. If men have no knowledge or belief of the eternal God, they will be very apt to think him such as themselves. How hard is it to form any thoughts of eternity! What men count slackness, is long-suffering, and that to us-ward; it is giving more time to his own people, to advance in knowledge and holiness, and in the exercise of faith and patience, to abound in good works, doing and suffering what they are called to, that they may bring glory to God. Settle therefore in your hearts that you shall certainly be called to give an account of all things done in the body, whether good or evil. And let a humble and diligent walking before God, and a frequent judging of yourselves, show a firm belief of the future judgment, though many live as if they were never to give any account at all. This day will come, when men are secure, and have no expectation of the day of the Lord. The stately palaces, and all the desirable things wherein wordly-minded men seek and place their happiness, shall be burned up; all sorts of creatures God has made, and all the works of men, must pass through the fire, which shall be a consuming fire to all that sin has brought into the world, though a refining fire to the works of God's hand. What will become of us, if we set our affections on this earth, and make it our portion, seeing all these things shall be burned up? Therefore make sure of happiness beyond this visible world.

Verses 11-18

From the doctrine of Christ's second coming, we are exhorted to purity and godliness. This is the effect of real knowledge. Very exact and universal holiness is enjoined, not resting in any low measure or degree. True Christians look for new heavens and a new earth; freed from the vanity to which things present are subject, and the sin they are polluted with. Those only who are clothed with the righteousness of Christ, and sanctified by the Holy Ghost, shall be admitted to dwell in this holy place. He is faithful, who has promised. Those, whose sins are pardoned, and their peace made with God, are the only safe and happy people; therefore follow after peace, and that with all men; follow after holiness as well as peace. Never expect to be found at that day of God in peace, if you are lazy and idle in this your day, in which we must finish the work given us to do. Only the diligent Christian will be the happy Christian in the day of the Lord. Our Lord will suddenly come to us, or shortly call us to him; and shall he find us idle? Learn to make a right use of the patience of our Lord, who as yet delays his coming. Proud, carnal, and corrupt men, seek to wrest some things into a seeming agreement with their wicked doctrines. But this is no reason why St. Paul's epistles, or any other part of the Scriptures, should be laid aside; for men, left to themselves, pervert every gift of God. Then let us seek to have our minds prepared for receiving things hard to be understood, by putting in practice things which are more easy to be understood. But there must be self-denial and suspicion of ourselves, and submission to the authority of Christ Jesus, before we can heartily receive all the truths of the gospel, therefore we are in great danger of rejecting the truth. And whatever opinions and thoughts of men are not according to the law of God, and warranted by it, the believer disclaims and abhors. Those who are led away by error, fall from their own stedfastness. And that we may avoid being led away, we must seek to grow in all grace, in faith, and virtue, and knowledge. Labour to know Christ more clearly, and more fully; to know him so as to be more like him, and to love him better. This is the knowledge of Christ, which the apostle Paul reached after, and desired to attain; and those who taste this effect of the knowledge of the Lord and Saviour Jesus Christ, will, upon receiving such grace from him, give thanks and praise him, and join in ascribing glory to him now, in the full assurance of doing the same hereafter, for ever.

1 John

This epistle is a discourse upon the principles of Christianity, in doctrine and practice. The design appears to be, to refute and guard against erroneous and unholy tenets, principles, and practices, especially such as would lower the Godhead of Christ, and the reality and power of his sufferings and death, as an atoning sacrifice; and against the assertion that believers being saved by grace, are not required to obey the commandments. This epistle also stirs up all who profess to know God, to have communion with him, and to believe in him, and that they walk in holiness, not in sin, showing that a mere outward profession is nothing, without the evidence of a holy life and conduct. It also helps forward and excites real Christians to communion with God and the Lord Jesus Christ, to constancy in the true faith, and to purity of life.

Chapter 1

Chapter Outline

The apostle prefaces his epistle to believers in general, with evident testimonies to Christ, for promoting their happiness and joy.   (1–4)

The necessity of a life of holiness, in order to communion with God, is shown.   (5–10)

Verses 1-4

That essential Good, that uncreated Excellence, which had been from the beginning, from eternity, as equal with the Father, and which at length appeared in human nature for the salvation of sinners, was the great subject concerning which the apostle wrote to his brethren. The apostles had seen Him while they witnessed his wisdom and holiness, his miracles, and love and mercy, during some years, till they saw him crucified for sinners, and afterwards risen from the dead. They touched him, so as to have full proof of his resurrection. This Divine Person, the Word of life, the Word of God, appeared in human nature, that he might be the Author and Giver of eternal life to mankind, through the redemption of his blood, and the influence of his new-creating Spirit. The apostles declared what they had seen and heard, that believers might share their comforts and everlasting advantages. They had free access to God the Father. They had a happy experience of the truth in their souls, and showed its excellence in their lives. This communion of believers with the Father and the Son, is begun and kept up by the influences of the Holy Spirit. The benefits Christ bestows, are not like the scanty possessions of the world, causing jealousies in others; but the joy and happiness of communion with God is all-sufficient, so that any number may partake of it; and all who are warranted to say, that truly their fellowship is with the Father, will desire to lead others to partake of the same blessedness.

Verses 5-10

A message from the Lord Jesus, the Word of life, the eternal Word, we should all gladly receive. The great God should be represented to this dark world, as pure and perfect light. As this is the nature of God, his doctrines and precepts must be such. And as his perfect happiness cannot be separated from his perfect holiness, so our happiness will be in proportion to our being made holy. To walk in darkness, is to live and act against religion. God holds no heavenly fellowship or intercourse with unholy souls. There is no truth in their profession; their practice shows its folly and falsehood. The eternal Life, the eternal Son, put on flesh and blood, and died to wash us from our sins in his own blood, and procures for us the sacred influences by which sin is to be subdued more and more, till it is quite done away. While the necessity of a holy walk is insisted upon, as the effect and evidence of the knowledge of God in Christ Jesus, the opposite error of self-righteous pride is guarded against with equal care. All who walk near to God, in holiness and righteousness, are sensible that their best days and duties are mixed with sin. God has given testimony to the sinfulness of the world, by providing a sufficient, effectual Sacrifice for sin, needed in all ages; and the sinfulness of believers themselves is shown, by requiring them continually to confess their sins, and to apply by faith to the blood of that Sacrifice. Let us plead guilty before God, be humble, and willing to know the worst of our case. Let us honestly confess all our sins in their full extent, relying wholly on his mercy and truth through the righteousness of Christ, for a free and full forgiveness, and our deliverance from the power and practice of sin.

Chapter 2

Chapter Outline

The apostle directs to the atonement of Christ for help against sinful infirmities.	(1, 2)
The effects of saving knowledge in producing obedience, and love to the brethren.	(3–11)
Christians addressed as little children, young men, and fathers.	(12–14)
All are cautioned against the love of this world, and against errors.	(15–23)
They are encouraged to stand fast in faith and holiness.	(24–29)

Verses 1, 2

When have an Advocate with the Father; one who has undertaken, and is fully able, to plead in behalf of every one who applies for pardon and salvation in his name, depending on his pleading for them. He is "Jesus," the Saviour, and "Christ," the Messiah, the Anointed. He alone is "the Righteous One," who received his nature pure from sin, and as our Surety perfectly obeyed the law of God, and so fulfilled all righteousness. All men, in every land, and through successive generations, are invited to come to God through this all-sufficient atonement, and by this new and living way. The gospel, when rightly understood and received, sets the heart against all sin, and stops the allowed practice of it; at the same time it gives blessed relief to the wounded consciences of those who have sinned.

Verses 3-11

What knowledge of Christ can that be, which sees not that he is most worthy of our entire obedience? And a disobedient life shows there is neither religion nor honesty in the professor. The love of God is perfected in him that keeps his commandments. God's grace in him attains its true mark, and produces its sovereign effect as far as may be in this world, and this is man's regeneration; though never absolutely perfect here. Yet this observing Christ's commands, has holiness and excellency which, if universal, would make the earth resemble heaven itself. The command to love one another had been in force from the beginning of the world; but it might be called a new command as given to Christians. It was new in them, as their situation was new in respect of its motives, rules, and obligations. And those who walk in hatred and enmity to believers, remain in a dark state. Christian love teaches us to value our brother's soul, and to dread every thing hurtful to his purity and peace. Where spiritual darkness dwells, in mind, the judgment, and the conscience will be darkened, and will mistake the way to heavenly life. These things demand serious self-examination; and earnest prayer, that God would show us what we are, and whither we are going.

Verses 12-14

As Christians have their peculiar states, so they have peculiar duties; but there are precepts and obedience common to all, particularly mutual love, and contempt of the world. The youngest sincere disciple is pardoned: the communion of saints is attended with the forgiveness of sins. Those of the longest standing in Christ's school need further advice and instruction. Even fathers must be written unto, and preached unto; none are too old to learn. But especially young men in Christ Jesus, though they are arrived at strength of spirit and sound sense, and have successfully resisted first trials and temptations, breaking off bad habits and connexions, and entered in at the strait gate of true conversion. The different descriptions of Christians are again addressed. Children in Christ know that God is their Father; it is wisdom. Those advanced believers, who know Him that was from the beginning, before this world was made, may well be led thereby to give up this world. It will be the glory of young persons to be strong in Christ, and his grace. By the word of God they overcome the wicked one.

Verses 15-17

The things of the world may be desired and possessed for the uses and purposes which God intended, and they are to be used by his grace, and to his glory; but believers must not seek or value them for those purposes to which sin abuses them. The world draws the heart from God; and the more the love of the world prevails, the more the love of God decays. The things of the world are classed according to the three ruling inclinations of depraved nature. 1. The lust of the flesh, of the body: wrong desires of the heart, the appetite of indulging all things that excite and inflame sensual pleasures. 2. The lust of the eyes: the eyes are delighted with riches and rich possessions; this is the lust of covetousness. 3. The pride of life: a vain man craves the grandeur and pomp of a vain-glorious life; this includes thirst after honour and applause. The things of the world quickly fade and die away; desire itself will ere long fail and cease, but holy affection is not like the lust that passes away. The love of God shall never fail. Many vain efforts have been made to evade the force of this passage by limitations, distinctions, or exceptions. Many have tried to show how far we may be carnally-minded, and love the world; but the plain meaning of these verses cannot easily be mistaken. Unless this victory over the world is begun in the heart, a man has no root in himself, but will fall away, or at most remain an unfruitful professor. Yet these vanities are so alluring to the corruption in our hearts, that without constant watching and prayer, we cannot escape the world, or obtain victory over the god and prince of it.

Verses 18-23

Every man is an antichrist, who denies the Person, or any of the offices of Christ; and in denying the Son, he denies the Father also, and has no part in his favour while he rejects his great salvation. Let this prophecy that seducers would rise in the Christian world, keep us from being seduced. The church knows not well who are its true members, and who are not, but thus true Christians were proved, and rendered more watchful and humble. True Christians are anointed ones; their names expresses this: they are anointed with grace, with gifts and spiritual privileges, by the Holy Spirit of grace. The great and most hurtful lies that the father of lies spreads in the world, usually are falsehoods and errors relating to the person of Christ. The unction from the Holy One, alone can keep us from delusions. While we judge favourably of all who trust in Christ as the Divine Saviour, and obey his word, and seek to live in union with them, let us pity and pray for those who deny the Godhead of Christ, or his atonement, and the new-creating work of the Holy Ghost. Let us protest against such antichristian doctrine, and keep from them as much as we may.

Verses 24-29

The truth of Christ, abiding in us, is a means to sever from sin, and unites us to the Son of God, Joh 15:3, 4. What value should we put upon gospel truth! Thereby the promise of eternal life is made sure. The promise God makes, is suitable to his own greatness, power, and goodness; it is eternal life. The Spirit of truth will not lie; and he teaches all things in the present dispensation, all things necessary to our knowledge of God in Christ, and their glory in the gospel. The apostle repeats the kind words, "little children;" which denotes his affection. He would persuade by love. Gospel privileges oblige to gospel duties; and those anointed by the Lord Jesus abide with him. The new spiritual nature is from the Lord Christ. He that is constant to the practice of religion in trying times, shows that he is born from above, from the Lord Christ. Then, let us beware of holding the truth in unrighteousness, remembering that those only are born of God, who bear his holy image, and walk in his most righteous ways.

Chapter 3

Chapter Outline

Verses 1, 2

Little does the world know of the happiness of the real followers of Christ. Little does the world think that these poor, humble, despised ones, are favourites of God, and will dwell in heaven. Let the followers of Christ be content with hard fare here, since they are in a land of strangers, where their Lord was so badly treated before them. The sons of God must walk by faith, and live by hope. They may well wait in faith, hope, and earnest desire, for the revelation of the Lord Jesus. The sons of God will be known, and be made manifest by likeness to their Head. They shall be transformed into the same image, by their view of him.

Verses 3-10

The sons of God know that their Lord is of purer eyes than to allow any thing unholy and impure to dwell with him. It is the hope of hypocrites, not of the sons of God, that makes allowance for gratifying impure desires and lusts. May we be followers of him as his dear children, thus show our sense of his unspeakable mercy, and express that obedient, grateful, humble mind which becomes us. Sin is the rejecting the Divine law. In him, that is, in Christ, was no sin. All the sinless weaknesses that were consequences of the fall, he took; that is, all those infirmities of mind or body which subject man to suffering, and expose him to temptation. But our moral infirmities, our proneness to sin, he had not. He that abides in Christ, continues not in the practice of sin. Renouncing sin is the great proof of spiritual union with, continuance in, and saving knowledge of the Lord Christ. Beware of self-deceit. He that doeth righteousness is righteous, and to be a follower of Christ, shows an interest by faith in his obedience and sufferings. But a man cannot act like the devil, and at the same time be a disciple of Christ Jesus. Let us not serve or indulge what the Son of God came to destroy. To be born of God is to be inwardly renewed by the power of the Spirit of God. Renewing grace is an abiding principle. Religion is not an art, a matter of dexterity and skill, but a new nature. And the regenerate person cannot sin as he did before he was born of God, and as others do who are not born again. There is that light in his mind, which shows him the evil and malignity of sin.

There is that bias upon his heart, which disposes him to loathe and hate sin. There is the spiritual principle that opposes sinful acts. And there is repentance for sin, if committed. It goes against him to sin with forethought. The children of God and the children of the devil have their distinct characters. The seed of the serpent are known by neglect of religion, and by their hating real Christians. He only is righteous before God, as a justified believer, who is taught and disposed to righteousness by the Holy Spirit. In this the children of God are manifest, and the children of the devil. May all professors of the gospel lay these truths to heart, and try themselves by them.

Verses 11-15

We should love the Lord Jesus, value his love, and therefore love all our brethren in Christ. This love is the special fruit of our faith, and a certain sign of our being born again. But none who rightly know the heart of man, can wonder at the contempt and enmity of ungodly people against the children of God. We know that we are passed from death to life: we may know it by the evidences of our faith in Christ, of which love to our brethren is one. It is not zeal for a party in the common religion, or affection for those who are of the same name and sentiments with ourselves. The life of grace in the heart of a regenerate person, is the beginning and first principle of a life of glory, whereof they must be destitute who hate their brother in their hearts.

Verses 16-21

Here is the condescension, the miracle, the mystery of Divine love, that God would redeem the church with his own blood. Surely we should love those whom God has loved, and so loved. The Holy Spirit, grieved at selfishness, will leave the selfish heart without comfort, and full of darkness and terror. By what can it be known that a man has a true sense of the love of Christ for perishing sinners, or that the love of God has been planted in his heart by the Holy Spirit, if the love of the world and its good overcomes the feelings of compassion to a perishing brother? Every instance of this selfishness must weaken the evidences of a man's conversion; when habitual and allowed, it must decide against him. If conscience condemn us in known sin, or the neglect of known duty, God does so too. Let conscience therefore be well-informed, be heard, and diligently attended to.

Verses 22-24

When believers had confidence towards God, through the Spirit of adoption, and by faith in the great High Priest, they might ask what they would of their reconciled Father. They would receive it, if good for them. And as good-will to men was proclaimed from heaven, so good-will to men, particularly to the brethren, must be in the hearts of those who go to God and heaven. He who thus follows Christ, dwells in Him as his ark, refuge, and rest, and in the Father through him. This union between Christ and the souls of believers, is by the Spirit he has given them. A man may believe that God is gracious before he knows it; yet when faith has laid hold on the promises, it sets reason to work. This Spirit of God works a change; in all true Christians it changes from the power of Satan to the power of God. Consider, believer, how it changes thy heart. Dost not thou long for peace with God? Wouldst thou not forego all the world for it? No profit, pleasure, or preferment shall hinder thee from following Christ. This salvation is built upon Divine testimony, even the Spirit of God.

Chapter 4

Chapter Outline

Believers cautioned against giving heed to every one that pretends to the Spirit.   (1–6)

Brotherly love enforced.   (7–21)

Verses 1-6

Christians who are well acquainted with the Scriptures, may, in humble dependence on Divine teaching, discern those who set forth doctrines according to the apostles, and those who contradict them. The sum of revealed religion is in the doctrine concerning Christ, his person and office. The false teachers spake of the world according to its maxims and tastes, so as not to offend carnal men. The world approved them, they made rapid progress, and had many followers such as themselves; the world will love its own, and its own will love it. The true doctrine as to the Saviour's person, as leading men from the world to God, is a mark of the spirit of truth in opposition to the spirit of error. The more pure and holy any doctrine is, the more likely to be of God; nor can we by any other rules try the spirits whether they are of God or not. And what wonder is it, that people of a worldly spirit should cleave to those who are like themselves, and suit their schemes and discourses to their corrupt taste?

Verses 7-13

The Spirit of God is the Spirit of love. He that does not love the image of God in his people, has no saving knowledge of God. For it is God's nature to be kind, and to give happiness. The law of God is love; and all would have been perfectly happy, had all obeyed it. The provision of the gospel, for the forgiveness of sin, and the salvation of sinners, consistently with God's glory and justice, shows that God is love. Mystery and darkness rest upon many things yet. God has so shown himself to be love, that we cannot come short of eternal happiness, unless through unbelief and impenitence, although strict justice would condemn us to hopeless misery, because we break our Creator's laws. None of our words or thoughts can do justice to the free, astonishing love of a holy God towards sinners, who could not profit or harm him, whom he might justly crush in a moment, and whose deserving of his vengeance was shown in the method by which they were saved, though he could by his almighty Word have created other worlds, with more perfect beings, if he had seen fit. Search we the whole universe for love in its most glorious displays? It is to be found in the person and the cross of Christ. Does love exist between God and sinners? Here was the origin, not that we loved God, but that he freely loved us. His love could not be designed to be fruitless upon us, and when its proper end and issue are gained and produced, it may be said to be perfected. So faith is perfected by its works. Thus it will appear that God dwells in us by his new-creating Spirit. A loving Christian is a perfect Christian; set him to any good duty, and he is perfect to it, he is expert at it. Love oils the wheels of his affections, and sets him on that which is helpful to his brethren. A man that goes about a business with ill will, always does it badly. That God dwells in us and we in him, were words too high for mortals to use, had not God put them before us. But how may it be known whether the testimony to this does proceed from the Holy Ghost? Those who are truly persuaded that they are the sons of God, cannot but call him Abba, Father. From love to him, they hate sin, and whatever disagrees with his will, and they have a sound and hearty desire to do his will. Such testimony is the testimony of the Holy Ghost.

Verses 14-21

The Father sent the Son, he willed his coming into this world. The apostle attests this. And whosoever shall confess that Jesus is the Son of God, God dwelleth in him, and he in God. This confession includes faith in the heart as the foundation; makes acknowledgment with the mouth to the glory of God and Christ, and profession in the life and conduct, against the flatteries and frowns of the world. There must be a day of universal judgment. Happy those who shall have holy boldness before the Judge at that day; knowing he is their Friend and Advocate! Happy those who have holy boldness in the prospect of that day, who look and wait for it, and for the Judge's appearance! True love to God assures believers of God's love to them. Love teaches us to suffer for him and with him; therefore we may trust that we shall also be glorified with him, 2Ti 2:12. We must distinguish between the fear of God and being afraid of him; the fear of God imports high regard and veneration for God. Obedience and good works, done from the principle of love, are not like the servile toil of one who unwillingly labours from dread of a master's anger. They are like that of a dutiful child, who does services to a beloved father, which benefit his brethren, and are done willingly. It is a sign that our love is far from perfect, when our doubts, fears, and apprehensions of God, are many. Let heaven and earth stand amazed at his love. He sent his word to invite sinners to partake of this great salvation. Let them take the comfort of the happy change wrought in them, while they give him the glory. The love of God in Christ, in the hearts of Christians from the Spirit of adoption, is the great proof of conversion. This must be tried by its effects on their temper, and their conduct to their brethren. If a man professes to love God, and yet indulges anger or revenge, or shows a selfish disposition, he gives his profession the lie. But if it is plain that our natural enmity is changed into affection and gratitude, let us bless the name of our God for this seal and earnest of eternal happiness. Then we differ from the false professors, who pretend to love God, whom they have not seen, yet hate their brethren, whom they have seen.

Chapter 5

Chapter Outline

Brotherly love is the effect of the new birth, which makes obedience to all God's commandments pleasant.   (1–5)

Reference to witnesses agreeing to prove that Jesus, the Son of God, is the true Messiah.   (6–8)

The satisfaction the believer has about Christ, and eternal life through him.   (9–12)

The assurance of God's hearing and answering prayer.   (13–17)

The happy condition of true believers, and a charge to renounce all idolatry.   (18–21)

Verses 1-5

True love for the people of God, may be distinguished from natural kindness or party attachments, by its being united with the love of God, and obedience to his commands. The same Holy Spirit that taught the love, will have taught obedience also; and that man cannot truly love the children of God, who, by habit, commits sin or neglects known duty. As God's commands are holy, just, and good rules of liberty and happiness, so those who are born of God and love him, do not count them grievous, but lament that they cannot serve him more perfectly. Self-denial is required, but true Christians have a principle which carries them above all hinderances. Though the conflict often is sharp, and the regenerate may be cast down, yet he will rise up and renew his combat with resolution. But all, except believers in Christ, are enslaved in some respect or other, to the customs, opinions, or interests of the world. Faith is the cause of victory, the means, the instrument, the spiritual armour by which we overcome. In and by faith we cleave to Christ, in contempt of, and in opposition to the world. Faith sanctifies the heart, and purifies it from those sensual lusts by which the world obtains sway and dominion over souls. It has the indwelling Spirit of grace, which is greater than he who dwells in the world. The real Christian overcomes the world by faith; he sees, in and by the life and conduct of the Lord Jesus on earth, that this world is to be renounced and overcome. He cannot be satisfied with this world, but looks beyond it, and is still tending, striving, and pressing toward heaven. We must all, after Christ's example, overcome the world, or it will overcome us to our ruin.

Verses 6-8

We are inwardly and outwardly defiled; inwardly, by the power and pollution of sin in our nature. For our cleansing there is in and by Christ Jesus, the washing of regeneration and the renewing of the Holy Ghost. Some think that the two sacraments are here meant: baptism with water, as the outward sign of regeneration, and purifying from the pollution of sin by the Holy Spirit; and the Lord's supper, as the outward sign of the shedding Christ's blood, and the receiving him by faith for pardon and justification. Both these ways of cleansing were represented in the old ceremonial sacrifices and cleansings. This water and blood include all that is necessary to our salvation. By the water, our souls are washed and purified for heaven and the habitation of saints in light. By the blood, we are justified, reconciled, and presented righteous to God. By the blood, the curse of the law being satisfied, the purifying Spirit is obtained for the internal cleansing of our natures. The water, as well as the blood, came out of the side of the sacrificed Redeemer. He loved the church, and gave himself for it, that he might sanctify and cleanse it with the washing of water by the word; that he might present it to himself a glorious church, Eph 5:25–27. This was done in and by the Spirit of God, according to the Saviour's declaration. He is the Spirit of God, and cannot lie. Three had borne witness to these doctrines concerning the person and the salvation of Christ. The Father, repeatedly, by a voice from heaven declared that Jesus was his beloved Son. The Word declared that He and the Father were One, and that whoever had seen him had seen the Father. And the Holy Ghost, who descended from heaven and rested on Christ at his baptism; who had borne witness to Him by all the prophets; and gave testimony to his resurrection and mediatorial office, by the gift of miraculous powers to the apostles. But whether this passage be cited or not, the doctrine of the Trinity in Unity stands equally firm and certain. To the doctrine taught by the apostles, respecting the person and salvation of Christ, there were three testimonies. 1. The Holy Spirit. We come into the world with a corrupt, carnal disposition, which is enmity to God. This being done away by the regeneration and new-creating of souls by the Holy Spirit, is a testimony to the Saviour. 2. The water: this sets forth the Saviour's purity and purifying power. The actual and active purity and holiness of his disciples are represented by baptism. 3. The blood which he shed: and this was our ransom, this testifies for Jesus Christ; it sealed up and finished the sacrifices of the Old Testament. The benefits procured by his blood, prove that he is the Saviour of the world. No wonder if he that rejects this evidence is judged a blasphemer of the Spirit of God. These three witnesses are for one and the same purpose; they agree in one and the same thing.

Verses 9-12

Nothing can be more absurd than the conduct of those who doubt as to the truth of Christianity, while in the common affairs of life they do not hesitate to proceed on human testimony, and would deem any one out of his senses who declined to do so. The real Christian has seen his guilt and misery, and his need of such a Saviour. He has seen the suitableness of such a Saviour to all his spiritual wants and circumstances. He has found and felt the power of the word and doctrine of Christ, humbling, healing, quickening, and comforting his soul. He has a new disposition, and new delights, and is not the man that he formerly was. Yet he finds still a conflict with himself, with sin, with the flesh, the world, and wicked powers. But he finds such strength from faith in Christ, that he can overcome the world, and travel on towards a better. Such assurance has the gospel believer: he has a witness in himself, which puts the matter out of doubt with him, except in hours of darkness or conflict; but he cannot be argued out of his belief in the leading truths of the gospel. Here is what makes the unbeliever's sin so awful; the sin of unbelief. He gives God the lie; because he believes not the record that God gave of his Son. It is in vain for a man to plead that he believes the testimony of God in other things, while he rejects it in this. He that refuses to trust and honour Christ as the Son of God, who disdains to submit to his teaching as Prophet, to rely on his atonement and intercession as High Priest, or to obey him as King, is dead in sin, under condemnation; nor will any outward morality, learning, forms, notions, or confidences avail him.

Verses 13-17

Upon all this evidence, it is but right that we believe on the name of the Son of God. Believers have eternal life in the covenant of the gospel. Then let us thankfully receive the record of Scripture. Always abounding in the work of the Lord, knowing that our labour is not in vain in the Lord. The Lord Christ invites us to come to him in all circumstances, with our supplications and requests, notwithstanding the sin that besets us. Our prayers must always be offered in submission to the will of God. In some things they are speedily answered; in others they are granted in the best manner, though not as requested. We ought to pray for others, as well as for ourselves. There are sins that war against spiritual life in the soul, and the life above. We cannot pray that the sins of the impenitent and unbelieving should, while they are such, be forgiven them; or that mercy, which supposes the forgiveness of sins, should be granted to them, while they wilfully continue such. But we may pray for their repentance, for their being enriched with faith in Christ, and thereupon for all other saving mercies. We should pray for others, as well as for ourselves, beseeching the Lord to pardon and recover the fallen, as well as to relieve the tempted and afflicted. And let us be truly thankful that no sin, of which any one truly repents, is unto death.

Verses 18-21

All mankind are divided into two parties or dominions; that which belongs to God, and that which belongs to the wicked one. True believers belong to God: they are of God, and from him, and to him, and for him; while the rest, by far the greater number, are in the power of the wicked one; they do his works, and support his cause. This general declaration includes all unbelievers, whatever their profession, station, or situation, or by whatever name they may be called. The Son leads believers to the Father, and they are in the love and favour of both; in union with both, by the indwelling and working of the Holy Spirit. Happy are those to whom it is given to know that the Son of God is come, and to have a heart to trust in and rely on him that is true! May this be our privilege; we shall thus be kept from all idols and false doctrines, and from the idolatrous love of worldly objects, and be kept by the power of God, through faith, unto eternal salvation. To this living and true God, be glory and dominion for ever and ever. Amen.

2 John

This epistle is like an abridgement of the first; it touches, in few words, on the same points. The Lady Electa is commended for her virtuous and religious education of her children; is exhorted to abide in the doctrine of Christ, to persevere in the truth, and carefully to avoid the delusions of false teachers. But chiefly the apostle beseeches her to practise the great commandment of Christian love and charity.

Chapter 1

Chapter Outline

The apostle salutes the elect lady and her children.	(1–3)
Express his joy in their faith and love.	(4–6)
Cautions them against deceivers.	(7–11)
And concludes.	(12, 13)

Verses 1-3

Religion turns compliments into real expressions of respect and love. And old disciple is honourable; an old apostle and leader of disciples is more so. The letter is to a noble Christian matron, and her children; it is well that the gospel should get among such: some noble persons are called. Families are to be encouraged and directed in their love and duties at home. Those who love truth and piety in themselves, should love it in others; and the Christians loved this lady, not for her rank, but for her holiness. And where religion truly dwells, it will abide for ever. From the Divine Persons of the Godhead, the apostle craves grace, Divine favour, and good-will, the spring of all good things. It is grace indeed that any spiritual blessing should be given to sinful mortals. Mercy, free pardon, and forgiveness; for those already rich in grace, need continual forgiveness. Peace, quietness of spirit, and a clear conscience, in assured reconciliation with God, together with all outward prosperity that is really for good: these are desired in truth and love.

Verses 4-6

It is good to be trained to early religion; and children may be beloved for their parents' sake. It gave great joy to the apostle to see children treading in their parents' steps, and likely in their turn to support the gospel. May God bless such families more and more, and raise up many to copy their example. How pleasing the contrast to numbers who spread irreligion, infidelity, and vice, among their children! Our walk is true, our converse right, when according to the word of God. This commandment of mutual Christian love, may be said to be a new one, in respect of its being declared by the Lord Christ; yet, as to the matter, it is old. And this is love to our own souls, that we obey the Divine commands. The foresight of the decay of this love, as well as of other apostacies, or fallings away, might engage the apostle to urge this duty, and this command, frequently and earnestly.

Verses 7-11

The deceiver and his deceit are described: he brings some error concerning the person or office of the Lord Jesus. Such a one is a deceiver and an antichrist; he deludes souls, and undermines the glory and kingdom of the Lord Christ. Let us not think it strange, that there are deceivers and opposers of the Lord Christ's name and dignity now, for there were such, even in the apostles' times. The more deceivers and deceits abound, the more watchful the disciples must be. Sad it is, that splendid attainments in the school of Christ, should ever be lost. The way to gain the full reward is, to abide true to Christ, and constant in religion to the end. Firm cleaving to Christian truth unites us to Christ, and thereby to the Father also; for they are one. Let us equally disregard such as abide not in the doctrine of Christ, and those who transgress his commands. Any who did not profess and preach the doctrine of Christ, respecting him as the Son of God, and salvation by him from guilt and sin, were not to be noticed and countenanced. Yet in obeying this command, we must show kindness and a good spirit to those who differ from us in lesser matters, but hold firmly the all-important doctrines of Christ's person, atonement, and holy salvation.

Verses 12, 13

The apostle refers many things to a personal meeting. Pen and ink were means of strengthening and comforting others; but to see each other is more so. The communion of saints should be maintained by all methods; and should tend to mutual joy. In communion with them we find much of our present joy, and look forward to happiness for ever.

3 John

This epistle is addressed to a converted Gentile. The scope is to commend his stedfastness in the faith, and his hospitality, especially to the ministers of Christ.

Chapter 1

Chapter Outline

The apostle commends Gaius for piety and hospitality. (1–8)

Cautions him against siding with Diotrephes, who was a turbulent spirit; but recommends Demetrius as a man of excellent character. (9–12)

He hopes soon to see Gaius. (13, 14)

Verses 1-8

Those who are beloved of Christ, will love the brethren for his sake. Soul prosperity is the greatest blessing on this side heaven. Grace and health are rich companions. Grace will employ health. A rich soul may be lodged in a weak body; and grace must then be exercised in submitting to such a dispensation. But we may wish and pray that those who have prosperous souls, may have healthful bodies; that their grace may shine where there is still more room for activity. How many professors there are, about whom the apostle's words must be reversed, and we must earnestly wish and pray that their souls might prosper, as their health and circumstances do! True faith will work by love. A good report is due from those who receive good; they could not but testify to the church, what they found and felt. Good men will rejoice in the soul prosperity of others; and they are glad to hear of the grace and goodness of others. And as it is a joy to good parents, it will be a joy to good ministers, to see their people adorn their profession. Gaius overlooked petty differences among serious Christians, and freely helped all who bore the image, and did the work of Christ. He was upright in what he did, as a faithful servant. Faithful souls can hear their own praises without being puffed up; the commendation of what is good in them, lays them at the foot of the cross of Christ. Christians should consider not only what they must do, but what they may do; and should do even the common actions of life, and of good-will, after a godly sort, serving God therein, and designing his glory. Those who freely make known Christ's gospel, should be helped by others to whom God gives the means. Those who cannot themselves proclaim it, may yet receive, help, and countenance those who do so.

Verses 9-12

Both the heart and mouth must be watched. The temper and spirit of Diotrephes was full of pride and ambition. It is bad not to do good ourselves; but it is worse to hinder those who would do good. Those cautions and counsels are most likely to be accepted, which are seasoned with love. Follow that which is good, for he that doeth good, as delighting therein, is born of God. Evil-workers vainly pretend or boast acquaintance with God. Let us not follow that which is proud, selfish, and of bad design, though the example may be given by persons of rank and power; but let us be followers of God, and walk in love, after the example of our Lord.

Verses 13, 14

Here is the character of Demetrius. A name in the gospel, or a good report in the churches, is better than worldly honour. Few are well spoken of by all; and sometimes it is ill to be so. Happy those whose spirit and conduct commend them before God and men. We must be ready to bear our testimony to them; and it is well when those who commend, can appeal to the consciences of such as know most of those who are commended. A personal conversation together often spares time and trouble, and mistakes which rise from letters; and good Christians may well be glad to see one another. The blessing is, Peace be to you; all happiness attend you. Those may well salute and greet one another on earth, who hope to live together in heaven. By associating with and copying the example of such Christians, we shall have peace within, and live at peace with the brethren; our communications with the Lord's people on earth will be pleasing, and we shall be numbered with them in glory everlasting.

Jude

This epistle is addressed to all believers in the gospel. Its design appears to be to guard believers against the false teachers who had begun to creep into the Christian church, and to scatter dangerous tenets, by attempting to lower all Christianity into a merely nominal belief and outward profession of the gospel. Having thus denied the obligations of personal holiness, they taught their disciples to live in sinful courses, at the same time flattering them with the hope of eternal life. The vile character of these seducers is shown, and their sentence is denounced, and the epistle concludes with warnings, admonitions, and counsels to believers.

Chapter 1

Chapter Outline

The apostle exhorts to stedfastness in the faith.	(1–4)
The danger of being infected by false professors, and the dreadful punishment which shall be inflicted on them and their followers.	(5–7)
An awful description of these seducers and their deplorable end.	(8–16)
Believers cautioned against being surprised at such deceivers arising among them.	(17–23)
The epistle ends with an encouraging doxology, or words of praise.	(24, 25)

Verses 1-4

Christians are called out of the world, from the evil spirit and temper of it; called above the world, to higher and better things, to heaven, things unseen and eternal; called from sin to Christ, from vanity to seriousness, from uncleanness to holiness; and this according to the Divine purpose and grace. If sanctified and glorified, all the honour and glory must be ascribed to God, and to him alone. As it is God who begins the work of grace in the souls of men, so it is he who carries it on, and perfects it. Let us not trust in ourselves, nor in our stock of grace already received, but in him, and in him alone. The mercy of God is the spring and fountain of all the good we have or hope for; mercy, not only to the miserable, but to the guilty. Next to mercy is peace, which we have from the sense of having obtained mercy. From peace springs love; Christ's love to us, our love to him, and our brotherly love to one another. The apostle prays, not that Christians may be content with a little; but that their souls and societies may be full of these things. None are shut out from gospel offers and invitations, but those who obstinately and wickedly shut themselves out. But the application is to all believers, and only to such. It is to the weak as well as to the strong. Those who have received the doctrine of this common salvation, must contend for it, earnestly, not furiously. Lying for the truth is bad; scolding for it is not better. Those who have received the truth must contend for it, as the apostles did; by suffering with patience and courage for it, not by making others suffer if they will not embrace every notion we call faith, or important. We ought to contend earnestly for the faith, in opposition to those who would corrupt or deprave it; who creep in unawares; who glide in like serpents. And those are the worst of the ungodly, who take encouragement to sin boldly, because the grace of God has abounded, and still abounds so wonderfully, and who are hardened by the extent and fulness of gospel grace, the design of which is to deliver men from sin, and bring them unto God.

Verses 5-7

Outward privileges, profession, and apparent conversion, could not secure those from the vengeance of God, who turned aside in unbelief and disobedience. The destruction of the unbelieving Israelites in the wilderness, shows that none ought to presume on their privileges. They had miracles as their daily bread; yet even they perished in unbelief. A great number of the angels were not pleased with the stations God allotted to them; pride was the main and direct cause or occasion of their fall. The fallen angels are kept to the judgment of the great day; and shall fallen men escape it? Surely not. Consider this in due time. The destruction of Sodom is a loud warning to all, to take heed of, and flee from fleshly lusts that war against the soul, 1Pe 2:11. God is the same holy, just, pure Being now, as then. Stand in awe, therefore, and sin not, Ps 4:4. Let us not rest in anything that does not make the soul subject to the obedience of Christ; for nothing but the renewal of our souls to the Divine image by the Holy Spirit, can keep us from being destroyed among the enemies of God. Consider this instance of the angels, and see that no dignity or worth of the creature is of avail. How then should man tremble, who drinketh iniquity like water! Job 15:16.

Verses 8-16

False teachers are dreamers; they greatly defile and grievously wound the soul. These teachers are of a disturbed mind and a seditious spirit; forgetting that the powers that be, are ordained of God, Ro 13:1. As to the contest about the body of Moses, it appears that Satan wished to make the place of his burial known to the Israelites, in order to tempt them to worship him, but he was prevented, and vented his rage in desperate blasphemy. This should remind all who dispute never to bring railing charges. Also learn hence, that we ought to defend those whom God owns. It is hard, if not impossible, to find any enemies to the Christian religion, who did not, and do not, live in open or secret contradiction to the principles of natural religion. Such are here compared to brute beasts, though they often boast of themselves as the wisest of mankind. They corrupt themselves in the things most open and plain. The fault lies, not in their understandings, but in their depraved wills, and their disordered appetites and affections. It is a great reproach, though unjust to religion, when those who profess it are opposed to it in heart and life. The Lord will remedy this in his time and way; not in men's blind way of plucking up the wheat with the tares. It is sad when men begin in the Spirit, and end in the flesh. Twice dead; they had been once dead in their natural, fallen state; but now they are dead again by the evident proofs of their hypocrisy. Dead trees, why cumber they the ground! Away with them to the fire. Raging waves are a terror to sailing passengers; but when they get into port, the noise and terror are ended. False teachers are to expect the worst punishments in this world and in that to come. They glare like meteors, or falling stars, and then sink into the blackness of darkness for ever. We have no mention of the prophecy of Enoch in any other part or place of Scripture; yet one plain text of Scripture, proves any point we are to believe. We find from this, that Christ's coming to judge was prophesied of, as early as the times before the flood. The Lord cometh: what a glorious time will that be! Notice how often the word "ungodly" is repeated. Many now do not at all refer to the terms godly, or ungodly, unless it be to mock at even the words; but it is not so in the language taught us by the Holy Ghost. Hard speeches of one another, especially if ill-grounded, will certainly come into account at the day of judgment. These evil men and seducers are angry at every thing that happens, and never pleased with their own state and condition. Their will and their fancy, are their only rule and law. Those who please their sinful appetites, are most prone to yield to ungovernable passions. The men of God, from the beginning of the world, have declared the doom denounced on them. Such let us avoid. We are to follow men only as they follow Christ. (Jud 1:17-23)

Verses 17-23

Sensual men separate from Christ, and his church, and join themselves to the devil, the world, and the flesh, by ungodly and sinful practices. That is infinitely worse than to separate from any branch of the visible church on account of opinions, or modes and circumstances of outward government or worship. Sensual men have not the spirit of holiness, which whoever has not, does not belong to Christ. The grace of faith is most holy, as it works by love, purifies the heart, and overcomes the world, by which it is distinguished from a false and dead faith. Our prayers are most likely to prevail, when we pray in the Holy Ghost, under his guidance and influence, according to the rule of his word, with faith, fervency, and earnestness; this is praying in the Holy Ghost. And a believing expectation of eternal life will arm us against the snares of sin: lively faith in this blessed hope will help us to mortify our lusts. We must watch over one another; faithfully, yet prudently reprove each other, and set a good example to all about us. This must be done with compassion, making a difference between the weak and the wilful. Some we must treat with tenderness. Others save with fear; urging the terrors of the Lord. All endeavours must be joined with decided abhorrence of crimes, and care be taken to avoid whatever led to, or was connected with fellowship with them, in works of darkness, keeping far from what is, or appears to be evil.

Verses 24, 25

God is able, and as willing as able, to keep us from falling, and to present us faultless before the presence of his glory. Not as those who never have been faulty, but as those who, but for God's mercy, and a Saviour's sufferings and merits, might most justly have been condemned long ago. All sincere believers were given him of the Father; and of all so given him he has lost none, nor will lose any one. Now, our faults fill us with fears, doubts, and sorrows; but the Redeemer has undertaken for his people, that they shall be presented faultless. Where there is no sin, there will be no sorrow; where there is the perfection of holiness, there will be the perfection of joy. Let us more often look up to Him who is able to keep us from falling, to improve as well as maintain the work he has wrought in us, till we shall be presented blameless before the presence of his glory.

Then shall our hearts know a joy beyond what earth can afford; then shall God also rejoice over us, and the joy of our compassionate Saviour be completed. To Him who has so wisely formed the scheme, and will faithfully and perfectly accomplish it, be glory and majesty, dominion and power, both now and for ever. Amen.

Revelation

The Book of the Revelation of St. John consists of two principal divisions. 1. Relates to "the things which are," that is, the then present state of the church, and contains the epistle of John to the seven churches, and his account of the appearance of the Lord Jesus, and his direction to the apostle to write what he beheld, ch. 1:9–20. Also the addresses or epistles to seven churches of Asia. These, doubtless, had reference to the state of the respective churches, as they then existed, but contain excellent precepts and exhortations, commendations and reproofs, promises and threatenings, suitable to instruct the Christian church at all times. 2. Contains a prophecy of "the things which shall be hereafter," and describes the future state of the church, from the time when the apostle beheld the visions here recorded. It is intended for our spiritual improvement; to warn the careless sinner, point out the way of salvation to the awakened inquirer, build up the weak believer, comfort the afflicted and tempted Christian, and, we may especially add, to strengthen the martyr of Christ, under the cruel persecutions and sufferings inflicted by Satan and his followers.

Chapter 1

Chapter Outline

The Divine origin, the design, and the importance of this book.	(1–3)
The apostle John salutes the seven churches of Asia.	(4–8)
Declares when, where, and how, the revelation was made to him.	(9–11)
His vision, in which he saw Christ appear.	(12–20)

Verses 1-3

This book is the Revelation of Jesus Christ; the whole Bible is so; for all revelation comes through Christ, and all relates to him. Its principal subject is to discover the purposes of God concerning the affairs of the church, and of the nations as connected therewith, to the end of the world. These events would surely come to pass; and they would begin to come to pass very shortly. Though Christ is himself God, and has light and life in himself, yet, as Mediator between God and man, he receives instructions from the Father. To him we owe the knowledge of what we are to expect from God, and what he expects from us. The subject of this revelation was, the things that must shortly come to pass. On all who read or hear the words of the prophecy, a blessing is pronounced. Those are well employed who search the Bible. It is not enough that we read and hear, but we must keep the things that are written, in our memories, in our minds, in our affections, and in practice, and we shall be blessed in the deed. Even the mysteries and difficulties of this book are united with discoveries of God, suited to impress the mind with awe, and to purify the soul of the reader, though he may not discern the prophetic meaning. No part of Scripture more fully states the gospel, and warns against the evil of sin.

Verses 4-8

There can be no true peace, where there is not true grace; and where grace goeth before, peace will follow. This blessing is in the name of God, of the Holy Trinity, it is an act of adoration. The Father is first named; he is described as the Jehovah who is, and who was, and who is to come, eternal, unchangeable. The Holy Spirit is called the seven spirits, the perfect Spirit of God, in whom there is a diversity of gifts and operations. The Lord Jesus Christ was from eternity, a Witness to all the counsels of God. He is the First-born from the dead, who will by his own power raise up his people. He is the Prince of the kings of the earth; by him their counsels are overruled, and to him they are accountable. Sin leaves a stain of guilt and pollution upon the soul. Nothing can fetch out this stain but the blood of Christ; and Christ shed his own blood to satisfy Divine justice, and purchase pardon and purity for his people. Christ has made believers kings and priests to God and his Father. As such they overcome the world, mortify sin, govern their own spirits, resist Satan, prevail with God in prayer, and shall judge the world. He has made them priests, given them access to God, enabled them to offer spiritual and acceptable sacrifices, and for these favours they are bound to ascribe to him dominion and glory for ever. He will judge the world. Attention is called to that great day when all will see the wisdom and happiness of the friends of Christ, and the madness and misery of his enemies. Let us think frequently upon the second coming of Christ. He shall come, to the terror of those who wound and crucify him by apostacy: he shall come, to the astonishment of the whole world of the ungodly. He is the Beginning and the End; all things are from him and for him; he is the Almighty; the same eternal and unchanged One. And if we would be numbered with his saints in glory everlasting, we must now willing submit to him receive him, and honour him as a saviour, who we believe will come to be our Judge. Alas, that there should be many, who would wish never to die, and that there should not be a day of judgment!

Verses 9-11

It was the apostle's comfort that he did not suffer as an evil-doer, but for the testimony of Jesus, for bearing witness to Christ as the Immanuel, the Saviour; and the Spirit of glory and of God rested upon this persecuted apostle. The day and time when he had this vision was the Lord's day, the Christian sabbath, the first day of the week, observed in remembrance of the resurrection of Christ. Let us who call him "Our Lord," honour him on his own day. The name shows how this sacred day should be observed; the Lord's day should be wholly devoted to the Lord, and none of its hours employed in a sensual, worldly manner, or in amusements. He was in a serious, heavenly, spiritual frame, under the gracious influences of the Spirit of God. Those who would enjoy communion with God on the Lord's day, must seek to draw their thoughts and affections from earthly things. And if believers are kept on the Lord's holy day, from public ordinances and the communion of saints, by necessity and not by choice, they may look for comfort in meditation and secret duties, from the influences of the Spirit; and by hearing the voice and contemplating the glory of their beloved Saviour, from whose gracious words and power no confinement or outward circumstances can separate them. An alarm was given as with the sound of the trumpet, and then the apostle heard the voice of Christ.

Verses 12-20

The churches receive their light from Christ and the gospel, and hold it forth to others. They are golden candlesticks; they should be precious and pure; not only the ministers, but the members of the churches; their light should so shine before men, as to engage others to give glory to God. And the apostle saw as though of the Lord Jesus Christ appeared in the midst of the golden candlesticks. He is with his churches always, to the end of the world, filling them with light, and life, and love. He was clothed with a robe down to the feet, perhaps representing his righteousness and priesthood, as Mediator. This vest was girt with a golden girdle, which may denote how precious are his love and affection for his people. His head and hairs white like wool and as snow, may signify his majesty, purity, and eternity. His eyes as a flame of fire, may represent his knowledge of the secrets of all hearts, and of the most distant events. His feet like fine brass burning in a furnace, may denote the firmness of his appointments, and the excellence of his proceedings. His voice as the sound of many waters, may represent the power of his word, to remove or to destroy. The seven stars were emblems of the ministers of the seven churches to which the apostle was ordered to write, and whom Christ upheld and directed. The sword represented his justice, and his word, piercing to the dividing asunder of soul and spirit, Heb 4:12. His countenance was like the sun, when it shines clearly and powerfully; its strength too bright and dazzling for mortal eyes to behold. The apostle was overpowered with the greatness of the lustre and glory in which Christ appeared. We may well be contented to walk by faith, while here upon earth. The Lord Jesus spake words of comfort; Fear not. Words of instruction; telling who thus appeared. And his Divine nature; the First and the Last. His former sufferings; I was dead: the very same whom his disciples saw upon the cross. His resurrection and life; I have conquered death, and am partaker of endless life. His office and authority; sovereign dominion in and over the invisible world, as the Judge of all, from whose sentence there is no appeal. Let us listen to the voice of Christ, and receive the tokens of his love, for what can he withhold from those for whose sins he has died? May we then obey his word, and give up ourselves wholly to him who directs all things aright.

Chapter 2

Chapter Outline

Verses 1-7

These churches were in such different states as to purity of doctrine and the power of godliness, that the words of Christ to them will always suit the cases of other churches, and professors. Christ knows and observes their state; though in heaven, yet he walks in the midst of his churches on earth, observing what is wrong in them, and what they want. The church of Ephesus is commended for diligence in duty. Christ keeps an account of every hour's work his servants do for him, and their labour shall not be in vain in the Lord. But it is not enough that we are diligent; there must be bearing patience, and there must be waiting patience. And though we must show all meekness to all men, yet we must show just zeal against their sins. The sin Christ charged this church with, is, not the having left and forsaken the object of love, but having lost the fervent degree of it that at first appeared. Christ is displeased with his people, when he sees them grow remiss and cold toward him. Surely this mention in Scripture, of Christians forsaking their first love, reproves those who speak of it with carelessness, and thus try to excuse indifference and sloth in themselves and others; our Saviour considers this indifference as sinful. They must repent: they must be grieved and ashamed for their sinful declining, and humbly confess it in the sight of God. They must endeavour to recover their first zeal, tenderness, and seriousness, and must pray as earnestly, and watch as diligently, as when they first set out in the ways of God. If the presence of Christ's grace and Spirit is slighted, we may expect the presence of his displeasure. Encouraging mention is made of what was good among them. Indifference as to truth and error, good and evil, may be called charity and meekness, but it is not so; and it is displeasing to Christ. The Christian life is a warfare against sin, Satan, the world, and the flesh. We must never yield to our spiritual enemies, and then we shall have a glorious triumph and reward. All who persevere, shall derive from Christ, as the Tree of life, perfection and confirmation in holiness and happiness, not in the earthly paradise, but in the heavenly. This is a figurative expression, taken from the account of the garden of Eden, denoting the pure, satisfactory, and eternal joys of heaven; and the looking forward to them in this world, by faith, communion with Christ, and the consolations of the Holy Spirit. Believers, take your wrestling life here, and expect and look for a quiet life hereafter; but not till then: the word of God never promises quietness and complete freedom from conflict here.

Verses 8-11

Our Lord Jesus is the First, for by him were all things made; he was before all things, with God, and is God himself. He is the Last, for he will be the Judge of all. As this First and Last, who was dead and is alive, is the believer's Brother and Friend, he must be rich in the deepest poverty, honourable amidst the lowest abasement, and happy under the heaviest tribulation, like the church of Smyrna. Many who are rich as to this world, are poor as to the next; and some who are poor outwardly, are inwardly rich; rich in faith, in good works, rich in privileges, rich in gifts, rich in hope. Where there is spiritual plenty, outward poverty may be well borne; and when God's people are made poor as to this life, for the sake of Christ and a good conscience, he makes all up to them in spiritual riches. Christ arms against coming troubles. Fear none of these things; not only forbid slavish fear, but subdue it, furnishing the soul with strength and courage. It should be to try them, not to destroy them. Observe, the sureness of the reward; "I will give thee:" they shall have the reward from Christ's own hand. Also, how suitable it is; "a crown of life:" the life worn out in his service, or laid down in his cause, shall be rewarded with a much better life, which shall be eternal. The second death is unspeakably worse than the first death, both in the agonies of it, and as it is eternal death: it is indeed awful to die, and to be always dying. If a man is kept from the second death and wrath to come, he may patiently endure whatever he meets with in this world.

Verses 12-17

The word of God is a sword, able to slay both sin and sinners. It turns and cuts every way; but the believer need not fear this sword; yet this confidence cannot be supported without steady obedience. As our Lord notices all the advantages and opportunities we have for duty in the places where we dwell, so he notices our temptations and discouragements from the same causes. In a situation of trials, the church of Pergamos had not denied the faith, either by open apostacy, or by giving way so as to avoid the cross. Christ commends their stedfastness, but reproves their sinful failures. A wrong view of gospel doctrine and Christian liberty, was a root of bitterness from which evil practices grew. Repentance is the duty of churches and bodies of men, as well as of particular persons; those who sin together, should repent together. Here is the promise of favour to those that overcome. The influences and comforts of the Spirit of Christ, come down from heaven into the soul, for its support. This is hidden from the rest of the world. The new name is the name of adoption; when the Holy Spirit shows his own work in the believer's soul, this new name and its real import are understood by him.

Verses 18-29

Even when the Lord knows the works of his people to be wrought in love, faith, zeal, and patience; yet if his eyes, which are as a flame of fire, observe them committing or allowing what is evil, he will rebuke, correct, or punish them. Here is praise of the ministry and people of Thyatira, by One who knew the principles from which they acted. They grew wiser and better. All Christians should earnestly desire that their last works may be their best works. Yet this church connived at some wicked seducers. God is known by the judgments he executes; and by this upon seducers, he shows his certain knowledge of the hearts of men, of their principles, designs, frame, and temper. Encouragement is given to those who kept themselves pure and undefiled. It is dangerous to despise the mystery of God, and as dangerous to receive the mysteries of Satan. Let us beware of the depths of Satan, of which those who know the least are the most happy. How tender Christ is of his faithful servants! He lays nothing upon his servants but what is for their good. There is promise of an ample reward to the persevering, victorious believer; also knowledge and wisdom, suitable to their power and dominion. Christ brings day with him into the soul, the light of grace and of glory, in the presence and enjoyment of him their Lord and Saviour. After every victory let us follow up our advantage against the enemy, that we may overcome and keep the works of Christ to the end.

Chapter 3

Chapter Outline

Verses 1-6

The Lord Jesus is He that hath the Holy Spirit with all his powers, graces, and operations. Hypocrisy, and lamentable decay in religion, are sins charged upon Sardis, by One who knew that church well, and all her works. Outward things appeared well to men, but there was only the form of godliness, not the power; a name to live, not a principle of life. There was great deadness in their souls, and in their services; numbers were wholly hypocrites, others were in a disordered and lifeless state. Our Lord called upon them to be watchful against their enemies, and to be active and earnest in their duties; and to endeavour, in dependence on the grace of the Holy Spirit, to revive and strengthen the faith and spiritual affections of those yet alive to God, though in a declining state. Whenever we are off our watch, we lose ground. Thy works are hollow and empty; prayers are not filled up with holy desires, alms-deeds not filled up with true charity, sabbaths not filled up with suitable devotion of soul to God. There are not inward affections suitable to outward acts and expressions; when the spirit is wanting, the form cannot long remain. In seeking a revival in our own souls, or the souls of others, it is needful to compare what we profess with the manner in which we go on, that we may be humbled and quickened to hold fast that which remains. Christ enforces his counsel with a dreadful threatening if it should be despised. Yet our blessed Lord does not leave this sinful people without some encouragement. He makes honourable mention of the faithful remnant in Sardis, he makes a gracious promise to them. He that overcometh shall be clothed in white raiment; the purity of grace shall be rewarded with the perfect purity of glory. Christ has his book of life, a register of all who shall inherit eternal life; the book of remembrance of all who live to God, and keep up the life and power of godliness in evil times. Christ will bring forward this book of life, and show the names of the faithful, before God, and all the angels, at the great day.

Verses 7-13

The same Lord Jesus has the key of government and authority in and over the church. He opens a door of opportunity to his churches; he opens a door of utterance to his ministers; he opens a door of entrance, opens the heart. He shuts the door of heaven against the foolish, who sleep away their day of grace; and against the workers of iniquity, how vain and confident soever they may be. The church in Philadelphia is commended; yet with a gentle reproof. Although Christ accepts a little strength, yet believers must not rest satisfied in a little, but strive to grow in grace, to be strong in faith, giving glory to God. Christ can discover this his favour to his people, so that their enemies shall be forced to acknowledge it. This, by the grace of Christ, will soften their enemies, and make them desire to be admitted into communion with his people. Christ promises preserving grace in the most trying times, as the reward of past faithfulness; To him that hath shall be given. Those who keep the gospel in a time of peace, shall be kept by Christ in an hour of temptation; and the same Divine grace that has made them fruitful in times of peace, will make them faithful in times of persecution. Christ promises a glorious reward to the victorious believer. He shall be a monumental pillar in the temple of God; a monument of the free and powerful grace of God; a monument that shall never be defaced or removed. On this pillar shall be written the new name of Christ; by this will appear, under whom the believer fought the good fight, and came off victorious.

Verses 14-22

Laodicea was the last and worst of the seven churches of Asia. Here our Lord Jesus styles himself, "The Amen;" one steady and unchangeable in all his purposes and promises. If religion is worth anything, it is worth every thing. Christ expects men should be in earnest. How many professors of gospel doctrine are neither hot nor cold; except as they are indifferent in needful matters, and hot and fiery in disputes about things of lesser moment! A severe punishment is threatened. They would give a false opinion of Christianity, as if it were an unholy religion; while others would conclude it could afford no real satisfaction, otherwise its professors would not have been heartless in it, or so ready to seek pleasure or happiness from the world. One cause of this indifference and inconsistency in religion is, self-conceit and self-delusion; "Because thou sayest." What a difference between their thoughts of themselves, and the thoughts Christ had of them! How careful should we be not to cheat our owns souls! There are many in hell, who once thought themselves far in the way to heaven. Let us beg of God that we may not be left to flatter and deceive ourselves. Professors grow proud, as they become carnal and formal. Their state was wretched in itself. They were poor; really poor, when they said and thought they were rich. They could not see their state, nor their way, nor their danger, yet they thought they saw it. They had not the garment of justification, nor sanctification: they were exposed to sin and shame; their rags that would defile them. They were naked, without house or harbour, for they were without God, in whom alone the soul of man can find rest and safety. Good counsel was given by Christ to this sinful people. Happy those who take his counsel, for all others must perish in their sins. Christ lets them know where they might have true riches, and how they might have them. Some things must be parted with, but nothing valuable; and it is only to make room for receiving true riches. Part with sin and self-confidence, that you may be filled with his hidden treasure. They must receive from Christ the white raiment he purchased and provided for them; his own imputed righteousness for justification, and the garments of holiness and sanctification. Let them give themselves up to his word and Spirit, and their eyes shall be opened to see their way and their end. Let us examine ourselves by the rule of his word, and pray earnestly for the teaching of his Holy Spirit, to take away our pride, prejudices, and worldly lusts. Sinners ought to take the rebukes of God's word and rod, as tokens of his love to their souls. Christ stood without; knocking, by the dealings of his providence, the warnings and teaching of his word, and the influences of his Spirit. Christ still graciously, by his word and Spirit, comes to the door of the hearts of sinners. Those who open to him shall enjoy his presence. If what he finds would make but a poor feast, what he brings will supply a rich one. He will give fresh supplies of graces and comforts. In the conclusion is a promise to the overcoming believer. Christ himself had temptations and conflicts; he overcame them all, and was more than a conqueror. Those made like to Christ in his trials, shall be made like to him in glory. All is closed with the general demand of attention. And these counsels, while suited to the churches to which they were addressed, are deeply interesting to all men.

Chapter 4

Chapter Outline

A vision of God, as on his glorious throne, around which were twenty-four elders and four living creatures. (1–8)

Whose songs, and those of the holy angels, the apostle heard. (9–11)

Verses 1-8

After the Lord Jesus had instructed the apostle to write to the churches "the things that are," there was another vision. The apostle saw a throne set in heaven, an emblem of the universal dominion of Jehovah. He saw a glorious One upon the throne, not described by human features, so as to be represented by a likeness or image, but only by his surpassing brightness. These seem emblems of the excellence of the Divine nature, and of God's awful justice. The rainbow is a fit emblem of that covenant of promise which God has made with Christ, as the Head of the church, and with all his people in him. The prevailing colour was a pleasant green, showing the reviving and refreshing nature of the new covenant. Four-and-twenty seats around the throne, were filled with four-and-twenty elders, representing, probably, the whole church of God. Their sitting denotes honour, rest, and satisfaction; their sitting about the throne signifies nearness to God, the sight and enjoyment they have of him. They were clothed in white raiment; the imputed righteousness of the saints and their holiness: they had on their heads crowns of gold, signifying the glory they have with him. Lightnings and voices came from the throne; the awful declarations God makes to his church, of his sovereign will and pleasure. Seven lamps of fire were burning before the throne; the gifts, graces, and operations of the Spirit of God in the churches of Christ, dispensed according to the will and pleasure of Him who sits upon the throne. In the gospel church, the laver for purification is the blood of the Lord Jesus Christ, which cleanses from all sin. In this all must be washed, to be admitted into the gracious presence of God on earth, and his glorious presence in heaven. The apostle saw four living creatures, between the throne and the circle of the elders, standing between God and the people. These seem to signify the true ministers of the gospel, because of their place between God and the people. This also is shown by the description given, denoting wisdom, courage, diligence, and discretion, and the affections by which they mount up toward heaven.

Verses 9-11

All true believers wholly ascribe their redemption and conversion, their present privileges and future hopes, to the eternal and most holy God. Thus rise the for-ever harmonious, thankful songs of the redeemed in heaven. Would we on earth do like them, let our praises be constant, not interrupted; united, not divided; thankful, not cold and formal; humble, not self-confident.

Chapter 5

Chapter Outline

A book sealed with seven seals, which could
be opened by none but Christ, who took the
book to open it.   (1–7)

Upon which all honour is ascribed to him,   (8–14)
as worthy to open it.

Verses 1-7

The apostle saw in the hand of Him that sat upon the throne, a roll of parchments in the form usual in those times, and sealed with seven seals. This represented the secret purposes of God about to be revealed. The designs and methods of Divine Providence, toward the church and the world, are stated, fixed, and made a matter of record. The counsels of God are altogether hidden from the eye and understanding of the creature. The several parts are not unsealed and opened at once, but after each other, till the whole mystery of God's counsel and conduct is finished in the world. The creatures cannot open it, nor read it; the Lord only can do so. Those who see most of God, are most desirous to see more; and those who have seen his glory, desire to know his will. But even good men may be too eager and hasty to look into the mysteries of the Divine conduct. Such desires, if not soon answered, turn to grief and sorrow. If John wept much because he could not look into the book of God's decrees, what reason have many to shed floods of tears for their ignorance of the gospel of Christ! of that on which everlasting salvation depends! We need not weep that we cannot foresee future events respecting ourselves in this world; the eager expectation of future prospects, or the foresight of future calamities, would alike unfit us for present duties and conflicts, or render our prosperous days distressing. Yet we may desire to learn, from the promises and prophecies of Scripture, what will be the final event to believers and to the church; and the Incarnate Son has prevailed, that we should learn all that we need to know. Christ stands as Mediator between God and both ministers and people. He is called a Lion, but he appears as a Lamb slain. He appears with the marks of his sufferings, to show that he pleads for us in heaven, in virtue of his satisfaction. He appears as a Lamb, having seven horns and seven eyes; perfect power to execute all the will of God, and perfect wisdom to understand it, and to do it in the most effectual manner. The Father put the book of his eternal counsels into the hand of Christ, and Christ readily and gladly took it into his hand; for he delights to make known the will of his Father; and the Holy Spirit is given by him to reveal the truth and will of God.

Verses 8-14

It is matter of joy to all the world, to see that God deals with men in grace and mercy through the Redeemer. He governs the world, not merely as a Creator, but as our Saviour. The harps were instruments of praise; the vials were full of odours, or incense, which signify the prayers of the saints: prayer and praise should always go together. Christ has redeemed his people from the bondage of sin, guilt, and Satan. He has not only purchased liberty for them, but the highest honour and preferment; he made them kings and priests; kings, to rule over their own spirits, and to overcome the world, and the evil one; and he makes them priests; giving them access to himself, and liberty to offer up spiritual sacrifices. What words can more fully declare that Christ is, and ought to be worshipped, equally with the Father, by all creatures, to all eternity! Happy those who shall adore and praise in heaven, and who shall for ever bless the Lamb, who delivered and set them apart for himself by his blood. How worthy art thou, O God, Father, Son, and Holy Ghost, of our highest praises! All creatures should proclaim thy greatness, and adore thy majesty.

Chapter 6

Chapter Outline

The opening of the seals, The first, second,   (1–8)
third, and fourth.

The fifth.   (9–11)

The sixth.   (12–17)

Verses 1-8

Christ, the Lamb, opens the first seal: observe what appeared. A rider on a white horse. By the going forth of this white horse, a time of peace, or the early progress of the Christian religion, seems to be intended; its going forth in purity, at the time when its heavenly Founder sent his apostles to teach all nations, adding, Lo! I am with you alway, even to the end of the world. The Divine religion goes out crowned, having the Divine favour resting upon it, armed spiritually against its foes, and destined to be victorious in the end. On opening the second seal, a red horse appeared; this signifies desolating judgments. The sword of war and persecution is a dreadful judgment; it takes away peace from the earth, one of the greatest blessings; and men who should love one another, and help one another, are set upon killing one another. Such scenes also followed the pure age of early Christianity, when, neglectful of charity and the bond of peace, the Christian leaders, divided among themselves, appealed to the sword, and entangled themselves in guilt. On opening the third seal, a black horse appeared; a colour denoting mourning and woe, darkness and ignorance. He that sat on it had a yoke in his hand. Attempts were made to put a yoke of superstitious observances on the disciples. As the stream of Christianity flowed further from its pure fountain, it became more and more corrupt. During the progress of this black horse, the necessaries of life should be at excessive prices, and the more costly things should not be hurt. According to prophetic language, these articles signified that food of religious knowledge, by which the souls of men are sustained unto everlasting life; such we are invited to buy, Isa 55:1. But when the dark clouds of ignorance and superstition, denoted by the black horse, spread over the Christian world, the knowledge and practice of true religion became scarce. When a people loathe their spiritual food, God may justly deprive them of their daily bread. The famine of bread is a terrible judgment; but the famine of the word is more so. Upon opening the fourth seal, another horse appeared, of a pale colour. The rider was Death, the king of terrors. The attendants, or followers of this king of terrors, hell, a state of eternal misery to all who die in their sins; and in times of general destruction, multitudes go down unprepared into the pit. The period of the fourth seal is one of great slaughter and devastation, destroying whatever may tend to make life happy, making ravages on the spiritual lives of men. Thus the mystery of iniquity was completed, and its power extended both over the lives and consciences of men. The exact times of these four seals cannot be ascertained, for the changes were gradual. God gave them power, that is, those instruments of his anger, or those judgments: all public calamities are at his command; they only go forth when God sends them, and no further than he permits.

Verses 9-11

The sight the apostle beheld at the opening the fifth seal was very affecting. He saw the souls of the martyrs under the altar; at the foot of the altar in heaven, at the feet of Christ. Persecutors can only kill the body; after that there is no more they can do; the soul lives. God has provided a good place in the better world, for those who are faithful unto death. It is not their own death, but the sacrifice of Christ, that gives them entrance into heaven. The cause in which they suffered, was for the word of God; the best any man can lay down his life for; faith in God's word, and the unshaken confession of that faith. They commit their cause to Him to whom vengeance belongs. The Lord is the comforter of his afflicted servants, and precious is their blood in his sight. As the measure of the sin of persecutors is filling up, so is the number of the persecuted, martyred servants of Christ. When this is fulfilled, God will send tribulation to those who trouble them, and unbroken happiness and rest to those that are troubled.

Verses 12-17

When the sixth seal was opened, there was a great earthquake. The foundations of churches and states would be terribly shaken. Such bold figurative descriptions of great changes abound in the prophecies of Scripture; for these events are emblems, and declare the end of the world and the day of judgment. Dread and terror would seize on all sorts of men. Neither grandeur, riches, valour, nor strength, can support men at that time. They would be glad to be no more seen; yea, to have no longer any being. Though Christ be a Lamb, he can be angry, and the wrath of the Lamb is exceedingly dreadful; for if the Redeemer himself, who appeases the wrath of God, be our enemy, where shall we find a friend to plead for us? As men have their day of opportunity, and their seasons of grace, so God has his day of righteous wrath. It seems that the overthrow of the paganism of the Roman empire is here meant. The idolaters are described as hiding themselves in their dens and secret caves, and vainly seeking to escape ruin. In such a day, when the signs of the times show those who believe in God's word, that the King of kings is approaching, Christians are called to a decided course, and to a bold confession of Christ and his truth before their fellowmen. Whatever they may have to endure, the short contempt of man is to be borne, rather than that shame which is everlasting.

Chapter 7

Chapter Outline

Verses 1-8

In the figurative language of Scripture, the blowing of the four winds together, means a dreadful and general destruction. But the destruction is delayed. Seals were used to mark for each person his own possessions. This mark is the witness of the Holy Ghost, printed in the hearts of believers. And the Lord would not suffer his people to be afflicted before they were marked, that they might be prepared against all conflicts. And, observe, of those who are thus sealed by the Spirit, the seal must be on the forehead, plainly to be seen alike by friends and foes, but not by the believer himself, except as he looks stedfastly in the glass of God's word. The number of those who were sealed, may be understood to stand for the remnant of people which God reserved. Though the church of God is but a little flock, in comparison with the wicked world, yet it is a society really large, and to be still more enlarged. Here the universal church is figured under the type of Israel.

Verses 9-12

The first fruits of Christ having led the way, the Gentiles converted later follow, and ascribe their salvation to God and the Redeemer, with triumph. In acts of religious worship we come nigh to God, and must come by Christ; the throne of God could not be approached by sinners, were it not for a Mediator. They were clothed with the robes of justification, holiness, and victory; and they had palms in their hands, as conquerors used to appear in their triumphs. Such a glorious appearance will the faithful servants of God make at last, when they have fought the good fight of faith, and finished their course. With a loud voice they gave to God and the Lamb the praise of the great salvation. Those who enjoy eternal happiness must and will bless both the Father and the Son; they will do it publicly, and with fervour. We see what is the work of heaven, and we ought to begin it now, to have our hearts much in it, and to long for that world where our praises, as well as our happiness, will be made perfect.

Verses 13-17

Faithful Christians deserve our notice and respect; we should mark the upright. Those who would gain knowledge, must not be ashamed to seek instruction from any who can give it. The way to heaven is through many tribulations; but tribulation, how great soever, shall not separate us from the love of God. Tribulation makes heaven more welcome and more glorious. It is not the blood of the martyrs, but the blood of the Lamb, that can wash away sin, and make the soul pure and clean in the sight of God; other blood stains, this is the only blood that makes the robes of the saints white and clean. They are happy in their employment; heaven is a state of service, though not of suffering; it is a state of rest, but not of sloth; it isa praising, delightful rest. They have had sorrows, and shed many tears on account of sin and affliction; but God himself, with his own gracious hand, will wipe those tears away. He deals with them as a tender father. This should support the Christian under all his troubles. As all the redeemed owe their happiness wholly to sovereign mercy; so the work and worship of God their Saviour is their element; his presence and favour complete their happiness, nor can they conceive of any other joy. To Him may all his people come; from him they receive every needed grace; and to him let them offer all praise and glory.

Chapter 8

Chapter Outline

The seventh seal is opened and seven angels appear with seven trumpets, ready to proclaim the purposes of God.	(1, 2)
Another angel casts fire on the earth, which produces terrible storms of vengeance.	(3–5)
The seven angels prepare to sound their trumpets.	(6)
Four sound them.	(7–12)
Another angel denounces greater woes to come.	(13)

Verses 1-6

The seventh seal is opened. There was profound silence in heaven for a space; all was quiet in the church, for whenever the church on earth cries through oppression, that cry reaches up to heaven; or it is a silence of expectation. Trumpets were given to the angels, who were to sound them. The Lord Jesus is the High Priest of the church, having a golden censer, and much incense, fulness of merit in his own glorious person. Would that men studied to know the fulness that is in Christ, and endeavoured to be acquainted with his excellency. Would that they were truly persuaded that Christ has such an office as that of Intercessor, which he now performs with deep sympathy. No prayers, thus recommended, was ever denied hearing and acceptance. These prayers, thus accepted in heaven, produced great changes upon earth. The Christian worship and religion, pure and heavenly in its origin and nature, when sent down to earth and conflicting with the passions and worldly projects of sinful men, produced remarkable tumults, here set forth in prophetical language, as our Lord himself declared, Lu 12:49.

Verses 7-13

The first angel sounded the first trumpet, and there followed hail and fire mingled with blood. A storm of heresies, a mixture of dreadful errors falling on the church, or a tempest of destruction. The second angel sounded, and a great mountain, burning with fire, was cast into the sea; and the third part of the sea became blood. By this mountain some understand leaders of the persecutions; others, Rome sacked by the Goths and Vandals, with great slaughter and cruelty. The third angel sounded, and there fell a star from heaven. Some take this to be an eminent governor; others take it to be some person in power who corrupted the churches of Christ. The doctrines of the gospel, the springs of spiritual life, comfort, and vigour, to the souls of men, are corrupted and made bitter by the mixture of dangerous errors, so that the souls of men find ruin where they sought refreshment. The fourth angel sounded, and darkness fell upon the great lights of heaven, that give light to the world, the sun, and the moon, and the stars. The guides and governors are placed higher than the people, and are to dispense light, and kind influences to them. Where the gospel comes to a people, and has not proper effects on their hearts and lives, it is followed with dreadful judgments. God gives alarm by the written word, by ministers, by men's own consciences, and by the signs of the times; so that if people are surprised, it is their own fault. The anger of God makes all comforts bitter, and even life itself burdensome. But God, in this world, sets bounds to the most terrible judgments. Corruption of doctrine and worship in the church are great judgments, and also are the usual causes and tokens of other judgments coming on a people. Before the other three trumpets were sounded, there was solemn warning how terrible the calamities would be that should follow. If lesser judgments do not take effect the church and the world must expect greater; and when God comes to punish the world, the inhabitants shall tremble before him. Let sinners take warning to flee from the wrath to come; let believers learn to value and to be thankful for their privileges; and let them patiently continue in well doing.

Chapter 9

Chapter Outline

The fifth trumpet is followed by a representation of another star as falling from heaven and opening the bottomless pit, out of which come swarms of locusts.	(1–12)
The sixth trumpet is followed by the loosing of four angels bound in the great river Euphrates.	(13–21)

Verses 1-12

Upon sounding the fifth trumpet, a star fell from heaven to the earth. Having ceased to be a minister of Christ, he who is represented by this star becomes the minister of the devil; and lets loose the powers of hell against the churches of Christ. On the opening of the bottomless pit, there arose a great smoke. The devil carries on his designs by blinding the eyes of men, by putting out light and knowledge, and promoting ignorance and error. Out of this smoke there came a swarm of locusts, emblems of the devil's agents, who promote superstition, idolatry, error, and cruelty. The trees and the grass, the true believers, whether young or more advanced, should be untouched. But a secret poison and infection in the soul, should rob many others of purity, and afterwards of peace. The locusts had no power to hurt those who had the seal of God. God's all-powerful, distinguishing grace will keep his people from total and final apostacy. The power is limited to a short season; but it would be very sharp. In such events the faithful share the common calamity, but from the pestilence of error they might and would be safe. We collect from Scripture, that such errors were to try and prove the Christians, 1Co 11:19. And early writers plainly refer this to the first great host of corrupters who overspread the Christian church.

Verses 13-21

The sixth angel sounded, and here the power of the Turks seems the subject. Their time is limited. They not only slew in war, but brought a poisonous and ruinous religion. The antichristian generation repented not under these dreadful judgments. From this sixth trumpet learn that God can make one enemy of the church a scourge and a plague to another. The idolatry in the remains of the eastern church and elsewhere, and the sins of professed Christians, render this prophecy and its fulfilment more wonderful. And the attentive reader of Scripture and history, may find his faith and hope strengthened by events, which in other respects fill his heart with anguish and his eyes with tears, while he sees that men who escape these plagues, repent not of their evil works, but go on with idolatries, wickedness, and cruelty, till wrath comes upon them to the utmost.

Chapter 10

Chapter Outline

The Angel of the covenant presents a little open book, which is followed with seven thunders.	(1–4)
At the end of the following prophecies, time should be no more.	(5–7)
A voice directs the apostle to eat the book; and tells him he must prophesy further.	(8–10)
	(11)

Verses 1-7

The apostle saw another representation. The person communicating this discovery probably was our Lord and Saviour Jesus Christ, or it was to show his glory. He veils his glory, which is too great for mortal eyes to behold; and throws a veil upon his dispensations. A rainbow was upon his head; our Lord is always mindful of his covenant. His awful voice was echoed by seven thunders; solemn and terrible ways of discovering the mind of God. We know not the subjects of the seven thunders, nor the reasons for suppressing them. There are great events in history, perhaps relating to the Christian church, which are not noticed in open prophecy. The final salvation of the righteous, and the final success of true religion on earth, are engaged for by the unfailing word of the Lord. Though the time may not be yet, it cannot be far distant. Very soon, as to us, time will be no more; but if we are believers, a happy eternity will follow: we shall from heaven behold and rejoice in the triumphs of Christ, and his cause on earth.

Verses 8-11

Most men feel pleasure in looking into future events, and all good men like to receive a word from God. But when this book of prophecy was thoroughly digested by the apostle, the contents would be bitter; there were things so awful and terrible, such grievous persecutions of the people of God, such desolations in the earth, that the foresight and foreknowledge of them would be painful to his mind. Let us seek to be taught by Christ, and to obey his orders; daily meditating on his word, that it may nourish our souls; and then declaring it according to our several stations. The sweetness of such contemplations will often be mingled with bitterness, while we compare the Scriptures with the state of the world and the church, or even with that of our own hearts.

Chapter 11

Chapter Outline

The state of the church is represented under the figure of a temple measured.	(1, 2)
Two witnesses prophesy is sackcloth.	(3–6)
They are slain, after which they arise and ascend to heaven.	(7–13)
Under the seventh trumpet, all antichristian powers are to be destroyed and there will be a glorious state of Christ's kingdom upon earth.	(14–19)

Verses 1, 2

This prophetical passage about measuring the temple seems to refer to Ezekiel's vision. The design of this measuring seems to be the preservation of the church in times of public danger; or for its trial, or for its reformation. The worshippers must be measured; whether they make God's glory their end, and his word their rule, in all their acts of worship. Those in the outer court, worship in a false manner, or with dissembling hearts, and will be found among his enemies. God will have a temple and an altar in the world, till the end of time. He looks strictly to his temple. The holy city, the visible church, is trodden under foot; is filled with idolaters, infidels, and hypocrites. But the desolations of the church are limited, and she shall be delivered out of all her troubles.

Verses 3-13

In the time of treading down, God kept his faithful witnesses to attest the truth of his word and worship, and the excellence of his ways, The number of these witnesses is small, yet enough. They prophesy in sackcloth. It shows their afflicted, persecuted state, and deep sorrow for the abominations against which they protested. They are supported during their great and hard work, till it is done. When they had prophesied in sackcloth the greatest part of 1260 years, antichrist, the great instrument of the devil, would war against them, with force and violence for a time. Determined rebels against the light rejoice, as on some happy event, when they can silence, drive to a distance, or destroy the faithful servants of Christ, whose doctrine and conduct torment them. It does not appear that the term is yet expired, and the witnesses are not a present exposed to endure such terrible outward sufferings as in former times; but such things may again happen, and there is abundant cause to prophesy in sackcloth, on account of the state of religion. The depressed state of real Christianity may relate only to the western church. The Spirit of life from God, quickens dead souls, and shall quicken the dead bodies of his people, and his dying interest in the world. The revival of God's work and witnesses, will strike terror into the souls of his enemies. Where there is guilt, there is fear; and a persecuting spirit, though cruel, is a cowardly spirit. It will be no small part of the punishment of persecutors, both in this world, and at the great day, that they see the faithful servants of God honoured and advanced. The Lord's witnesses must not be weary of suffering and service, nor hastily grasp at the reward; but must stay till their Master calls them. The consequence of their being thus exalted was a mighty shock and convulsion in the antichristian empire. Events alone can show the meaning of this. But whenever God's work and witnesses revive, the devil's work and witnesses fall before him. And that the slaying of the witnesses is future, appears to be probable.

Verses 14-19

Before the sounding of the seventh and last trumpet, there is the usual demand of attention. The saints and angels in heaven know the right of our God and Saviour to rule over all the world. But the nations met God's wrath with their own anger. It was a time in which he was beginning to reward his people's faithful services, and sufferings; and their enemies fretted against God, and so increased their guilt, and hastened their destruction. By the opening the temple of God in heaven, may be meant, that there was a more free communication between heaven and earth; prayer and praises more freely and frequently going up, graces and blessings plentifully coming down. But it rather seems to refer to the church of God on earth. In the reign of antichrist, God's law was laid aside, and made void by traditions and decrees; the Scriptures were locked up from the people, but now they are brought to the view of all. This, like the ark, is a token of the presence of God returned to his people, and his favour toward them in Jesus Christ, as the Propitiation for their sins. The great blessing of the Reformation was attended with very awful providences; as by terrible things in righteousness God answered the prayers presented in his holy temple now opened.

Chapter 12

Chapter Outline

A description of the church of Christ and of Satan, under the figures of a woman and of a great red dragon.	(1–6)
Michael and his angels fight against the devil and his angels, who are defeated.	(7–12)
The dragon persecutes the church.	(13, 14)
His vain endeavours to destroy her, He renews his war against her seed.	(14–17)

Verses 1-6

The church, under the emblem of a woman, the mother of believers, was seen by the apostle in vision, in heaven. She was clothed with the sun, justified, sanctified, and shining by union with Christ, the Sun of Righteousness. The moon was under her feet; she was superior to the reflected and feebler light of the revelation made by Moses. Having on her head a crown of twelve stars; the doctrine of the gospel, preached by the twelve apostles, is a crown of glory to all true believers. As in pain to bring forth a holy family; desirous that the conviction of sinners might end in their conversion. A dragon is a known emblem of Satan, and his chief agents, or those who govern for him on earth, at that time the pagan empire of Rome, the city built upon seven hills. As having ten horns, divided into ten kingdoms. Having seven crowns, representing seven forms of government. As drawing with his tail a third part of the stars in heaven, and casting them down to the earth; persecuting and seducing the ministers and teachers. As watchful to crush the Christian religion; but in spite of the opposition of enemies, the church brought forth a manly issue of true and faithful professors, in whom Christ was truly formed anew; even the mystery of Christ, that Son of God who should rule the nations, and in whose right his members partake the same glory. This blessed offspring was protected of God.

Verses 7-11

The attempts of the dragon proved unsuccessful against the church, and fatal to his own interests. The seat of this war was in heaven; in the church of Christ, the kingdom of heaven on earth. The parties were Christ, the great Angel of the covenant, and his faithful followers; and Satan and his instruments. The strength of the church is in having the Lord Jesus for the Captain of their salvation. Pagan idolatry, which was the worship of devils, was cast out of the empire by the spreading of Christianity. The salvation and strength of the church, are only to be ascribed to the King and Head of the church. The conquered enemy hates the presence of God, yet he is willing to appear there, to accuse the people of God. Let us take heed that we give him no cause to accuse us; and that, when we have sinned, we go before the Lord, condemn ourselves, and commit our cause to Christ as our Advocate. The servants of God overcame Satan by the blood of the Lamb, as the cause. By the word of their testimony: the powerful preaching of the gospel is mighty, through God, to pull down strong holds. By their courage and patience in sufferings: they loved not their lives so well but they could lay them down in Christ's cause. These were the warriors and the weapons by which Christianity overthrew the power of pagan idolatry; and if Christians had continued to fight with these weapons, and such as these, their victories would have been more numerous and glorious, and the effects more lasting. The redeemed overcame by a simple reliance on the blood of Christ, as the only ground of their hopes. In this we must be like them. We must not blend any thing else with this.

Verses 12-17

The church and all her friends might well be called to praise God for deliverance from pagan persecution, though other troubles awaited her. The wilderness is a desolate place, and full of serpents and scorpions, uncomfortable and destitute of provisions; yet a place of safety, as well as where one might be alone. But being thus retired could not protect the woman. The flood of water is explained by many to mean the invasions of barbarians, by which the western empire was overwhelmed; for the heathen encouraged their attacks, in the hope of destroying Christianity. But ungodly men, for their worldly interests, protected the church amidst these tumults, and the overthrow of the empire did not help the cause of idolatry. Or, this may be meant of a flood of error, by which the church of God was in danger of being overwhelmed and carried away. The devil, defeated in his designs upon the church, turns his rage against persons and places. Being faithful to God and Christ, in doctrine, worship, and practice, exposes to the rage of Satan; and will do so till the last enemy shall be destroyed.

Chapter 13

Chapter Outline

It obliges all to worship its image, and   (16–18)
receive its mark, as persons devoted to it.

Verses 1-10

The apostle, standing on the shore, saw a savage beast rise out of the sea; a tyrannical, idolatrous, persecuting power, springing up out of the troubles which took place. It was a frightful monster! It appears to mean that worldly, oppressing dominion, which for many ages, even from the times of the Babylonish captivity, had been hostile to the church. The first beast then began to oppress and persecute the righteous for righteousness' sake, but they suffered most under the fourth beast of Daniel, (the Roman empire,) which has afflicted the saints with many cruel persecutions. The source of its power was the dragon. It was set up by the devil, and supported by him. The wounding the head may be the abolishing pagan idolatry; and the healing of the wound, introducing popish idolatry, the same in substance, only in a new dress, but which as effectually answers the devil's design. The world admired its power, policy and success. They paid honour and subjection to the devil and his instruments. It exercised infernal power and policy, requiring men to render that honour to creatures which belongs to God alone. Yet the devil's power and success are limited. Christ has a chosen remnant, redeemed by his blood, recorded in his book, sealed by his Spirit; and though the devil and antichrist may overcome the body, and take away the natural life, they cannot conquer the soul, nor prevail with true believers to forsake their Saviour, and join his enemies. Perseverance in the faith of the gospel and true worship of God, in this great hour of trial and temptation, which would deceive all but the elect, is the character of those registered in the book of life. This powerful motive and encouragement to constancy, is the great design of the whole Revelation.

Verses 11-18

Those who understand the first beast to denote a worldly power, take the second to be also a persecuting and assumed power, which acts under the disguise of religion, and of charity to the souls of men. It is a spiritual dominion, professing to be derived from Christ, and exercised at first in a gentle manner, but soon spake like the dragon. Its speech betrayed it; for it gives forth those false doctrines and cruel decrees, which show it to belong to the dragon, and not to the Lamb. It exercised all the power of the former beast. It pursues the same design, to draw men from worshipping the true God, and to subject the souls of men to the will and control of men. The second beast has carried on its designs, by methods whereby men should be deceived to worship the former beast, in the new shape, or likeness made for it. By lying wonders, pretended miracles. And by severe censures. Also by allowing none to enjoy natural or civil rights, who will not worship that beast which is the image of the pagan beast. It is made a qualification for buying and selling, as well as for places of profit and trust, that they oblige themselves to use all their interest, power, and endeavour, to forward the dominion of the beast, which is meant by receiving his mark. To make an image to the beast, whose deadly wound was healed, would be to give form and power to his worship, or to require obedience to his commands. To worship the image of the beast, implies being subject to those things which stamp the character of the picture, and render it the image of the beast. The number of the beast is given, so as to show the infinite wisdom of God, and to exercise the wisdom of men. The number is the number of a man, computed after the usual manner among men, and it is 666. What or who is intended by this, remains a mystery. To almost every religious dispute this number has yet been applied, and it may reasonably be doubted whether the meaning has yet been discovered. But he who has wisdom and understanding, will see that all the enemies of God are numbered and marked out for destruction; that the term of their power will soon expire, and that all nations shall submit to our King of righteousness and peace.

Chapter 14

Chapter Outline

Verses 1-5

Mount Sion is the gospel church. Christ is with his church, and in the midst of her in all her troubles, therefore she is not consumed. His presence secures perseverance. His people appear honourably. They have the name of God written in their foreheads; they make a bold and open profession of their faith in God and Christ, and this is followed by suitable actings. There were persons in the darkest times, who ventured and laid down their lives for the worship and truth of the gospel of Christ. They kept themselves clean from the wicked abominations of the followers of antichrist. Their hearts were right with God; and they were freely pardoned in Christ; he is glorified in them, and they in him. May it be our prayer, our endeavour, our ambition, to be found in this honourable company. Those who are really sanctified and justified are meant here, for no hypocrite, however plausible, can be accounted to be without fault before God. (Rev 14:6-13)

Verses 6-13

The progress of the Reformation appears to be here set forth. The four proclamations are plain in their meaning; that all Christians may be encouraged, in the time of trial, to be faithful to their Lord. The gospel is the great means whereby men are brought to fear God, and to give glory to him. The preaching of the everlasting gospel shakes the foundations of antichrist in the world, and hastens its downfal. If any persist in being subject to the beast, and in promoting his cause, they must expect to be for ever miserable in soul and body. The believer is to venture or suffer any thing in obeying the commandments of God, and professing the faith of Jesus. May God bestow this patience upon us. Observe the description of those that are and shall be blessed: such as die in the Lord; die in the cause of Christ, in a state of union with Christ; such as are found in Christ when death comes. They rest from all sin, temptation, sorrow, and persecution; for there the wicked cease from troubling, there the weary are at rest. Their works follow them: do not go before as their title, or purchase, but follow them as proofs of their having lived and died in the Lord: the remembrance of them will be pleasant, and the reward far above all their services and sufferings. This is made sure by the testimony of the Spirit, witnessing with their spirits, and the written word.

Verses 14-20

Warnings and judgments not having produced reformation, the sins of the nations are filled up, and they become ripe for judgments, represented by a harvest, an emblem which is used to signify the gathering of the righteous, when ripe for heaven, by the mercy of God. The harvest time is when the corn is ripe; when the believers are ripe for heaven, then the wheat of the earth shall be gathered into Christ's garner. And by a vintage. The enemies of Christ and his church are not destroyed, till by their sin they are ripe for ruin, and then he will spare them no longer. The wine-press is the wrath of God, some terrible calamity, probably the sword, shedding the blood of the wicked. The patience of God towards sinners, is the greatest miracle in the world; but, though lasting, it will not be everlasting; and ripeness in sin is a sure proof of judgment at hand.

Chapter 15

Chapter Outline

A song of praise is sung by the church.	(1–4)
Seven angels with the seven plagues; and to them one of the living creatures gives seven golden vials full of the wrath of God.	(5–8)

Verses 1-4

Seven angels appeared in heaven; prepared to finish the destruction of antichrist. As the measure of Babylon's sins was filled up, it finds the full measure of Divine wrath. While believers stand in this world, in times of trouble, as upon a sea of glass mingled with fire, they may look forward to their final deliverance, while new mercies call forth new hymns of praise. The more we know of God's wonderful works, the more we shall praise his greatness as the Lord God Almighty, the Creator and Ruler of all worlds; but his title of Emmanuel, the King of saints, will make him dear to us. Who that considers the power of God's wrath, the value of his favour, or the glory of his holiness, would refuse to fear and honour him alone? His praise is above heaven and earth.

Verses 5-8

In the judgments God executes upon antichrist and his followers, he fulfils the prophecies and promises of his word. These angels are prepared for their work, clothed with pure and white linen, their breasts girded with golden girdles, representing the holiness, and righteousness, and excellence of these dealings with men. They are ministers of Divine justice, and do every thing in a pure and holy manner. They were armed with the wrath of God against his enemies. Even the meanest creature, when armed with the anger of God, will be too hard for any man in the world. The angels received the vials from one of the four living creatures, one of the ministers of the true church, as in answer to the prayers of the ministers and people of God. Antichrist could not be destroyed without a great shock to all the world, and even the people of God would be in trouble and confusion while the great work was doing. The greatest deliverances of the church are brought about by awful and astonishing steps of Providence; and the happy state of the true church will not begin till obstinate enemies shall be destroyed, and lukewarm or formal Christians are purified. Then, whatever is against Scripture being purged away, the whole church shall be spiritual, and the whole being brought to purity, unity, and spirituality, shall be firmly established.

Chapter 16

Chapter Outline

Verses 1-7

We are to pray that the will of God may be done on earth as it is done in heaven. Here is a succession of terrible judgments of Providence; and there seems to be an allusion to several of the plagues of Egypt. The sins were alike, and so were the punishments. The vials refer to the seven trumpets, which represented the rise of antichrist; and the fall of the enemies of the church shall bear some resemblance to their rise. All things throughout their earth, their air, their sea, their rivers, their cities, all are condemned to ruin, all accursed for the wickedness of that people. No wonder that angels, who witness or execute the Divine vengeance on the obstinate haters of God, of Christ, and of holiness, praise his justice and truth; and adore his awful judgments, when he brings upon cruel persecutors the tortures they made his saints and prophets suffer.

Verses 8-11

The heart of man is so desperately wicked, that the most severe miseries never will bring any to repent, without the special grace of God. Hell itself is filled with blasphemies; and those are ignorant of the history of human nature, of the Bible, and of their own hearts, who do not know that the more men suffer, and the more plainly they see the hand of God in their sufferings, the more furiously they often rage against him. Let sinners now seek repentance from Christ, and the grace of the Holy Spirit, or they will have the anguish and horror of an unhumbled, impenitent, and desperate heart; thus adding to their guilt and misery through all eternity. Darkness is opposed to wisdom and knowledge, and forebodes the confusion and folly of the idolaters and followers of the beast. It is opposed to pleasure and joy, and signifies anguish and vexation of spirit.

Verses 12-16

This probably shows the destruction of the Turkish power, and of idolatry, and that a way will be made for the return of the Jews. Or, take it for Rome, as mystical Babylon, the name of Babylon being put for Rome, which was meant, but was not then to be directly named. When Rome is destroyed, her river and merchandise must suffer with her. And perhaps a way will be opened for the eastern nations to come into the church of Christ. The great dragon will collect all his forces, to make one desperate struggle before all be lost. God warns of this great trial, to engage his people to prepare for it. These will be times of great temptation; therefore Christ, by his apostle, calls on his professed servants to expect his sudden coming, and to watch that they might not be put to shame, as apostates or hypocrites. However Christians differ, as to their views of the times and seasons of events yet to be brought to pass, on this one point all are agreed, Jesus Christ, the Lord of glory, will suddenly come again to judge the world. To those living near to Christ, it is an object of joyful hope and expectation, and delay is not desired by them.

Verses 17-21

The seventh and last angel poured forth his vial, and the downfal of Babylon was finished. The church triumphant in heaven saw it and rejoiced; the church in conflict on earth saw it and became triumphant. God remembered the great and wicked city; though for some time he seemed to have forgotten her idolatry and cruelty. All that was most secure was carried away by the ruin. Men blasphemed: the greatest judgments that can befal men, will not bring to repentance without the grace of God. To be hardened against God, by his righteous judgments, is a certain token of sure and utter destruction.

Chapter 17

Chapter Outline

Verses 1-6

Rome clearly appears to be meant in this chapter. Pagan Rome subdued and ruled with military power, not by art and flatteries. She left the nations in general to their ancient usages and worship. But it is well known that by crafty and politic management, with all kinds of deceit of unrighteousness, papal Rome has obtained and kept her rule over kings and nations. Here were allurements of worldly honour and riches, pomp and pride, suited to sensual and worldly minds. Prosperity, pomp, and splendour, feed the pride and lusts of the human heart, but are no security against the Divine vengeance. The golden cup represents the allurements, and delusions, by which this mystical Babylon has obtained and kept her influence, and seduced others to join her abominations. She is named, from her infamous practices, a mother of harlots; training them up to idolatry and all sorts of wickedness. She filled herself with the blood of the saints and martyrs of Jesus. She intoxicated herself with it; and it was so pleasant to her, that she never was satisfied. We cannot but wonder at the oceans of Christian blood shed by men called Christians; yet when we consider these prophecies, these awful deeds testify to the truth of the gospel. And let all beware of a splendid, gainful, or fashionable religion. Let us avoid the mysteries of iniquity, and study diligently the great mystery of godliness, that we may learn humility and gratitude from the example of Christ. The more we seek to resemble him, the less we shall be liable to be deceived by antichrist.

Verses 7-14

The beast on which the woman sat was, and is not, and yet is. It was a seat of idolatry and persecution, and is not; not in the ancient form, which was pagan: yet it is; it is truly the seat of idolatry and tyranny, though of another sort and form. It would deceive into stupid and blind submission all the inhabitants of the earth within its influence, except the remnant of the elect. This beast was seven heads, seven mountains, the seven hills on which Rome stands; and seven kings, seven sorts of government. Five were gone by when this prophecy was written; one was then in being; the other was yet to come. This beast, directed by the papacy, makes an eighth governor, and sets up idolatry again. It had ten horns, which are said to be ten kings who had as yet no kingdoms; they should not rise up till the Roman empire was broken; but should for a time be very zealous in her interest. Christ must reign till all enemies be put under his feet. The reason of the victory is, that he is the King of kings, and Lord of lords. He has supreme dominion and power over all things; all the powers of earth and hell are subject to his control. His followers are called to this warfare, are fitted for it, and will be faithful in it.

Verses 15-18

God so ruled the hearts of these kings, by his power over them, and by his providence, that they did those things, without intending it, which he purposed and foretold. They shall see their folly, and how they have been bewitched and enslaved by the harlot, and be made instruments in her destruction. She was that great city which reigned over the kings of the earth, when John had this vision; and every one knows Rome to be that city. Believers will be received to the glory of the Lord, when wicked men will be destroyed in a most awful manner; their joining together in sin, will be turned to hatred and rage, and they will eagerly assist in tormenting each other. But the Lord's portion is his people; his counsel shall stand, and he will do all his pleasure, to his glory, and the happiness of all his servants.

Chapter 18

Chapter Outline

Another angel from heaven proclaims the fall of mystical Babylon.	(1–3)
A voice from heaven admonishes the people of God, lest they partake of her plagues.	(4–8)
The lamentations over her.	(9–19)
The church called upon to rejoice in her utter ruin.	(20–24)

Verses 1-8

The downfal and destruction of the mystical Babylon are determined in the counsels of God. Another angel comes from heaven. This seems to be Christ himself, coming to destroy his enemies, and to shed abroad the light of his gospel through all nations. The wickedness of this Babylon was very great; she had forsaken the true God, and set up idols, and had drawn all sorts of men into spiritual adultery, and by her wealth and luxury kept them in her interest. The spiritual merchandise, by which multitudes have wickedly lived in wealth, by the sins and follies of mankind, seems principally intended. Fair warning is given to all that expect mercy from God, that they should not only come out of this Babylon, but assist in her destruction. God may have a people even in Babylon. But God's people shall be called out of Babylon, and called effectually, while those that partake with wicked men in their sins, must receive of their plagues. (Rev 18:9-19)

Verses 9-19

The mourners had shared Babylon's sensual pleasures, and gained by her wealth and trade. The kings of the earth, whom she flattered into idolatry, allowing them to be tyrannical over their subjects, while obedient to her; and the merchants, those who trafficked for her indulgences, pardons, and honours; these mourn. Babylon's friends partook her sinful pleasures and profits, but are not willing to share her plagues. The spirit of antichrist is a worldly spirit, and that sorrow is a mere worldly sorrow; they do not lament for the anger of God, but for the loss of outward comforts. The magnificence and riches of the ungodly will avail them nothing, but will render the vengeance harder to be borne. The spiritual merchandise is here alluded to, when not only slaves, but the souls of men, are mentioned as articles of commerce, to the destroying the souls of millions. Nor has this been peculiar to the Roman antichrist, and only her guilt. But let prosperous traders learn, with all their gains, to get the unsearchable riches of Christ; otherwise; even in this life, they may have to mourn that riches make to themselves wings and fly away, and that all the fruits their souls lusted after, are departed from them. Death, at any rate, will soon end their commerce, and all the riches of the ungodly will be exchanged, not only for the coffin and the worm, but for the fire that cannot be quenched.

Verses 20-24

That which is matter of rejoicing to the servants of God on earth, is matter of rejoicing to the angels in heaven. The apostles, who are honoured and daily worshipped at Rome in an idolatrous manner, will rejoice in her fall. The fall of Babylon was an act of God's justice. And because it was a final ruin, this enemy should never molest them any more; of this they were assured by a sign. Let us take warning from the things which brought others to destruction, and let us set our affections on things above, when we consider the changeable nature of earthly things.

Chapter 19

Chapter Outline

Verses 1-10

Praising God for what we have, is praying for what is yet further to be done for us. There is harmony between the angels and the saints in this triumphant song. Christ is the Bridegroom of his ransomed church. This second union will be completed in heaven; but the beginning of the glorious millennium (by which is meant a reign of Christ, or a state of happiness, for a thousand years on earth) may be considered as the celebration of his espousals on earth. Then the church of Christ, being purified from errors, divisions, and corruptions, in doctrine, discipline, worship, and practice, will be made ready to be publicly owned by him as his delight and his beloved. The church appeared; not in the gay, gaudy dress of the mother of harlots, but in fine linen, clean and white. In the robes of Christ's righteousness, imputed for justification, and imparted for sanctification. The promises of the gospel, the true sayings of God, opened, applied, and sealed by the Spirit of God, in holy ordinances, are the marriage-feast. This seems to refer to the abundant grace and consolation Christians will receive in the happy days which are to come. The apostle offered honour to the angel. The angel refused it. He directed the apostle to the true and only object of religious worship; to worship God, and him alone. This plainly condemns the practice of those who worship the elements of bread and wine, and saints, and angels; and of those who do not believe that Christ is truly and by nature God, yet pay him a sort of worship. They stand convicted of idolatry by a messenger from heaven. These are the true sayings of God; of Him who is to be worshipped, as one with the Father and the Holy Spirit.

Verses 11-21

Christ, the glorious Head of the church, is described as on a white horse, the emblem of justice and holiness. He has many crowns, for he is King of kings, and Lord of lords. He is arrayed in a vesture dipped in his own blood, by which he purchased his power as Mediator; and in the blood of his enemies, over whom he always prevails. His name is "The Word of God;" a name none fully knows but himself; only this we know, that this Word was God manifest in the flesh; but his perfections cannot be fully understood by any creature. Angels and saints follow, and are like Christ in their armour of purity and righteousness. The threatenings of the written word he is going to execute on his enemies. The ensigns of his authority are his name; asserting his authority and power, warning the most powerful princes to submit, or they must fall before him. The powers of earth and hell make their utmost effort. These verses declare important events, foretold by the prophets. These persons were not excused because they did what their leaders bade them. How vain will be the plea of many sinners at the great day! We followed our guides; we did as we saw others do! God has given a rule to walk by, in his word; neither the example of the most, nor of the chief, must influence us contrary thereto: if we do as the most do, we must go where the most go, even into the burning lake.

Chapter 20

Chapter Outline

Satan loosed, Gog and Magog. (7–10)

The last and general resurrection. (11–15)

Verses 1-3

Here is a vision, showing by a figure the restraints laid on Satan himself. Christ, with Almighty power, will keep the devil from deceiving mankind as he has hitherto done. He never wants power and instruments to break the power of Satan. Christ shuts by his power, and seals by his authority. The church shall have a time of peace and prosperity, but all her trials are not yet over.

Verses 4-6

Here is an account of the reign of the saints, for the same space of time as Satan is bound. Those who suffer with Christ, shall reign with him in his spiritual and heavenly kingdom, in conformity to him in his wisdom, righteousness, and holiness: this is called the first resurrection, with which none but those who serve Christ, and suffer for him, shall be favoured. The happiness of these servants of God is declared. None can be blessed but those that are holy; and all that are holy shall be blessed. We know something thing of what the first death is, and it is very awful; but we know not what this second death is. It must be much more dreadful; it is the death of the soul, eternal separation from God. May we never know what it is: those who have been made partakers of a spiritual resurrection, are saved from the power of the second death. We may expect that a thousand years will follow the destruction of the antichristian, idolatrous, persecuting powers, during which pure Christianity, in doctrine, worship, and holiness, will be made known over all the earth. By the all-powerful working of the Holy Spirit, fallen man will be new-created; and faith and holiness will as certainly prevail, as unbelief and unholiness now do. We may easily perceive what a variety of dreadful pains, diseases, and other calamities would cease, if all men were true and consistent Christians. All the evils of public and private contests would be ended, and happiness of every kind largely increased. Every man would try to lighten suffering, instead of adding to the sorrows around him. It is our duty to pray for the promised glorious days, and to do every thing in our public and private stations which can prepare for them.

Verses 7-10

While this world lasts, Satan's power in it will not be wholly destroyed, though it may be limited and lessened. No sooner is Satan let loose, than he again begins deceiving the nations, and stirring them up to make war with the saints and servants of God. It would be well if the servants and ministers of Christ were as active and persevering in doing good, as his enemies in doing mischief. God will fight this last and decisive battle for his people, that the victory may be complete, and the glory be to himself.

Verses 11-15

After the events just foretold, the end will speedily come; and there is no mention of any thing else, before the appearing of Christ to judge the world. This will be the great day: the Judge, the

Lord Jesus Christ, will then put on majesty and terror. The persons to be judged are the dead, small and great; young and old, low and high, poor and rich. None are so mean, but they have some talents to account for; and none so great, as to avoid having to account for them. Not only those alive at the coming of Christ, but all the dead. There is a book of remembrance both for good and bad: and the book of the sinner's conscience, though formerly secret, will then be opened. Every man will recollect all his past actions, though he had long forgotten many of them. Another book shall be opened, the book of the Scriptures, the rule of life; it represents the Lord's knowledge of his people, and his declaring their repentance, faith, and good works; showing the blessings of the new covenant. By their works men shall be justified or condemned; he will try their principles by their practices. Those justified and acquitted by the gospel, shall be justified and acquitted by the Judge, and shall enter into eternal life, having nothing more to fear from death, or hell, or wicked men; for these are all destroyed together. This is the second death; it is the final separation of sinners from God. Let it be our great concern to see whether our Bibles justify or condemn us now; for Christ will judge the secrets of all men according to the gospel. Who shall dwell with devouring flames?

Chapter 21

Chapter Outline

A new heaven, and new earth: the new Jerusalem where God dwells, and banishes all sorrow from his people.	(1–8)
Its heavenly origin, glory, and secure defence.	(9–21)
Its perfect happiness, as enlightened with the presence of God and the Lamb, and in the free access of multitudes, made holy.	(22–27)

Verses 1-8

The new heaven and the new earth will not be separate from each other; the earth of the saints, their glorified, bodies, will be heavenly. The old world, with all its troubles and tumults, will have passed away. There will be no sea; this aptly represents freedom from conflicting passions, temptations, troubles, changes, and alarms; from whatever can divide or interrupt the communion of saints. This new Jerusalem is the church of God in its new and perfect state, the church triumphant. Its blessedness came wholly from God, and depends on him. The presence of God with his people in heaven, will not be interrupt as it is on earth, he will dwell with them continually. All effects of former trouble shall be done away. They have often been in tears, by reason of sin, of affliction, of the calamities of the church; but no signs, no remembrance of former sorrows shall remain. Christ makes all things new. If we are willing and desirous that the gracious Redeemer should make all things new in order hearts and nature, he will make all things new in respect of our situation, till he has brought us to enjoy complete happiness. See the certainty of the promise. God gives his titles, Alpha and Omega, the Beginning and the End, as a pledge for the full performance. Sensual and sinful pleasures are muddy and poisoned waters; and the best earthly comforts are like the scanty supplies of a cistern; when idolized, they become broken cisterns, and yield only vexation. But the joys which Christ imparts are like waters springing from a fountain, pure, refreshing, abundant, and eternal. The sanctifying consolations of the Holy Spirit prepare for heavenly happiness; they are streams which flow for us in the wilderness. The fearful durst not meet the difficulties of religion, their slavish fear came from their unbelief; but those who were so dastardly as not to dare to take up the cross of Christ, were yet so desperate as to run into abominable wickedness. The agonies and terrors of the first death will lead to the far greater terrors and agonies of eternal death.

Verses 9-21

God has various employments for his holy angels. Sometimes they sound the trumpet of Divine Providence, and warn a careless world; sometimes they discover things of a heavenly nature of the heirs of salvation. Those who would have clear views of heaven, must get as near to heaven as they can, on the mount of meditation and faith. The subject of the vision is the church of God in a perfect, triumphant state, shining in its lustre; glorious in relation to Christ; which shows that the happiness of heaven consists in intercourse with God, and in conformity to him. The change of emblems from a bride to a city, shows that we are only to take general ideas from this description. The wall is for security. Heaven is a safe state; those who are there, are separated and secured from all evils and enemies. This city is vast; here is room for all the people of God. The foundation of the wall; the promise and power of God, and the purchase of Christ, are the strong foundations of the safety and happiness of the church. These foundations are set forth by twelve sorts of precious stones, denoting the variety and excellence of the doctrines of the gospel, or of the graces of the Holy Spirit, or the personal excellences of the Lord Jesus Christ. Heaven has gates; there is a free admission to all that are sanctified; they shall not find themselves shut out. These gates were all of pearls. Christ is the Pearl of great price, and he is our Way to God. The street of the city was pure gold, like transparent glass. The saints in heaven tread gold under foot. The saints are there at rest, yet it is not a state of sleep and idleness; they have communion, not only with God, but with one another. All these glories but faintly represent heaven.

Verses 22-27

Perfect and direct communion with God, will more than supply the place of gospel institutions. And what words can more full express the union and co-equality of the Son with the Father, in the Godhead? What a dismal world would this be, if it were not for the light of the sun! What is there in heaven that supplies its place? The glory of God lightens that city, and the Lamb is the Light thereof. God in Christ will be an everlasting Fountain of knowledge and joy to the saints in heaven. There is no night, therefore no need of shutting the gates; all is at peace and secure. The whole shows us that we should be more and more led to think of heaven as filled with the glory of God, and enlightened by the presence of the Lord Jesus. Nothing sinful or unclean, idolatrous, or false and deceitful, can enter. All the inhabitants are made perfect in holiness. Now the saints feel a sad mixture of corruption, which hinders them in the service of God, and interrupts their communion with him; but, at their entrance into the holy of holies, they are washed in the laver of Christ's blood, and presented to the Father without spot. None are admitted into heaven who work abominations. It is free from hypocrites, such as make lies. As nothing unclean can enter heaven, let us be stirred up by these glimpses of heavenly things, to use all diligence, and to perfect holiness in the fear of God.

Chapter 22

Chapter Outline

A description of the heavenly state, under the figures of the water and the tree of life, and of the throne of God and the Lamb.	(1–5)
The truth and certain fulfilling of all the prophetic visions, The Holy Spirit, and the bride, the church, invite, and say, Come.	(6–19)
The closing blessing.	(20, 21)

Verses 1-5

All streams of earthly comfort are muddy; but these are clear, and refreshing. They give life, and preserve life, to those who drink of them, and thus they will flow for evermore. These point to the quickening and sanctifying influences of the Holy Spirit, as given to sinners through Christ. The Holy Spirit, proceeding from the Father and the Son, applies this salvation to our souls by his new-creating love and power. The trees of life are fed by the pure waters of the river that comes from the throne of God. The presence of God in heaven, is the health and happiness of the saints. This tree was an emblem of Christ, and of all the blessings of his salvation; and the leaves for the healing of the nations, mean that his favour and presence supply all good to the inhabitants of that blessed world. The devil has no power there; he cannot draw the saints from serving God, nor can he disturb them in the service of God. God and the Lamb are here spoken of as one. Service there shall be not only freedom, but honour and dominion. There will be no night; no affliction or dejection, no pause in service or enjoyment: no diversions or pleasures or man's inventing will there be wanted. How different all this from gross and merely human views of heavenly happiness, even those which refer to pleasures of the mind!

Verses 6-19

The Lord Jesus spake by the angel, solemnly confirming the contents of this book, particularly of this last vision. He is the Lord God faithful and true. Also by his messengers; the holy angels showed them to holy men of God. They are things that must shortly be done; Christ will come quickly, and put all things out of doubt. And by the integrity of that angel who had been the apostle's interpreter. He refused to accept religious worship from John, and reproved him for offering it.

This presents another testimony against idolatrous worship of saints and angels. God calls every one to witness to the declarations here made. This book, thus kept open, will have effect upon men; the filthy and unjust will be more so, but it will confirm, strengthen, and further sanctify those who are upright with God. Never let us think that a dead or disobedient faith will save us, for the First and the Last has declared that those alone are blessed who do his commandments. It is a book that shuts out form heaven all wicked and unrighteous persons, particularly those who love and make lies, therefore cannot itself be a lie. There is no middle place or condition. Jesus, who is the Spirit of prophecy, has given his churches this morning-light of prophecy, to assure them of the light of the perfect day approaching. All is confirmed by an open and general invitation to mankind, to come and partake freely of the promises and of the privileges of the gospel. The Spirit, by the sacred word, and by convictions and influence in the sinner's conscience, says, Come to Christ for salvation; and the bride, or the whole church, on earth and in heaven, says, Come and share our happiness. Lest any should hesitate, it is added, Let whosoever will, or, is willing, come and take of the water of life freely. May every one who hears or reads these words, desire at once to accept the gracious invitation. All are condemned who should dare to corrupt or change the word of God, either by adding to it, or taking from it.

Verses 20, 21

After discovering these things to his people on earth, Christ seems to take leave of them, and return to heaven; but he assures them it shall not be long before he comes again. And while we are busy in the duties of our different stations of life; whatever labours may try us, whatever difficulties may surround us, whatever sorrows may press us down, let us with pleasure hear our Lord proclaiming, Behold, I come quickly; I come to put an end to the labour and suffering of my servants. I come, and my reward of grace is with me, to recompense, with royal bounty, every work of faith and labour of love. I come to receive my faithful, persevering people to myself, to dwell for ever in that blissful world. Amen, even so, come, Lord Jesus. A blessing closes the whole. By the grace of Christ we must be kept in joyful expectation of his glory, fitted for it, and preserved to it; and his glorious appearance will be joyful to those who partake of his grace and favour here. Let all add, Amen. Let us earnestly thirst after greater measures of the gracious influences of the blessed Jesus in our souls, and his gracious presence with us, till glory has made perfect his grace toward us. Glory be to the Father, and to the Son, and to the Holy Ghost; as it was in the beginning, is now, and ever shall be, world without end. Amen.

Indexes

Index of Scripture References

Genesis

44:18-34 45:1-15 45:1-15 45:16-24 45:16-24 45:25-28 45:25-28 46:1-4 46:1-4 46:5-27
46:5-27 46:28-34 46:28-34 47:1-6 47:1-6 47:7-12 47:7-12 47:13-26 47:13-26 47:27-31
47:27-31 48:1-7 48:1-7 48:8-22 48:8-22 49:1 49:1 49:2 49:2 49:3-7 49:3-7 49:8-12
49:8-12 49:10 49:13-18 49:13-18 49:19-21 49:19-21 49:22-27 49:22-27 49:28-33
49:28-33 50:1-6 50:1-6 50:7-14 50:7-14 50:15-21 50:15-21 50:22-26 50:22-26

Exodus

1:1-7 1:1-7 1:8-14 1:8-14 1:15-22 1:15-22 2:1-4 2:1-4 2:5-10 2:5-10 2:11-15 2:11-15
2:16-22 2:16-22 2:23-25 2:23-25 3:1-6 3:1-6 3:7-10 3:7-10 3:11-15 3:11-15 3:11-15
3:14 3:16-22 3:16-22 4:1-9 4:1-9 4:10-17 4:10-17 4:18-23 4:18-23 4:24-31 4:24-31
5:1-9 5:1-9 5:10-23 5:10-23 6:1-9 6:1-9 6:10-13 6:10-13 6:14-30 6:14-30 7:1-7 7:1-7
7:8-13 7:8-13 7:14-25 7:14-25 7:20 8:1-15 8:1-15 8:16-19 8:16-19 8:20-32 8:20-32
9:1-7 9:1-7 9:8-12 9:8-12 9:13-21 9:13-21 9:22-35 9:22-35 10:1-11 10:1-11 10:12-20
10:12-20 10:21-29 10:21-29 11:1-3 11:1-3 11:4-10 11:4-10 12:1-20 12:1-20 12:21-28
12:21-28 12:29-36 12:29-36 12:37-42 12:37-42 12:43-51 12:43-51 12:46 13:1-10
13:1-10 13:2-10 13:11-16 13:11-16 13:11-16 13:17-20 13:17-20 13:21 13:21 13:22
13:22 14:1-9 14:1-9 14:10-14 14:10-14 14:13 14:15-20 14:15-20 14:21-31 14:21-31
15:1-21 15:1-21 15:22-27 15:22-27 16:1-12 16:1-12 16:13-21 16:13-21 16:18 16:18
16:22-31 16:22-31 16:23 16:32-36 16:32-36 17:1-7 17:1-7 17:8-16 17:8-16 17:14
18:1-6 18:1-6 18:7-12 18:7-12 18:13-27 18:13-27 19:1-8 19:1-8 19:9-15 19:9-15
19:16-25 19:16-25 20 20:1 20:1 20:2 20:2 20:3-11 20:3-11 20:12-17 20:12-17
20:18-21 20:18-21 20:22-26 20:22-26 21:1-11 21:1-11 21:12-21 21:12-21 21:22-36
21:22-36 22:18 23 23:1-9 23:1-9 23:10-19 23:10-19 23:20-33 23:20-33 24:1-8 24:1-8
24:7 24:9-11 24:9-11 24:9-11 24:12-18 24:12-18 25:1-9 25:1-9 25:10-22 25:10-22
25:10-22 25:23-30 25:23-30 25:31-40 25:31-40 25:40 26:1-6 26:1-6 26:7-14 26:7-14
26:7-14 26:15-30 26:15-30 26:31-37 26:31-37 27:1-8 27:1-8 27:9-19 27:9-19 27:20
27:20 27:21 27:21 28:1-5 28:1-5 28:6-14 28:6-14 28:15-30 28:15-30 28:31-39 28:31-39
28:40-43 28:40-43 29:1-37 29:1-37 29:38-46 29:38-46 30:1-10 30:1-10 30:11-16
30:11-16 30:17-21 30:17-21 30:22-38 30:22-38 31:1-11 31:1-11 31:12-17 31:12-17
31:18 31:18 32 32:1-6 32:1-6 32:7-14 32:7-14 32:15-20 32:15-20 32:21-29 32:21-29
32:30-35 32:30-35 33:1-6 33:1-6 33:7-11 33:7-11 33:12-23 33:12-23 34:1-4 34:1-4
34:5-9 34:5-9 34:10-17 34:10-17 34:18-27 34:18-27 34:24 34:28-35 34:28-35 35:1-3
35:1-3 35:4-19 35:4-19 35:20-29 35:20-29 35:30-35 35:30-35 38:1-8 38:1-8 38:9-20
38:9-20 38:9-20 38:21-31 38:21-31 39:1-31 39:1-31 39:32-43 39:32-43 40:1-15 40:1-15
40:16-33 40:16-33 40:34-38 40:34-38

Leviticus

1:1 1:1 1:2 1:2 1:3-9 1:3-9 1:10-17 1:10-17 2:1-11 2:1-11 2:12-16 2:12-16 3:1-5
3:1-5 3:6-17 3:6-17 4:1-12 4:1-12 4:13-21 4:13-21 4:22-26 4:22-26 4:27-35 4:27-35
5:1-13 5:1-13 5:14-19 5:14-19 6:1-7 6:1-7 6:8-13 6:8-13 6:14-23 6:14-23 6:24-30
6:24-30 7:1-10 7:1-10 7:11-27 7:11-27 7:28-34 7:28-34 7:35-38 7:35-38 7:35-38
8:1-13 8:1-13 8:14-36 8:14-36 9:1-21 9:1-21 9:22-24 9:22-24 9:23 9:24 10:1 10:1
10:2 10:2 10:3-7 10:3-7 10:8-11 10:8-11 10:12-20 10:12-20 13:1-17 13:1-17 13:18-44
13:18-44 13:24 13:45 13:45 13:46 13:46 13:47-59 13:47-59 14:1-9 14:1-9 14:10-32
14:10-32 14:33-53 14:33-53 14:54-57 14:54-57 16:1-14 16:1-14 16:15-34 16:15-34
16:15-34 17:1-9 17:1-9 17:10-16 17:10-16 18:18 19:2 19:3 19:4 19:9 19:11 19:12

19:13 19:14 19:15 19:17 19:17 19:18 19:31 19:32 19:33 19:35 20:1-9 20:1-9
20:10-27 20:10-27 22:24 23:1-3 23:1-3 23:4-14 23:4-14 23:15-22 23:15-22 23:23-32
23:23-32 23:33-44 23:33-44 24:1-9 24:1-9 24:10-23 24:10-23 25:1-7 25:1-7 25:8-22
25:8-22 25:23-34 25:23-34 25:35-38 25:35-38 25:39-55 25:39-55 26:1-13 26:1-13
26:14-39 26:14-39 26:14-39 26:17 26:21-24 26:37 26:40-46 26:40-46 27:1-13 27:1-13
27:14-25 27:14-25 27:26-33 27:26-33 27:34 27:34

Numbers

1:1-43 1:1-43 1:44-46 1:44-46 1:47-54 1:47-54 3:1-13 3:1-13 3:14-39 3:14-39 3:40-51
3:40-51 4:1-3 4:1-3 4:4-20 4:4-20 4:21-33 4:21-33 4:34-49 4:34-49 5:1-10 5:1-10
5:11-31 5:11-31 6:1-21 6:1-21 6:22-27 6:22-27 6:22-27 7:1-9 7:1-9 7:10-89 7:10-89
8:1-4 8:1-4 8:5-26 8:5-26 9:1-14 9:1-14 9:15-23 9:15-23 10:1-10 10:1-10 10:11-28
10:11-28 10:11-28 10:29-32 10:29-32 10:33-36 10:33-36 11:1-3 11:1-3 11:4-9 11:4-9
11:10-15 11:10-15 11:16-23 11:16-23 11:24-30 11:24-30 11:31-35 11:31-35 12:1-9
12:1-9 12:10-16 12:10-16 13:1-20 13:1-20 13:21-25 13:21-25 13:26-33 13:26-33 14
14:1-4 14:1-4 14:5-10 14:5-10 14:11-19 14:11-19 14:11-19 14:20-35 14:20-35 14:29
14:36-39 14:36-39 14:40-45 14:40-45 15:1-21 15:1-21 15:22-29 15:22-29 15:30-36
15:30-36 15:37-41 15:37-41 15:38 16:1-11 16:1-11 16:12-15 16:12-15 16:16-22
16:16-22 16:23-34 16:23-34 16:35-40 16:35-40 16:41-50 16:41-50 17:1-7 17:1-7
17:8-13 17:8-13 18:1-7 18:1-7 18:8-19 18:8-19 18:20 18:20-32 18:20-32 18:31 19:1-10
19:1-10 19:11-22 19:11-22 20:1-13 20:1-13 20:14-21 20:14-21 20:22-29 20:22-29
21:1-3 21:1-3 21:4-9 21:4-9 21:6-9 21:10-20 21:10-20 21:21-35 21:21-35 22:1-14
22:1-14 22:15-21 22:15-21 22:22-35 22:22-35 22:36-41 22:36-41 23:1-10 23:1-10
23:11-30 23:11-30 24:1-9 24:1-9 24:10-14 24:10-14 24:10-14 24:15-25 24:15-25 25:1-5
25:1-5 25:6-15 25:6-15 25:16-18 25:16-18 26:1-51 26:1-51 26:52-56 26:52-56 26:52-56
26:57-62 26:57-62 26:63-65 26:63-65 27:1-11 27:1-11 27:12-14 27:12-14 27:15-23
27:15-23 27:15-23 28:1-8 28:1-8 28:9-15 28:9-15 28:16-31 28:16-31 28:16-31 29:1-11
29:1-11 29:12-40 29:12-40 30:1 30:1 30:2 30:2 30:3-16 30:3-16 31:1-6 31:1-6 31:7-12
31:7-12 31:13-18 31:13-38 31:19-24 31:25-47 31:25-47 31:39-24 31:48-54 31:48-54
32 32:1-5 32:1-5 32:6-15 32:6-15 32:14 32:16-27 32:16-27 32:28-42 32:28-42 33:1-49
33:1-49 33:50-56 33:50-56 34:1-15 34:1-15 34:16-29 34:16-29 34:16-29 35 35:1-8
35:1-8 35:9-34 35:9-34 36:1-4 36:1-4 36:5-12 36:5-12 36:5-12 36:13 36:13

Deuteronomy

1:1-8 1:1-8 1:6-8 1:9-18 1:9-18 1:19-46 1:19-46 1:22 2:1-7 2:1-7 2:8-23 2:8-23
2:24-37 2:24-37 3:1-11 3:1-11 3:12-20 3:12-20 3:21-29 3:21-29 4:1 4:1-23 4:1-23
4:24-40 4:24-40 4:40 4:41-49 4:41-49 5:1-5 5:1-5 5:6-22 5:6-22 5:14 5:23-33 5:23-33
6:1-3 6:1-3 6:4 6:4 6:4-9 6:5 6:5 6:6-16 6:6-16 6:7 6:17-25 6:17-25 7 7:1-11
7:1-11 7:12-26 7:12-26 8:1-9 8:1-9 8:3 8:10-20 8:10-20 9:1-6 9:1-6 9:7-29 9:7-29
10:1-11 10:1-11 10:12-22 10:12-22 11 11:1-7 11:1-7 11:8-17 11:8-17 11:13-21
11:18-25 11:18-25 11:26-32 11:26-32 12:1-4 12:1-4 12:5-32 12:5-32 13:1-5 13:1-5
13:6-11 13:6-11 13:12-18 13:12-18 14:1-21 14:1-21 14:22-29 14:22-29 15:1-11 15:1-11
15:12-18 15:12-18 15:19-23 15:19-23 16:1-17 16:1-17 16:18-22 16:18-22 17:1-7 17:1-7
17:8-13 17:8-13 17:14-20 17:14-20 18:1-8 18:1-8 18:9-14 18:9-14 18:11 18:15-22
18:15-22 19 19:1-13 19:1-13 19:14 19:14 19:15-21 19:15-21 20:1-9 20:1-9 20:10-12
20:10-20 21:1-9 21:1-9 21:10-14 21:10-14 21:15-17 21:15-17 21:18-21 21:18-21 21:22

21:22 21:23 21:23 21:23 22:1-4 22:1-4 22:5-12 22:5-12 22:13-30 22:13-30 23:1-8
23:1-8 23:9-14 23:9-14 23:15-25 23:15-25 23:25 24:1-4 24:1-4 24:5-13 24:5-13
24:14-22 24:14-22 25:1-3 25:1-3 25:2 25:3 25:4 25:4 25:5-10 25:5-12 25:5-12
25:13-16 25:13-16 25:17-19 25:17-19 25:19 26:1-11 26:1-11 26:12-15 26:12-15
26:16-19 26:16-19 27 27:1-10 27:1-10 27:11-26 27:11-26 28:1-14 28:1-14 28:15-44
28:15-44 28:45-68 28:45-68 28:53-57 28:63 29:1-9 29:1-9 29:10-21 29:10-21 29:22-28
29:22-28 29:23 29:29 29:29 29:29 30:1-10 30:1-10 30:11-14 30:11-14 30:15-20
30:15-20 31:1-8 31:1-8 31:9-13 31:9-13 31:14-22 31:14-22 31:22-30 31:23-30 32:1
32:1 32:2 32:2 32:3-6 32:3-6 32:7-14 32:7-14 32:13 32:14 32:15-18 32:15-18 32:19-25
32:19-25 32:26-38 32:26-38 32:39-43 32:39-43 32:44-47 32:44-47 32:48-52 32:48-52
33:1-5 33:1-5 33:6-23 33:6-23 33:24 33:24 33:25 33:25 33:26-29 33:26-29 34:1-4
34:1-4 34:5-8 34:5-8 34:9-12 34:9-12

Joshua

1:1-4 1:1-4 1:4 1:5-9 1:5-9 1:10-15 1:10-15 1:16-18 1:16-18 2:1-7 2:1-7 2:8-21
2:8-21 2:9 2:22-24 2:22-24 3:1-6 3:1-6 3:7-13 3:7-13 3:14-17 3:14-17 4:1-9 4:1-9
4:10-19 4:10-19 4:20-24 4:20-24 5:1-9 5:1-9 5:10 5:10-12 5:10-12 5:13-15 5:13-15
6:1-5 6:1-5 6:2 6:6-16 6:6-16 6:17-27 6:17-27 7:1-5 7:1-5 7:6-9 7:6-9 7:10-5 7:10-15
7:16-26 7:16-26 8:1 8:1 8:2 8:2 8:3-22 8:3-22 8:23-29 8:23-29 8:30-35 8:30-35 9:1
9:1 9:2 9:2 9:3-13 9:3-13 9:3-13 9:14-21 9:14-21 9:22-27 9:22-27 10:1-6 10:1-6
10:7-14 10:7-14 10:15-27 10:15-27 10:28-43 10:28-43 11:1-9 11:1-9 11:10-14 11:10-14
11:10-14 11:15-23 11:15-23 12:1-6 12:1-6 12:7-24 12:7-24 13:1-6 13:1-6 13:7-33
13:7-33 14:1-5 14:1-5 14:6-15 14:6-15 15:1-12 15:1-12 15:13-19 15:13-19 15:16-19
15:20-63 15:20-63 17:1-6 17:1-6 17:7-13 17:7-13 17:14-18 17:14-18 18:1 18:1 18:2-10
18:2-10 18:11-28 18:11-28 19:1-9 19:1-9 19:10-16 19:10-16 19:17-51 19:17-51 20:1-6
20:1-6 20:7-9 20:7-9 21:1-8 21:1-8 21:9-42 21:9-42 21:9-42 21:43-45 21:43-45
21:43-45 22:1-9 22:1-9 22:10-20 22:10-20 22:21-29 22:21-29 22:30-34 22:30-34
23:1-10 23:1-10 23:11-16 23:11-16 24:1-14 24:1-14 24:15 24:15-28 24:15-28 24:29-33
24:29-33

Judges

1:1-4 1:1-4 1:1-8 1:1-8 1:5-7 1:5-7 1:7 1:8-16 1:8-16 1:9-20 1:9-20 1:14 1:15
1:17-23 1:17-23 1:17-23 1:21-36 1:21-36 1:24 1:24 1:25 1:25 2:1-5 2:1-5 2:6-23
2:6-23 3:1-7 3:1-7 3:8-11 3:8-11 3:12-30 3:12-30 3:31 3:31 4:1-3 4:1-3 4:4-9 4:4-9
4:10-16 4:10-16 4:17-24 4:17-24 5:1-5 5:1-5 5:6-11 5:6-11 5:12-23 5:12-23 5:24-31
5:24-31 6:1-6 6:1-6 6:7-10 6:7-10 6:11-24 6:11-24 6:25-32 6:25-32 6:33-40 6:33-40
7:1-8 7:1-8 7:9-15 7:9-15 7:16-22 7:16-22 7:23-25 7:23-25 8:1-3 8:1-3 8:4-12 8:4-12
8:13-17 8:13-17 8:18-21 8:18-21 8:22-28 8:22-28 8:29-35 8:29-35 9:1-6 9:1-6 9:7-21
9:7-21 9:22-29 9:22-29 9:30-49 9:30-49 9:50-57 9:50-57 9:50-57 10:1-5 10:1-5 10:6-9
10:6-9 10:10-18 10:10-18 11:1-11 11:1-11 11:12-28 11:12-28 11:29-40 11:29-40 12:1-7
12:1-7 12:8-15 12:8-15 13:1-7 13:1-7 13:8-14 13:8-14 13:15-23 13:15-23 13:24 13:24
13:25 13:25 14:1-4 14:1-4 14:5-9 14:5-9 14:10-20 14:10-20 15:1-8 15:1-8 15:9-17
15:9-17 15:18-20 15:18-20 16:1 16:1-3 16:1-3 16:4-17 16:4-17 16:18-21 16:18-21
16:22-24 16:22-24 16:25-31 16:25-31 17:1-6 17:1-6 17:7-13 17:7-13 18 20:28

Ruth

3:16-28 3:16-28 4:1-19 4:1-19 4:20-28 4:20-28 4:29-34 4:29-34 5:1-9 5:1-9 5:10-18
5:10-18 6 6:1-10 6:1-10 6:11-14 6:11-14 6:15-38 6:15-38 7:1-12 7:1-12 7:13-47
7:13-47 7:48-51 7:48-51 8:1-11 8:1-11 8:12-21 8:12-21 8:22-53 8:22-53 8:54-61
8:54-61 8:62-66 8:62-66 9:1-9 9:1-9 9:10-14 9:10-14 9:15-28 9:15-28 10 10:1-13
10:1-13 10:14-29 10:14-29 11:1-8 11:1-8 11:9-13 11:9-13 11:9-13 11:14-25 11:14-25
11:26-40 11:26-40 11:41-43 11:41-43 12:1-15 12:1-15 12:16-24 12:16-24 12:25-33
12:25-33 13:1-10 13:1-10 13:11-22 13:11-22 13:23-34 13:23-34 14:1-6 14:1-6 14:7-20
14:7-20 14:21-31 14:21-31 15:1-8 15:1-8 15:3 15:9-24 15:9-24 15:25-34 15:25-34
16:1-14 16:1-14 16:15-28 16:15-28 16:29-34 16:29-34 17:1-7 17:1-7 17:8-16 17:8-16
17:8-16 17:17-24 17:17-24 18:1-16 18:1-16 18:17-20 18:17-20 18:21-40 18:21-40
18:41-46 18:41-46 19:1-8 19:1-8 19:9-13 19:9-13 19:14-18 19:14-18 19:19-21 19:19-21
20:1-11 20:1-11 20:12-21 20:12-21 20:22-30 20:22-30 20:31-43 20:31-43 21:1-4 21:1-4
21:5-16 21:5-16 21:17-29 21:17-29 22 22:1-14 22:1-14 22:15-28 22:15-28 22:29-40
22:29-40 22:41-50 22:41-50 22:49 22:51-53 22:51-53

2 Kings

1:1-8 1:1-8 1:9-18 1:9-18 2:1-8 2:1-8 2:9-12 2:9-12 2:13-18 2:13-18 2:19-25 2:19-25
3:1-5 3:1-5 3:6-19 3:6-19 3:20-27 3:20-27 4:1-7 4:1-7 4:8-17 4:8-17 4:18-37 4:18-37
4:38-44 4:38-44 5:1-8 5:1-8 5:9-14 5:9-14 5:15-19 5:15-19 5:20-27 5:20-27 6:1-7
6:1-7 6:8-12 6:8-12 6:13-23 6:13-23 6:24-33 6:24-33 7:1 7:1 7:2 7:2 7:3-11 7:3-11
7:12-20 7:12-20 8:1-6 8:1-6 8:7-15 8:7-15 8:16-24 8:16-24 8:25-29 8:25-29 9:1-10
9:1-10 9:11-15 9:11-15 9:16-29 9:16-29 9:30-37 9:30-37 10:1-14 10:1-14 10:15-28
10:15-28 10:29-36 10:29-36 11 11:1-12 11:1-12 11:13-16 11:13-16 11:17-21 11:17-21
12:1-16 12:1-16 12:17-21 12:17-21 13:1-9 13:1-9 13:10-19 13:10-19 13:20-25 13:20-25
14:1-7 14:1-7 14:8-14 14:8-14 14:15-22 14:15-22 14:15-22 14:23-29 14:23-29 14:25
15:1-7 15:1-7 15:8-31 15:8-31 15:32-38 15:32-38 16:1-9 16:1-9 16:10-16 16:10-16
16:17-20 16:17-20 17 17:1-6 17:1-6 17:7-23 17:7-23 17:24-41 17:24-41 18:1-8 18:1-8
18:9-16 18:9-16 18:17-37 18:17-37 19:1-7 19:1-7 19:8-19 19:8-19 19:20-34 19:20-34
19:20-34 19:35-37 19:35-37 20:1-11 20:1-11 20:12-21 20:12-21 21:1-9 21:1-9 21:10-18
21:10-18 21:19-26 21:19-26 22:1-10 22:1-10 22:11-20 22:11-20 23:1-3 23:1-3 23:4-14
23:4-14 23:15-24 23:15-24 23:25-30 23:25-30 23:31-37 23:31-37 23:31-37 24:1-7
24:1-7 24:8-20 24:8-20 24:8-20 25:1-7 25:1-7 25:8-21 25:8-21 25:22-30 25:22-30

1 Chronicles

1:1-27 1:1-27 1:28-54 1:28-54 4:9 4:10 11:1-9 11:1-9 11:10-47 11:10-47 12:1-22
12:1-22 12:22 12:23-40 12:23-40 13:1-5 13:1-5 13:6-14 13:6-14 13:6-14 15:1-24
15:1-24 15:25-29 15:25-29 16:1-6 16:1-6 16:7-36 16:7-36 16:37-43 16:37-43 17:19
22:1-5 22:1-5 22:6-16 22:6-16 22:17-19 22:17-19 22:17-19 23:1-23 23:1-23 23:24-32
23:24-32 27:1-15 27:1-15 27:16-34 27:16-34 28:1-10 28:1-10 28:11-21 28:11-21 29:1-9
29:1-9 29:10-19 29:10-19 29:20-25 29:20-25 29:26-30 29:26-30

2 Chronicles

5:1-10 5:1-10 5:11-14 5:11-14 9:1-12 9:1-12 9:13-31 9:13-31 11:1-12 11:1-12 11:13
11:13-23 11:13-23 11:14 20:1-13 20:1-13 20:14-19 20:14-19 20:20-30 20:20-30
20:31-37 20:31-37 21:1-11 21:1-11 21:12-20 21:12-20 24:1-14 24:1-14 24:15-27
24:15-27 25:1-13 25:1-13 25:14-16 25:14-16 25:17-28 25:17-28 26:1-15 26:1-15
26:16-23 26:16-23 29:1-19 29:1-19 29:20-36 29:20-36 30:1-12 30:1-12 30:13-20

30:13-20 30:21-27 30:21-27 32:1-23 32:1-23 32:24-33 32:24-33 33:1-20 33:1-20
33:21-25 33:21-25 33:21-25 35:1-19 35:1-19 35:20-27 35:20-27 36:1-21 36:1-21 36:22
36:22 36:23 36:23

Ezra

1:1-4 1:1-4 1:5-11 1:5-11 2:1-35 2:1-35 2:36-63 2:36-63 2:64-70 2:64-70 3:1-7 3:1-7
3:8-13 3:8-13 4:1-5 4:1-5 4:6-24 4:6-24 4:6-24 5:1 5:1 5:2 5:2 5:3-17 5:3-17 6
6:1-12 6:1-12 6:13-22 6:13-22 7 7:1-10 7:1-10 7:11-26 7:11-26 7:27 7:27 7:28 7:28
8:1-20 8:1-20 8:21-23 8:21-23 8:24-30 8:24-30 8:31-36 8:31-36 9:1-4 9:1-4 9:5-15
9:5-15 10:1-5 10:1-5 10:6-14 10:6-14 10:15-44 10:15-44

Nehemiah

2:1-8 2:1-8 2:9-18 2:9-18 2:19 2:19 2:20 2:20 4:1-6 4:1-6 4:7-15 4:7-15 4:16-23
4:16-23 5:1-5 5:1-5 5:6-13 5:6-13 5:14-19 5:14-19 6:1-9 6:1-9 6:10-14 6:10-14
6:15-19 6:15-19 7:1-4 7:1-4 7:5-73 7:5-73 8:1-8 8:1-8 8:9-12 8:9-12 8:13-18 8:13-18
9:1-3 9:1-3 9:4-38 9:4-38 10:1-31 10:1-31 10:32-39 10:32-39 12:1-26 12:1-26 12:27-43
12:27-43 12:44-47 12:44-47 13:1-9 13:1-9 13:10-14 13:10-14 13:15-22 13:15-22
13:23-31 13:23-31

Esther

1:1-9 1:1-9 1:10-22 1:10-22 2:1-20 2:1-20 2:21-23 2:21-23 3:1-6 3:1-6 3:7-15 3:7-15
4:1-4 4:1-4 4:5-17 4:5-17 5:1-8 5:1-8 5:9-14 5:9-14 6:1-3 6:1-3 6:4-11 6:4-11
6:12-14 6:12-14 7:1-6 7:1-6 7:7-10 7:7-10 8:1 8:1 8:2 8:2 8:3-14 8:3-14 8:15-17
8:15-17 9:1-19 9:1-19 9:20-32 9:20-32

Job

1 1:1-5 1:1-5 1:6-12 1:6-12 1:13-19 1:13-19 1:20-22 1:20-22 1:20-22 2:1-6 2:1-6
2:7-10 2:7-10 2:11-13 2:11-13 3:1-10 3:1-10 3:11-19 3:11-19 3:20-26 3:20-26 4:1-6
4:1-6 4:7-11 4:7-11 4:12-21 4:12-21 5:1-5 5:1-5 5:6-16 5:6-16 5:17-27 5:17-27 6:1-7
6:1-7 6:8-13 6:8-13 6:14-30 6:14-30 7:1-6 7:1-6 7:7-16 7:7-16 7:17-21 7:17-21 8:1-7
8:1-7 8:8-19 8:8-19 8:14 8:20-22 8:20-22 9:1-13 9:1-13 9:14-21 9:14-21 9:22-24
9:22-24 9:25-35 9:25-35 9:34 10:1-7 10:1-7 10:8-13 10:8-13 10:14-22 10:14-22 11:1-6
11:1-6 11:7-12 11:7-12 11:13-20 11:13-20 12:1-5 12:1-5 12:6-11 12:6-11 12:12-25
12:12-25 12:12-25 13:1-12 13:1-12 13:13-22 13:13-22 13:23-28 13:23-28 14:1-6 14:1-6
14:7-15 14:7-15 14:16-22 14:16-22 15:1-16 15:1-16 15:16 15:17-35 15:17-35 16:1-5
16:1-5 16:6-16 16:6-16 16:17-22 16:17-22 17:1-9 17:1-9 17:10-16 17:10-16 18:1-4
18:1-4 18:5-10 18:5-10 18:11-21 18:11-21 19:1-7 19:1-7 19:8-22 19:8-22 19:8-22
19:23-29 19:23-29 20:1-9 20:1-9 20:10-22 20:10-22 20:23-29 20:23-29 21 21:1-6
21:1-6 21:7-16 21:7-16 21:17-26 21:17-26 21:27-34 21:27-34 22:1-4 22:1-4 22:5-14
22:5-14 22:15-20 22:15-20 22:21-30 22:21-30 23:1-7 23:1-7 23:8-12 23:8-12 23:13-17
23:13-17 24:1-12 24:1-12 24:13-17 24:13-17 24:18-25 24:18-25 26:1-4 26:1-4 26:5-14
26:5-14 27:1-6 27:1-6 27:7-10 27:7-10 27:11-23 27:11-23 27:11-23 28:1-11 28:1-11
28:12-19 28:12-19 28:20-28 28:20-28 28:20-28 29:1-6 29:1-6 29:7-17 29:7-17 29:18-25
29:18-25 30:1-14 30:1-14 30:15-31 30:15-31 31:1-8 31:1-8 31:7 31:9-15 31:9-15
31:13 31:14 31:16-23 31:16-23 31:24-32 31:24-32 31:33-40 31:33-40 32:1 32:1-5
32:1-5 32:2 32:6-14 32:6-14 32:15-22 32:15-22 33:1-7 33:1-7 33:8-13 33:8-13 33:14-18
33:14-18 33:19-28 33:19-28 33:25 33:29-33 33:29-33 34:1-9 34:1-9 34:10-15 34:10-15
34:16-30 34:16-30 34:19 34:31-37 34:31-37 35:1-8 35:1-8 35:9-13 35:9-13 35:14-16

Psalms

Proverbs

15:20 15:21 15:22 15:23 15:24 15:25 15:26 15:27 15:28 15:29 15:30 15:31 15:32
15:33 16:1 16:2 16:3 16:4 16:5 16:6 16:7 16:7 16:8 16:9 16:11 16:12 16:13 16:14
16:15 16:16 16:17 16:18 16:19 16:21 16:22 16:23 16:24 16:25 16:26 16:27 16:28
16:29 16:30 16:31 16:32 16:33 17:1 17:2 17:3 17:4 17:5 17:6 17:7 17:8 17:9
17:10 17:11 17:12 17:13 17:14 17:15 17:16 17:17 17:18 17:19 17:20 17:21 17:22
17:23 17:24 17:25 17:26 17:27 17:28 18:1 18:2 18:3 18:4 18:5 18:6 18:7 18:8
18:9 18:10 18:11 18:12 18:13 18:14 18:15 18:16 18:17 18:18 18:19 18:20 18:21
18:22 18:23 18:24 19:1 19:2 19:3 19:3 19:3 19:4 19:5 19:6 19:7 19:8 19:9 19:10
19:11 19:12 19:13 19:14 19:15 19:16 19:17 19:18 19:19 19:20 19:21 19:22 19:23
19:24 19:25 19:26 19:27 19:28 19:29 20:1 20:2 20:3 20:4 20:5 20:6 20:7 20:8
20:9 20:10 20:11 20:12 20:13 20:14 20:15 20:16 20:17 20:17 20:18 20:19 20:20
20:21 20:22 20:23 20:24 20:25 20:26 20:27 20:28 20:29 20:30 21:1 21:2 21:3
21:4 21:5 21:6 21:7 21:8 21:9 21:10 21:11 21:12 21:13 21:14 21:15 21:16 21:17
21:18 21:19 21:20 21:21 21:22 21:23 21:24 21:24 21:25 21:26 21:27 21:28 21:29
21:30 21:31 22:1 22:2 22:3 22:4 22:5 22:6 22:7 22:8 22:9 22:10 22:11 22:12
22:13 22:14 22:15 22:16 22:17-21 22:22 22:23 22:24 22:25 22:26 22:27 22:28
23:1-3 23:4 23:5 23:6-8 23:9 23:10 23:11 23:12-16 23:17 23:18 23:19-28 23:29-35
23:29-35 24:1 24:2 24:3-6 24:7-9 24:10 24:11 24:12 24:13 24:14 24:15 24:16 24:17
24:18 24:19 24:20 24:21 24:22 24:23-26 24:27 24:28 24:29 24:30-34 25:1-3 25:4
25:5 25:6 25:7 25:8 25:8-10 25:11 25:12 25:13 25:14 25:15 25:16 25:17 25:18
25:19 25:20 25:21 25:22 25:23 25:24 25:25 25:26 25:27 25:28 26:1 26:2 26:3
26:4 26:5 26:6-9 26:10 26:11 26:12 26:13 26:14 26:15 26:16 26:17 26:18 26:19
26:20-22 26:23 26:24-26 26:27 26:28 27:1 27:2 27:3 27:4 27:5 27:6 27:6 27:7
27:8 27:9 27:10 27:11 27:12 27:13 27:14 27:15 27:16 27:17 27:18 27:19 27:20
27:21 27:22 27:23-27 28:1 28:2 28:3 28:4 28:5 28:6 28:7 28:8 28:9 28:10 28:11
28:12 28:13 28:13 28:14 28:15 28:16 28:17 28:18 28:19 28:20 28:21 28:22 28:23
28:24 28:25 28:26 28:27 28:28 29:1 29:2 29:3 29:4 29:5 29:6 29:7 29:8 29:9
29:10 29:11 29:12 29:13 29:14 29:15 29:16 29:17 29:18 29:19 29:20 29:21 29:22
29:23 29:23 29:24 29:25 29:25 29:26 29:27 30:1-6 30:4 30:7-9 30:10 30:11-14
30:15-17 30:18-20 30:21-23 30:24-28 30:29-33 31:1-9 31:1-9 31:10-31 31:10-31 31:26
31:27

Ecclesiastes
1:4 2:18 2:19 7:1 7:29 9:2 9:10 10:4 11:4

Song of Solomon
1:3 4:16

Isaiah
5:19 7:9 8:12 8:18 8:19 8:20 10:5 11:15 12:3 17 21:10 25:6 26:4 28:20 30:7
32:2 38 40:3 40:11 42:1 42:4 43:2 45:7 46:1 48:10 50:4 50:10 53:8 53:9 53:9
53:11 55:1 55:1 55:2 56:10 57:21 60:10 66:23

Jeremiah
3:23 5:31 6:16 9:23-24 17:9 17:9 17:11 25:22 31:33 32:5 34:3 34:18 34:19 40
49:16

Ezekiel
12:13 16:49 20:37 27:17 36:26

Daniel
12:2

Hosea
4:5 11:1 12:4 12:5 13:9

Amos
2:1-8 2:1-8 2:9-16 2:9-16 3:1-8 3:1-8 3:3 3:9-15 3:9-15 4:1-5 4:1-5 4:6-13 4:6-13
5:1-6 5:1-6 5:7-17 5:7-17 5:18-27 5:18-27 6:1-7 6:1-7 6:6 6:8-14 6:8-14 7:1-9 7:1-9
7:10-17 7:10-17 8:1-3 8:1-3 8:4-10 8:4-10 8:11-14 8:11-14 9:1-10 9:1-10 9:11-15
9:11-15 9:13-15

Obadiah
1:1-16 1:1-16 1:17-21 1:17-21

Jonah
1:1-3 1:1-3 1:4-7 1:4-7 1:8-12 1:8-12 1:13-17 1:13-17 2:1-9 2:1-9 2:10 2:10 3:1-4
3:1-4 3:5-10 3:5-10 4:1-4 4:1-4 4:5-11 4:5-11

Micah
1:1-7 1:1-7 1:8-16 1:8-16 2:1-5 2:1-5 2:6-11 2:6-11 2:12 2:12 2:13 2:13 3:1-8
3:1-8 3:9-12 3:9-12 4:1-8 4:1-8 4:9-13 4:9-13 5 5:1-6 5:1-6 5:2 5:7-15 5:7-15
6:1-5 6:1-5 6:6 6:6-8 6:6-8 6:7 6:9-16 6:9-16 7:1-7 7:1-7 7:8-13 7:8-13 7:14-20
7:14-20

Nahum
1:1-8 1:1-8 1:9-15 1:9-15 2:1-10 2:1-10 2:11-13 2:11-13 3:1-7 3:1-7 3:8-19 3:8-19

Habakkuk
1:1-11 1:1-11 1:12-17 1:12-17 2:1-4 2:1-4 2:5-14 2:5-14 2:6 2:15 2:15-20 2:15-20
2:16 3:1 3:1 3:2 3:2 3:3-15 3:3-15 3:16-19 3:16-19

Zephaniah
1:1-6 1:1-6 1:5 1:7-13 1:7-13 1:14-18 1:14-18 2:1-3 2:1-3 2:4-15 2:4-15 3:1-7 3:1-7
3:8-13 3:8-13 3:14-20 3:14-20

Haggai
1:1-11 1:1-11 1:12-15 1:12-15 2:1-9 2:1-9 2:10-19 2:10-19 2:20-23 2:20-23

Zechariah
1:1-6 1:1-6 1:7-17 1:7-17 1:18-21 1:18-21 2:1-5 2:1-5 2:6-9 2:6-9 2:10-13 2:10-13
3:1-5 3:1-5 3:6-10 3:6-10 4:1-7 4:1-7 4:8-10 4:8-10 4:11-14 4:11-14 4:11-14 5:1-4
5:1-4 5:5-11 5:5-11 6:1-8 6:1-8 6:9-15 6:9-15 7:1-7 7:1-7 7:8-14 7:8-14 8:1-8 8:1-8
8:4 8:5 8:9-17 8:9-17 8:18-23 8:18-23 9:1-8 9:1-8 9:9 9:9-11 9:9-17 9:12 9:12-17
10:1-5 10:1-5 10:6-12 10:6-12 11:1-3 11:1-3 11:4-14 11:4-14 11:8 11:12 11:15-17
11:15-17 11:17 12:1-8 12:1-8 12:9-14 12:9-14 13:1 13:1 13:1-6 13:1-6 13:7-9 13:7-9
14:1-7 14:1-7 14:8-15 14:8-15 14:16 14:16-21 14:16-21 14:18

Malachi
1:1-5 1:1-5 1:6-14 1:6-14 1:11 2:1-9 2:1-9 2:10 2:10-17 2:10-17 3:1-6 3:1-6 3:7-12
3:7-12 3:13-18 3:13-18 4:1-3 4:1-3 4:4-6 4:4-6

Matthew
1:1-17 1:1-17 1:18-25 1:18-25 1:21 1:23 2:1-8 2:1-8 2:5 2:9-12 2:9-12 2:13-15
2:13-15 2:16-18 2:16-18 2:19-23 2:19-23 3:1-6 3:1-6 3:7-12 3:7-12 3:13-17 3:13-17
4:1-11 4:1-11 4:4 4:6 4:12-17 4:12-17 4:18-22 4:18-22 4:23-25 4:23-25 5 5:1 5:1

Mark

14:43-52   14:43-52   14:53-65   14:53-65   14:66-72   14:66-72   15:1-14   15:1-14   15:15-21
15:15-21   15:22-32   15:22-32   15:33-41   15:33-41   15:42-47   15:42-47   16:1-8   16:1-8
16:9-13   16:9-13   16:14-18   16:14-18   16:19   16:19   16:20   16:20

Luke

1:1-4   1:1-4   1:5-25   1:5-25   1:26-38   1:26-38   1:32   1:39-56   1:39-56   1:57-66   1:57-66
1:67-80   1:67-80   2:1-7   2:1-7   2:8   2:8-20   2:8-20   2:21-24   2:21-24   2:25-35   2:25-35
2:36-40   2:36-40   2:41-52   2:41-52   3:1-14   3:1-14   3:15-20   3:15-20   3:21   3:21   3:22   3:22
3:23-38   3:23-38   4:1-13   4:1-13   4:14-30   4:14-30   4:31-44   4:31-44   5:1-11   5:1-11   5:12-16
5:12-16   5:17-26   5:17-26   5:27-39   5:27-39   6:1-5   6:1-5   6:6-11   6:6-11   6:12-19 6:12-19
6:20-26   6:20-26   6:27-36   6:27-36   6:37-49   6:37-49   7:1-10   7:1-10   7:11-18   7:11-18
7:19-35   7:19-35   7:36-50   7:36-50   7:38   8:1-3   8:1-3   8:4-21   8:4-21   8:22-40   8:22-40
8:41-56   8:41-56   9:1-9   9:1-9   9:10-17   9:10-17   9:18-27   9:18-27   9:28-36   9:28-36   9:35
9:37-42   9:37-42   9:43-50   9:43-50   9:51-56   9:51-56   9:54   9:57-62   9:57-62   10:1-16
10:1-16   10:17-24   10:17-24   10:25-37   10:25-37   10:27   10:38-42   10:38-42   11   11:1-4
11:1-4   11:5-13   11:5-13   11:13   11:14-26   11:14-26   11:20   11:27   11:27   11:28   11:28
11:29-36   11:29-36   11:37-54   11:37-54   11:39   12:1-12   12:1-12   12:13-21   12:13-21
12:16-21   12:22-40   12:22-40   12:33   12:41-53   12:41-53   12:49   12:54-59   12:54-59 13:1-5
13:1-5   13:6-9   13:6-9   13:10-17   13:10-17   13:18-22   13:18-22   13:23-30   13:23-30   13:25
13:31-35   13:31-35   14:1-6   14:1-6   14:7-14   14:7-14   14:15-24   14:15-24   14:25-35 14:25-35
15:1-10   15:1-10   15:11-16   15:11-16   15:17-24   15:17-24   15:25-32   15:25-32   16:1-12
16:1-12   16:12   16:13-18   16:13-18   16:19-31   16:19-31   16:25   17:1-10   17:1-10 17:11-19
17:11-19   17:20-37   17:20-37   17:26   17:27   18:1   18:1-8   18:1-8   18:9-14   18:9-14   18:15-17
18:15-17   18:18-30   18:18-30   18:31-34   18:31-34   18:35-43   18:35-43   19:1-10   19:1-10
19:11-27   19:11-27   19:28-40   19:28-40   19:41-48   19:41-48   20:1-8   20:1-8   20:9-19 20:9-19
20:20-26   20:20-26   20:27-38   20:27-38   20:37   20:39-47   20:39-47   21:1-4   21:1-4   21:5-28
21:5-28   21:29-38   21:29-38   21:34   21:34   22:1-6   22:1-6   22:7-18   22:7-18   22:19   22:19
22:20   22:20   22:21-38   22:21-38   22:39-46   22:39-46   22:47-53   22:47-53   22:54-62 22:54-62
22:63-71   22:63-71   23:1-5   23:1-5   23:6-12   23:6-12   23:11   23:13-25   23:13-25   23:26-31
23:26-31   23:32-43   23:32-43   23:44-49   23:44-49   23:50-56   23:50-56   24:1-12   24:1-12
24:13-27   24:13-27   24:28-35   24:28-35   24:36-49   24:36-49   24:50-53   24:50-53

John

1:1   1:1   1:1   1:1-5   1:1-5   1:6-14   1:6-14   1:13   1:14   1:15-18   1:15-18   1:18   1:19-28
1:19-28   1:29   1:29   1:29-36   1:29-36   1:30   1:37   1:37-42   1:37-42   1:43-51   1:43-51   1:51
2:1-11   2:1-11   2:12-22   2:12-22   2:13-17   2:23-25   2:23-25   3:1-8   3:1-21   3:8   3:11-13
3:14   3:15   3:22-36   3:22-36   3:29   4:1-3   4:1-3   4:4-26   4:4-26   4:21   4:27-42   4:27-42
4:34   4:43-54   4:43-54   5:1-9   5:1-9   5:10-16   5:10-16   5:17-23   5:17-23   5:23   5:24-29
5:24-47   5:30-38   5:39   5:39-44   5:45-47   6:1-14   6:1-14   6:15   6:15-21   6:15-21   6:22-27
6:22-27   6:27   6:28-35   6:28-65   6:36-46   6:47-51   6:48   6:51   6:52-59   6:53   6:55   6:60-65
6:66-71   6:66-71   7:1-13   7:1-13   7:14-24   7:14-39   7:25-30   7:31-36   7:37-39   7:38   7:38
7:39   7:40-53   7:40-53   8:1-11   8:1-11   8:12   8:12   8:12-16   8:12-59   8:17-20   8:21-29
8:30-36   8:32   8:37-40   8:41   8:41-47   8:48-53   8:54-59   8:56   9:1-7   9:1-7   9:8-12   9:8-12
9:13-17   9:13-17   9:18-23   9:18-23   9:24-34   9:24-34   9:35-38   9:35-38   9:39-41   9:39-41
10:1-5   10:1-5   10:6-9   10:6-9   10:10-18   10:10-18   10:16   10:19-21   10:19-21   10:22-30
10:22-30   10:31-38   10:31-38   10:39-42   10:39-42   11:1-6   11:1-6   11:7-10   11:7-10   11:11-16

11:11-16 11:17-32 11:17-32 11:33-46 11:33-46 11:47-53 11:47-53 11:52 11:54-57
11:54-57 12:1-11 12:1-11 12:12-19 12:12-19 12:20-26 12:20-26 12:27-33 12:27-33
12:28 12:34-36 12:34-36 12:37-43 12:37-43 12:44-50 12:44-50 12:48 13:1-17 13:1-17
13:18-30 13:18-30 13:31-35 13:31-38 13:36-38 14:1-11 14:1-11 14:3 14:6 14:7
14:12-17 14:12-17 14:18-24 14:18-31 14:25-27 14:28-31 15:1-8 15:1-8 15:3 15:4
15:9-17 15:9-17 15:14 15:18-25 15:18-25 15:26 15:26 15:27 15:27 16:1-6 16:1-6
16:7 16:7-15 16:7-15 16:8 16:16-22 16:16-22 16:23-27 16:23-27 16:28-33 16:28-33
17:1-5 17:1-5 17:2 17:3 17:6-10 17:6-10 17:11-16 17:11-26 17:17-19 17:19 17:20-23
17:24-26 18:1-12 18:1-12 18:11 18:13-27 18:13-27 18:28-32 18:28-40 18:33-40 19:1-18
19:1-18 19:19-30 19:19-30 19:28 19:31-37 19:31-37 19:33 19:38-42 19:38-42 20:1-10
20:1-10 20:11-18 20:11-18 20:19-25 20:19-25 20:26-29 20:26-29 20:30 20:30 20:31
20:31 20:31 21:1-14 21:1-14 21:15-19 21:15-19 21:20-24 21:20-24 21:22 21:25 21:25

Acts

1:1-5 1:1-5 1:6-11 1:6-11 1:12-14 1:12-14 1:15-26 1:15-26 2 2:1-4 2:1-4 2:2 2:4
2:5-13 2:5-13 2:14-21 2:14-36 2:22-36 2:24 2:25-31 2:37-41 2:37-41 2:40 2:42-47
2:42-47 3:1-11 3:1-11 3:12-18 3:12-26 3:19-21 3:22-26 4:1-4 4:1-4 4:5-14 4:5-14
4:15-22 4:15-22 4:23-31 4:23-31 4:32-37 4:32-37 5:1-11 5:1-11 5:12-16 5:12-16
5:17-25 5:17-25 5:26-33 5:26-33 5:34-42 5:34-42 6:1-7 6:1-7 6:8-15 6:8-15 7:1-16
7:1-50 7:17-29 7:30-41 7:42-50 7:51-53 7:51-53 7:54-60 7:54-60 8:1-4 8:1-4 8:5-13
8:5-13 8:13-25 8:14-25 8:14-25 8:26-40 8:26-40 9:1-9 9:1-9 9:6 9:10-22 9:10-22
9:23-31 9:23-31 9:32-35 9:32-35 9:36-43 9:36-43 10:1-8 10:1-8 10:9-18 10:9-18
10:19-33 10:19-33 10:34 10:34-43 10:34-43 10:44-48 10:44-48 11:1-18 11:1-18 11:16
11:19-24 11:19-24 11:25-30 11:25-30 12:1-5 12:1-5 12:6-11 12:6-11 12:12 12:12-19
12:12-19 12:20-25 12:20-25 13:1-3 13:1-3 13:4-13 13:4-13 13:13 13:14-31 13:14-41
13:32-37 13:38-41 13:42-52 13:42-52 14:1-7 14:1-7 14:8-18 14:8-18 14:19-28 14:19-28
15:1-6 15:1-6 15:7-21 15:7-21 15:22-35 15:22-35 15:36-41 15:36-41 16:1-5 16:1-5
16:6-15 16:6-15 16:10 16:11 16:16-24 16:16-24 16:25-34 16:25-34 16:31 16:35-40
16:35-40 17:1-9 17:1-9 17:10-15 17:10-15 17:16-21 17:16-21 17:22-31 17:22-31
17:32-34 17:32-34 18:1-6 18:1-6 18:7-11 18:7-11 18:12-17 18:12-17 18:18-23 18:18-23
18:24-28 18:24-28 19:1-7 19:1-7 19:8-12 19:8-12 19:13-20 19:13-20 19:21-31 19:21-31
19:32-41 19:32-41 20:1-6 20:1-6 20:7-12 20:7-12 20:13-16 20:13-16 20:17-27 20:17-27
20:27 20:28-38 20:28-38 21:1-7 21:1-7 21:8-18 21:8-18 21:13 21:19-26 21:19-26
21:27-40 21:27-40 22:1-11 22:1-11 22:12-21 22:12-21 22:14 22:21 22:22-30 22:22-30
23:1-5 23:1-5 23:6-11 23:6-11 23:12-24 23:12-24 23:25-35 23:25-35 24:1-9 24:1-9
24:10-21 24:10-21 24:22-27 24:22-27 25:1-12 25:1-12 25:13-27 25:13-27 25:16 26:1-11
26:1-11 26:12-23 26:12-23 26:13 26:24-32 26:24-32 26:28 27:1-11 27:1-11 27:12-20
27:12-20 27:21-29 27:21-29 27:30-38 27:30-38 27:39-44 27:39-44 28 28:1-10 28:1-10
28:11-16 28:11-16 28:17-22 28:17-22 28:23-31 28:23-31

Romans

1:1-7 1:1-7 1:8-15 1:8-15 1:16 1:16 1:16 1:17 1:17 1:18-25 1:18-32 1:26-32 2:1-16
2:1-16 2:16 2:17-24 2:17-29 2:25-29 2:28 2:29 3:1-8 3:1-8 3:9-18 3:9-18 3:17 3:19
3:19 3:20 3:20 3:21-26 3:21-31 3:27-31 4:1-12 4:1-12 4:13-22 4:13-22 4:23-25
4:23-25 4:24 5:1-5 5:1-5 5:6-11 5:6-11 5:8 5:11 5:12-14 5:12-14 5:15-19 5:15-19
5:19 5:20 5:20 5:21 5:21 6:1 6:1 6:2 6:2 6:3-10 6:3-10 6:6 6:6 6:11-15 6:11-15

6:12 6:13 6:16-20 6:16-20 6:21-23 6:21-23 7:1-6 7:1-6 7:7-13 7:7-13 7:11 7:14
7:14-17 7:14-25 7:18-22 7:23-25 8:1 8:1-9 8:1-9 8:3 8:3 8:3 8:5 8:5-9 8:7 8:10-17
8:10-17 8:14 8:18-25 8:18-25 8:26 8:26 8:27 8:27 8:28-31 8:28-31 8:30 8:32-39
8:32-39 8:37 9:1-5 9:1-5 9:6-13 9:6-13 9:12-15 9:14-24 9:14-24 9:16 9:25-29 9:25-29
9:30-33 9:30-33 10:1-4 10:1-4 10:5-11 10:5-11 10:12-17 10:12-17 10:15 10:16
10:18-21 10:18-21 11:1 11:1-10 11:1-10 11:9 11:10 11:11-21 11:11-21 11:22-32
11:22-32 11:33 11:33-36 11:33-36 12:1 12:1 12:2 12:2 12:3-8 12:3-8 12:9-16 12:9-16
12:17-21 12:17-21 12:18 13:1 13:1-7 13:1-7 13:4 13:8-10 13:8-10 13:11-14 13:11-14
14:1-6 14:1-13 14:7-13 14:8 14:14-18 14:14-23 14:19-23 15:1 15:1-7 15:1-7 15:2
15:8-13 15:8-13 15:11 15:14-21 15:14-21 15:22-29 15:22-29 15:30-33 15:30-33 16:1-16
16:1-16 16:17-20 16:17-20 16:20 16:21-24 16:21-24 16:25-27 16:25-27

1 Corinthians

1:1-9 1:1-9 1:10-16 1:10-16 1:17 1:17-25 1:17-25 1:26-31 1:26-31 2:1-5 2:1-5 2:6-9
2:6-9 2:9 2:9 2:10-16 2:10-16 2:13 3:1-4 3:1-4 3:5-9 3:5-9 3:10-15 3:10-15 3:16
3:16 3:16 3:17 3:17 3:18-23 3:18-23 4:1-6 4:1-6 4:7-13 4:7-13 4:9 4:14-21 4:14-21
5:1-8 5:1-8 5:7 5:7 5:7 5:8 5:9-13 5:9-13 6:1-8 6:1-8 6:9-11 6:9-11 6:12-20 6:12-20
7:1-9 7:1-9 7:2 7:10-16 7:10-16 7:17-24 7:17-24 7:25-35 7:25-35 7:33 7:34 7:36-40
7:36-40 8:1-6 8:1-6 8:7-13 8:7-13 9:1-14 9:1-14 9:9 9:15-23 9:15-23 9:24-27 9:24-27
10:1 10:1-5 10:1-5 10:2 10:4 10:6-14 10:6-14 10:9 10:9 10:13 10:15-22 10:15-22
10:23-33 10:23-33 11:1 11:1 11:2-16 11:2-16 11:17-22 11:17-22 11:19 11:23-26
11:23-34 11:27-34 12:1-11 12:1-11 12:7 12:7-21 12:12-26 12:12-26 12:12-26 12:27-30
12:27-31 12:29 12:30 12:31 13:1-3 13:1-3 13:4-7 13:4-7 13:5 13:8-13 13:8-13 14
14:1-5 14:1-5 14:6-14 14:6-14 14:15-25 14:15-25 14:26-33 14:26-33 14:34-40 14:34-40
15:1-11 15:1-11 15:12-19 15:12-19 15:20-34 15:20-34 15:26 15:35-50 15:35-50
15:51-54 15:51-58 15:55-58 15:58 16:1-9 16:1-9 16:2 16:10-12 16:10-12 16:13-18
16:13-18 16:19-24 16:19-24

2 Corinthians

1:1-11 1:1-11 1:12-14 1:12-14 1:15-24 1:15-24 2:1-4 2:1-4 2:5-11 2:5-11 2:12-17
2:12-17 2:16 3:1-11 3:1-11 3:3 3:12-18 3:12-18 3:18 4:1-7 4:1-7 4:6 4:6 4:7 4:8-12
4:8-12 4:13-18 4:13-18 5:1 5:1-8 5:1-8 5:9 5:9-15 5:9-15 5:16-21 5:16-21 5:18 5:19
5:21 6:1-10 6:1-10 6:2 6:11-18 6:11-18 6:17 7:1-4 7:1-4 7:5-11 7:5-11 7:12-16
7:12-16 8:1-6 8:1-6 8:7-9 8:7-9 8:9 8:9 8:10-15 8:10-15 8:16-24 8:16-24 9:1-5 9:1-5
9:6-15 9:6-15 9:7 9:7 10:1-6 10:1-6 10:7-11 10:7-11 10:12-18 10:12-18 11:1-4
11:1-14 11:5-15 11:5-15 11:16-21 11:16-21 11:22-33 11:22-33 12:1-6 12:1-6 12:7-10
12:7-10 12:9 12:9 12:10 12:11-21 12:11-21 13:1-6 13:1-6 13:7-10 13:7-10 13:11-14
13:11-14 13:14

Galatians

1:1-5 1:1-5 1:6-9 1:6-9 1:10-14 1:10-14 1:15-24 1:15-24 1:16 2:1-10 2:1-10 2:11-14
2:11-14 2:15-19 2:15-21 2:20 2:21 3:1-5 3:1-5 3:6-9 3:6-14 3:10-14 3:13 3:15-18
3:15-18 3:17 3:19-22 3:19-25 3:23-25 3:26-29 3:26-29 4:1-7 4:1-7 4:4 4:8-11 4:8-11
4:12-18 4:12-18 4:19 4:19 4:20 4:20 4:21-27 4:21-31 4:28-31 4:31 5:1 5:1-6 5:1-12
5:7-12 5:8 5:13-15 5:13-15 5:16-26 5:16-26 6:1-5 6:1-5 6:6 6:6-11 6:6-11 6:7-9
6:12-15 6:12-15 6:16-18 6:16-18

Ephesians

1:1 1:1-8 1:2 1:3-8 1:4 1:4 1:9-14 1:9-14 1:15-23 1:15-23 2:1-10 2:1-10 2:4 2:5
2:9 2:11 2:11-13 2:11-13 2:12 2:14-18 2:14-22 2:19-22 2:20 2:21 3:1-7 3:1-7 3:8-12
3:8-12 3:13-19 3:13-19 3:18 3:20 3:20 3:20 3:21 3:21 4:1-6 4:1-6 4:7-16 4:7-16
4:8 4:17-24 4:17-24 4:17-24 4:25-28 4:25-32 4:29-32 5:1 5:1 5:2 5:2 5:3-14 5:3-14
5:8 5:15-21 5:15-21 5:22-33 5:22-33 5:25-27 6 6:1-4 6:1-4 6:5-9 6:5-9 6:9 6:10-18
6:10-18 6:19-24 6:19-24 6:19-24

Philippians

1:1-7 1:1-7 1:8-11 1:8-11 1:12-20 1:12-20 1:13 1:21-26 1:21-26 1:27-30 1:27-30
1:29 2:1-4 2:1-4 2:5-11 2:5-11 2:12-18 2:12-18 2:14 2:17 2:17 2:19-30 2:19-30
2:19-30 2:21 3:1-11 3:1-11 3:5 3:12-21 3:12-21 3:12-21 4:1 4:1 4:2-9 4:2-9 4:10-19
4:10-19 4:11-18 4:20-23 4:20-23 4:22

Colossians

1:1-8 1:1-8 1:9-14 1:9-14 1:9-14 1:15-23 1:15-23 1:21 1:24-29 1:24-29 1:26 2:1-7
2:1-7 2:5 2:8-17 2:8-17 2:9 2:18 2:18-23 2:18-23 3:1-4 3:1-4 3:5-11 3:5-11 3:12-17
3:12-17 3:18-25 3:18-25 4:1 4:1 4:1 4:2-6 4:2-6 4:7-9 4:7-9 4:10 4:10-18 4:10-18

1 Thessalonians

1:1-5 1:1-5 1:6-10 1:6-10 2:1-6 2:1-12 2:7-12 2:13-16 2:13-16 2:17-20 2:17-20 3:1-5
3:1-5 3:6-10 3:6-10 3:11-13 3:11-13 4:1-8 4:1-8 4:9-12 4:9-12 4:13-18 4:13-18 5:1-5
5:1-11 5:6-11 5:12-15 5:12-22 5:16-22 5:23-28 5:23-28

2 Thessalonians

1:1-4 1:1-4 1:5-10 1:5-12 1:8 1:11 1:12 2:1 2:1-4 2:1-4 2:5-12 2:5-12 2:13-15
2:13-17 2:16 2:17 3:1-5 3:1-5 3:6-15 3:6-15 3:10 3:10 3:16-18 3:16-18

1 Timothy

1:1-4 1:1-4 1:5-11 1:5-11 1:12-17 1:12-17 1:18-20 1:18-20 2:1 2:1-7 2:1-7 2:2
2:8-15 2:8-15 3:1-7 3:1-7 3:3 3:5 3:8-13 3:8-13 3:14-16 3:14-16 3:16 4:1-5 4:1-5
4:6-10 4:6-16 4:11-16 5:1 5:1 5:2 5:2 5:3-8 5:3-8 5:4 5:6 5:9-16 5:9-16 5:17-25
5:17-25 6:1-5 6:1-5 6:3 6:6-10 6:6-10 6:6-10 6:11-16 6:11-16 6:17 6:17-21 6:17-21
6:18

2 Timothy

1:1-5 1:1-5 1:6-14 1:6-14 1:15-18 1:15-18 1:15-18 2:1-7 2:1-7 2:8-13 2:8-13 2:12
2:14-21 2:14-21 2:22-26 2:22-26 3:1 3:1-9 3:1-9 3:10-13 3:10-13 3:14-17 3:14-17
4:1-5 4:1-5 4:6-8 4:6-8 4:9-13 4:9-13 4:14-18 4:14-18 4:18 4:19-22 4:19-22

Titus

1:1-4 1:1-4 1:5-9 1:5-9 1:10-16 1:10-16 2:1-8 2:1-8 2:9 2:9 2:10 2:10 2:11-15
2:11-15 2:12 2:14 2:14 3:1-7 3:1-7 3:5 3:8-11 3:8-11 3:12-15 3:12-15

Philemon

1:1-7 1:1-7 1:8-14 1:8-22 1:15-22 1:23-25 1:23-25

Hebrews

1:1 1:1-3 1:1-3 1:2 1:2 1:4-14 1:4-14 1:6 2:1-4 2:1-4 2:5-9 2:5-9 2:6-8 2:10
2:10-13 2:10-13 2:11 2:12 2:14 2:14-18 2:14-18 2:16 3:1 3:1-6 3:1-6 3:7-13 3:7-13
3:13 3:14-19 3:14-19 4:1 4:1-10 4:1-10 4:2 4:11-16 4:11-16 4:12 4:16 5:1-10 5:1-10
5:7 5:11-14 5:11-14 6:1-8 6:1-8 6:8 6:9 6:9 6:10 6:10 6:10 6:11-20 6:11-20 6:18
6:18 7:1-3 7:1-3 7:3 7:4 7:4-10 7:4-10 7:11-25 7:11-25 7:14 7:14 7:19 7:26-28
7:26-28 8:1-6 8:1-6 8:7-10 8:7-13 8:7-13 9:1-5 9:1-5 9:6-10 9:6-10 9:7 9:8 9:11-14

9:11-22 9:12 9:15-22 9:23-28 9:23-28 10:1 10:1-10 10:1-18 10:2 10:3 10:11-18
10:19-25 10:19-25 10:22 10:22 10:23 10:26-31 10:26-31 10:29 10:32-39 10:32-39
11 11:1-3 11:1-3 11:4 11:4-7 11:4-7 11:5 11:6 11:6 11:7 11:8 11:8-19 11:8-19
11:13 11:13 11:14 11:14 11:14 11:16 11:20-31 11:20-31 11:21 11:23 11:31 11:32
11:32-38 11:32-38 11:39 11:39 11:39 11:40 11:40 12:1 12:1-11 12:1-11 12:2 12:3
12:12-17 12:12-17 12:13 12:15 12:16 12:18-29 12:18-29 12:24 12:28 13:1-6 13:1-6
13:2 13:5 13:7-15 13:7-15 13:11-13 13:13 13:14 13:16-21 13:16-21 13:22-25 13:22-25

James

1:1-11 1:1-11 1:5 1:12-18 1:12-18 1:14 1:19-21 1:19-21 1:22-25 1:22-25 1:26 1:26
1:27 1:27 2:1-13 2:1-13 2:10 2:14-26 2:14-26 2:24 2:25 3:1-12 3:1-12 3:13 3:13-18
3:13-18 4:1-10 4:1-10 4:7 4:11-17 4:11-17 4:15 4:15 5:1-6 5:1-6 5:2 5:3 5:3 5:7-11
5:7-11 5:12-18 5:12-18 5:19 5:19 5:20 5:20

1 Peter

1:1-9 1:1-9 1:2 1:10-12 1:10-12 1:11 1:13-16 1:13-16 1:15 1:16 1:17-25 1:17-25
1:23 2:1-10 2:1-10 2:5 2:5 2:5 2:6-8 2:11 2:11 2:11 2:12 2:12 2:13-17 2:13-17
2:18-25 2:18-25 2:20 3:1-7 3:1-7 3:8-13 3:8-13 3:14-22 3:14-22 3:20 3:21 4:1-6
4:1-6 4:7-11 4:7-11 4:8 4:9 4:10 4:10 4:12-19 4:12-19 5:1-4 5:1-4 5:5-9 5:5-9 5:8
5:10-14 5:10-14 5:13

2 Peter

1:1-11 1:1-11 1:12-15 1:12-15 1:14 1:16-21 1:16-21 1:19 1:19 1:19 1:21 1:21 2:1-9
2:1-9 2:5 2:10 2:10-16 2:10-16 2:17-22 2:17-22 2:22 3:1 3:1-4 3:1-4 3:1-7 3:3 3:4
3:5-10 3:5-10 3:11-18 3:11-18 3:14

1 John

1:1-4 1:1-4 1:5-10 1:5-10 1:8 1:9 2:1 2:1 2:2 2:2 2:3-11 2:3-11 2:12-14 2:12-14
2:15-17 2:15-23 2:18-23 2:24-29 2:24-29 2:27 3:1 3:1 3:2 3:2 3:3-10 3:3-10 3:11-15
3:11-15 3:12 3:15 3:16-21 3:16-21 3:22-24 3:22-24 4:1-6 4:1-6 4:7-13 4:7-21 4:8
4:14-21 4:16 5:1-5 5:1-5 5:3 5:6-8 5:6-8 5:9-12 5:9-12 5:11 5:13-17 5:13-17 5:18-21
5:18-21 5:20

2 John

1:1-3 1:1-3 1:4-6 1:4-6 1:7-11 1:7-11 1:8 1:12 1:12 1:13 1:13

3 John

1:1-8 1:1-8 1:9-12 1:9-12 1:13 1:13 1:14 1:14

Revelation

1:1-3 1:1-3 1:4-8 1:4-8 1:5 1:5 1:6 1:6 1:6 1:8 1:9-11 1:9-11 1:9-20 1:12-20
1:12-20 1:18 2:1-7 2:1-7 2:7 2:8-11 2:8-11 2:12-17 2:12-17 2:17 2:18-29 2:18-29
3:1-6 3:1-6 3:7-13 3:7-13 3:11 3:14-22 3:14-22 3:20 3:20 3:20 4:1-8 4:1-8 4:8
4:9-11 4:9-11 5:1-7 5:1-7 5:8-14 5:8-14 6:1-8 6:1-8 6:9-11 6:9-11 6:12-17 6:12-17
7 7:1-3 7:1-8 7:4-8 7:9-12 7:9-12 7:13-17 7:13-17 8:1 8:1-6 8:2 8:3 8:3-5 8:6
8:7-12 8:7-13 8:13 9:1-12 9:1-12 9:13-21 9:13-21 10:1-4 10:1-7 10:5-7 10:8-10
10:8-11 10:11 11:1 11:1 11:2 11:2 11:3-6 11:3-13 11:7-13 11:14-19 11:14-19 12:1-6
12:1-6 12:7-11 12:7-12 12:12-17 12:13 12:14 12:14-17 13:1-10 13:1-10 13:8 13:11-15
13:11-18 13:16-18 14:1-5 14:1-5 14:6-13 14:6-13 14:6-13 14:14-16 14:14-20 14:17-20
15:1-4 15:1-4 15:5-8 15:5-8 16:1-7 16:1-7 16:8-11 16:8-11 16:12-16 16:12-16 16:15
16:17-21 16:17-21 17:1-6 17:1-6 17:7-14 17:7-18 17:15-18 18:1-3 18:1-8 18:4 18:4

Index of Scripture Commentary

34:1-4 34:5-9 34:10-17 34:18-27 34:28-35 35:1-3 35:4-19 35:20-29 35:30-35 38:1-8
38:9-20 38:21-31 39:1-31 39:32-43 40:1-15 40:16-33 40:34-38

Leviticus

1:1 1:2 1:3-9 1:10-17 2:1-11 2:12-16 3:1-5 3:6-17 4:1-12 4:13-21 4:22-26 4:27-35
5:1-13 5:14-19 6:1-7 6:8-13 6:14-23 6:24-30 7:1-10 7:11-27 7:28-34 7:35-38 8:1-13
8:14-36 9:1-21 9:22-24 10:1 10:2 10:3-7 10:8-11 10:12-20 13:1-17 13:18-44 13:45
13:46 13:47-59 14:1-9 14:10-32 14:33-53 14:54-57 16:1-14 16:15-34 17:1-9 17:10-16
20:1-9 20:10-27 23:1-3 23:4-14 23:15-22 23:23-32 23:33-44 24:1-9 24:10-23 25:1-7
25:8-22 25:23-34 25:35-38 25:39-55 26:1-13 26:14-39 26:40-46 27:1-13 27:14-25
27:26-33 27:34

Numbers

1:1-43 1:44-46 1:47-54 3:1-13 3:14-39 3:40-51 4:1-3 4:4-20 4:21-33 4:34-49 5:1-10
5:11-31 6:1-21 6:22-27 7:1-9 7:10-89 8:1-4 8:5-26 9:1-14 9:15-23 10:1-10 10:11-28
10:29-32 10:33-36 11:1-3 11:4-9 11:10-15 11:16-23 11:24-30 11:31-35 12:1-9 12:10-16
13:1-20 13:21-25 13:26-33 14:1-4 14:5-10 14:11-19 14:20-35 14:36-39 14:40-45
15:1-21 15:22-29 15:30-36 15:37-41 16:1-11 16:12-15 16:16-22 16:23-34 16:35-40
16:41-50 17:1-7 17:8-13 18:1-7 18:8-19 18:20-32 19:1-10 19:11-22 20:1-13 20:14-21
20:22-29 21:1-3 21:4-9 21:10-20 21:21-35 22:1-14 22:15-21 22:22-35 22:36-41 23:1-10
23:11-30 24:1-9 24:10-14 24:15-25 25:1-5 25:6-15 25:16-18 26:1-51 26:52-56 26:57-62
26:63-65 27:1-11 27:12-14 27:15-23 28:1-8 28:9-15 28:16-31 29:1-11 29:12-40 30:1
30:2 30:3-16 31:1-6 31:7-12 31:13-18 31:19-24 31:25-47 31:48-54 32:1-5 32:6-15
32:16-27 32:28-42 33:1-49 33:50-56 34:1-15 34:16-29 35:1-8 35:9-34 36:1-4 36:5-12
36:13

Deuteronomy

1:1-8 1:9-18 1:19-46 2:1-7 2:8-23 2:24-37 3:1-11 3:12-20 3:21-29 4:1-23 4:24-40
4:41-49 5:1-5 5:6-22 5:23-33 6:1-3 6:4 6:5 6:6-16 6:17-25 7:1-11 7:12-26 8:1-9
8:10-20 9:1-6 9:7-29 10:1-11 10:12-22 11:1-7 11:8-17 11:18-25 11:26-32 12:1-4
12:5-32 13:1-5 13:6-11 13:12-18 14:1-21 14:22-29 15:1-11 15:12-18 15:19-23 16:1-17
16:18-22 17:1-7 17:8-13 17:14-20 18:1-8 18:9-14 18:15-22 19:1-13 19:14 19:15-21
20:1-9 20:10-12 21:1-9 21:10-14 21:15-17 21:18-21 21:22 21:23 22:1-4 22:5-12
22:13-30 23:1-8 23:9-14 23:15-25 24:1-4 24:5-13 24:14-22 25:1-3 25:4 25:5-12
25:13-16 25:17-19 26:1-11 26:12-15 26:16-19 27:1-10 27:11-26 28:1-14 28:15-44
28:45-68 29:1-9 29:10-21 29:22-28 29:29 30:1-10 30:11-14 30:15-20 31:1-8 31:9-13
31:14-22 31:23-30 32:1 32:2 32:3-6 32:7-14 32:15-18 32:19-25 32:26-38 32:39-43
32:44-47 32:48-52 33:1-5 33:6-23 33:24 33:25 33:26-29 34:1-4 34:5-8 34:9-12

Joshua

1:1-4 1:5-9 1:10-15 1:16-18 2:1-7 2:8-21 2:22-24 3:1-6 3:7-13 3:14-17 4:1-9 4:10-19
4:20-24 5:1-9 5:10-12 5:13-15 6:1-5 6:6-16 6:17-27 7:1-5 7:6-9 7:10-15 7:16-26 8:1
8:2 8:3-22 8:23-29 8:30-35 9:1 9:2 9:3-13 9:14-21 9:22-27 10:1-6 10:7-14 10:15-27
10:28-43 11:1-9 11:10-14 11:15-23 12:1-6 12:7-24 13:1-6 13:7-33 14:1-5 14:6-15
15:1-12 15:13-19 15:20-63 17:1-6 17:7-13 17:14-18 18:1 18:2-10 18:11-28 19:1-9
19:10-16 19:17-51 20:1-6 20:7-9 21:1-8 21:9-42 21:43-45 22:1-9 22:10-20 22:21-29
22:30-34 23:1-10 23:11-16 24:1-14 24:15-28 24:29-33

Judges

1:1-4 1:1-8 1:5-7 1:8-16 1:9-20 1:17-23 1:21-36 1:24 1:25 2:1-5 2:6-23 3:1-7 3:8-11
3:12-30 3:31 4:1-3 4:4-9 4:10-16 4:17-24 5:1-5 5:6-11 5:12-23 5:24-31 6:1-6 6:7-10
6:11-24 6:25-32 6:33-40 7:1-8 7:9-15 7:16-22 7:23-25 8:1-3 8:4-12 8:13-17 8:18-21
8:22-28 8:29-35 9:1-6 9:7-21 9:22-29 9:30-49 9:50-57 10:1-5 10:6-9 10:10-18 11:1-11
11:12-28 11:29-40 12:1-7 12:8-15 13:1-7 13:8-14 13:15-23 13:24 13:25 14:1-4 14:5-9
14:10-20 15:1-8 15:9-17 15:18-20 16:1-3 16:4-17 16:18-21 16:22-24 16:25-31 17:1-6
17:7-13

Ruth

1:1-5 1:6-14 1:15-18 1:19-22 2:1-3 2:4-16 2:17-23 3:1-5 3:6-13 3:14-18 4:1-8 4:9-12
4:13-22

1 Samuel

1:1-8 1:9-18 1:19-28 2:1-10 2:11-26 2:27-36 3:1-10 3:11-18 3:19-21 4:1-9 4:10 4:11
4:12-18 4:19-22 5:1-5 5:6-12 6:1-9 6:10-18 6:19-21 7:1-4 7:5 7:6 7:7-12 7:13-17
8:1-3 8:4-9 8:10-22 9:1-10 9:11-17 9:18-27 10:1-8 10:9-16 10:17-27 11:1-11 11:12-15
12:1-5 12:6-15 12:16-25 13:1-7 13:8-14 13:15-23 14:1-15 14:16-23 14:24-35 14:36-46
14:47-52 15:1-9 15:10-23 15:24-31 15:32-35 16:1-5 16:6-13 16:14-23 17:1-11 17:12-30
17:31-39 17:40-47 17:48-58 18:1-5 18:6-11 18:12-30 19:1-10 19:11-24 20:1-10 20:11-23
20:24-34 20:35-42 21:1-9 21:10-15 22:1-5 22:6-19 22:20-23 23:1-6 23:7-13 23:14-18
23:19-29 24:1-7 24:8-15 24:16-22 25:1 25:2-11 25:12-17 25:18-31 25:32-39 25:39-44
26:1-12 26:13-20 26:21-25 27:1-7 27:8-12 28:1-6 28:7-19 28:20-25 29:1-5 29:6-11
30:1-6 30:7-15 30:16-20 30:21-31 31:1-7 31:8-13

2 Samuel

1:1-10 1:11-16 1:17-27 2:1-7 2:8-17 2:18-24 2:25-32 3:1-6 3:7-21 3:22-39 4:1-7
4:8-12 5:1-5 5:6-10 5:11-16 5:17-25 6:1-5 6:6-11 6:12-19 6:20-23 7:1-3 7:4-17
7:18-29 8:1-8 8:9-14 8:15-18 9:1-8 9:9-13 10:1-5 10:6-14 10:15-19 11:1-5 11:6-13
11:14-27 12:1-14 12:15-25 12:26-31 13:1-20 13:21-29 13:30-39 14:1-20 14:21-24
14:25-27 14:28-33 15:1-6 15:7-12 15:13-23 15:24-30 15:31-37 16:1-4 16:5-14 16:15-23
17:1-21 17:22-29 18:1-8 18:9-18 18:19-33 19:1-8 19:9-15 19:16-23 19:24-30 19:31-39
19:40-43 20:1-3 20:4-13 20:14-22 20:23-26 21:1-9 21:10-14 21:15-22 23:1-7 23:8-39
24:1-9 24:10-15 24:16 24:17 24:18-25

1 Kings

1:1-4 1:5-10 1:11-31 1:32-53 2:1-4 2:5-11 2:12-25 2:26-34 2:35-46 3:1-4 3:5-15
3:16-28 4:1-19 4:20-28 4:29-34 5:1-9 5:10-18 6:1-10 6:11-14 6:15-38 7:1-12 7:13-47
7:48-51 8:1-11 8:12-21 8:22-53 8:54-61 8:62-66 9:1-9 9:10-14 9:15-28 10:1-13
10:14-29 11:1-8 11:9-13 11:14-25 11:26-40 11:41-43 12:1-15 12:16-24 12:25-33
13:1-10 13:11-22 13:23-34 14:1-6 14:7-20 14:21-31 15:1-8 15:9-24 15:25-34 16:1-14
16:15-28 16:29-34 17:1-7 17:8-16 17:17-24 18:1-16 18:17-20 18:21-40 18:41-46 19:1-8
19:9-13 19:14-18 19:19-21 20:1-11 20:12-21 20:22-30 20:31-43 21:1-4 21:5-16 21:17-29
22:1-14 22:15-28 22:29-40 22:41-50 22:51-53

2 Kings

1:1-8 1:9-18 2:1-8 2:9-12 2:13-18 2:19-25 3:1-5 3:6-19 3:20-27 4:1-7 4:8-17 4:18-37
4:38-44 5:1-8 5:9-14 5:15-19 5:20-27 6:1-7 6:8-12 6:13-23 6:24-33 7:1 7:2 7:3-11
7:12-20 8:1-6 8:7-15 8:16-24 8:25-29 9:1-10 9:11-15 9:16-29 9:30-37 10:1-14 10:15-28
10:29-36 11:1-12 11:13-16 11:17-21 12:1-16 12:17-21 13:1-9 13:10-19 13:20-25 14:1-7

14:8-14 14:15-22 14:23-29 15:1-7 15:8-31 15:32-38 16:1-9 16:10-16 16:17-20 17:1-6
17:7-23 17:24-41 18:1-8 18:9-16 18:17-37 19:1-7 19:8-19 19:20-34 19:35-37 20:1-11
20:12-21 21:1-9 21:10-18 21:19-26 22:1-10 22:11-20 23:1-3 23:4-14 23:15-24 23:25-30
23:31-37 24:1-7 24:8-20 25:1-7 25:8-21 25:22-30

1 Chronicles

1:1-27 1:28-54 11:1-9 11:10-47 12:1-22 12:23-40 13:1-5 13:6-14 15:1-24 15:25-29
16:1-6 16:7-36 16:37-43 22:1-5 22:6-16 22:17-19 23:1-23 23:24-32 27:1-15 27:16-34
28:1-10 28:11-21 29:1-9 29:10-19 29:20-25 29:26-30

2 Chronicles

5:1-10 5:11-14 9:1-12 9:13-31 11:1-12 11:13-23 20:1-13 20:14-19 20:20-30 20:31-37
21:1-11 21:12-20 24:1-14 24:15-27 25:1-13 25:14-16 25:17-28 26:1-15 26:16-23
29:1-19 29:20-36 30:1-12 30:13-20 30:21-27 32:1-23 32:24-33 33:1-20 33:21-25
35:1-19 35:20-27 36:1-21 36:22 36:23

Ezra

1:1-4 1:5-11 2:1-35 2:36-63 2:64-70 3:1-7 3:8-13 4:1-5 4:6-24 5:1 5:2 5:3-17 6:1-12
6:13-22 7:1-10 7:11-26 7:27 7:28 8:1-20 8:21-23 8:24-30 8:31-36 9:1-4 9:5-15 10:1-5
10:6-14 10:15-44

Nehemiah

2:1-8 2:9-18 2:19 2:20 4:1-6 4:7-15 4:16-23 5:1-5 5:6-13 5:14-19 6:1-9 6:10-14
6:15-19 7:1-4 7:5-73 8:1-8 8:9-12 8:13-18 9:1-3 9:4-38 10:1-31 10:32-39 12:1-26
12:27-43 12:44-47 13:1-9 13:10-14 13:15-22 13:23-31

Esther

1:1-9 1:10-22 2:1-20 2:21-23 3:1-6 3:7-15 4:1-4 4:5-17 5:1-8 5:9-14 6:1-3 6:4-11
6:12-14 7:1-6 7:7-10 8:1 8:2 8:3-14 8:15-17 9:1-19 9:20-32

Job

1:1-5 1:6-12 1:13-19 1:20-22 2:1-6 2:7-10 2:11-13 3:1-10 3:11-19 3:20-26 4:1-6
4:7-11 4:12-21 5:1-5 5:6-16 5:17-27 6:1-7 6:8-13 6:14-30 7:1-6 7:7-16 7:17-21 8:1-7
8:8-19 8:20-22 9:1-13 9:14-21 9:22-24 9:25-35 10:1-7 10:8-13 10:14-22 11:1-6 11:7-12
11:13-20 12:1-5 12:6-11 12:12-25 13:1-12 13:13-22 13:23-28 14:1-6 14:7-15 14:16-22
15:1-16 15:17-35 16:1-5 16:6-16 16:17-22 17:1-9 17:10-16 18:1-4 18:5-10 18:11-21
19:1-7 19:8-22 19:23-29 20:1-9 20:10-22 20:23-29 21:1-6 21:7-16 21:17-26 21:27-34
22:1-4 22:5-14 22:15-20 22:21-30 23:1-7 23:8-12 23:13-17 24:1-12 24:13-17 24:18-25
26:1-4 26:5-14 27:1-6 27:7-10 27:11-23 28:1-11 28:12-19 28:20-28 29:1-6 29:7-17
29:18-25 30:1-14 30:15-31 31:1-8 31:9-15 31:16-23 31:24-32 31:33-40 32:1-5 32:6-14
32:15-22 33:1-7 33:8-13 33:14-18 33:19-28 33:29-33 34:1-9 34:10-15 34:16-30 34:31-37
35:1-8 35:9-13 35:14-16 36:1-4 36:5-14 36:15-23 36:24-33 37:1-13 37:14-20 37:21-24
38:1-3 38:4-11 38:12-24 38:25-41 40:1-5 40:6-14 40:15-24 42:1-6 42:7-9 42:10-17

Psalms

1:1-3 1:4-6 2:1-6 2:7-9 2:10-12 3:1-3 3:4-8 4:1-5 4:6-8 5:1-6 5:7-12 6:1-7 6:8-10
7:1-9 7:10-17 8:1 8:2 8:3-9 9:1-10 9:11-20 10:1-11 10:12-18 17:1-7 17:8-15 18:1-19
18:20-28 18:29-50 19:1-6 19:7-10 19:11-14 21:1-6 21:7-13 22:1-10 22:11-21 22:22-31
24:1-6 24:7-10 25:1-7 25:8-14 25:15-22 27:1-6 27:7-14 28:1-5 28:6-9 30:1-5 30:6-12
31:1-8 31:9-18 31:19-24 32:1 32:2 32:3-7 32:8-11 33:1-11 33:12-22 34:1-10 34:11-22
35:1-10 35:11-16 35:17-28 36:1-4 36:5-12 37:1-6 37:7-20 37:21-33 37:34-40 38:1-11

Proverbs

16:15 16:16 16:17 16:18 16:19 16:21 16:22 16:23 16:24 16:25 16:26 16:27 16:28
16:29 16:30 16:31 16:32 16:33 17:1 17:2 17:3 17:4 17:5 17:6 17:7 17:8 17:9
17:10 17:11 17:12 17:13 17:14 17:15 17:16 17:17 17:18 17:19 17:20 17:21 17:22
17:23 17:24 17:25 17:26 17:27 17:28 18:1 18:2 18:3 18:4 18:5 18:6 18:7 18:8
18:9 18:10 18:11 18:12 18:13 18:14 18:15 18:16 18:17 18:18 18:19 18:20 18:21
18:22 18:23 18:24 19:1 19:2 19:3 19:4 19:5 19:6 19:7 19:8 19:9 19:10 19:11
19:12 19:13 19:14 19:15 19:16 19:17 19:18 19:19 19:20 19:21 19:22 19:23 19:24
19:25 19:26 19:27 19:28 19:29 20:1 20:2 20:3 20:4 20:5 20:6 20:7 20:8 20:9
20:10 20:11 20:12 20:13 20:14 20:15 20:16 20:17 20:18 20:19 20:20 20:21 20:22
20:23 20:24 20:25 20:26 20:27 20:28 20:29 20:30 21:1 21:2 21:3 21:4 21:5 21:6
21:7 21:8 21:9 21:10 21:11 21:12 21:13 21:14 21:15 21:16 21:17 21:18 21:19
21:20 21:21 21:22 21:23 21:24 21:25 21:26 21:27 21:28 21:29 21:30 21:31 22:1
22:2 22:3 22:4 22:5 22:6 22:7 22:8 22:9 22:10 22:11 22:12 22:13 22:14 22:15
22:16 22:17-21 22:22 22:23 22:24 22:25 22:26 22:27 22:28 23:1-3 23:4 23:5 23:6-8
23:9 23:10 23:11 23:12-16 23:17 23:18 23:19-28 23:29-35 24:1 24:2 24:3-6 24:7-9
24:10 24:11 24:12 24:13 24:14 24:15 24:16 24:17 24:18 24:19 24:20 24:21 24:22
24:23-26 24:27 24:28 24:29 24:30-34 25:1-3 25:4 25:5 25:6 25:7 25:8-10 25:11
25:12 25:13 25:14 25:15 25:16 25:17 25:18 25:19 25:20 25:21 25:22 25:23 25:24
25:25 25:26 25:27 25:28 26:1 26:2 26:3 26:4 26:5 26:6-9 26:10 26:11 26:12 26:13
26:14 26:15 26:16 26:17 26:18 26:19 26:20-22 26:23 26:24-26 26:27 26:28 27:1
27:2 27:3 27:4 27:5 27:6 27:7 27:8 27:9 27:10 27:11 27:12 27:13 27:14 27:15
27:16 27:17 27:18 27:19 27:20 27:21 27:22 27:23-27 28:1 28:2 28:3 28:4 28:5
28:6 28:7 28:8 28:9 28:10 28:11 28:12 28:13 28:14 28:15 28:16 28:17 28:18 28:19
28:20 28:21 28:22 28:23 28:24 28:25 28:26 28:27 28:28 29:1 29:2 29:3 29:4 29:5
29:6 29:7 29:8 29:9 29:10 29:11 29:12 29:13 29:14 29:15 29:16 29:17 29:18 29:19
29:20 29:21 29:22 29:23 29:24 29:25 29:26 29:27 30:1-6 30:7-9 30:10 30:11-14
30:15-17 30:18-20 30:21-23 30:24-28 30:29-33 31:1-9 31:10-31

Amos
2:1-8 2:9-16 3:1-8 3:9-15 4:1-5 4:6-13 5:1-6 5:7-17 5:18-27 6:1-7 6:8-14 7:1-9
7:10-17 8:1-3 8:4-10 8:11-14 9:1-10 9:11-15

Obadiah
1:1-16 1:17-21

Jonah
1:1-3 1:4-7 1:8-12 1:13-17 2:1-9 2:10 3:1-4 3:5-10 4:1-4 4:5-11

Micah
1:1-7 1:8-16 2:1-5 2:6-11 2:12 2:13 3:1-8 3:9-12 4:1-8 4:9-13 5:1-6 5:7-15 6:1-5
6:6-8 6:9-16 7:1-7 7:8-13 7:14-20

Nahum
1:1-8 1:9-15 2:1-10 2:11-13 3:1-7 3:8-19

Habakkuk
1:1-11 1:12-17 2:1-4 2:5-14 2:15-20 3:1 3:2 3:3-15 3:16-19

Zephaniah
1:1-6 1:7-13 1:14-18 2:1-3 2:4-15 3:1-7 3:8-13 3:14-20

Haggai